GERMANY AND
THE AXIS POWERS

GERMANY AND THE AXIS POWERS

From Coalition to Collapse

Richard L. DiNardo

Foreword by Dennis Showalter

University Press of Kansas

© 2005 by the University Press of Kansas

Published by the University Press of Kansas (Lawrence, Kansas 66049),
which was organized by the Kansas Board of Regents and is operated
and funded by Emporia State University, Fort Hays State University,
Kansas State University, Pittsburg State University, the University of
Kansas, and Wichita State University

Library of Congress Cataloging-in-Publication Data

DiNardo, R. L.
Germany and the Axis : powers from coalition to collapse /
Richard L. DiNardo ; foreword by Dennis Showalter.
p. cm. — (Modern war studies)
Includes bibliographical references and index.
ISBN 0-7006-1412-5 (cloth : alk. paper)
1. World War, 1939–1945—Diplomatic history. 2. World War,
1939–1945—Germany. 3. Germany—Foreign relations—1933–1945.
I. Title. II. Series.
D751.D56 2005
940.53′2443—dc22
2005025666

British Library Cataloguing-in-Publication Data is available.
Printed in the United States of America

10 8 6 4 2 1 3 5 7

The paper used in this publication meets the minimum requirements of
the American National Standard for Permanence of Paper for Printed
Library Materials Z39.48-1984.

FOR MY PARENTS

CONTENTS

A photograph section appears following page 83.

FOREWORD

Germany's commitment to total war in 1914–1918 and 1939–1945 resulted in a significant gap between its commitments and its resources. Alliance relationships were correspondingly important as a means of bridging those gaps. Alliances were important for another reason as well. Germany, the last of the great European powers to emerge from the process of unification, was correspondingly inexperienced at the high politics of international relations. Heavy-handed diplomatic bumbling did as much as deliberate policy to set the Second Reich on the path to the Great War. Hitler's Foreign Office was significantly unable to offer a convincing counterpoint to the Führer's ideologically driven belligerence during the 1930s. Despite its shortcomings at negotiating and persuading, Germany was able both times to secure allies once the shooting started. But could Germany manage alliance relationships effectively? Could it coordinate the complex relationships of states with interests, aims, and not least histories that often made them at best uneasy bedfellows?

In a comprehensive overview that has no counterpart in either English or German literature, Richard DiNardo addresses the subject of German alliances from a military perspective. His relegation of diplomatic and political factors to secondary roles is appropriate. In both world wars, the Reich's alliances were fundamentally military connections. Even the Dual Alliance with Austria-Hungary, long publicly touted as a fundamental bonding of Europe's Germanic empires in "Nibelungen fidelity," rapidly lost after 1914 any meaningful sense of being a "special relationship" in the Anglo-American fashion. Instead Berlin treated Vienna as a "hollow ally," whose deteriorating army required the "corset stays" of German troops to hold it together and whose incompetent government must be kept in line by German pressure. It was scarcely a promising precedent for a later, even more demanding conflict.

DiNardo makes solid use of both archival and published material in a comprehensive demonstration that by the standards of the World War II Grand Coalition of the United States, Britain, and the Soviet Union, to say nothing of the Anglo-American alliance, the Axis was hardly a relationship at all. Japan's connection was so remote and so limited that DiNardo appropriately excludes it from consideration. In a European context, the Axis was a product of bandwagoning. The Third Reich's ostensible partners, Italy,

Romania, Hungary, Finland, local clients like Slovakia and Croatia, and fellow travelers like Vichy France, did not follow Hitler from a common ideological adherence to Fascism. Nor did they share a common commitment to save Europe from Bolshevism. They hoped, rather, to benefit specifically from Hitler's New Order. Italy's Benito Mussolini sought an independent imperium in the Mediterranean. Romania's Ion Antonescu wanted primacy in the Balkans, while Hungary proposed to balance the ambitions of its longtime rival in that region. Finland hoped for security against a repetition of the Russian invasion of 1939. And no one wished to be the last rat to board the ship.

Hitler and his generals were reluctant and unable to create a unified high command even for their own armed services, to say nothing of incorporating allies who as a rule trusted neither each other nor Germany. It is scarcely surprising that the Axis was most effective and most functional when its members worked chimney-style, waging "parallel war" with each partner pursuing its own ends with its own means. DiNardo presents the German use of allies in Operation *Barbarossa* in this context, as being more or less appropriate to their interests, capacities, and limitations. He especially credits the often-overlooked Romanian contributions to the victories of Army Group South. That balance, however, did not survive the first winter of what still should be called the Russo-German War. By 1942, a Germany seeking to compensate for its own deficiencies in men and material put increasing pressure on allies unable to replace their losses, let alone increase their commitments. The result was not merely alienation but heightened interest in negotiating a way out of an impossible situation. Only in North Africa, where Erwin Rommel was far better than his reputation in working with the Italians, did Germany conduct anything remotely resembling successful alliance warmaking—and then for only a short time, under emergency conditions.

In specific contexts the Germans were badly handicapped by a lack of officers whose skills and abilities could be translated to coalition contexts—even linguists were in short supply in an army that was never particularly interested in developing an alliance capacity. At division levels and below, though individual relationships were often harmonious, German officers nevertheless frequently came across as arrogant and intrusive, more didactic than helpful even in the operational issues that were Germany's forte. DiNardo pays particular attention to the often-overlooked aspects of the air and naval connections of Germany with its partners. Here cooperation was frequently more harmonious, partly because the underlying conditions of air and sea war were common to all participants and partly because the Luftwaffe and the Kriegsmarine also increasingly operated on shoestrings. On the whole, however, Nazi Germany's doctrinal commitment to short wars and its growing internal disorganization left far too little slack for dealing with the frictions and tensions of alliance relationships.

Germany also failed badly in providing equipment, both finished products and manufacturing licenses. There was no Axis counterpart to the ubiquitous Sherman tank, which by 1945 made up more than half the British inventory in northwestern Europe, or even the humble jeep. In part this reflected Germany's own shortages, but it also manifested a determination to extort the greatest possible profit from allies whose own budgets were seriously fragile, and whose economic and industrial developments were nowhere near able to meet the material demands of modern war.

Alliance warfare is always difficult, always frustrating, always dependent on interlocking networks of compromise and conciliation at personal, professional, and political levels. Autonomous warmaking is correspondingly attractive. A state can define and pursue its interests and its principles without regard for the interests or sensibilities of partners and clients. It may take as much or as little of a conflict as it wills, or is able to sustain. That, however, is a Platonic ideal, rarely achieved and often proving an illusion. States, even powerful states, correspondingly seek to cover their backs while sharing costs and risks.

So it was with Germany in two world wars. Yet the German experience also indicates that the dynamics of alliances are shaped by symmetry. Alliances are at bottom sustained by the significant sharing of risk and effort. Significant imbalances of strength and commitment work to transform them into a different kind of relationship. At best it will be patronage, as when a dynamic United States sustained more and more of an exhausted Britain's war effort in 1944–1945. At worst it devolves into clientage, where the lesser members' only real leverage is to threaten collapse. In a famous aphorism Winston Churchill declared that "the only thing worse than fighting with allies is fighting without them." DiNardo's work provocatively suggests that the ultimately disastrous fate of the European Axis reflected a synergy of weakness and arrogance in the membership.

Dennis Showalter

ACKNOWLEDGMENTS

A book of this size cannot be completed in a short time, nor can it be completed alone. Perhaps the first person who should be acknowledged here is Bill Dean. Back in 1993, he asked me to deliver a paper on this topic at a conference held in Norwich University. One could say that things steadily spun out of control from there.

Professionally, while working on this book, I benefited from the help of any number of friends and colleagues. Dennis Showalter and Robert Citino read the work in manuscript and made numerous helpful comments and suggestions. After the manuscript was accepted for publication, Rob agreed to prepare all the maps in the book. During my two-year stint at the Air War College at Maxwell AFB, Alabama, I was able to discuss this topic, and many others, with my friend Jim Corum. Jim also gave me some excellent material, especially on the Luftwaffe. Another valued friend and colleague here was Dan Hughes, with whom I collaborated on an article dealing with this subject. Over the years I have had the opportunity to discuss German military history at length with Gerhard Weinberg and have profited greatly from his wisdom and insight. Brian Sullivan and Albert Nofi provided a great deal of knowledge on the Italian armed forces. In addition, Al helped with the translation of some of the Italian material. I am grateful to the staff at the National Archives at College Park, Maryland. A deep debt of gratitude is also owed to the staff of the Alfred M. Gray Research Center at the Marine Corps Base Quantico, Virginia, and to Richard Sommers and the staff at the Military History Institute in Carlisle, Pennsylvania. I would also like to thank all my friends and colleagues at the Marine Corps Command and Staff College for their help and support. Finally, I am most thankful to the Marine Corps University Foundation for its generous financial support to cover several research trips to Germany.

On the other side of the Atlantic, a number of people are owed thanks. Jürgen Förster was always generous with his time and knowledge on this subject, especially over many a beer. My sojourns to Germany were made all the more pleasant by my friends there, especially Rolli and Annie Foerster, Detlef and Johanna Vogel, Klaus Maier, and Horst Boog and his *Stammtisch* at the Grosser Meyerhof in Freiburg. I am very much indebted to Dr. Manfred Kehrig, the former director of the Bundesarchiv-Militärarchiv. He was kind enough to actually take the time to arrange my lodging there when I made my first trip. I also must express my gratitude to the staff of the Bundesarchiv-Militärarchiv, especially Frau Helga Waibel and Frau Ulrike Notzke. These two able and efficient ladies always took great care of me at the archive and were most patient in putting up with my badly spoken German.

I am most grateful for the support of my friends and family along the way. My thanks to Scott, Mary, Sheila, Janice, Irving, Valerie, Karl, Karen, Jay, Kathy, Martin, Mary Jane, Bill, Carol, Jen, Pat, Betty, and especially Monica. Two people deserve special mention. Cynthia Whittaker, my old teacher and friend of more than thirty years, has been one of the great influences in my life. The other is the late David Syrett, my *Doktorvater*. It is one of my great disappointments that this work was completed only after his sudden passing in October 2004.

My family has always been a source of support, however mysterious my choice of career may have seemed. So I would like to thank my brothers, Robert and Jerry, along with their wives, JoAnn and Vinece, and my nephews, Michael and Thomas, and niece, Ann Marie. Most of all, I would like to thank my parents, Louis and Ann DiNardo. It is with love and gratitude that I dedicate this book to them.

Although a great many people have been mentioned, I alone am responsible for any mistakes and omissions in this book.

Introduction

A coalition is excellent as long as all interests of each member are the same. But in all coalitions the interests of the allies coincide only up to a certain point. As soon as one of the allies has to make sacrifices for the attainment of a large common objective, one cannot usually count on the coalition's efficacy.

Helmuth Graf von Moltke[1]

The military profession has always been in something of a paradoxical situation in regard to failure. In civilian society, failure is usually the predecessor of success. Many successful individuals in business, for example, normally fail a number of times before they succeed. This can be true of military establishments as well. It is one of the truisms of military history that military establishments learn the most from defeat.[2] Yet if there is one thing both governments and military establishments can scarcely afford, it is failure. Therefore, it is generally better to study the failures of others. In this regard, a military study of Germany as a conductor of coalition warfare provides a great opportunity to study failure, because the Axis failed as a coalition at so many levels of warfare.

Since Germany was of course the senior partner in the Axis, the focus of this study will be on Germany and its conduct of World War II as a coalition war. As such, I will focus on a number of issues. The first of these is presented as a question. Was Germany inept at conducting coalition warfare? At first glance, this might seem to be a question that should not even be asked, since the answer should be obvious, given the outcome of the war. To simply leave it at that, however, would be insufficient, because it begs a whole number of questions. Was Germany better at conducting coalition warfare at some levels of war than others? Were some services better at working with their allies than others? Were the problems confronting Germany and its Axis allies similar to those faced by the Allies, or were they different? Did the German military learn anything in this regard from the experience of the First World War? To what degree did Nazi ideology and the Holocaust play a role in Germany's conduct of coalition warfare?

Another element that comes into question here is the performance of the Axis allied forces. Over the past few years, the common perception of the

Romanian forces in World War II has been changed, at least in the English-speaking world, by the work of Mark Axworthy and his associates.[3] Likewise, the common perception of the Italian armed forces has been subject to a wide spectrum of revision, ranging from the rather radical views of James Sadkovich to the more balanced judgments of Brian Sullivan, MacGregor Knox, and Lucio Ceva.[4]

Another issue that requires examination is the opinion the Germans held of their allies. Traditional scholarship has generally treated this question in a rather facile manner, simply saying that the Germans regarded their allies, especially the Italians, Hungarians, and Romanians, with disgust. More recent scholarship, however, has shown that this issue is somewhat more complex.[5] In this respect a comparison must be made of how well the Germans were able to work with their allies in North Africa as opposed to the eastern front. Was Axis coalition warfare more effective in one theater, and if so, why?

This study seeks to be a work of military history. Although the diplomatic history of the period has been covered brilliantly by the likes of Gerhard Weinberg and others, it is necessary to delve once again into the depths of Adolf Hitler's diplomacy.[6] German foreign policy, however, will be peripheral to the core of the book. It will be dealt with only in cases where it clearly influenced Germany's conduct of coalition warfare. This also means that this study will focus largely on Germany and four countries, namely, Italy, Romania, Hungary, and Finland. Japan will figure to some degree, particularly in the formulation of strategy. Bulgaria's part in this work will be minimal, because that nation took very little active part in the war. While Spain and Slovakia sent units of varying size to support the German war effort on the eastern front, they will receive little comment. To be sure, the story of the Spanish Blue Division is an interesting one, especially in its cultural aspects. It will receive some attention, but the subject has already been covered elsewhere in some detail.[7]

This does not mean, however, that I will eschew sources that normally come to hand in diplomatic history. The volumes of German foreign policy documents published by the U.S. government contain numerous documents of military interest up to the end of 1941, including private correspondence of high-level officials.[8] They will be used in this study. Much more of the research presented here, however, will be based on the reports of German liaison officers, military attachés, and members of military missions posted to the Axis allied countries.[9]

This work also proceeds from the assumption that the reader knows a good deal about the Second World War. Although this study will discuss coalition warfare in the context of the various campaigns of the war, the campaigns themselves will not be discussed in the kind of cut-and-thrust detail that students of the Second World War find so appealing. Rather, this will be much more of an analytical exercise.

Taken altogether this study hopes to examine as fairly and as extensively as possible Germany's conduct of World War II as a coalition war at a variety of levels. Whether it will say anything "new" is a matter that ultimately must be left to the discretion of the reader. If it broadens your understanding of the Second World War or, more important, makes you rethink much of what you had heretofore held to be true, then this book has served its purpose.

Having offered that caveat, let us now proceed to the beginning of our story. Military establishments do not fight wars, nor exist, in vacuums. They are the product of decades or even centuries of tradition, and they do develop a particular style of war fighting. They are also reflections of the societies they represent, up to and including that society's social values and racial attitudes. Military establishments also seek to incorporate the lessons they learn from previous wars into their thinking. In some areas, particularly in operational doctrine, the German army and air force excelled in incorporating the experiences gained in the First World War.[10] With this in mind, we must begin with a survey of the Prussian and later the Imperial German Army's experience in coalition warfare.

1

Prussia, Germany, and Coalition War, 1740–1933

It is traditional in European politics for states to make offensive and defensive pacts for mutual support—though not to the point of fully espousing one another's interests and quarrels.   Carl von Clausewitz[1]

It is useless to stipulate common operations in advance, because in practice they will not be carried out.   Helmuth Graf von Moltke[2]

I . . . wrote to Waldersee and pleaded with him not to allow any friction to arise, that we must play with open cards in order that we follow the lessons of all coalition wars.   Karl Graf von Kaganeck, 4 August 1914[3]

It is in our interest that we understand and support our ally and its army.
Hans von Seeckt, ca. December 1917[4]

THE HISTORY OF THE GERMAN ARMY and its Prussian antecedent in regard to coalition warfare prior to 1914 is, like that of most powers, a very limited one. Frederick the Great did not fight any of his wars in a really close coalition with other powers. Theoretically at least, Frederick was allied with France in the First and Second Silesian Wars and with Britain in the Seven Years' War. In the actual event, neither Frederick nor the French proved entirely trustworthy allies, and in the Seven Years' War the English provided subsidies, but not much else. In fact, Frederick came to regard the Treaty of Westminster, signed 27 January 1756, as "the worst mistake of my career," as it helped propel an irate France into an alliance with Austria.[5]

On the other hand, Frederick almost certainly profited from the fact that he fought against a coalition. This was best illustrated in the aftermath of Frederick's disastrous defeat at Kunersdorf, when the Austro-Russian forces of Field Marshal Leopold Daun and General P. S. Saltykov went their separate ways, even though they almost had Frederick at their mercy.[6] Ultimately, what saved Prussia was the combination of Frederick's magnificent spirit and the diverging goals of his enemies.[7]

When Prussia finally did engage in a war as part of a coalition, it was with the Austrians against the French in the opening stages of the French revolutionary wars. Of all the powers in the First Coalition, however, Prussia was the first to quit, withdrawing from the war by the Treaty of Basle, signed on 16 May 1795.

After a little more than a decade of inaction, Prussia signed an alliance with Russia in 1806, an agreement that was financially backed by Britain. Having done that, Prussia, in the words of Gunther Rothenberg, "trying to act as if it were still the Frederician state," decided to take the field against Napoleon without waiting for the Russians.[8] This decision, made largely by Queen Louise and the pro-war party in Prussia, led to a catastrophe of almost unimaginable proportions at Napoleon's hands in 1806.[9]

Prussia's next experience in the realm of coalition warfare was more successful but still fraught with problems. After Napoleon's defeat in Russia and Major General Johan David Ludwig Yorck's signing of the Convention of Tauroggen with the Russians, Prussia allied itself with Russia in the Treaty of Kalisch on 28 February 1813. The treaty itself was the result of a Prussian demand for a formal agreement, given Prime Minister Karl August von Hardenberg's worries about the mercurial temperament of Russia's Czar Alexander I.[10] The two allies, joined by Sweden and financed by Britain, fought an inconclusive campaign against Napoleon in the spring of 1813. Although a Russian general, Ludwig Adolf von Wittgenstein, was the allied commander in chief and ideally could give orders to Prussian commanders, reality was another matter. The senior Prussian general, Friedrich Wilhelm von Bülow, often received contradictory orders from the Prussian king Friedrich Wilhelm III and Wittgenstein, and Bülow usually chose to obey his monarch. Given this kind of arrangement, it is not surprising that the campaign against Napoleon in the spring of 1813 was inconclusive.[11]

In the summer of 1813 Austria and Sweden joined the coalition, with Austria becoming the leader of the allies. The allies often clashed over war aims, especially territorial adjustments. The allied commander, Austria's Prince Karl Philip zu Schwarzenberg, found giving orders to recalcitrant allies as difficult as it had been for Wittgenstein. As for strategy, the best the allies could come up with was the so-called Trachenberg Plan, which called for the allies to attack only when Napoleon was not present.[12] Despite such impediments, the campaign ultimately resulted first in Napoleon's defeat at Leipzig in October 1813, followed by the successful invasion of France in 1814, culminating in the occupation of Paris and Napoleon's first abdication.[13] That, aside from the brief Hundred Days' interlude in 1815, marked the end of Prussia's active participation in a war as part of a coalition.

Between 1815 and 1871, the Prussian army devoted little if any time, thought, or energy to coalition warfare. Clausewitz devoted very little space to the subject in *On War*. Although Prussia was allied with Italy against Austria in 1866, the war that followed was more of a "parallel" war than a coalition war. Theoretically at least, Prussia and Italy were supposed to coordinate their respective mobilizations and offensives. In the event, confusion and infighting in the Italian High Command led to a delay that lasted into late June 1866, something that infuriated the Prussians.[14] When the war finally opened, Prussia fought its war against Austria and won, while Italy fought its war against Austria and won because Prussia had won its war. There was never any real coordination, however, between the Prussian and Italian forces. Likewise, the Franco-Prussian War cannot really be considered a coalition war, although there were some aspects of the war that would be part and parcel of any coalition war. The south German states fought on the side of Prussia, and their armies were subsumed into the Prussian war effort as a corps-size unit that was subordinated to Crown Prince Friedrich Wilhelm's Third Army. The Bavarian army, for example, had a liaison officer attached to the crown prince's headquarters. The south German forces certainly did require careful handling, which tested the considerable political and diplomatic skills of the crown prince.[15]

The developing international situation of the late nineteenth century, however, meant that more attention had to be devoted to coalition warfare. The German army did this only in a limited sense. After 1879 Field Marshal Helmuth Graf von Moltke, chief of the general staff, generally developed his war plans in close consultation with his Austrian allies, and developed a fairly close relationship with his Austrian counterpart, Field Marshal Friedrich Baron Beck-Rzikowsky. These generally called for a defensive stand in the west against France, while an Austro-German offensive would drive the Russians out of Poland.[16] As the plans were refined over the years, Moltke dutifully kept the Austrians informed of any changes. Although staff talks were initiated in 1882 and continued to occur intermittently for a decade, Moltke neither endorsed nor attempted to create a mechanism for combined planning between the Germans and Austrians.[17]

The eastern bent of German war planning continued during the brief tenure of General Alfred Graf von Waldersee as chief of the general staff.[18] In general, however, the nature of coalition planning in Germany took a very ominous turn after Moltke's retirement in 1888 and Otto von Bismarck's dismissal by Wilhelm II in 1890. To be sure, there had always been a gap between the political and military sides of the German-Austrian equation even during the respective tenures of Moltke and Bismarck. During the German Wars of Unification, for example, the Prussians pursued an approach to civil-military relations that was more akin to that espoused by Jomini than by Clausewitz. Moltke often bristled at what he felt were attempts by Bismarck to meddle in military matters. Bismarck, for his part, generally resisted efforts by the military, to include at times even Wilhelm I, to exert influence on peace negotiations. Later on the chancellor, for example, kept the news of the Reinsurance Treaty with Russia from Moltke until military circumstances forced Bismarck to divulge its existence to him.[19]

Once both Moltke and Bismarck were gone, however, this gap became a veritable chasm that eventually reflected an almost complete disconnect in German political-military relations. On the political side, after Bismarck's dismissal Wilhelm II made political promises to Austria "almost to the point of irresponsibility."[20] Yet at the same time, with the advent of General Alfred Graf von Schlieffen as chief of the general staff in 1891, both Germany's strategic planning and approach to coalition warfare took a very different turn.

Fearful of an open-ended campaign in the east and convinced that a decisive battle of annihilation similar to the one fought by Hannibal at Cannae in 216 B.C. against the Romans was possible against the French, Schlieffen altered the focus of Germany's war planning accordingly. German war planning was now focused on the west, a shift that culminated in the advent of the Schlieffen Plan. In addition, planning, and the educational system designed to produce planners, became increasingly focused on the operational, technological, and tactical aspects.[21]

As the focus of German planning shifted west, the military side of the Austrian alliance suffered accordingly. Contact between the two general staffs, which had been infrequent during Moltke's tenure, now virtually disappeared. During Schlieffen's tenure as chief of the general staff, there was a period of about ten years during which there were no contacts at all between the two general staffs. Contact between Schlieffen and his Austrian counterpart, Field Marshal Franz Count Conrad von Hötzendorf, was limited only to the most perfunctory forms.[22]

Things improved only marginally under Schlieffen's successor, Colonel General Helmuth von Moltke, a nephew of the victor of 1866 and 1870. While contacts with the Austrians resumed upon Moltke's appointment, and Moltke enjoyed a good personal relationship with Conrad, the Germans were not entirely forthcoming with the Austrians.[23] Although Moltke did promise Conrad that there would be German involvement in offensive operations against Russia in case of a war involving Germany, Austria, and Russia, Moltke carefully evaded committing himself to sending a fixed number of troops or to a definitive plan of operations.[24]

To some degree, the Germans may have been spooked by the Redl affair. The chief of the Russian Intelligence Bureau in Warsaw had discovered that Colonel Alfred Redl, an officer on the Austrian General Staff, was a homosexual. The Russians successfully blackmailed Redl into giving them information on Austrian deployments and war plans. He also provided information to Italy. Exposed by the combined efforts of the intelligence section of the Austrian General Staff and the Austrian state police, Redl was arrested on 24 May 1913 at a Vienna hotel. After a brief interrogation in the hotel room, Redl shot himself in the early morning hours of 25 May 1913, on direct orders from Conrad.[25]

It is difficult to tell how much the Germans knew about the extent of Redl's activities, although they were aware of the broad outlines of the affair. The Germans were rather unsettled at the fact that Redl had served in the Intelligence Section of the Austrian General Staff; German suspicions were not allayed when questions put to the Austrians about the matter received evasive answers. On 18 June 1913, for example, the best Conrad could do was to rather lamely assure Moltke that Redl could not have betrayed "the whole of their private correspondence."[26]

Given the Redl affair, it would be understandable if the Germans were to some degree circumspect regarding what they would do in case of a full-scale war in Europe. In their dealings with the Austrians the Germans were not just circumspect but even disingenuous. Throughout the period 1906–1913, Conrad clearly expected a joint offensive with the Germans. In a 19 March 1909 letter to Conrad, Moltke promised an attack on the Narew River to support the planned Austrian offensive between the Bug and Vistula rivers. Conrad took this pledge seriously enough to insist that Moltke sign a written confirmation of it every year thereafter. Moltke continued to do this, even though he had indicated to Conrad in a 10 February 1913 letter that Austria's fate "will not be decided on the Bug, but definitely on the Seine." The Austrians then could accuse Moltke of taking the pledge for an eastern offensive much less seriously than Conrad.[27]

The Germans also had one other ally who figured in their war plans, at least in a theoretical sense, namely, Italy. Italy had become the third member of the Triple Alliance in 1882, and Italian forces were gradually worked into German war plans, at least in a nominal sense. While Moltke's war plans in the 1880s included an Italian army eventually deploying in Alsace, he did not regard Italy as a major military factor in his plans.[28] When the Schlieffen Plan took shape, it did call for the Italians to send forces to the Rhine to strengthen the German left. By 1914 the plan called for Italy to send three army corps and two cavalry divisions to the Rhine.[29]

After 1908, however, Italy began to slowly back out of the Triple Alliance. Although the last version of the Schlieffen Plan did include Italian participation, Schlieffen himself, in his last memorandum written in retirement on 28 December 1912, clearly no longer regarded Italy as a "working member" of the Triple Alliance. Likewise, it seems clear from Moltke's consistent strengthening of the left wing that he did not seriously expect the Italians to show up in 1914.[30] Actual Italian participation was considered even less likely after the Italian army chief of staff, General Alberto Pollio, suffered a fatal heart attack on the same day that Franz Ferdinand was assassinated in Sarajevo. Both the German military attaché to Vienna, Karl Graf von Kaganeck, and Moltke's deputy, Georg von Waldersee, regarded Pollio's death as a disaster. Pollio, married to an Austrian and fluent in German, had long been the most powerful advocate of the German alliance in Italy. Given Italian objectives, it is quite possible that the Italian government would have stayed out of war in 1914 even had Pollio lived. With his death, however, it was clearly assumed that Italy would adopt some sort of neutrality in case of war.[31] Even though the Italian declaration of neutrality was somewhat expected, Moltke still denounced the action to Conrad in the bitterest of terms. After the eventual miscarriage of the Schlieffen Plan, Moltke wrote in November 1914 of Italy's announcement of neutrality that "nowhere in history is a more shameful broken promise to be found."[32]

Thus when *"der Tag"* came in August 1914, the Germans would fight, initially at least, with Austria alone on its side. Given the state of German-Austrian military relations in 1914, it is not surprising that things went wrong. Even before the July crisis, Moltke surprised Conrad at their last prewar meeting at Carlsbad in May 1914 by telling Conrad that the German army would be ready to deploy its major strength to the east six weeks after the start of operations, about a month after the deadline Moltke had previously agreed to in 1909. His skepticism aroused, when the crisis broke Conrad raised with Kaganeck the question of what Germany would do in the case of a French declaration of neutrality in the event of a war between Russia and Austria-Hungary.[33] The Austrians were, to say the least, rather surprised when they learned the full extent of the Schlieffen Plan. Kaganeck pleaded with Waldersee that the Germans should "play with open cards" in dealing with the Austrians, but he was ultimately disregarded. Matters were made worse by the slowness with which the allies exchanged liaison officers. The Germans and Austrians did not agree to exchange deployment officers until 4 August.[34] In the Austrian case Conrad's representative, Count Josef von Stürgkh, did not receive his final instructions until the night of the sixth and did not leave Vienna until the next morning.[35] These delays, plus

Conrad's own rather considerable errors and bad judgments, led to a very confused situation on the eastern front and contributed in no small part to the disaster suffered by the Austrians in 1914 at the hands of the Russians.[36]

The worsening of military relations between Germany and Austria-Hungary also manifested itself in the vexatious matter of a unified high command in the east. An Austrian proposal for a unified command in the east had been put forth as early as 1893 by Conrad but was turned down by Schlieffen, whose focus was already shifting westward.[37] The issue of a unified command in the east came down to a simple but unstated problem of trust and proportion. The Germans could not trust an Austrian commander to defend East Prussia, while the shifting of Germany's major effort to the west guaranteed that a German could not hold the position of commander of all German-Austrian forces in the east.

Once all the war plans had miscarried to one degree or another, and it became clear that the war was going to last far longer than anyone had expected, Germany and Austria moved a little toward mounting combined operations on the eastern front, but not exactly with complete trust in each other. Conrad was still bitter at the Germans for not launching an offensive in the aftermath of Tannenberg to relieve pressure on the Austrians in Galicia, while the Germans thought Conrad was being something of an ingrate to expect more from them. In a letter to the chief of Francis Joseph's Military Chancery, Artur Baron von Bolfras, Conrad denounced his German allies as "disloyal" and "egotistical."[38]

In 1915 the Germans and Austrians launched a successful combined offensive at Gorlice-Tarnów, but the unusual command arrangement insisted on by the Germans undoubtedly rankled the Austrians. The offensive would be conducted by the German Eleventh and Austrian Fourth Armies. The German Eleventh Army commander, General (eventually Field Marshal) August von Mackensen, had tactical control of the Austrian Fourth Army. Theoretically, Mackensen answered to Conrad and the Austrian High Command. Conrad, however, could not issue orders to Mackensen unless he received the prior approval of his German counterpart, General Erich von Falkenhayn, who had succeeded Moltke on 14 September 1914.[39]

The fact that relations with the Austrians went as smoothly as they did during the operation was due in no small part to Mackensen himself. His "elegant appearance and courtly charm" won the hearts of the Austrians. On the eve of Gorlice-Tarnów, for example, the old hussar made a personal visit to his Austrian colleague Archduke Joseph Ferdinand, something that would almost never have happened with the far more abrasive and aloof personalities of Hindenberg and Ludendorff.[40]

Starting on 2 May 1915, the offensive shattered the Russian defenses. Mackensen ruffled a good many Austrian feathers when German troops took the fortress of Przemsyl, whose fall in March 1915 cost the Austrians hundreds of thousands of casualties. This was compounded when Mackensen announced the fall of Przemsyl in a rather tactless message to Vienna through his nominal Austrian superior, Archduke Friedrich. Mackensen quickly rectified that mistake, however, by arranging for Austrian troops to take Lemberg, thus giving Austrian morale a major boost and earning him warm congratulations from both Wilhelm II and Francis Joseph.[41]

In October 1915 Mackensen, again operating in a command system like that used in the Gorlice operation, led a force composed of German, Austro-Hungarian, and Bulgarian troops against Serbia. In a rapid campaign, Serbia was overrun. Mackensen again showed a deft touch by having Belgrade occupied by Austrian troops, an act that won the personal affection of Francis Joseph.[42] The following year, Mackensen would again command a combined force of German, Austro-Hungarian, Bulgarian, and Turkish troops in dealing with the crisis created by Romania's intervention. Romania was laid low by Mackensen's forces in a campaign that could only be described as brilliant in any number of ways.[43]

Generally, cooperation between the Germans and Austrians was better at the lower echelons of command. One advantage the Central powers enjoyed in this case was a common language. Although Austrian staff officers disliked at times the patronizing attitude of some German officers, they undoubtedly were impressed by the performance of German arms.[44] Stürgkh attributed the arrogant and patronizing attitude of some German officers to north German Prussianism versus the more southern German attitude of the Austrians.[45]

Some German officers, however, were very sympathetic to the plight of the Austrians. Mackensen's ability to work with the Austrians has already been mentioned. Another notable officer was Hans von Seeckt. A highly regarded officer who was a graduate of the Kriegsakademie and a member of the Great General Staff, in 1914 Seeckt was a colonel serving as chief of staff for the III Corps. After serving with distinction on the western front from August 1914 to January 1915, Seeckt was sent to the eastern front. For much of 1915 and 1916, he served as Mackensen's chief of staff. In June 1916, during the Austro-Hungarian emergency caused by the success of the Brussilov offensive, Seeckt took command of the Austrian Seventh Army and led it for the better part of a month. In July 1916 Seeckt, by then a major general, became chief of staff for an Austro-German army group commanded by Austrian archduke Joseph. With this kind of experience behind him, at the end of 1917 Seeckt wrote a very thoughtful and sympathetic appraisal of the Austro-Hungarian army and its soldiers.[46]

At the highest levels of command, however, the German-Austrian alliance broke down badly, both militarily and politically. Criticism of the Germans by Austrian military officials was soon echoed on the political side by Austrian diplomats.[47] Although on occasions the two general staffs could cooperate, such as when the Austrians quickly dispatched eight 305mm mortars to assist the Germans in destroying Belgian and French forts in August 1914, this was the exception more than the rule.[48] In general, however, there was never any attempt to rationally plan a combined strategy. General Maximilian von Prittwitz, commander of the German Eighth Army in East Prussia in 1914, had not even been included in any discussions between the Germans and Austrians before the war. There were also long periods in which the German and Austrian military chiefs did not even speak to each other, let alone communicate regularly. This often meant that each ally was at times totally in the dark about matters that might be of common concern. Conrad, for example, was told nothing of the progress of the western campaign in 1914, the retreat from the Marne, or the relief of Moltke.[49]

While relations between the Germans and Austrians were poor during Moltke's tenure as chief of the general staff, they were good compared with what followed. On 2 December 1914 an Austrian delegation headed by Conrad met a German delegation headed by Wilhelm II and Falkenhayn at Breslau. Although the ostensible purpose of the meeting was to decide on a course to pursue in regard to the war in the east, nothing was either decided or accomplished. About the only thing that did happen was Wilhelm's taking advantage of this opportunity to indulge his penchant for the ridiculous, telling Conrad that his fondest hope now was to make peace with the French so he could capture the British Expeditionary Force.[50]

Theoretically, the advent of Falkenhayn should have augured a period of closer relations between the allies. Although Falkenhayn was considered a "westerner" in the realm of German strategic thought, by the beginning of 1915 he regarded elimination of the Russian threat to Austria-Hungary as critical.[51] With more attention being paid to the eastern front, there should have been closer cooperation between the Austrians and the Germans. In fact, the opposite occurred. Part of this estrangement was personal. On 28 October 1914 Falkenhayn invited Conrad to come to Berlin. Conrad responded to the invitation by sending one of his staff officers, Lieutenant Colonel Rudolf Kundmann, to represent him, an inexcusable snub that the proud and prickly Prussian was not likely to forget.[52] In addition, stung by what he regarded as German betrayals in 1914, Conrad grew increasingly angry and mistrustful as Falkenhayn sent more German forces east, but correspondingly demanded a preponderant role in planning. This was clearly illustrated in the three meetings subsequent to the 2 December 1914 Breslau meeting. Conrad met with Falkenhayn at Oppeln on 19 December 1914, in Berlin on 1 January 1915, and again at Breslau a few days later. Although Conrad did secure some German help for continued Austro-Hungarian operations in the Carpathians with Ludendorff's help, Falkenhayn showed little if any interest in Conrad's ideas.[53]

Thereafter, high-level contacts between the two allies became almost non-existent. Some of this was due to the simple fact that Falkenhayn and Conrad had very different styles of communication. Conrad generally preferred to communicate ideas in a written form, either a letter or a more formal memorandum. If the ideas required further discussion, this could be done on a personal basis at a face-to-face meeting. Ever the antithesis of Conrad, Falkenhayn disliked meetings, thinking them a time-wasting exercise. In fact, to try to minimize his travel time to such meetings with Conrad, Falkenhayn had an automobile specially modified to drive much faster than the standard cars of the day. Falkenhayn much preferred to discuss ideas at length over the telephone, a device Conrad disliked and distrusted.[54]

As a result, during critical periods in 1915 and 1916, Falkenhayn and Conrad did not have any communications at all, while their personal relationship had deteriorated to the point of "open enmity" by the end of 1915.[55] This led to a series of unfortunate events. In 1915 Austria unilaterally attacked Montenegro without informing the Germans, an action the Germans had absolutely opposed.[56] This became particularly serious in 1916, when Falkenhayn committed German men and material to what became the bloodbath of Verdun. For his part, Conrad stripped men and material to pursue an offensive against Italy, but with still inadequate forces. This resulted in a major crisis on the Russian front when the Brussilov offensive crushed the Austro-Hungarian Seventh Army in June 1916. A situation such as that which existed at the start of 1916 called for as close cooperation as possible between Germany and Austria-Hungary. That was not the case. In fact, Falkenhayn went so far as to give misleading information to Conrad's military representative regarding German plans for Verdun, while the Austrians lied to Kaganeck about Conrad's plans for Italy. As a result, Falkenhayn and Conrad pursued their own plans with a degree of disorganization that was clearly evident to Kaganeck.[57]

A definitive answer to the question of an overall unified command in the east also continued to elude the Germans and Austrians. Between November 1914 and July 1916, several proposals for a unified command in the east were bruited about, but none were adopted. In the crisis created by the Brussilov offensive in the summer of 1916, Wilhelm II divided the eastern front into two equal halves, the northern half being commanded by Hindenburg and the southern half by Archduke Joseph. Each commander had control over all units in their area, regardless of nationality.[58] This arrangement lasted until September, when the crisis was mastered.

After Falkenhayn's dismissal and the advent of the Hindenburg and Ludendorff as the ruling duumvirate, a unified command structure was finally agreed to in 1916, in which directives would be issued from the German General Staff through the nominal overall commander on the eastern front, Wilhelm II. The Austrians did exert a sort of veto power, since Wilhelm's issuing the requisite orders depended on the approval of Austrian emperor Francis Joseph. This arrangement did produce success, especially in Romania, an operation that was agreed on by both general staffs and was brilliantly conducted by the combination of Falkenhayn and Mackensen, employing troops from every member of the Central powers under Mackensen's overall command.[59]

The arrangement fell apart, however, when Francis Joseph died on 21 November 1916. His successor, Karl, quickly dismantled it and returned to the more nebulous arrangements that had obtained earlier. Karl evidently took this step to effectively assert his rights as an equal of Wilhelm II as well as asserting Austrian sovereignty. The Germans and Austrians would never again come close to creating a unified command.[60]

A good part of the political breakdown in the alliance can be traced to disagreements over the disposition of Poland, which by the end of 1915 was almost entirely in either German or Austrian hands. At the outbreak of war, both Germany and Austria-Hungary decided to mount an operation to subvert Russian political control in Poland. The two general staffs agreed to the text of a proclamation announcing that the forces of the Central powers were there to liberate Poland from the Russian yoke.[61] As the 1915 campaign brought most of Poland under German or Austrian control, the two governments came up with very different ideas on how to proceed. For their part, the Austrians desired the creation of a Polish kingdom that would be ruled by an Austrian archduke, a prospect that did not thrill Ludendorff.[62] The conditions stipulated by Bethmann, however, virtually ensured that such an arrangement would be unsatisfactory to Austria-Hungary even if its desired Polish kingdom was formed. First, although the Austrians would have nominal control politically over the area, the Germans would insist on conditions that would make the economy and transportation system dependent on Germany. Second, as Gerhard Ritter noted, the only way Poland could remain in Austrian hands was if the Austro-German alliance was extended into perpetuity.[63] This was not about to happen as both the Austrians and the Germans thought this an unsatisfactory arrangement. Some Germans, notably Ludendorff and Falkenhayn in a rare moment of agreement, regarded Austria as a "corpse" and a thoroughly unsatisfactory ally.[64] For their part, the Austrians realized early on that Austria, because of its military inferiority, would be eternally confined to junior partner status at best.[65]

There was also some political disagreement over Italy. In 1915, as the threat of Italian intervention drew nearer, the Germans and Austrians differed over how to deal with the threat. The Germans urged the Austrians to try to buy off the Italians with border territories. Such a concession would not matter much to Austria, as only 2 percent of the dual monarchy's population was Italian. Conrad felt, probably with some justification, that this would only encourage the Italians to raise the price. He was also tactless enough to suggest to Falkenhayn that since Germany was urging Austria to cede the Tyrol to Italy, perhaps Germany might want to give Alsace-Lorraine back to France.[66] In any case, although the Germans regarded Italy's behavior in both 1914 and 1915 as swinish, they did not regard Italy's entry into the war as a severe threat against Austria, nor as something in which Germany should involve itself. A week before Italy declared war on Austria-Hungary—but not Germany—Ludendorff, for example, wrote to Moltke that Italian morale was such that it would not survive one serious defeat.[67] For his part, in his memoirs Falkenhayn explained that an immediate declaration of war on Italy would have been overly hasty. Falkenhayn said that Germany's yearlong delay kept lines of communication open to the outside world and rather dubiously claimed that it imposed no strain on the alliance.[68] More likely, the German delay may have been due to Germany's irritation with Austria-Hungary over the Montenegro affair, and to a serious underestimation of both Italian capability and resolve. For his part, Conrad, especially after 1915, wanted to scale back the effort on the eastern front and devote more attention to Italy. This stemmed partly from Conrad's own attitude but also from the fact that the war with Italy was a good deal more popular with the Austro-Hungarian troops than the war with Russia. It was also better suited to Austro-Hungarian capabilities.[69]

With the advent of the duumvirate of Hindenburg and Ludendorff, the alliance broke down completely. Even Karl's replacing Conrad with General Artur Arz von Straussenberg in early 1917 did little to lessen the tension between the respective general staffs.[70] Although the Germans and Austrians were able to win a combined victory at Caporetto (or Karfreit, as the Austrians referred to it), it was preceded by acrimonious squabbling, marked by

German fears that a victory over the Italians would only give the Austrians the position they needed to make a separate peace. German fears were seemingly confirmed when Austria-Hungary failed to send any units to aid the German army in its last offensives in the spring of 1918.[71] The Austrians, for their part, increasingly resented their growing economic dependence on Germany, and their having to submit to a German-dominated Mitteleuropa.[72] Although the Austrian emperor Karl did attempt to negotiate a separate peace, nothing came of it. Karl's efforts were defeated by a combination of rising ethnic nationalism, a hardening of Entente attitudes toward Austria-Hungary, and clumsy Austrian diplomacy, especially in the Sixtus affair.[73] Consequently, Germany and Austria-Hungary ended the war as they had begun it, allies in a technical sense but in reality alone.

Some attention must be given to Germany's military relations with its other major Central powers partner, Ottoman Turkey. The first German military mission had gone to Turkey in the aftermath of the Russo-Turkish War of 1877–1878. In 1913 Germany sent another military mission to Turkey, largely at the behest of the Young Turks and the urging of the German ambassador, Freiherr von Wangenheim. Headed by General Otto Liman von Sanders, it consisted of forty-two officers, mostly of field-grade rank, who were then placed in either command or staff positions in Turkish units. Their task was to bring the Turkish army up to German training standards and thus ensure that in a war the Entente powers, especially Russia, would not be able to simply carve up Turkey.[74]

At the higher levels there was some considerable friction between Liman and the Turkish war minister, Enver Pasha. Ideally Enver and Liman should have gotten along well. Before becoming defense minister, Enver had served as the Turkish military attaché in Berlin, and he was fluent in German.[75] He was, however, given to acting in a high-handed manner at times. This in turn irritated Liman, who felt that some of Enver's actions, such as dismissing Colonel Ali Risa Bei as commander of the Eighth Infantry Division, impinged on his prerogatives.[76]

There were problems at the lower levels, however, between the members of the German military mission and the Turks, principally in regard to language. Almost none of the German officers spoke Turkish, and the soldiers assigned to them as interpreters did not have enough facility with German to really qualify for such a position. Colonel (later Major General) Hans Kannengiesser, for example, had as an interpreter one Zia Bey. Although assigned as an interpreter, Zia Bey was a Bosnian who spoke Turkish, German, and French equally poorly.[77] Matters were not helped by the Germans' lack of understanding of Turkish culture and society.

Nonetheless, cooperation between the Turks and the Germans during the war was reasonably good. Although the ablest Turkish field commander, Mustapha Kemal, had opposed the coming of the German military mission in 1913, he and Liman proved a combination formidable enough to fend off the Allied amphibious operation at Gallipoli.[78] At the top, the Germans were fortunate in having Field Marshal Colmar Freiherr von der Goltz as the chief German military adviser to the sultan. A veteran of the first German military mission to Turkey, Goltz had served in Turkey from 1882 to 1895.[79] Goltz always proceeded from the sensible basis that one could not expect Turks to be Germans, and that one must make the best possible use of the native fighting qualities of the Turks. Karl Dönitz, the World War II commander of the German U-boat arm, always regarded Goltz as a master of coalition warfare. Liman thought his death on 6 April 1916 from typhus to be a major loss.[80] German-Turkish cooperation was good enough so that after the Russian breakthrough at Lutsk in July 1916, Turkish troops were deployed to the eastern front.[81] Nevertheless, in the overall scheme of things, Turkey would always be a sideshow for Germany during World War I.

As noted previously, German-Austrian cooperation was very poor, especially at the higher levels of command, both politically and militarily. Although there were some instances of cooperation, these were the exceptions rather than the rule. Part of this breakdown may be explained by the system of German military planning that developed in the post-Waldersee era. Military planning became so divided that the army and the navy developed separate war plans without regard to what the other was doing.[82] Given the fact that the German military establishment could not manage any kind of interservice planning, it should not be entirely surprising that the same problems appeared in the much more difficult area of planning for a coalition war.

Another part of the explanation lay in the attitudes of the German leadership toward Austria-Hungary. Stürgkh's opinion that German and Austrian attitudes simply illustrated the cultural differences between south Germans and the Prussian-dominated north Germans have already been noted.[83] Other attitudes were darker. Wilhelm II was utterly convinced that the Austro-Hungarian Empire was ridden with racially inferior elements. In 1887 Wilhelm, then still crown prince, confided to a couple of Austrian call girls that Austria-Hungary was racially corrupt. Crown Prince Rudolph in particular was, according to Wilhelm, completely under Jewish influence. The kaiser was also absolutely convinced that Europe was as threatened by the "Slavic Peril" as it was by the "Yellow Peril."[84] An ardent admirer of all facets of Houston Stewart Chamberlain's thinking, the kaiser was also as anti-Catholic as he was anti-Semitic or anti-Slavic.[85] Thus for the kaiser, Austria-Hungary's official Catholicism made it an untrustworthy ally.

Such attitudes were not confined to the kaiser and his immediate entourage. Walter Görlitz has argued that what Pan-Germanism existed in the German General Staff was strongest among the officers of bourgeois origin who were becoming an increasing presence in the organization.[86] Clearly the influence of these ideas and their adjunct, social Darwinism, affected the noble members of the general staff as well. Schlieffen gave some evidence of this in his own writings.[87] Racial attitudes were much more evident in the younger Moltke. An ardent social Darwinist, Moltke had imbibed deeply from the works of writers such as Ernst Haeckel, Houston Stewart Chamberlain, and Rudolf Steiner, among others. In a letter to his wife dated 22 July 1913, Moltke saw the coming war as a struggle between "Germandom and Slavdom."[88] Not content with confiding such thoughts only to his wife, Moltke was tactless enough to have expressed the same ideas in a 10 February 1913 letter to Conrad. Moltke went on to say that in case of a war, it was the duty of the Germanic states to carry forward the banner of the spirit of German culture (*Geistkultur*).[89] One could only imagine the reaction of Conrad, who responded five days later by pointing out that some 47 percent of the Austro-Hungarian Empire's inhabitants were Slavic. Moltke's fears could only have been increased at the onset of the July 1914 crisis when Kaganeck wrote to him on 1 July, outlining the deleterious effect that Serbian nationalist propaganda was having on the South Slavic troops in the Austro-Hungarian army. Even Mackensen, a relative liberal by the standards of Wilhelmine Germany, was given to such thinking.[90]

Such attitudes could only harden with the advent of Erich Ludendorff as the de facto dictator of Germany in late 1916. Ludendorff's stance toward Austria-Hungary became evident as early as September 1914, when he refused to see Austrian military representatives who had been sent by Conrad to discuss future plans for a coordinated Austro-German offensive.[91] Ludendorff's letters to Moltke consistently refer to the "worthlessness" or "wretchedness" of the Austrians, calling them a "nation of whiners" (*Jammervolk*). This was probably one of the few things on which Ludendorff and Falkenhayn agreed.[92]

Such attitudes could only have hardened when he left the eastern front and direct contact with the Austrians for the more insular atmospheres of first Berlin and then western front headquarters at Spa, Belgium. Thus a man such as Seeckt, with his long experience and his familiarity with and sympathy for Austria-Hungary, noted that because of the heavy losses of officers in the first years of the war, Jews were allowed to be commissioned as officers. He saw this as a positive step, especially in Hungary, where newly commissioned Jewish officers got caught up in the patriotic spirit of the time and performed well in combat. One could imagine how Ludendorff would have reacted to this, given his well-established low regard for anything connected to the Austro-Hungarian army.[93]

Taken altogether, Germany had not distinguished itself in conducting coalition warfare. It should be pointed out, however, that in World War I the Allies did not exactly distinguish themselves either. Although the Allies did not let their political objectives diverge so widely as to affect their conduct of the war, their conduct of coalition warfare was not very effective. The issue of coalition command was not solved until the crisis of 1918, when Ferdinand Foch was appointed supreme commander of the Allied forces. Prior to that time, Anglo-French combined operations were discussed at high-level conferences, but practical operations never got beyond nebulous promises of cooperation between the commander of the British Expeditionary Force, Field Marshal Sir Douglas Haig, and the chief of the French General Staff, Marshal Joseph Joffre.[94] Even after Foch's appointment as supreme commander, his authority was somewhat limited, and Allied commanders such as John Pershing were often inclined to regard Foch's orders more as suggestions. After the war the French, however imperfectly, paid some attention to the issues involved in conducting coalition warfare at the National War College.[95] When war broke out in 1939, the Allies sought to replicate the arrangements that had served them well enough in 1918.

In coalition warfare, as in so many other areas, World War I had given the Germans a wealth of experience. Yet it seems clear that the Germans paid very little attention, if any, to the problems of coalition warfare. To be sure, a number of officers who were deeply involved in the issues of coalition warfare, such as Stürgkh and Cramon, did write memoirs. With exercises such as these, however, their goal was often to obscure as much as it was to reveal, especially about the major figures in the war.

The postwar writings of commanders also shed little light on this subject. Ludendorff's writings were a clear example. In his memoirs, Ludendorff decried the lack of military unity in the Central powers. In his rather bizarre book *Der totale Krieg*, he noted the relative superiority of the Allied command arrangements, even with their flaws.[96] Ludendorff's postwar ideas on this subject, however, vary quite a bit with his wartime opinions of a unified command, as we have seen.

German military periodical literature was relatively silent on coalition warfare. During the interwar period, the pages of the premier German military periodical, *Militär Wochenblatt*, featured a large number of officers debating the major military issues of the day, such as the uses of emerging technologies such as tanks and aircraft. Coalition warfare drew the attention of only one officer, General Georg Wetzell, who was the editor of *Militär Wochenblatt* during the 1930s. In late 1937 he serialized his book on Germany and coalition warfare in World War I in a series of articles in *Militär Wochenblatt* that dealt with the issue of coalition warfare from the Bismarckian period up through the end of World War I. Although conventional in its approach (Bismarck and Moltke were incapable of error) and marked by his own biases, especially in regard to Falkenhayn, Wetzell's pieces were rather thoughtful. In his concluding article, Wetzell presciently suggested that in the future, all wars would be coalition wars, requiring commanders of great vision, with complete understanding of both the political and the military situation.[97]

Aside from Wetzell's articles, there was the occasional encomium to World War I commanders such as Conrad or August von Mackensen, but that was all. Even an article that attempted to place World War I in a historical context said nothing about coalition warfare.[98] The fact that very little about coalition warfare appeared in the pages of German military periodicals is notable, especially in the case of *Militärwissenschaftliche Rundschau,* given the publication's intended audience. Founded in late 1935 and edited by the general staff, *Militärwissenschaftliche Rundschau* was a journal for senior officers. Its pages were often home to some of Germany's premier military thinkers, including Heinz Guderian, Walter Nehring, and Wilhelm Ritter von Leeb. Thus it seems clear that while there was what one could call a climate of opinion regarding any number of tactical and operational issues, the same could not be said for coalition warfare.

Another area where coalition warfare seemed to be ignored was in German professional military education. Captain (later General) Albert C. Wedemeyer, in his after-action report on his assignment as a student at the Kriegsakademie, reported no study at all of coalition warfare.[99] Given the emphasis of the Kriegsakademie, the cornerstone of German professional military education, on combat tactics and operations, this is perhaps not surprising.

Somewhat more promising was the Wehrmachtakademie Founded in 1935 at the urging of Army General (later Field Marshal) Walter von Reichenau, supported by Luftwaffe General Walter Wever, the Wehrmachtakademie was supposed to be attended by a small number of senior officers from the three services. Staffed largely by civilian professors from German universities, the school was to provide an education that would take students far beyond the narrow perspective of their own services.[100] The joint aspect of warfare was dealt with, to give one example, in a rather lengthy presentation of how the lack of joint command structure among the armed services affected the conduct of the war by the belligerents on both sides of World War I.[101]

Coalition warfare received attention as well. Speakers brought in to address the class included military attachés and ambassadors to foreign countries. As at the Kriegsakademie, students also had to learn a foreign language. Ultimately, supporters of the school hoped it would become the premier institution of professional military education in Germany for teaching senior officers such topics as civil-military relations, economic aspects of war, and the need for a unified command structure in both joint and coalition warfare.[102]

Unfortunately for the Germans, this was not to be. Although the Luftwaffe High Command placed great value on the Wehrmachtakademie, the commander in chief of the Luftwaffe, Reichsmarschal Hermann Göring, had opposed its creation, fearing that any joint school would in reality be dominated by the army. It went forward anyway, however, as the war minister, Field Marshal Werner von Blomberg, was an ardent supporter of the Wehr-machtakademie. After his removal by Hitler in 1938, however, combined with Wever's death two years earlier on 3 June 1936, the Wehrmacht-akademie no longer enjoyed any support from the higher echelons of the armed forces, and the school was closed in 1938.[103]

The lack of interest in coalition warfare manifested itself in other ways as well, although here it would seem clear that the Luftwaffe enjoyed a better record than the army. In coalition warfare, especially in a European sense, language is an important issue. It pays to know the language of one's ally. In this context, it is interesting to note the difference between the Luftwaffe and the army. In 1932, while military cooperation between the Soviet Union and Germany was still ongoing, relatively few German officers attempted to learn Russian. That year foreign language exams for officers were administered by Wehrkreis III in Berlin. Of the 178 officers who took examinations, only 34 took Russian, which came in a poor third behind English and French. Only one officer took the Italian examination, and no one took an examination for either Romanian or Hungarian. This later came back to haunt the army, which was consistently short of Romanian interpreters throughout the war.[104] By contrast, in the Luftwaffe by 1939, of some 220 officers on the general staff, the largest number had passed examinations in French or English, but 28 knew Italian, 23 knew Spanish, 17 knew Russian, and 17 knew other languages.[105] In this case the Luftwaffe almost certainly profited not only from the secret military cooperation with the Soviet Union but also from the secret cooperation with the Italians in 1933–1934. The agreement, engineered by Göring and Italian aviation minister Italo Balbo, resulted in the Germans having some 150 pilots trained in Italy during that brief period.[106]

To the army at least, the matter of language did not seem to be a critical criterion for the selection of German military attachés or officers who would be involved in conducting coalition operations. In Germany, according to General Enno von Rintelen, German military attaché to Italy from 1936 to 1943, the selection of military attachés was based on the following criteria. An officer had to have good military bearing, social agility (which also extended to his wife), good general training, general staff experience, and sound military judgment. When told of his selection as military attaché to Italy, Rintelen objected to the chief of the Foreign Armies Section, General Heinrich von Stülpnagel, that he did not know a word of Italian. Stülpnagel responded by telling Rintelen that he would learn the language soon enough.[107]

The Prussian and later imperial German experiences with coalition warfare did not augur well for the future. Prussia had only a mixed record of success in conducting coalition warfare, and the record of the German Empire was lamentable in this regard, especially after Bismarck and the elder Moltke passed from the scene. After the rise of Schlieffen, German-Austrian relations were marked by the combination of political and diplomatic ineptitude, particularly on the part of Wilhelm II, while military relations became increasingly estranged. Although military relations improved somewhat under the younger Moltke in terms of direct contact between the respective general staffs, they were marred by a disingenuousness that evolved into an escalating pattern of deceit and dishonesty on the part of both Germany and Austria.

Having garnered a wealth of valuable, if painful, experience in coalition warfare during World War I, the Germans proceeded not to make any use of it. In a classic case of failing to learn from history, the German military made no attempt to incorporate the experience of coalition warfare into its system of professional military education. The only attempt to do this, the creation of the Wehrmachtakademie, withered on the vine because of interservice suspicion. Likewise, the pages of German military periodicals, normally abounding with lively debate on a variety of issues, were virtually silent on this topic. Instead, writing on this subject was generally confined to former general officers penning their memoirs, many of which were of dubious value at best. While this inattention to coalition warfare was perhaps understandable during the 1920s, given Germany's relative diplomatic isolation outside of the Rappallo agreement with the Soviet Union, the failure to study coalition warfare after 1933 was incomprehensible. After all, by that time Germany was led by a man who in his writings at least was calling for an alliance with a country whose leader possessed an ideology and persona congenial to his own. It is to this relationship we now turn.

2

Hitler, Diplomacy, and Coalition Warfare

From His Appointment as Chancellor to the Battle of Britain

In this period—I openly admit—I conceived the profoundest admiration for the great man south of the Alps, who, full of ardent love for his people, made no pacts with the enemies of Italy, but strove for their annihilation by all ways and means.   Adolf Hitler, 1924[1]

Hitler is like a gramophone with seven records, and that when he played them all he began again at the beginning.   Benito Mussolini[2]

Have you ever watched a cat while it studies its prey and then, with a leap, is upon it? . . . I intend to act in the same way.
Benito Mussolini, 21 April 1940[3]

The Italian aircraft were no match for the modern English fighters, not even for the Hurricanes.   Albert Kesselring[4]

IN DEALING WITH THE SUBJECT OF Germany and coalition warfare in World War II, it is necessary to delve briefly into the personality of Adolf Hitler. Although this area has been covered many times before by a wide range of historians, a reexamination is a must here if we are to understand the manner in which Germany conducted coalition warfare. Since the Nazi dictatorship was as much personal as ideological, it is necessary to start at the top and examine Hitler's ideas about foreign policy, coalitions, and the factors that shape them. This will also allow some brief comparisons with Germany's prior experiences in coalition warfare.

The first notable thing about Hitler in this regard is his utter lack of knowledge about the world. Being rather indifferently educated, he neither spoke nor read any language other than German. Nor was he well traveled. Prior to his first trip to Venice to meet Mussolini on 14 June 1934, Hitler had never been to a non-German-speaking country. This was true for much of his entourage as well.[5]

Hitler set down his ideas on foreign policy during the summer of 1928 in a book that, like *Mein Kampf,* he dictated to one of his secretaries. The book, which remained unpublished during Hitler's lifetime for several reasons, was essentially a broad outline of his concepts for how the new German *völkisch* state envisioned in *Mein Kampf* should conduct foreign policy. Hitler's ideas on the goals and conduct of foreign policy were relatively simple. Continuing in the vein he had advocated in *Mein Kampf,* Hitler considered it absolutely essential that a racially superior German state obtain Lebensraum in eastern Europe, especially Poland and Russia for its burgeoning population. That this would entail war or perhaps a series of wars was considered natural and even beneficial. While Hitler's foreign policy was always tinged with opportunism, its wellsprings were clearly ideological.[6] In the last chapter of the book, when Hitler calls for an alliance with Italy, his reasoning is clearly based on ideology more than anything else.[7]

As for the day-to-day conduct of foreign policy, Hitler pursued a bilateral approach. In his massive study of Hitler's foreign policy, Gerhard Weinberg noted that Hitler always avoided multilateral arrangements, preferring instead a series of bilateral agreements, which he could later break at his leisure.[8] In addition, the bilateral approached appealed to Hitler's style of personal diplomacy, which in some ways was reminiscent of that of Wilhelm II. Hitler did not look on the foreign policy of a country as something that could be shaped by a variety of forces, some of them very impersonal. Rather, for Hitler the personal was political. Foreign policy was something that was shaped, or should be shaped, by the greatest man in the country, who would presumably be the leader. This comes through very clearly in Hitler's *Tischgespräche (Table Talk).* Whatever observations he might have about the Italians or the Romanians as peoples were ultimately irrelevant. Hitler could not see either country going on without the great leader, in these cases Mussolini and Antonescu, respectively, to guide the helm.[9] In no case was Hitler's penchant for personal and ideological diplomacy more evident than in his long and complex relationship with Benito Mussolini.

Hitler's attraction to Mussolini was clearly of an ideological nature. He had followed the Duce's career with interest right from the beginning. To the very end of his life Hitler always acknowledged his ideological debt to Mussolini, beginning with his tribute to him in *Mein Kampf* as the premier anti-Marxist in Europe. In Hitler's words, "The brownshirt would probably not have existed without the blackshirt."[10] For Hitler, Mussolini's force of personality mattered more than everything else that militated against an alliance with Italy. The Duce was the leading personality in Italy, and that, plus Fascist ideology, would overcome contrary factors such as the lack of common interests between the two countries, Hitler's absolute contempt for the Italian royal family, and lingering bitterness on the part of both countries from the First World War.[11]

The ideological nature of Hitler's call for an Italian alliance and Mussolini's eventual response to it were also symptomatic of something else the two of them shared, namely, a fundamental misunderstanding of the nature and purpose of the Italian armed forces. For Hitler, armed forces served two essential purposes. The first was to provide a unifying institution, which in Hitler's case would be for the future German *völkisch* state. As Hitler stated in *Mein Kampf,* "The German army does not exist to be a school for the preservation of tribal peculiarities, but should rather be a school for the mutual understanding and adaptation of all Germans."[12] The second, given his ideas on Lebensraum, was to conquer and occupy territory for the state.[13] To a great degree, Mussolini shared this view of the purpose of the armed forces. The critical difference here was ideological. The Duce's outlook on the conquering of territory was more connected to traditional European power politics. Mussolini's notions about remaking the Italian people smacked more of Ernst Jünger than the *völkisch* ideology espoused by Hitler.[14]

The problem here was that neither Hitler (understandably at least) nor Mussolini (much less understandably) fully understood the nature of the Italian armed forces, especially the Regio Esercito. In its essence, the purpose of the Italian army was to maintain the internal political position of the Savoy dynasty. Mussolini's attempts to replace the army with organizations of a more ideological bent, such as the Fascist Militia, failed. This left Mussolini with a military establishment, especially an officer corps, whose loyalty he would never fully command.[15]

Mussolini's side of the equation was equally complex. There is no doubt that Mussolini disliked Hitler personally. Much of this stemmed from their first meeting in Venice on 14 June 1934. Hitler, worried about ongoing tensions between him and the Sturmabteilung (SA), which would be resolved in the Night of the Long Knives, made a very poor impression on the patronizing Mussolini.[16] Matters worsened considerably with the failed Nazi putsch against the Austrian government of Engelbert Dollfuss, a move Mussolini strenuously opposed, even to the point of deploying troops on the border between Austria and Italy.[17] Thereafter, as Hitler gained power internationally and the nature of the relationship changed, Mussolini found Hitler steadily more difficult to take. This was especially true when it came to the Führer's rambling monologues. Mussolini once described Hitler to Marshal Pietro Badoglio as "a gramophone with seven records, and that when he played them all he began again at the beginning." Likewise, Hitler's fascination with Italian art left Mussolini bored almost to distraction.[18]

Mussolini's misgivings about Hitler and the Nazis were shared by some of his top advisers. Perhaps the two most notable of them were foreign minister Dino Grandi and aviation minister Italo Balbo. While Grandi urged a policy that would allow Italy to demand concessions from both France and Germany, he always preferred a pro-French policy. Balbo, while impressed by German technology and strength, and a personal friend of Hermann Göring, was also very much anti-German in his outlook. While Grandi was irritated by the tendency to treat Fascism and Nazism as two sides of the same coin, Balbo's political outlook was based much more on the nineteenth-century political liberalism and nationalism of the Risorgimento. His anti-German views were also heavily influenced by his heroic service in World War I and by his revulsion at the vicious anti-Semitism of the Nazis.[19]

On the other hand, several things made an alliance with Germany seem necessary, if not attractive. The primary consideration was to some degree ideological, especially on Mussolini's part. Hitler had, of course, paid tribute to Mussolini as the premier anti-Marxist in Europe in *Mein Kampf*. Mussolini did share Hitler's anti-Bolshevism, although there were differences in the details. Like Hitler, Mussolini was also driven by a combination of nationalist imperialism and "vitalistic-biological" ideas, which both of them took seriously, although Mussolini tended to stress the former a good deal more than the latter.[20]

The ideological argument for supporting an alliance with Germany found favor with some of Mussolini's advisers. The most notable were Roberto Farinacci, former head of the Fascist Party, the mindless Achille Starace, party secretary from late 1931, and the brutal former governor of Cyrenaica, Attilio Teruzzi.[21] The most important member of the pro-German faction among Mussolini's advisers, however, was the Duce's son-in-law, foreign minister (after June 1936), and clear heir apparent by 1933, Count Galeazzo Ciano. Ciano was ardently pro-German, as would be seen by his efforts to bring Germany and Italy closer together after his appointment as foreign minister, his unquestioning acceptance of the German *Anschluss* with Austria, and his expectation that the dismissal of Hjalmar Schacht as the German economics minister would lead to a further "nazification" of the government.[22]

The final arguments for an alliance between Italy and Germany came from Mussolini's gauging of the relative strengths of the European powers. Mussolini was utterly convinced that Germany was on the road to becoming the dominant power in Europe, an opinion that was shared by a number of his advisers. In demographic, economic, and military strength, Mussolini believed that the trends were clearly in Germany's favor.[23] Equally persuasive to Mussolini was not only German strength but what he regarded as the weakness and duplicity of the British and French. Clearly, Mussolini believed that Great Britain was a declining power well on the downward slope, and the same held true for France.[24] Finally, Mussolini's program of expansion in the Mediterranean was bound to lead to conflict with Britain and France, regardless of the common misgivings they all may have shared about Germany. In any conflict of this nature Germany would be a vital ally for Italy. Certainly in this regard Anglo-French policy toward Italy in the wake of the invasion of Ethiopia in 1935 played a crucial part in the collapse of the Stresa front and moved Mussolini in the direction of Hitler.[25] The result would be the agreement signed on 23 October 1936 between Italy and Germany, which Mussolini described as the "Axis" around which the other European states would revolve.[26]

Aside from Hitler himself, several other elements were deeply involved in diplomacy and, by extension, coalition warfare. The first of these was, of course, the Foreign Ministry. Populated by professional diplomats, the Foreign Ministry proved every bit as willing to do the Führer's bidding as committed Nazi ideologues.[27] While the story of the German Foreign Ministry and its role in Hitler's diplomacy is an interesting one, it lies beyond the focus of this study, which is on the military side of coalition warfare.

The other major factors in Germany's conduct of coalition warfare were the armed services themselves, and their importance went far beyond mere military concerns. The armed forces had certainly exerted influence in German diplomacy in the Weimar period, as witnessed by the secret Russo-German military cooperation that had been part of the Rappallo Treaty between Germany and the Soviet Union.[28] Since each service had its own ministry, the heads of each service could make decisions in a variety of areas that would have an impact on coalition warfare. The most notable of these concerned the purchase of German weapons and equipment by Germany's allies. Decisions regarding types of equipment, models of weapons or aircraft, and what would be provided in return were often made by service ministries, at least before Albert Speer gained full control over armaments production late in the war. Here the most important of the services was the Luftwaffe, with its corpulent chief, Reichmarschall Hermann Göring.

Aside from being the commander in chief of the Luftwaffe and the minister of aviation, Göring was also the head of the Four Year Plan, and was thus one of the major power brokers in the German economy. Through the holding company Reichswerke Hermann Göring, he was able to extend his influence, if not outright control, over significant portions of the economies of Austria, Czechoslovakia, and especially Romania.[29]

Being relatively well traveled, Göring had made personal contacts in a number of countries, and he used one of these in one of Nazi Germany's first foreign military ventures. The military cooperation between the Weimar Republic and the Soviet Union has already been noted. Less well known is the cooperation between the still secret Luftwaffe and the Regia Aeronautica in 1933–1934. Beginning with his first visit to Rome in 1931, Göring developed a close personal friendship with Balbo. Along with Giuseppe Renzetti, an Italian economic official and high-ranking Fascist Party official, in April 1933 they worked out a plan for the training of Luftwaffe pilots in Italy. Although both Mussolini and the German Foreign Ministry had considerable misgivings about Göring, by the fall of 1934 almost 150 pilots had been trained in Italy.[30] The cooperation of the two air forces proved somewhat prophetic, as Germany's first experience with coalition warfare prior to 1940 would indeed involve the Italians to some degree.

During the interwar period, the Spanish civil war provided the military establishments of several European countries with a veritable laboratory to test both weapons and ideas on how to use them. This was certainly the case in regard to the uses of tanks and aircraft, and the Germans clearly profited not only from learning the right lessons about the employment of airpower but also from not learning the wrong lessons about the employment of armor units in light of the Italian experience at Guadalajara.[31] This applied to coalition warfare as well.

Germany's initial involvement in the Spanish civil war was at the behest of the Nationalist leader, General Francisco Franco, who requested German assistance to airlift Nationalist troops from Morocco to Spain.[32] After that, Hitler decided to limit German involvement in Spain; for him, German involvement there would be an investment but not a commitment. The dividends of this investment would become manifest in a greatly enhanced German position in the Spanish economy.[33] The major German presence would be provided by the Luftwaffe's Condor Legion. Even the economic assistance to the Nationalists was limited, totaling only some 150 million reichmarks through the end of May 1937.[34] Fascist Italy, on the other hand, took a much different approach. Benito Mussolini decided that the Italian commitment in Spain would be on a massive scale, whether Franco wanted it or not.[35] The Italians ultimately sent four divisions (with the title of Corpo Truppe Volontarie, or CTV) plus air and naval units, a force that by 20 December 1937 had swollen to no less than 40,000 men. The Italian presence in Spain became so large it ultimately consumed about two-thirds of Italy's total military budget in the period from 1935 to 1940. The CTV would also suffer some 12,000 casualties in the course of the war.[36]

The Spanish civil war presented the Germans with the problem of working with both the Spanish and the Italians. To command the Condor Legion, Hitler selected General Wolfram von Richthofen. A visionary in the field of close air support and one of the Luftwaffe's ablest field commanders in World War II, Richthofen was also a good choice from a coalition standpoint. He was fluent in Italian and had served as air attaché to Italy from 1929 to 1932. With his Italian-language experience, he was able to pick up Spanish fairly quickly.[37]

On the whole, German cooperation with the Nationalist forces in Spain was quite successful, despite a rocky start. The first German aid to Franco was in the form of antiaircraft guns. The only problem was that the German Luftwaffe corporal who was to instruct the Spanish in their use spoke no Spanish.[38] Once established, the Condor Legion was able to effectively support Nationalist operations, especially in the north. The Germans were successful in this endeavor for two reasons. First, the relatively small scale of the German effort kept the problems associated with coalition warfare to a minimum. The total German presence in Spain numbered between 5,000 and 6,000 men, of which more than 80 percent were in the Condor Legion.[39] Thus the Germans did not have to find or train a large number of interpreters. Equally important was the fact that the Germans realized, from Hitler on down, that this was not their war. They consequently kept a relatively low profile, thus avoiding incidents that might have proved embarrassing to the Spanish. Thus, even when Franco declared himself in agreement with Mussolini's proposal for the creation of a combined Italo-German General Staff to run the Nationalist side of the civil war, the proposal was turned down.[40]

Cooperation with the Italians was another matter. The initial cooperative steps taken by both Germany and Italy were of a diplomatic and economic nature. In August 1936 the respective propaganda ministers, Joseph Goebbels and Dino Alfieri, were able to come up with a jointly formulated series of statements to justify German and Italian intervention in Spain in the name of anticommunism. By late August the chiefs of the respective intelligence services, Admiral Wilhelm Canaris and Colonel (later General) Mario Roatta, were able to agree on a material aid package for the Nationalists.[41]

Actual military cooperation was another matter. Although the bombers of both the Condor Legion and the Regia Aeronautica took part in the November 1936 bombing of Madrid, they evidently flew separate missions.[42] Politically, the Pact of Steel was still on relatively shaky footing, and there was much Italian suspicion of German behavior, especially when the possibility arose of a cease-fire being brokered by Anglo-German cooperation in the summer of 1937.[43] Operationally, the Italians tended to be rather secretive about their own plans and intentions, which caused problems, especially in the conduct of combined air operations.[44] Also, given later events, it is notable that, here at least, the Germans were much more tactful than the Italians in their dealings with the Spanish. This was exemplified by the Italians' demand that their troops lead the Nationalist entrance into Barcelona on 26 January 1939. Ciano felt that the Italian troops deserved the honor, regardless of Spanish sensibilities.[45]

Another point of irritation between the Germans and the Italians concerned the failure, or at least the reluctance, of the Italians to follow up or at least take heed of German advice. The classic example of this was again Barcelona. The Italian air force contingent wanted to mount a deliberate terror bombing campaign against the city, along classic Douhetian lines. The Germans advised against this, believing that such an operation would only harden resistance. The Italians disregarded warnings both from the Germans and from Franco and proceeded to bomb the city at Mussolini's express orders. The Duce was delighted at the heavy civilian casualties, which he felt would give the Italians a reputation for ruthlessness.[46] As both the Germans and the rather indignant Franco had feared, the bombing did indeed harden and probably prolonged resistance. Certainly Richthofen left Spain with a great deal of frustration when it came to dealing with the Italians.[47]

The German military, as noted previously, had paid remarkably little attention to the lessons afforded them in coalition warfare in World War I. It seemed, however, that the experience in Spain had indicated that if Germany were to enter another war as part of a coalition, things might be done not much differently by the Germans than had been done in the past. In many ways, the military conduct of the Spanish civil war by Germany and Italy resembled what would happen in 1940, when Italy entered World War II with the intention of fighting a "parallel war." With the Nazi-Soviet Pact of 23 August 1939 and the initial German successes from the fall of 1939 to the spring and summer of 1940, however, it appeared that the Wehrmacht might not have to deal with such problems at all.

Germany's entry into World War II in terms of coalition warfare was very different from that of World War I. Germany, by Hitler's design, had begun the war on his terms, although a year later than he had originally intended.[48] Also, unlike in World War I, Germany began the war without any active allies militarily. Japan was still somewhat irritated over the Nazi-Soviet Pact, which had proved embarrassing to the Japanese government.[49] In any case, it was in Japan's interest to simply just await events. A German victory in the west would allow the Japanese to make major gains in Southeast Asia for minimal effort.[50] In addition, Hitler now had the unlikeliest of diplomatic partners, namely, Josef Stalin's Soviet Union, although this was an alliance Hitler always considered temporary at best, to be broken at a time when it would be most profitable to do so. In the actual event the Red Army took part in the dismembering of Poland but never participated with the Germans in a coalition operation.[51]

Mussolini had refrained from committing Italy to war in September 1939. Dissatisfied with simply declaring neutrality, a term he despised, he instead made his contribution to diplomatic euphemistic terminology by calling Italy's position "nonbelligerence." This was the Duce's way of ostensibly reassuring Hitler that this, while not participation in the war, was also not neutrality. Mussolini also promised to act on Hitler's request to pin down as many Allied forces as possible in whatever way available that was short of war. Nonetheless, as late as 2 September 1939 the Duce was still pushing for any kind of settlement that would be favorable to Germany.[52]

Mussolini refrained from entering the war in 1939 for two reasons. The first was Italy's state of almost complete unpreparedness, something that was known to Italians and Germans alike. Aside from material deficiencies, especially in the army, the brutal fact was that owing to the financial drains imposed on Italy by the Ethiopian War and by aiding the Nationalists in the Spanish civil war, the Italian government was virtually broke by early 1939. Felice Guarnari, the Italian minister of exchange and currency, announced as early as 1938 that the government was broke. His successor, Raffaello Riccardi, also pointed this out at a meeting of the Supreme Defense Committee in early February 1940.[53] All he received for his courage was a dismissive comment by Badoglio that Riccardi should essentially mind his own business. Riccardi's cause also may not have been helped by the fact that he received the warm support of Balbo, who by that time was certainly not on good terms with Mussolini.[54] For their part, the Germans were well aware of the financial straits Italy was in. Both a Luftwaffe orientation booklet on the Italian armed forces and a German navy report on the state of the Italian navy noted that Italy's tautly stretched finances would effectively prevent the nation from entering the war.[55]

The other reason Mussolini avoided war was that, in some ways, he was acting according to the dictates of traditional Italian strategy. Ever since Italy's entry into the world of European power politics as a unified country in the late nineteenth century, successive Italian governments had operated under the policy that Brian Sullivan has described as the strategy of the "decisive weight." By throwing Italy's weight into the scales of a European war on the winning side at the moment of decision, its leaders hoped to attain their goals in a short "war of rapid decision" while ignoring such things as popular sentiment, not to mention Italy's eternally difficult situation in terms of raw materials. This was essentially the manner by which the Italian government of Antonio Salandra had entered World War I, although to some degree at the prodding of King Vittorio Emmanuaele III and the chief of the Italian General Staff, General Luigi Cadorna, as well. The result was that although Italy did emerge with some gains from the Versailles conference, the war was neither rapid nor decisive. Its sheer bloodiness, however, coupled with the shattering defeat at Caporetto, pushed Italy to the very edge of disaster. Nevertheless, ultimate success in World War I had convinced Mussolini to act in the very same way. He would wait and see.[56]

The initial stance of nonbelligerence by Italy drew different responses from Hitler, depending on whom one reads. According to Walter Warlimont, Hitler was most disappointed in Italian nonbelligerence in 1939. If Hitler was disappointed, however, he certainly did not show it in his correspondence with Mussolini, in which the Führer showed himself to be the very soul of understanding in regard to Mussolini's position.[57]

The attitude of the German High Command toward Italy's refraining from war was probably one of relief. As noted earlier, informed circles in all of the German armed services were very well aware of the material and financial problems confronting the Italians.[58] Nonetheless, when the Italians presented a laundry list of items they would need from Germany, especially in the way of raw materials, even the Germans were surprised. Mussolini asked for some 6 million tons of coal, 7 million tons of oil, and 2 million tons of steel, and this constituted only a part of a very long list. In addition to raw materials, Mussolini asked for some 150 batteries of 90mm antiaircraft guns to protect the Turin-Genoa-Milan industrial area. In his diary, Ciano described the list as "enough to kill a bull—if a bull could read it."[59] For his part, Hitler responded by saying that Germany could supply only some of the items on the list, as well as thirty batteries of heavy antiaircraft guns. Hitler reassuringly added that he understood the Duce's position.[60]

Other German leaders were enthused that Italy was not in the war. Colonel General (later Field Marshal) Fedor von Bock regarded Italian nonbelligerence as fairly typical behavior. Since Wilhelm Keitel, the chief of the Armed Forces High Command (Oberkommando der Wehrmacht, or OKW), regarded Italy's later entry into the war as more of a "burden than a relief," it can safely be assumed that he thought of Italian nonbelligerence as more of a relief than a burden.[61]

Financial and material exigencies notwithstanding, Mussolini was clearly anxious to enter the war, and Hitler was equally anxious to have him in it. After the conquest of Poland, Hitler wanted an immediate attack on France. One of the reasons for this was, as Hitler told chief of the general staff Colonel General Franz Halder on 10 October 1939, that "an offensive is the only way to sweep Italy into action on our side."[62]

Aside from the ideological affinities, Mussolini was drawn to Hitler for two reasons having mostly to do with traditional power politics. As noted previously, during the period 1938–1940 Mussolini was acting under the assumption of the strategy of the decisive weight. It is fairly clear, however, that he had already decided that Germany would win. Deeply impressed by German military might, especially after his 1937 visit to Berlin, he was absolutely positive that Germany would emerge triumphant. These impulses were only sharpened by German military success in Poland in 1939. The Duce's pro-German impulses were equally reinforced by what Mussolini regarded as the contemptuous behavior of the Allies.[63] Conversely, by the fall and winter of 1939–1940 most of Mussolini's advisers who had counseled a more cautious approach toward Germany had been either effectively silenced or removed far from the seat of power. Balbo, for example, who had viewed Germany with some suspicion from the start, had been virtually exiled to North Africa in 1934 for a variety of reasons. His untimely death at the hands of mistaken Italian antiaircraft gunners on 28 June 1940 deprived Mussolini of one of the saner voices who at times could come within earshot of the Duce.[64] In his diary, Ciano consistently took an anti-German line, but evidently such ideas never went beyond the pages of that document.[65]

The second reason Mussolini was drawn to Hitler was the kind of war the Italian leader expected to fight, and the kind of peace that would be obtained in the victorious aftermath. Mussolini expected that Italy, even as an ally of Germany, would be able to wage a "parallel war," like prior Italian governments. This had been the case in 1866 with Italy's alliance with Prussia, and it was also the case with Italy in World War I. Mussolini clearly expected to fight on the side of Germany along the same lines.[66] In addition, Mussolini's war aims were very traditional in outlook, in that they involved the simple acquisition of territory.

Consistent with his strategy and the belief that Germany would be victorious, Mussolini frantically instituted a series of measures to make Italy as ready as possible for war. The first step, and one of the most important, was Mussolini's firing of General Alberto Pariani as chief of the general staff and General Giuseppe Valle as chief of the general staff of the air force.[67]

Described by Badoglio as a man of "lively but undisciplined intelligence," and by Fascist leader Luigi Federzoni as a "cold blooded maniac," Pariani had virtually crippled the Regio Esercito with a series of poorly thought out organizational schemes, especially the "binary division," which reduced the existing Italian divisions to the status of weak brigades. The equipment situation was also very poor, especially in antitank weapons, antiaircraft guns, and artillery.[68] Pariani's successor, Marshal Rodolfo Graziani, would have his hands full trying to undo the damage done during Pariani's tenure.

Valle had been undersecretary for air from 1933 to 1939 and chief of staff for the Regia Aeronautica from 1929 to 1939. His reign had been marked by a series of disastrous decisions, especially regarding the kind of aircraft the Italian air force should buy. This was particularly true in the realm of fighter aircraft. By 1939–1940, the mainstay of the Regia Aeronautica's fighter force was still the Fiat CR 42 biplane, a machine that was inferior in every respect, even though Valle claimed that it was the technological equal of the latest German and British designs. The CR 42's successors, the Fiat G 50 and the Macchi MC 200, while at least all metal monoplane fighters, were not significant improvements.[69] The bomber force was in slightly better shape, but like so many other air forces of the interwar period, the Regia Aeronautica suffered from the ideological dominance of the strategic bombing doctrines of Giulio Douhet. Although the Italians came to appreciate the value of dive-bombing during the Spanish civil war, the attempt to develop the Savioia-Marchetti SM-84 and the Breda 88 as dive-bombers had clearly failed by July 1940.[70] The best that Valle's successor, General Francesco Pricolo, could do was to buy German Ju-87 dive-bombers almost immediately after Italy's entry into the war, a matter that will be dealt with in a bit more detail later.[71]

Mussolini also sought to stockpile as much raw material as possible, but this effort was also a failure. Promised German deliveries of coal and iron dropped off sharply during the winter of 1939–1940, although Hitler attributed this to the terrible winter. Efforts to obtain raw materials from other sources were also unavailing as the Western powers, especially Britain, held all the cards. Britain had seized a number of German coal ships that were bound for Italy. A number of Italian colliers were also seized, and even though they were eventually released, their freedom was granted only after weeks of delay.[72] In addition, by controlling Gibraltar and the Suez Canal, Britain was in a position to close both ends of the Mediterranean to shipping headed for Italy. Before the war, Italy annually imported up to 22 million tons of goods. Of this about 84 percent came by sea, and of that amount, some 66 percent came by Gibraltar or the Suez Canal.[73] Thus Italy was still in a parlous state when Hitler and Mussolini met at the Brenner Pass on 18 March 1940.

On 8 March 1940 Hitler sent a nine-page letter to Mussolini, which was hand delivered to the Duce by German foreign minister Joachim von Ribbentropp. At the end of the letter, which was a broad survey of the military situation of Germany vis-à-vis the Allies, Hitler expressed interest in a personal meeting. Ribbentropp then made the idea into a formal proposal on the eleventh to Ciano and Mussolini, and they accepted immediately.[74]

On 18 March 1940 Hitler and Mussolini met face-to-face for the fourth time at the Brenner Pass. The conference and its aftermath are important to this study because they illuminate the manner in which Hitler conducted both diplomacy and coalition warfare. The only participants present at the meeting were Hitler, Mussolini, Ciano, Ribbentropp and Dr. Paul Schmidt, who was Hitler's interpreter. Schmidt's interpreting duties were not very onerous, as Mussolini was somewhat conversant in German, so he wrote a detailed summary of the conversation for the German Foreign Ministry. The meeting was not so much a conversation but a lengthy monologue by Hitler, although Ciano noted that it was delivered in a restrained tone, without the Führer's typical histrionics.[75]

Knowing of Mussolini's desire to enter the war, Hitler appealed to him to act as the decisive weight. He should time Italy's entry for the moment when it would conclusively tip the scales in favor of the Axis.[76] When it came to specifics, however, Hitler was a study in evasiveness if not outright mendacity. Although Hitler did indicate that France would be attacked, "this presupposed the breaching of large sections of the Maginot Line." He also gave absolutely no indication of the impending attack on Norway.[77] Likewise, when Hitler assented on 4 April 1940 to the resumption of staff talks between OKW and its Italian counterpart (Commando Supremo), Hitler again enjoined OKW to make no mention of the impending operations against either Norway or France, even though the talks were to deal with the problems that would arise from Italy's entry into the war against the Western allies.[78] This kind of behavior would be repeated consistently throughout the war.

When Hitler did attack Norway in April 1940, far from drawing Mussolini's ire at not being told, it only whetted the Duce's desire to get into the war. The only thing Mussolini asked was that Hitler keep him informed, as he had promised at their Brenner Pass meeting.[79] Hitler certainly did this, sending detailed messages to Mussolini outlining the course of operations. As impressed as Mussolini was by German boldness, he was equally impressed by the reaction of the French and the British, which he regarded as utterly craven.[80]

Mussolini's appetite was further encouraged when Hitler launched the German army on its conquest of France and the Low Countries on 10 May 1940. As usual, Hitler told Mussolini of the impending operations only the day before but then, as he had promised, followed through with several other messages that made Mussolini increasingly anxious to enter the war.[81] As early as 13 May 1940, Mussolini was convinced that the Allies were defeated; six days later Mussolini informed Hitler that the Italian people were "convinced that the period of non-belligerency cannot last much longer."[82] Although Mussolini was to waver slightly over the next few days, by the end of May he was certain that Germany had won and that the Allies were broken. On 26 May 1940 he informed Badoglio and Balbo over their objections that Italy would come into the war. Four days later he informed Hitler that Italy would enter the war as early as 5 June 1940, but he ultimately delayed Italy's entry at Hitler's request until the tenth. Notably, Hitler's reaction to Mussolini's plan to open with a declaration of war against France was one of almost utter contempt.[83]

For Germany, Italy's entry into the war posed several new problems as well as advantages. On the positive side, Italy could add its impressive-looking naval strength to that of Germany. It must be remembered, however, that although the Italian navy's performance in World War II was disappointing on the whole, at the outset of the war the Regia Marina was clearly regarded as the most modern of all the Italian services, especially its surface ships. It was hoped that Italy would indeed try to engage Britain on the sea and in the air.[84] Hitler was personally enthused by Italy's entry into the war, since he would be standing shoulder to shoulder with Mussolini, his closest comrade-in-arms.[85]

The minuses were much greater. If Hitler was not aware of it, the high commands of the various services certainly knew of Italy's parlous financial state, which has already been commented on. The next significant minus was Italy's lack of raw materials. Italy was short of almost every major strategic raw material. Italy once again requested raw materials from Germany after the declaration of war, but in much smaller amounts this time than the massive list put forth in August 1939. Italian shortfalls would have to be made up by Germany or other countries such as Romania, whose economic interests were tied closely with Germany.[86]

Another issue was the Italian request for finished weapons and equipment. As noted previously, when Mussolini declared nonbelligerence in 1939, one of the issues involved Germany's inability to deliver the 150 batteries of heavy antiaircraft guns requested by the Italians. With Italy's entry into the war such requests were now renewed, especially after a Royal Air Force

(RAF) Bomber Command raid on Turin left fourteen civilians dead and thirty wounded.[87] Not much, however, could be done about that. As a token of personal esteem, Hitler did give Mussolini two railroad cars with light antiaircraft guns for his personal protection. Nothing else was really done, however, by the Germans with the exception of the Luftwaffe, which did enter into negotiations with the Italians for the purchase of Ju-87 dive-bombers.[88]

Even this effort had drawbacks. In August 1939, for example, Germany had sent models of not only the Ju-87 but also the He-111 and the Me-109 to Italy for technical and flight tests. When the war broke out, however, these aircraft were recalled to Germany, and all cooperation ended. Any new proposal for cooperation in the realm of aircraft technology now had to go via diplomatic channels. Likewise, there was also a distinct lessening in the area of exchanges of intelligence and technical information.[89]

Other than that, however, the best that could be done was to put the Italians at the top of the list of countries to whom captured equipment (mostly French) could be sold or distributed. OKW would be the responsible agency for distribution. The Italians would be at the head of the list, followed by the Romanians, Bulgarians, and Hungarians. The Finns were effectively excluded from receiving any aid; the provisions of the Nazi-Soviet Pact made it impossible for the Germans to provide any real aid to the Finns, whatever German sympathies might be.[90]

In terms of conducting coalition warfare, there would be no mechanism to direct combined operations. There was never to be any organization comparable to the Anglo-American Combined Chiefs of Staff, whose mission was to develop common strategies and plans to implement them. This was satisfactory to both Germany and Italy. Mussolini, confronted with a divided high command beset by rivalries between major figures such as Badoglio and Balbo who distrusted the Germans, wanted Italy to wage a "parallel war."[91] Hitler and his military chiefs distrusted the Duce's military advisers, and Hitler always maintained a notorious secretiveness about his military plans in any case.[92] This even applied to the distribution of propaganda. Although Hitler's propaganda minister Joseph Goebbels was personally fond of such noted Fascist luminaries as Farinacci and Dino Alfieri, no German-Italian cooperation in this area was really formulated. When such attempts or gestures did occur, they had almost a comic-opera air about them. When Farinacci sent 5,000 books to be distributed to German soldiers, Goebbels noted in his diary that the content of the books was "anti-Fascist," so he disposed of them quietly.[93]

For military cooperation, a series of service-based liaison organizations were established. At the top, the respective attachés in Rome and Berlin,

General Enno von Rintelen and General Efesio Marras, each became the general attached to supreme headquarters. Rintelen was thus attached to Commando Supremo and Marras to OKW, although Warlimont noted that Marras was rarely seen at OKW. Rintelen did receive daily briefings at Commando Supremo, although he complained that the Italians were stingy with information about army strength and plans. In addition, despite Badoglio's insistence that Rintelen deal only with him, he was usually able to have extensive discussions with Mussolini and other Italian military leaders, the contents of which were invariably reported back to OKW, with a copy going to the Army High Command (Oberkommando des Heeres, or OKH).[94] Strategic matters were usually discussed at meetings between Hitler and Ciano or Keitel and his Italian counterpart, first Badoglio and later General Ugo Cavallero. Finally, Hitler and Mussolini occasionally met in a series of conferences, which were usually held at the Brenner Pass aboard either Hitler's or Mussolini's private train. During the period before his dismissal of Badoglio, Mussolini brought Ciano with him, but he would not take a military adviser.[95]

Below the high command level, each service also exchanged representatives to act as liaison officers. In Germany's case, it would seem here that the Luftwaffe was the best prepared to act immediately in this regard. On 11 June 1940 the Luftwaffe established a liaison staff attached to the headquarters of the Regia Aeronautica in Rome. Headed by General Max Ritter von Pohl, it consisted of five officers and one noncommissioned officer, assisted by a small number of enlisted personnel, who were drawn from Luftgaukommando (Air District Headquarters) VII. For transport the staff had three cars and a light aircraft.[96] It was Pohl who immediately conducted conversations with Pricolo on the Italian purchase of Stukas and other logistical issues. In addition to the negotiations for the Italian purchase of Ju-87s, a separate combined staff was set up to conduct exchanges of information regarding intelligence and aircraft technology.[97]

The German navy had been conducting limited exchanges of intelligence and technical information with the Italian navy before Italy's entry into the war.[98] Once Italy formally entered the war, the German navy established official liaison with the Regia Marina, with the naval attaché, Admiral Eberhard Weichold, being posted to Italian navy headquarters on 28 June 1940. He had, however, only a small staff to assist him. Because Rintelen was an army general, he handled army matters that cropped up in Rome.[99]

Italy's entry into the war did not create much of an opportunity for the respective armies to cooperate. The Italian offensive was undertaken by Army Group West under Crown Prince Umberto with limited forces in a great hurry, and as a result could make no headway. Little ground was taken, and the Italian troops, unprepared to fight in the snow-covered Alps, suffered heavily from frostbite.[100] General Mario Roatta hatched a plan to have the Germans transport Italian battalions to areas behind the French lines which the Germans had occupied, but against which the Italians had territorial claims. This idea, however, dismissed by Halder as the "cheapest kind of fraud," was disapproved by Badoglio, and so nothing came of it.[101] Matters were not helped by German-Italian disagreements over issues regarding French possessions in North Africa, although they were papered over in a series of intentionally vaguely worded agreements signed by Roatta and the head of the German Armistice Commission, General Karl-Heinrich von Stülpnagel.[102]

Italy's entry into the war did create two opportunities for the Germans and Italians to operate together, namely, at sea and in the air. Mussolini, interested in demonstrating to Hitler his seriousness about the war with Britain, offered to send ground troops to France to take part in Operation *Sea Lion*, the projected invasion of Britain, an offer Hitler declined on logistical grounds, much to Mussolini's annoyance.[103] Not about to take no for an answer, in a 17 July 1940 letter to Hitler Mussolini offered the assistance of Italian naval and air forces against Britain. This time the Führer accepted the Duce's offer on 25 July 1940, at a conference with his OKW advisers. Grand Admiral Erich Raeder, commander in chief of the German navy, wanted operations to be coordinated in that the Italians be trained to incorporate the lessons previously learned by German U-boats. Raeder also suggested creating a liaison staff from Grand Admiral Karl Dönitz's staff which would be posted to the Italian submarine command staff, an idea that Hitler approved. Finally, the Italians would be responsible for refueling their own submarines.[104]

Once Hitler agreed to the naval cooperation, the responsibility for its execution fell to the commander of the German U-boat arm, Grand Admiral Karl Dönitz. Things got off to a positive start, since Dönitz enjoyed a good relationship with his Italian counterpart, Admiral Angelo Parona. Both agreed that the overall direction of operations, the allocation of operational areas, and the form of any direct cooperation would be left to Dönitz and his staff. Parona would have a wide degree of latitude in his freedom of action and responsibility. Dönitz thought it important that Italian submarine crews should feel that they were being commanded by Italians and fighting alongside the Germans on an equal basis.[105]

The procedure to bring the Italians together with their German allies was a complex one. First, a suitable base had to be agreed on. In this case Bordeaux was the choice. Since the base would be in German-held territory, the

Germans would be responsible for building the infrastructure needed to base the Italian submarines and provide antiaircraft defenses, and the Italians were responsible for their own logistics.[106] Once that was in the final stages, the Italian boats and crews would move from their Italian bases to their new one in occupied France.

All this took quite a bit of time. Although the initial offer had been made by Mussolini and accepted by Hitler in July 1940 and the details agreed on in August, the first Italian submarine did not arrive in Bordeaux until 4 September 1940. The transfer of Italian submarines was accomplished without the loss of one boat, even though it involved a passage through the Straits of Gibraltar, which reflected well on Italian seamanship.[107] Once at the new base, the Italian crews were sent on to the Baltic for training while the officers would have the opportunity to go out as observers on German U-boat patrols. Both Dönitz and Parona were in agreement on this; both understood that the Italian crews would have a lot to learn about operations in the Atlantic.[108]

Although three Italian submarines, Commander Mario Leoni's *Malaspina,* Commander Giulio Ghiglieri's *Barbarigo,* and Commander Riccardo Boris's *Dandolo,* had been operating in the Atlantic during August and September 1940, the first combined German-Italian submarine operation did not begin until October 1940, by which time twenty-seven Italian submarines were based at Bordeaux.[109] Dönitz hoped that even if they did not sink ships, the Italian submarines could at least provide timely reconnaissance information to their German counterparts. The first operation, conducted between 10 October and 30 November 1940, was a failure from a coalition standpoint. During this period Italian submarines sank only four ships totaling 17,921 tons, while the Germans sank some eighty ships.[110]

There were several reasons for the failure of the operation. First, Italian submarines were poorly suited to conditions in the Atlantic. Their large conning towers and large deck guns rendered them unsuitable for German-style U-boat operations, which involved having U-boats making night attacks while surfaced. Dönitz noted that Italian submarines, built for the relatively placid waters of the Mediterranean, did not have a diesel air supply mast in their conning towers, so that while running on the surface the conning tower hatch had to be left open. In heavy seas, waves would break over the conning tower, and seawater would enter the boat, damaging the electrical equipment. The Italian crews also had not mastered the kind of radio procedures that Dönitz demanded, so that in the operation intelligence arrived late, if at all. Finally, it was hard to break old habits. Italian skippers, like those of so many other navies between the wars, had been trained to take up station and then lie in wait for the enemy, rather than aggressively search for him. When an enemy ship did come in sight, the preference was for a cautious submerged attack.[111]

Once the combined German-Italian submarine operation had broken down, Dönitz withdrew the Italian submarines. At Bordeaux, Parona had the Italian submarines fitted with smaller conning towers, while the crews were given additional training. When the Italian submarines had been re-fitted, Dönitz sent them out again in January 1941. This time Dönitz assigned the Italians to their own operational sector. Here the results proved more satisfactory. The best score was racked up by the *Torelli,* skippered by Commander Primo Longobardo, which sank four ships totaling 17,489 tons in two weeks.[112] Based on the promising results of January 1941, Dönitz decided to mount another combined operation against the North Atlantic convoys beginning in February. This operation, conducted between February and May 1941, also failed for some of the same reasons outlined earlier.[113]

With the breakdown of the second combined German-Italian submarine operation, Dönitz and Parona agreed to abandon tactical cooperation. Matters were also influenced by the fact that after the Italian defeats in North Africa in December 1940 and January 1941, most of the Italian submarines were recalled to the Mediterranean. By mid-1941 only about ten of the original twenty-seven boats were still based at Bordeaux. Dönitz assigned these to the following areas: west of Gibraltar, south of the German area of operations in the North Atlantic, and the area off Freetown. Later on, six Italian submarines participated in Dönitz's U-boat offensive in the Caribbean, sinking some twelve ships before being withdrawn in August 1942. Dönitz noted that two of the Italian skippers, Lieutenant Commander Gianfranco Gazzana-Priaroggia and Commander Carlo Feccia di Cossato, were awarded the Knight's Cross.[114]

Aside from naval support, Mussolini had also wanted to send a squadron of aircraft to participate in the war against Britain, an offer Hitler accepted around 11 or 12 August 1940.[115] By the end of August 1940, plans were in hand for the installation of units of the Regia Aeronautica (later known as the Corpo Aereo Italiano, or CAI), in the area of operations of General (later Field Marshal) Albert Kesselring's Second Air Fleet. The task of constructing the necessary facilities for the basing of the Italians was undertaken by the Luftgaukommando for Belgium and northern France. Heading the effort would be Major General von Kotze, who would be responsible for the construction of the requisite facilities for basing the Italians. He would essentially act as an intermediary between the Luftgaukommando and the CAI, being the head of the German liaison staff to the CAI.[116]

This cooperation between the Luftwaffe and the Regia Aeronautica was really the doing more of the Führer and the Duce. Certainly it generated very little enthusiasm among their military staffs and field commanders involved. Badoglio, as late as 9 October 1940, was still voicing objections to the dispatching of the CAI to Belgium. He argued that Italian pilots would have difficulty living in the harsh weather conditions of northwestern Europe and, with the period of bad weather setting in, would be confined to inactivity during the winter months. Instead, Badoglio felt that both aircraft and pilots would be much more gainfully employed in the Mediterranean during the winter and could then, if circumstances allowed, be committed to action over England in the spring of 1941.[117] Any number of German commanders were not exactly thrilled at the prospect of the CAI's arrival, either. Kesselring, who would exercise operational command over the CAI, thought them a nuisance and was delighted when they left.[118]

The objections of Badoglio, Kesselring, and others notwithstanding, preparations went ahead for the arrival of the CAI. On 10 September 1940 the liaison staff to the CAI was established. It was headed by Kotze, who would be assisted by a small staff drawn from the Second Air Fleet. Major Paul Gottschling was the operations officer, assisted by Major Hohenlindegg. The liaison staff would have a bomber officer and a fighter officer, as well as an intelligence officer. Interpreting duties would be handled by First Lieutenant Philipp De La Cerda and three enlisted men. The liaison staff had four principal tasks: first, to establish and maintain liaison with the CAI; second, to transmit orders from the Second Air Fleet to the CAI and to provide advice; third, to oversee the construction of facilities for the basing of the CAI; and, finally, to transmit the logistical needs of the CAI to the Luftgaukommando for Belgium and northern France, as well as to the headquarters of the Regia Aeronautica in Rome.[119] The 3,750 officers and men, as well as the aircraft, were set to arrive by train on 25 or 26 September 1940.[120]

The deployment of the CAI proceeded accordingly in stages. The men and aircraft arrived on time, followed by supplies. By 7 October 1940 the CAI, based in Dijon, had some 10,852 gallons of aviation fuel and sufficient quarters to house 80 officers and 120 men, and facilities to handle up to 100 aircraft. The plan was to have the Regia Aeronautica's Fifty-sixth Fighter Wing, consisting of one squadron of CR 42s and one squadron of G 50s, go through a training program leading up to a series of combined exercises involving the Fifty-sixth Fighter Wing and units of the German II Air Corps. Later on an Italian bomber wing of two squadrons of Fiat BR 20 bombers would be committed.[121]

In this case, German-Italian cooperation proved an absolute failure. Such exercises that did take place could be carried out only in ideal weather, something that was quite rare in that part of Europe at that time of the year. In addition, the Italian fighters proved no match for either the Hurricane or the Spitfire. The imbalance could only be redressed by the appearance of the Macchi 202 fighter, but that was still two years away, or by technology exchange between the respective air forces, a topic to be addressed later.[122]

It would seem that the CAI flew three raids against the British. On 29 October 1940, while the Third Air Fleet's raids against Portsmouth drew off most of the British fighters, fifteen BR 20 bombers, escorted by seventy-three fighters, attacked Ramsgate. Some eleven tons of bombs (ninety-two bombs) were dropped on the port facilities, inflicting some damage.[123] Then on the night of 5–6 November 1940, eight bombers from the CAI dropped a little over six tons of bombs on Harwich with no loss.[124] The next time the CAI went out on 11 November 1940, it was not so fortunate. Of the ten BR 20s sent out, three were shot down, along with three CR 42s. One British source noted that the bomber crews were carrying tin hats and bayonets.[125]

The 11 November 1940 raid against Harwich marked the end of the CAI's participation in the air war over England. Thereafter, the only interaction between the Second Air Fleet and the CAI essentially concerned training, where the Germans would provide training for Italian pilots in both blind and instrument flying.[126]

With the onset of bad weather and the shifting of German intentions to the east, the CAI's presence in Belgium made even less sense than before. The matter was clinched by the Italian disaster in North Africa. As soon as the first reports of Graziani's defeat became known, Badoglio's successor, General (later Marshal) Ugo Cavallero, passed a request through Rintelen to Göring for the return of the CAI from Belgium.[127] Thus the CAI was withdrawn from Belgium and France and sent back to Italy. The liaison staff was accordingly dissolved on 19 January 1941. De La Cerda and the staff intelligence officer, Major Ludwig Graf von Isenburg, went on to other assignments involving liaison functions with the Italians. The rest of the staff were returned to their parent formations, being either the Second Air Fleet or the Luftgaukommando for Belgium and northern France.[128]

The other area in which the Luftwaffe and the Regia Aeronautica cooperated was in the sale of aircraft, particularly dive-bombers, to the Italians. The Italians had come to appreciate the value of dive-bombing during the Spanish civil war and were quite impressed with the performance of the Ju-87. As a result, the Italians attempted to develop their own dive-bomber program, which failed because the SM-84 was not really up to demands required for a dive-bomber. This left the Italians with the choice of buying the Ju-87. After the initial conversations between Pricolo and Pohl, Pricolo and the Italian air attaché in Berlin, Colonel Teucchi, held extensive talks in Berlin with Göring about Italy's purchase of Ju-87Bs from Germany. Test flights were conducted at Graz in August 1940. The first Italian Stuka Group (Ninety-seventh) was formed on 11 November 1940 and would eventually be composed of about fourteen aircraft, all either the Ju-87B or Ju-87R models.[129] Aside from buying German-built aircraft, a more promising approach would have been to mate Italian air frames with German engines. This would come later in the war and would fail for a variety of reasons to be discussed later in this work.

Thus ended Germany's first experience in coalition warfare in World War II. On the whole, the cooperation between the German navy and the Italian navy in the battle of the Atlantic could be considered mildly successful. Dönitz was able to take the measure of Italian strengths and weaknesses, then employed them in situations where they could produce results. The German-Italian effort was aided by the fact that Dönitz and Parona established a good personal relationship. However small the Italian contribution, it was a contribution nonetheless. For Dönitz the sinking of merchant ships was the only thing that mattered, the goal being between 600,000 and 700,000 tons per month.[130] Thus any ship the Italians sank was a contribution, given Dönitz's strategy.[131] The Italian contribution in the Caribbean should not be underestimated, as Dönitz himself was never in a position to employ more than a handful of U-boats at any one time in his operations in North American waters.

The record of German-Italian aerial cooperation was more mixed. To be sure, only the Luftwaffe seemed to be ready for coalition warfare, establishing a liaison staff in Rome almost immediately after the Italian declaration of war.[132] The deployment of the CAI to the Second Air Fleet's area of operations was another matter. Badoglio's objections to the operation, which were well-founded, should have been pressed home more with Mussolini, just as German military skepticism should have pressed more with Hitler. In fact, one could argue that the decision to deploy the CAI set the pattern for several future events in which Hitler would acquiesce to an ill-conceived idea by Mussolini.[133] In the actual event, the effort involved in deploying the CAI was simply not commensurate with the results.

In some ways, however, the Luftwaffe benefited from the experience with the CAI. First, it allowed the Luftwaffe to develop some officers with experience in coalition operations. In fact, some members of the liaison staff who worked with the CAI would later figure with varying degrees of prominence in the Mediterranean. Also, the scale of the effort did not overtax the Luftwaffe's ability to conduct such operations. The number of interpreters, for example, was kept to a minimum. In addition, the Luftwaffe and the Regia Aeronautica learned enough that given the vast technological, logistical, and organizational differences between them, the creation of mixed German-Italian air units was out of the question, at least for the immediate future. Finally, some progress was made in the realm of exchanging intelligence and information on aircraft technology.[134]

The level of German involvement in coalition warfare was about to change, however, in a drastic way. Germany's participation in coalition warfare would expand into two theaters and would set the stage for the appearance of one of the most captivating personalities of World War II.

3

Desert Sands I

The Mediterranean and North Africa,
June 1940–February 1942

Italy is rich in manpower, but poorer by nature in raw materials than other great powers. Since the Italians are inherently aggressive and are constrained to end a war in a short time so as not to be overpowered by an enemy superior in raw materials, Italy has developed the doctrine of the war of rapid decision.

Unsigned article, 1939[1]

Mussolini . . . is convinced that we shall have victory and peace by the end of next month. For this reason he wants to move fast in Egypt.

Galeazzo Ciano, 18 August 1940[2]

Unquestionably, the Italian is ready to sacrifice his life for his fatherland and perform heroic deeds in an attack, or to endure the greatest privations in the hot sand of the desert; but to hold out in difficult places when alone and to defend oneself to the last cartridge is not for him.

Enno von Rintelen, 2 January 1941[3]

The Italian soldier has shown good individual performance and regularly shows himself to be modest and willing to help.

Erwin Rommel, February 1942[4]

THE ONSET OF WAR IN THE MEDITERRANEAN presented Germany with opportunities but also exposed some vulnerabilities. With the British holding both ends of the Mediterranean, namely, Gibraltar and the Suez Canal, they had entrée into the area. Potential allies in the Balkans, especially Greece and Yugoslavia, could provide numerous naval and air bases from which the long coastline of Italy could be threatened.[5] The best way to deal with these matters, with Italian participation in the war now a reality, was by the occupation of the North African coast, most notably Egypt and the Suez Canal. Mussolini, regarding the end of the war as imminent, was certainly pushing his generals for an early offensive into Egypt.

The question of the role of the Middle East in Axis planning has been hotly debated over the years. More traditional scholarship, led by Gerhard

46

Weinberg, has argued that the failure to pursue an offensive in the Middle East, combined with a Japanese offensive into the Indian Ocean in early 1942, cost the Axis powers their best chance to both act in concert and inflict the most serious damage on Britain possible, short of an outright invasion.[6] The opposite view holds that, given Hitler's overriding interest in the conquest of the Soviet Union, North Africa could never have been anything more than a sideshow. Even with the elimination of Malta in the spring of 1942 and supposing that Rommel did reach Alexandria and the Suez Canal, the size of the German commitment to Russia would have minimized the impact of and ability to exploit success in the Middle East.[7]

Both views are partially correct. While Weinberg's concept of a German-Japanese linkup in the area of the Indian Ocean seems somewhat far-fetched, especially in view of the shoestring nature of Axis logistics in general and German logistics in particular, he is quite correct in suggesting that ignoring it was a mistake. Although Klaus Schmider is right to stress the overriding importance of Russia in Hitler's thinking, he is wrong to dismiss the possible impact an Axis victory in the Mediterranean could have had, especially early on in the war.

The vulnerabilities of Italy upon its entry into the war have been enumerated. The best way these vulnerabilities could have been dealt with, however, was by the occupation of Egypt and the Suez Canal. If this had been done when the British were most vulnerable, namely, in the summer and fall of 1940, its impact would have been considerable. An early occupation of Egypt and the Suez Canal would have benefited Germany in several ways. First, it would have made continued British possession of Malta very difficult, if not impossible. Second, it would have confined British activities in the Mediterranean to the occasional long-range air raid or naval foray into the western or central Mediterranean. Even if the Italians did become embroiled in Greece (as will be discussed in the next chapter), the British would still have no way to effectively intervene in the Balkans. Thus the German strategic flank, even allowing for the eventual unwanted Italian meddling in Greece, would still be relatively secure. Finally, possession of the canal would facilitate the exchange of vital economic raw materials between Germany and Japan for at least some period of time. Even if the Axis could not retain the Suez area permanently, occupation of the canal for any time would allow the Axis the opportunity, if necessary, to destroy or at least block the canal, thus denying it to the British.

That none of these things materialized was due to a combination of poor timing on the part of both Axis powers, the complete absence of a combined planning mechanism, a wide divergence between Mussolini and his generals over the ability of the Italian army to undertake a campaign in North Africa, and the failure of the Axis powers to share technological information. From the start, Germany clearly regarded the Mediterranean as an Italian theater of war. At no time during Ciano's meeting with Hitler in Berlin on 7 July 1940, attended by several high-ranking diplomats from both countries, did the prospect of sending German help to North Africa come up. Nor did Hitler broach the subject in his 13 July 1940 letter to Mussolini.[8]

This thinking had changed somewhat by August 1940, at least on the part of the Germans. As early as 7 August 1940, OKW was discussing the idea of dispatching a German "expeditionary force," essentially a panzer corps, to support the Italian advance to the Nile Delta. By 23 August Hitler also wanted to send a German force to North Africa, but limited only to a "mixed armored brigade." By the twenty-sixth the discussion had expanded the unit to one perhaps of division size.[9]

The other tangible form of help Germany could send was airpower. While discussions were ongoing about sending an armored unit to assist the Italians, Hitler was also considering sending assistance in the form of Luftwaffe units, most notably Stukas. Once again, however, nothing was done immediately. Although models of the latest German aircraft, including the Me 109, Ju 87, and He 111, had been sent to Italy for technical and flight tests in August 1939, with the outbreak of war, as noted previously, all the models were sent back to Germany, and the exchange of technical information lessened considerably.[10]

As noted earlier, the Germans did sell a small number of Stukas to the Regia Aeronautica. Valuable time had been lost, however, so the actual training of Italian pilots did not begin until September 1940. The Stukas were assembled into a small group (ultimately totaling fourteen aircraft), which became operational in late November 1940.[11] The Stukas sold to the Italians by the Germans, however, were the older Ju 87B model, as opposed to the newer Ju 87D, which came into service in late 1940. The Italian group had some Ju 87R models, which were really designed for antishipping missions, but these were clearly in the minority.[12]

As the summer of 1940 wore on, discussions continued, but time slipped away in a welter of indecision, exacerbated by a command structure that was clumsy, to say the least. As noted earlier, military relations between the Italians and Germans were conducted in a bilateral manner that was essentially service based. There was no combined planning mechanism that joined the two staffs on a permanent basis.[13] This deficiency was exacerbated by the fact that within the two countries themselves, the services and command staffs spent little time talking to each other. In 1925 Mussolini had appointed Badoglio to the position of chief of the Supreme General Staff, but he did not create a staff to support Badoglio's position. Instead, Badoglio had to work largely through the army staff, even though he had the authority, theoretically at least, to issue directives to the navy and the air force, both of which complained bitterly. Subsequent reorganizations by Mussolini did little to curtail the independence exercised by the services. These divisions then expanded as each service staff came up with rather different ideas on how a war would be conducted.[14] In Germany, OKW and OKH were often at loggerheads over a variety of issues. The OKM and OKL also often weighed in with input. All this caused the decision-making process to move at a pace that at times could only be described as glacial.

Matters were not helped by Hitler's own indecision. As noted previously, consideration had been given to the idea of sending an armored unit to support the impending Italian offensive into Egypt. Hitler was still considering the matter at the end of August and had not even made up his mind about sending air units. Eventually, around mid-September 1940, a formal offer of German assistance was made to the Italians.[15] Even though these units would have to be transported by sea, this topic did not come up in Hitler's conferences with Raeder. The only matters that were discussed in conversations between the two at this time involving the navy and the Mediterranean were the planning for the operation against Gibraltar and the treatment of French colonies in Northwest Africa.[16]

In any event, the initial Italian response to the German offer was an ambiguous refusal. Badoglio was noncommittal on the subject, while the chief of the Transport Section of the Italian General Staff, General Mario Roatta, cited logistical problems. The ports in Cyrenaica were unsuitable for unloading tanks and other heavy equipment, and sending the units to Tripoli and then moving them up to the front overland would consume too much fuel.[17] In addition, Graziani's offensive into Egypt, which started on 13 September 1940, seemed to proceed without a hitch, although Mussolini was much displeased with Graziani's snail-like pace. After moving forward at the rate of about twelve miles a day, Graziani brought the Italian Tenth Army to a halt at Sidi Barrani, some sixty miles inside the Egyptian border but still eighty miles short of the first major Italian objective, Mersa Matruh. Graziani then hunkered down into a series of fortified camps and started to build a modern road behind him, as well as a water pipeline and even an aqueduct.[18] By the end of September Graziani was still demanding more time to complete these projects, much to the disgust of Mussolini. It was also apparent by the end of

September 1940, with such delicate problems as Spain and Northwest Africa pressing, that Hitler and Mussolini needed another face-to-face conference at the Brenner Pass, which indeed took place on 4 October 1940.

The meeting opened with a quick (for Hitler) explanation about the reasons for not launching *Sea Lion*. After a brief discussion about Spain, the main topic of the meeting was broached, which was the disposition of the French colonies in North Africa and the various German, Italian, and Spanish claims regarding them. For Hitler, the key issues were the obtaining of naval bases along the coast of Northwest Africa and persuading Spain to enter the war. The primary worry of both Mussolini and his generals was the security of the Italian rear area in Tripolitania against any kind of French surprise thrust.[19]

The conference then turned to active operations in North Africa. Mussolini opened by stating that explicit orders had been given to Graziani to commence the second phase of the offensive between 10 and 15 October, which would reach Mersa Matruh by the end of October. After another operational pause, the third phase of the offensive, aimed at the Nile Delta, would begin, hopefully about mid-November. Here Mussolini, overruling his generals, tentatively accepted German assistance. What would be needed most would be German tanks, motor vehicles, and aircraft, especially dive-bombers. Losses had been small thus far, and while the Italian supply of oil for the navy and aviation gasoline was limited to about thirteen months' worth, it would be enough to allow Italy to carry out these operations. Having reached a relatively broad consensus on these issues, the meeting broke up in an atmosphere of great cordiality. Hitler went off to see Franco at Hendaye, while Mussolini returned to Rome with Ciano.[20]

For all the talk and good feelings at this Brenner Pass meeting, very little that was of any real use to the Axis followed. In fact, quite the opposite occurred. First, it is important to note that at the Brenner Pass meeting on 4 October, Mussolini and Hitler brought with them only their respective foreign ministers. None of their top military advisers were in attendance.[21] Thus, when it came to discussing the practical side to these ideas, no one was available. The German navy, for example, even after the taking of Sidi Barrani, anticipated that the Italians would probably have to pause for "many weeks" before resuming the advance into Egypt. For his part, Badoglio had to wait for Mussolini's report on the conference to be sent to him on 5 October before he went to see Pohl in Rome on the ninth. There he pointed out the absolute necessity for conference between him and Keitel.[22] This request was then passed up the chain to Berlin, which came back with the word, given to Badoglio by Rintelen on the fourteenth, that no meeting was possible until after another political meeting had been set up to determine the future conduct of the war, much to Badoglio's irritation.[23]

The next issue to be decided was the dispatch of an armored unit of still indeterminate size to North Africa. Halder noted in his diary on 7 October the beginning of talks with OKW on this question.[24] A little more than three weeks later the issue seemed to have been decided. The Third Panzer Division was to be earmarked for North Africa, along with the VIII Air Corps. To prepare for this, General Wilhelm, Ritter von Thoma, inspector-general of panzer troops for the German army, made an exploratory visit to North Africa in early October 1940. In addition, the National Defense Section of OKW also raised the proposal for the creation of a mixed Italo-German unit. In any case, all German units sent to North Africa would be under Graziani's command. The Naval High Command, however, did not expect any German troops to be dispatched to North Africa until the beginning of 1941 at the earliest.[25]

Matters were made worse by the fact that Hitler's subsequent diplomatic efforts in regard to Spain came to naught. After a satisfactory meeting with Pierre Laval, the foreign minister of the Vichy French government, Hitler met with Franco at Hendaye on the Franco-Spanish border on 23 October. Franco stated that Spain was willing to enter the war but ultimately on conditions that Hitler was most unwilling to agree to. Likewise, Franco found Hitler's conditions, especially regarding Spain's position in North Africa, unacceptable.[26]

Matters continued at this glacial pace into November for two reasons. First, Axis attention was fixed by the ill-fated Italian invasion of Greece, an event that is discussed in the next chapter. Second, and most infuriating to both Mussolini and Badoglio, was Graziani's absolute failure to accomplish anything positive in North Africa. At the Brenner Pass meeting, Mussolini had stated that he would order Graziani to commence the second phase of the Italian offensive, which was to begin between 10 and 15 October 1940. In his meeting with Pohl on the ninth, Badoglio indicated that he expected Graziani to capture Mersa Matruh in two to three weeks.[27]

Graziani, however, did no such thing. Instead, on the sixteenth he sent a report to Mussolini via Ciano that he would not be ready to move again for another two months. Badoglio approved of Graziani's dilatory behavior, although in his postwar memoirs he was rather less supportive of Graziani. Mussolini's initial response was to tell Hitler nothing of this in his letter of 19 October 1940 to the Führer.[28] Even in matters where progress could have been made on both sides, it was not. The OKW diary noted on 24 October 1940 that there were still no liaison arrangements between the Italian forces

operating in North Africa and the Luftwaffe, which was now looking seriously at the possibility of operating in the Mediterranean and over Libya.[29]

Although both Hitler and Mussolini had agreed to the participation of at
least one German panzer division in North Africa, the Italian generals on the
spot were considerably less enthusiastic about that prospect than the Duce.
On 24 October Halder recorded that Thoma's report from North Africa
was not encouraging. The Italian command in North Africa did not see eye
to eye with Commando Supremo in Rome on anything, especially strategy.
According to Thoma, at least, the Italians, knowing that German units were
going to arrive, were inclined to hang back and let the Germans do the work
in taking Mersa Matruh initially and then the Nile Delta. The Germans, for
their part, felt that the capture of Mersa Matruh was essential, to provide a
major supply base from which to launch the next offensive to the delta.[30]

With the Italian invasion of Greece, some sort of high-level military meeting was necessary. After a 30 October meeting between Rintelen and Badoglio in Rome, a meeting between Badoglio and Keitel was set for 14 and 15
November 1940 at Innsbruck. Three days later, Ciano visited Hitler at the
Obersalzberg. The meeting between Badoglio and Keitel produced relatively
limited results. Much of the discussion was taken up with the deteriorating
Italian situation in Greece. As for North Africa, the two men agreed to what
had already been agreed to, namely, that a German panzer division would be
sent to North Africa for the final drive on the Nile Delta. The date for Mersa
Matruh's capture was now set for December. That would be followed on
with air attacks on the Suez Canal, if the Germans could provide the requisite Ju 87s and Ju 88s. With the weather in northwestern Europe worsening,
Badoglio once again called for the return of the CAI from Belgium. Finally,
in regard to North Africa, Badoglio once again indicated the interest of Italy
in Germany's obtaining clear and unequivocal agreements with France that
would provide a guarantee of security for the Italian rear in Libya. Nothing
was done, however, in the way of combined planning for operations.[31]

Like their other meetings, the one between Hitler and Ciano on 18 November was attended only by Ribbentropp and Schmidt, who performed the
interpreting duties; no military advisers were present. Here, at least, there
was some correlation between diplomatic and military activity. Although
most of the meeting was taken up with matters in the Balkans, some time
was spent on North Africa.[32] Two days later, Hitler provided his view of
matters in a somewhat reproachful letter to Mussolini. Hitler still urged
Mussolini to take Mersa Matruh as soon as possible, so that air bases could
be established. The offensive to the Suez Canal and the Nile Delta, however,
would have to be put off for a year. As to the air war, Hitler now essentially

sided with Badoglio over the transfer of the CAI from Belgium to the Mediterranean. In addition, Hitler also proposed to dispatch German aircraft to the Mediterranean, the size of the Luftwaffe presence to be determined after subsequent discussions with Göring. Since there was now going to be a German presence in the area, Hitler sensibly proposed the division of the theater into an Italian air operations area, which would cover Albania, Greece, and Libya, and a German one, which would extend east from the Italian area to Alexandria and the Suez Canal.[33] The Duce, rather chastened by his recent setbacks in Greece, agreed with Hitler's proposals, adding that in regard to the proposed division of the Mediterranean between the Regia Aeronautica and the Luftwaffe, representatives from the general staffs of the respective air forces should meet to work out the technical details. In this case, the Axis powers moved rather more swiftly. The necessary arrangements were made, and Hitler's directive concerning the commitment of the X Air Corps to the Mediterranean was issued on 10 December 1940.[34]

One event that did not enter any of the discussions outlined here was the raid mounted by the British Mediterranean Fleet against the Italian navy's capital ships based in Taranto. On the night of 11–12 November 1940, a group of twenty Swordfish torpedo planes from HMS *Illustrious* attacked Taranto. Several ships were damaged, and the battleship *Cavour* was knocked out for the rest of the war. British losses amounted to only two aircraft shot down. Only the German navy, however, seemed to take note of the raid in its war diary. It was not discussed at any of the meetings outlined here, nor in the correspondence between Hitler and Mussolini. It did not even rate a mention in the diaries of either Halder or OKW.[35] This would tend to support the contention of some historians that the attack's importance was vastly overrated by the British. It would also confirm the idea that Germany regarded the Mediterranean as an Italian theater of war.[36] Axis planning, such as it was, proceeded as if the attack had never occurred. The days of leisurely planning and even slower action, however, came to an abrupt halt following a series of British actions that brought Italy to the edge of strategic disaster by mid-December 1940.

At the beginning of December 1940, Graziani still held the positions he had occupied at the conclusion of his initial advance. The Italian Tenth Army, under the tactical command of General Mario Berti, had deployed his forward units in a series of fortified but mutually unsupported positions around Sidi Barrani. Graziani had spent the interval writing letters to Mussolini explaining why he could not move forward. The army lacked vehicles and maintenance personnel. He complained with some justice that many vehicles, guns, tanks, and supplies earmarked for North Africa were now being sent to Greece. This was doubly irritating to Graziani, since he had been kept completely in the dark even as to the very existence of the plan to attack Greece. What was far worse, however, was the fact that Graziani was almost wholly oblivious to the dangerous situation the Tenth Army was in.[37]

With the passing of the summer, the likelihood of a German landing operation against the English coast had receded considerably. The British command, egged on by Churchill, strongly reinforced the Commonwealth forces in Egypt, first with tanks and aircraft from England, then with troops from India and Australia.[38] With these forces in hand and under relentless pressure from Churchill to produce a victory, the British general officer commanding in the Middle East, General Sir Archibald Wavell, decided to launch a limited attack with units of the British Eighth Army against the Italian Tenth Army units in the area of Sidi Barrani.

Originally conceived as a quick five-day raid to destroy the isolated Italian camps at Nibeiwa and Tummar, the British attack began on 9 December 1940. Led by Wavell's best armor commander, the aggressive Richard O'Connor, over the next two days the camps were successfully stormed against poorly organized resistance.[39] Having accomplished his opening moves, O'Connor quickly turned his attention to the major Italian position at Sidi Barrani, which fell on the eleventh. In the space of a few days O'Connor had inflicted a major defeat on the Italian forces in Egypt. The Tenth Army suffered about 40,000 casualties, the vast majority of whom were captured. The haul included several general officers, seventy-three tanks, and 237 guns.[40]

Disaster metastasized into catastrophe when Wavell, seeking to maximize his advantage, extended O'Connor's raid into a general offensive. Over roughly the next two months, Wavell's offensive, with O'Connor in tactical command, rolled the Italian Tenth Army from Sidi Barrani all the way back to Beda Fomm, where much of the remaining Italian force was destroyed on 6–7 February 1941. By the end of the battle of Beda Fomm, Tenth Army losses were staggering. Ten divisions had been destroyed and 130,000 prisoners taken, including twenty-three generals. Immense quantities of equipment had been lost, including almost 400 light and medium tanks and 845 medium and heavy guns. British losses were slightly less than 2,000.[41]

News of the disaster reached Rome rather quickly. By 10 December both Mussolini and Ciano were well aware that Graziani had suffered a disaster. Ciano noted in his diary that the Duce took the tidings of Graziani's defeat very calmly. Mussolini's unruffled reaction to this, however, lasted only about two days. On the twelfth Graziani sent a telegram that indicated he might withdraw all the way to Tripoli, which left Mussolini deeply shaken.[42] After a few more days, during which Graziani's outlook improved only slightly, morale broke down completely. The clearest evidence of this was the panic-stricken telegram sent by Graziani to Mussolini on 14 December, effectively blaming Mussolini for the deteriorating situation in Africa. Then Graziani's wife, in a state of near hysteria, saw Ciano on the fifteenth. Graziani had sent her a letter containing his will, claiming that "one cannot break steel armor with fingernails alone," and demanding massive German intervention in Libya.[43]

Italian discomfiture in Africa was completed in February 1941 when a British force based in Kenya attacked Ethiopia and landings were made on the coast of Italian-occupied British Somaliland and Eritrea. Although the poorly supplied Italian forces led by the Duke of Aosta put up a lively defense, the British rapidly overran Italy's possessions in East Africa and put Emperor Haile Selassie back upon his throne in Ethiopia.[44]

Reaction in Italy was varied, but only in terms of whom to blame. Certainly one issue on which Mussolini and his generals agreed was that Graziani had lost his nerve. Many were of the opinion that Graziani had not been the same man after he had been wounded in an assassination attempt at Addis Ababa.[45] Despite this correct assessment of Graziani, Mussolini kept him on in command. Ultimately it would be Graziani himself who would ask Mussolini to relieve him on 8 February 1941.[46] Beyond that, Commando Supremo was rent with dissension; generals plotted against each other, while Mussolini had become ever more mistrustful of his generals with very few exceptions. One of the first to go was Badoglio. Critical of Mussolini, especially after things had gone wrong, he was also the victim of a smear campaign orchestrated largely by Farinacci. On 26 November 1940, Badoglio handed in his resignation.[47]

Badoglio's replacement would be General (later Marshal) Ugo Cavallero, a retired officer who had compiled a reasonably good record militarily and who had been a manager of the Ansaldo steelworks, a set of credentials unmatched in Italy. He was also fluent in both German and English. His deputy at Commando Supremo would be General Alfredo Guzzoni, who cut an unimpressive figure physically but was generally a very competent officer.[48]

Although these changes were made partly in response to the deteriorating Italian position in the Balkans, a subject to be discussed in the next chapter, the changes made here were critical to the conduct of the war in North Africa. Most important, after Cavallero's appointment, meetings with German leaders had a much greater level of Italian military involvement. During Badoglio's time at Commando Supremo, he never attended meetings between Hitler and Mussolini. Usually, the only person Mussolini had with him was Ciano. From Cavallero's appointment on, he was present at three of the major meetings between Hitler and Mussolini, namely, those of June and August 1941 and April 1942. When he could not be present, Guzzoni attended in Cavallero's stead. One other thing Cavallero tried to do, in the end unsuccessfully, was to limit the amount of contact between Mussolini and Rintelen and later Kesselring. This allowed Rintelen to gain a fair picture of both the thinking and the morale at Commando Supremo. After the war, Rintelen wrote that military relations between Italy and Germany were much better after Cavallero's appointment, although it still took time for the relationship to improve.[49]

With the situation in Libya careening out of control and Rintelen sending back messages almost daily detailing the mood of the Italian High Command, it was clear that something had to be done. The first tangible German help that could arrive on the scene was in the form of the Luftwaffe's X Air Corps, commanded by General Hans Geisler, with Major Martin Harlinghausen as his chief of staff. These two men were the Luftwaffe's preeminent experts on aerial warfare against shipping. The X Air Corps' initial mission was to mount attacks against Royal Navy ships at Alexandria, shipping passing through the Suez Canal as well as the narrows between Sicily and North Africa. This was clearly reflected in the composition of the X Air Corps, which by 14 December 1940 contained a number of Ju 87s and Ju 88s, as well as He 111s capable of dropping torpedoes and mines. The X Air Corps, however, would not be able to exert any real influence until a sufficient number of operational fighters had been assembled.[50]

The next thing Hitler did was to try to reassure the Italians and shore up their morale. On 31 December 1940 Hitler wrote Mussolini and provided an overall assessment of the war. When it came to North Africa, Hitler cautioned Mussolini that no large-scale counterattack could be expected until at least March. In the meantime, a blocking unit (*Sperrverband*) well armed with antitank weapons would be sent to assist the Italians. The battle would really have to be carried to the British by the Luftwaffe for the time being. The Führer then reassured the Duce that his people "will only emerge hardened from the first reverses." Hitler then closed by inviting Mussolini, with very diplomatic language, to come to Germany for a conference. In the meantime, Hitler issued Directive Number 22 on 11 January to initiate the sending of German troops to North Africa.[51]

Hitler's letter seemed to have the desired effect only in part. While it certainly heartened Mussolini and the Italian High Command, the Duce declined Hitler's invitation on 1 January 1941. He quickly reversed himself, however, as news of the loss of Bardia on the third with 30,000 men and a large number of guns arrived the next day, along with news of further defeats in Albania. With Italian morale once again being badly shaken with the loss of Bardia, Mussolini agreed to a conference with Hitler at Berchtesgaden on 20 January 1941.[52]

This meeting between Hitler and Mussolini marked something of a first for the Axis leaders. It would be the first time such a meeting would also be attended by high-level military advisers on both sides. Hitler was attended by Ribbentrop, Keitel, Jodl, and Rintelen; Mussolini was accompanied by Ciano, Guzzoni (at that time Cavallero was in Albania), and Marras. In addition, the conference was preceded by a lengthy discussion between Keitel and Guzzoni on 19 January.[53]

Unlike previous meetings, this actually produced some immediate positive results for the Axis partners. Although much of the meeting was taken up with the topic of the Balkans, some clear and positive decisions were taken in regard to North Africa. Hitler went out of his way to reassure the Italians that the situation there was above all a matter for the Italian commanders, although he did urge them to hold the positions there as far forward as possible, largely as a way of preventing any perfidy by the French. A German unit would be dispatched to North Africa as soon as possible, while the Italians would bolster their own forces with a mobile corps of one motorized division and one armored division. No firm command arrangements, however, were decided upon. Diplomatically, the Italians would make another attempt to bring Spain into the war.[54]

The execution of the decisions reached at the *Berghof* produced mixed results for the Axis. The Italian diplomatic effort to entice the wily Franco into the war proved no more successful than previous German efforts. Mussolini regarded Franco's attitude as one of considerable ingratitude.[55] The shoring up of the Italian position in North Africa was more successful. The losses of Derna and Tobruk convinced the two leading German officers in the spot, Rintelen and Major General Hans Freiherr von Funck, that negative measures such as a blocking unit would not be sufficient. Some type of armored counterattack was needed by either a German panzer unit or a mixed Italo-German armored unit of corps size, under a German commander and staff. If this were not to occur and only a passive defense of Tripoli was to be mounted, Rintelen suggested that no German troops be committed to North Africa. Rintelen also argued, like his navy colleague Weichold, that the German generals posted to the various Italian headquarters be given the ability to exert "operational influence" over decisions.[56]

This turned out not to be necessary, since in this case the Germans and Mussolini were thinking along similar lines. Some of the Italian generals

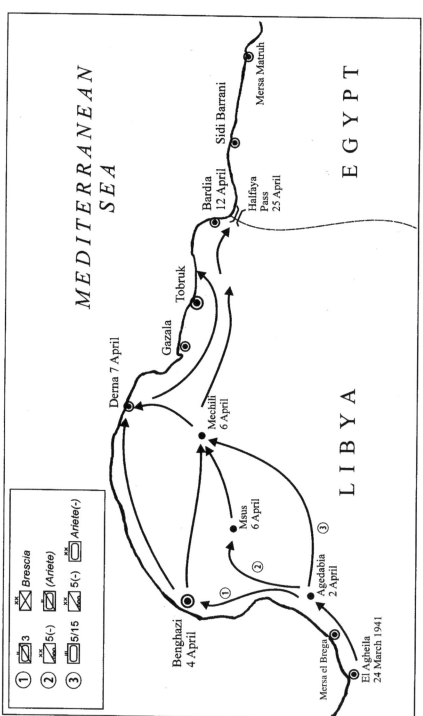

MEDITERRANEAN SEA

EGYPT

LIBYA

Mersa Matruh

Sidi Barrani

Bardia
12 April

Halfaya
Pass
25 April

Tobruk

Gazala

Derna 7 April

Mechili
6 April

Msus
6 April

Benghazi
4 April

Agedabia
2 April

Mersa el Brega

El Agheila
24 March 1941

① ▨ 3   ⊠ Brescia
② ▨ 5(-)   ▨ (Ariete)
③ ▢ 5/15   ▨ 5(-) ▢ Ariete(-)

Rommel's Drive across the Desert, February–April 1941

wanted to establish the defenses of Tripoli between Misurata and Homs, relatively close to the city. Rintelen, meeting the Duce in private at 9:00 A.M. on 9 February 1941, argued, in accordance with his instructions from OKW, that the defense line should be established between Misurata and Sirte, thus forcing the British to fight with the desert at their backs. Mussolini agreed with this position and was further reassured by Rintelen that a forward defense of Tripoli would effectively prevent any kind of French action against the Italian rear. Later that day Rintelen was informed by Guzzoni that Mussolini had issued the necessary orders and that Commando Supremo had agreed that the Italo-German mobile force, which was to be positioned behind the right flank of the line, should be placed under the command of a German general. He was also informed confidentially of Graziani's impending relief.[57]

The German general selected to lead the German units in North Africa was Erwin Rommel. Originally Funck was to have the command, but he was thought to be too gloomy in his outlook, judging from the tone of his reports from Africa. Hitler selected Rommel for several reasons. The first was Rommel's personal connection to Hitler, having been commander of the Führer's headquarters during the Polish campaign. Second, his record in command of the Seventh Panzer Division during the 1940 campaign was brilliant. It established Rommel as one of Germany's most daring field commanders, a fact Hitler stressed in his 5 February 1941 letter to Mussolini. Finally, Hitler felt that Axis forces in North Africa needed some inspirational leadership, which he believed Rommel would provide in abundance.[58]

The story of Rommel's arrival and his immediate offensive operations, which exceeded his orders, is too well known to bear a full recounting here. Suffice to say that by the middle of April 1941, the Italo-German forces under Rommel's command had retaken Cyrenaica and trapped the Australian Ninth Division in Tobruk.[59] Although Rommel could not take the heavily fortified and well-defended port, he was able to fend off the first British attempt to relieve the Tobruk garrison.[60] From the point of view of this study, the introduction of German ground and air forces into North Africa presented the Germans with a number of problems in terms of coalition warfare that bear fuller examination.

The first major issue to be examined here concerns command arrangements. Theoretically at least, since it was OKH that supplied the units that came to constitute the Deutsche Afrika Korps (DAK), Rommel was subject to the directives of Halder and the Army General Staff. In fact, Halder had given Rommel his instructions personally on 7 February 1941. Tactically, Rommel was to be subordinate to the local Italian commander in Libya.[61]

The first concept for command arrangements was suggested by Cavallero at a meeting with Rintelen on 18 December 1940. In the interests of unity of command, Cavallero suggested having Mussolini in command, at least in a nominal sense, with a German chief of staff. Nothing came from this, however, and the command structure that evolved was anything but unified. Aside from OKH, OKW also envisioned a place for itself in terms of making decisions regarding the Mediterranean. Orders were regularly passed to Rommel by Hitler and OKW through Rintelen, and these were often directly counter to the orders sent by OKH.[62] This situation was ideal for the independent-minded Rommel to get his own way. Early on he accomplished this by getting the approval of Mussolini, who by this time was extremely mistrustful of his own generals. A classic example of this occurred in his very first operation. Rommel's instructions stated that he should launch only a limited attack in the area of Agedabia. The attack, to be conducted by the Italo-German mobile force, would be controlled by General Italo Gariboldi, the commander of the Italian Fifth Army. Rommel, meeting with Mussolini and Rintelen on 23 March, demanded that he personally command the attack force, in essence demanding a free hand. Mussolini did not make an official decision but unofficially gave Rommel the go-ahead "with the present measures and plans." This was also in accordance with what Mussolini had already indicated to Hitler a month earlier.[63]

That was all the headstrong Swabian needed. The successful attack at El Agheila and the subsequent capture of Mersa el Brega gave him the impetus to exceed his orders and then extend his offensive. Orders trying to limit his advance by his nominal superiors could be parried by claims that orders from other headquarters had priority, or ultimately by saying that he had the Führer's backing.[64]

To try to prevent a repetition of this confusion, and to create a more settled chain of command in North Africa, on 20 May 1941 OKW issued a document to define command relationships in this theater. Copies went to Army, Navy, and Luftwaffe High Commands, as well as to Rintelen and each liaison staff at Italian headquarters. While acknowledging that the Mediterranean was an Italian theater and that the supply of the German forces in North Africa was dependent on the Italians, the DAK commander was essentially given a free hand, although lip service was paid to the idea that he was tactically subordinate to the Italian commander in North Africa. The DAK commander could also receive orders directly from OKH. The chief of staff of the DAK was to report to both the Italian commander in North Africa and the German general at Italian headquarters (Rintelen). Rintelen, in turn, would secure the necessary agreements from the various service headquarters. In addition, Rintelen would continue to report to OKH.[65]

In effect, however, this did very little to create a clear chain of command in the area. The organization of supply services was still chaotic, owing to a plethora of agencies. Halder believed that having one agency in Rome responsible for the supply of Axis forces in North Africa would solve the problem, but he saw little prospect of that happening.[66] Thus, Keitel and Cavallero had a great many subjects to discuss in Rome on 29 August 1941. During the meeting, the question of command in North Africa came up again. Now Keitel and Cavallero agreed that the two fronts in North Africa, namely, the besieging force at Tobruk and the covering force posted mainly at Sollum, would be subject to a British attack aimed at relieving Tobruk. In such an eventuality, only one commander should be responsible for handling these battles. Both men agreed that it should be Rommel, tactical subordination to the Italian commander in North Africa (now General Ettore Bastico) notwithstanding. To further strengthen Rommel's position, his force was redesignated as Panzer Group Africa, and Rommel himself was promoted to general of panzer troops on 1 July. This would give him the ability to exercise a degree of authority over some of the Italian formations, most notably the armored and motorized divisions of General Gastone Gambara's XX Corps.[67] Thus Rommel would always have the ability to disregard any chain of command that might be established, by either OKW or Commando Supremo. This state of affairs continued in the Mediterranean even after the appointment of Kesselring as *Ober Befehlshaber* (OB) South, an event to be discussed shortly in more detail.

Coordination between the other services was also a difficult nut to crack. As noted previously, the first major Luftwaffe presence in the Mediterranean was provided by the X Air Corps, based in Sicily. To provide direct support to the DAK in North Africa, two Stuka groups, as well as two squadrons from Kampf Geschwader 26 (KG 26), a squadron of Me 110 fighters from Zerstorer Geschwader (ZG 26), and some flak batteries were transferred to North Africa. These were placed under the command of a senior Luftwaffe officer, in this case Major General Stefan Fröhlich, who was designated as *Fliegerführer Afrika*. His job was to ensure close cooperation with the army, although he was tactically subordinate to the German X Air Corps.[68]

The job of developing close cooperation with the Italian Fifth Air Fleet belonged to First Lieutenant Philipp De La Cerda, who was posted as liaison officer from *Fliegerführer Afrika* to the Italian Fifth Air Fleet. His selection for the post was probably based on his previous association with the CAI in Belgium. De La Cerda immediately found himself in a difficult position. First, the commander of the Italian Fifth Air Fleet, General Aimone Cat, was unhappy with De La Cerda's mere presence. Cat believed that all he needed for liaison with the Germans was an interpreter. He looked on a liaison officer as an unwanted intrusion on Italian prerogatives. In addition, the Italians were very much put off by De La Cerda's rather junior rank. They felt that assigning only a first lieutenant as a liaison officer to a headquarters commanded by a senior general officer was something of an insult. Finally, coordination could be difficult because the Italian armed forces were afflicted with the same kind of internal organizations that affect all military establishments. One of the matters De La Cerda was supposed to coordinate with the Italian Fifth Air Fleet was flak defense for the North African ports. In the Italian armed forces, however, all flak units belonged to the Italian army, not the air force. In dealing with these units, De La Cerda generally had to work with Rommel's liaison officer to the Italian command in North Africa, Lieutenant Colonel Heinz Heggenreiner. While this was not necessarily an insurmountable obstacle, it did make coordination in that kind of circumstance difficult.[69]

For the conduct of the air war in the Mediterranean at the higher levels of warfare, a series of negotiations was held between the Regia Aeronautica and Pohl's liaison staff. The result was an agreement signed in Rome on 31 August 1941. With the experience of the CAI behind them, both air forces thought it not practical to create mixed Italo-German units. Instead, the airspace in the central and eastern Mediterranean was divided into German and Italian sectors. The X Air Corps would be responsible for the sector from just west of Derna all the way to the Nile Delta and the Suez Canal. The area west of that, which would cover the Axis convoy routes from Italy to Tripoli and Benghazi, would be covered by the Italians. The line of demarcation, however, was not rigid, so each air force could operate in the other's sector. This would ultimately allow both air forces to launch attacks on Malta. Regular procedures for the exchange of plans, information, and impending operations were set up, although the Germans did have something of a veto over any Italian operation that could disrupt an impending German one. Arrangements also were made for basing the German X Air Corps in Sicily, and a regular set of command relationships was set up.[70]

Cooperation between the German navy and the Regia Marina centered around a different set of concerns. Here the main issue was logistics. Since the Axis forces in North Africa would have to be supplied mainly by sea, attention here focused on the critical areas of available merchant shipping, the number and capacity of ports on both ends of the journey, and the protection of the convoys from attacks by British naval and air forces. In all these areas, at least initially, Italy was woefully unprepared.

In 1940 the Italian merchant marine possessed some 3,318,129 tons of shipping. This amount probably would have been sufficient to maintain the Italian position in the Mediterranean and Africa for a short war. Italy's weaknesses in this regard, however, were quite apparent. Given the raw material situation and the priorities of both Mussolini and Cavagnari in ship construction, very few resources were devoted to building merchant ships. Thus, even in a short war the merchant marine would be a wasting asset. Matters were made far worse when Mussolini decided to declare war while one-third of the merchant fleet, some 220 ships totaling 1,226,000 tons, including 46 tankers, was outside of the Mediterranean.[71]

For the Axis forces in North Africa, the seaborne supply route was a well-established one. A convoy would be assembled in Naples, then sail to Palermo in Sicily as a stopover point, and then move on to Tripoli. The escort for the convoys used to carry out Operation *Sunflower* was an Italo-German effort. The Italian navy provided the naval escort, while aerial escort was provided by both the Italian air force and the German X Air Corps. This was done, however, under a cooperative arrangement, as the Italians had refused a German proposal to create a unified air command, headed by the commander of the German X Air Corps. Although forewarned by Luftwaffe signals decoded by *Ultra*, the British forces in Malta were too weak to effectively interfere with the movement of the DAK to Italy, as the island had been heavily attacked throughout January by both Axis air forces.[72]

The port of Tripoli had relatively modern facilities but was rather small. Only about four ships could be unloaded at one time there. In addition, the normal time required to unload a ship was about four days, although that could be cut in half with an accelerated unloading schedule.[73] The capture of Benghazi certainly improved the supply situation, but only in a limited sense. Although some kind of supplies could be brought into Benghazi and later Derna, most heavy equipment could not. This was something that Rommel had difficulty grasping. On 27 February 1941, with an eye toward the future, Rommel outlined his desire that tanks be transported from Italy directly to Benghazi instead of Tripoli, something OKW considered an impossibility.[74]

By the summer of 1941, the Axis forces had the ports of Tripoli, Benghazi, and Derna as the terminal points for the two seaborne routes from Italy. The first, as noted previously, ran from Naples to Tripoli via Sicily. The second ran from Taranto to either Benghazi or Derna. The fact that both of these were relatively fixed made them vulnerable to attack by British submarines and aircraft based at Malta. The British would also attempt to interdict convoy traffic with two surface squadrons, Force K, based at Malta, and Force H, based at Alexandria.

The introduction of the DAK to Africa meant that the German navy would have to cooperate more closely than before with its Italian counterpart. One element of this cooperation resulted in a decision that would have disastrous consequences for the Axis. One of the German navy's biggest concerns was communications security. Weichold believed that the British were reading Italian naval codes. Likewise, Hitler did not want to give the Italians any kind of secret information about German plans because he thought the Italian royal family would leak it to the British. The Germans were able to persuade the Italians to adopt the Enigma machine as their standard coding device. This turned out to be a terrific boon to the Allies, since while Italian naval codes had been secure, the Allies had been breaking and reading German naval codes. A great deal of signals intelligence was also gleaned from the Luftwaffe.[75]

As 1941 wore on, sustaining the Axis forces in North Africa became steadily more difficult. The critical nature of the situation in early 1941, aided by the lack of serious opposition, allowed men, equipment, and supplies to flow relatively unimpeded from Italy to North Africa. Early in the spring, however, this situation deteriorated for several reasons. First, the impending operations in the Balkans by both German and Italian forces meant a diversion of shipping from the Mediterranean to the Adriatic and the Aegean to support that effort. Although the relatively rapid conquest of the Balkans would free up enough shipping to transport the Fifteenth Panzer Division to North Africa in May 1941, the Italian merchant marine would have to divide its efforts between sustaining the forces in North Africa and those in the Balkans. This draining away of both attention and resources would be intensified after the onset of Operation *Barbarossa*. This would also effectively prevent the planned equipping of the Italian infantry divisions in North Africa with some 3,000 motor vehicles, thus giving them at least a slightly higher degree of operational mobility.[76]

The Axis supply situation in North Africa was also severely undermined by the corresponding revival of British naval and air strength in the Mediterranean. On 28 March 1941 two British forces, Force H and Force B, met Admiral Angelo Iachino's Italian fleet off Cape Matapan, where it was trying to disrupt British convoy traffic to and from Greece. The British, aided by *Ultra*, radar-controlled gunnery, poor Italian fire control techniques, and erroneous intelligence given to Iachino from the Luftwaffe, were able to best the Italians in a confused engagement.[77] To some degree the loss of several cruisers was offset by both prior and subsequent events. On 26 March Italian frogmen, using small motorboats packed with explosives, successfully attacked several ships in Suda Bay, sinking the cruiser HMS *York*. Then, on the thirtieth, the Italian submarine *Ambra* torpedoed and sank the light cruiser HMS *Bonaventure*.[78]

Although Cape Matapan was perhaps not quite as decisive a victory as some British students of the war like to portray it, the action had serious logistical consequences for the Axis forces in Africa.[79] Certainly Hitler did not seem to grasp the consequences of the battle. Hitler, with the sortie of the *Bismarck* imminent, refused to send German U-boats to the Mediterranean. Instead, in another nod to the notion of "parallel war," he and the navy staff urged the withdrawal of most of the Italian submarines operating at Bordeaux to the Mediterranean, again a clear sign that the middle sea was an Italian theater of war.[80]

The victory at Matapan, however, combined with a long-feared shortage of oil for the Regia Marina, allowed the British to take a much more aggressive posture in the central Mediterranean. On 16 April 1941 the Fourteenth Destroyer Flotilla, newly based at Malta, on the strength of *Ultra* decrypts, intercepted and destroyed a convoy bound for Tripoli, losing only one destroyer in the process.[81] Although the evacuation of Crete and continued Axis air activity over Malta resulted in a number of British destroyers leaving Malta, shipping losses increased, particularly from submarines. While the drain was worrisome but not prohibitive in May and June, losses rose sharply during the late summer and reached crisis levels during the fall of 1941.[82] Temporary expedients, such as flying in replacements and flying out wounded and those no longer fit for service in North Africa, could not alleviate the crisis in supply, especially in terms of fuel.[83] Consequently, although Rommel had sufficient supplies stockpiled to beat off rather easily the first two attempts to relieve Tobruk, Operation *Brevity* in May and Operation *Battleaxe* in June, by November 1941 he was facing a logistical crisis that could seriously affect his ability to conduct operations.

Under pressure from Prime Minister Winston Churchill, the new British commander in North Africa, General Sir Claude Auchinleck, launched Operation *Crusader*, the third attempt to relieve the port of Tobruk, on 18 November 1941. After a series of confusing battles, punctuated by Rommel's rash "dash to the wire" in late November, the Axis forces in North Africa, having suffered serious losses especially in tanks, had to abandon their positions around Tobruk, as well as the garrisons at Sollum and Halfaya Pass, and retreat back toward Tripoli. A series of events, however, allowed Rommel to quickly turn the tables by the end of 1941, and by the end of February 1942 his counteroffensive had once again recovered Benghazi and brought the Axis forces in North Africa to a halt along a line from the coast south that stretched to Ain-el-Gazala. There the front would remain inactive until May 1942.[84]

In terms of land warfare, Rommel probably got more out of the Italian units under his command than he expected, certainly more than the British would care to admit. Certainly there were cultural and linguistic problems that had to be overcome. This started with the commanders themselves who did not speak Italian or German, including Rommel, who did not speak Italian. One of the more important people in Rommel's headquarters was his interpreter, Wilifried Armbruster, who was able to convey not only Rommel's thoughts precisely in Italian but also the tone in which they were delivered.[85]

Although liaison staffs were posted with every major Italian formation, communication remained a problem. Most German army officers could not speak Italian. Occasionally a unit such as the Fifteenth Panzer Division might boast of several interpreters on its staff, but this was rare.[86] Graduates of the Kriegsakademie generally preferred English or French. The German army drew the majority of its Italian interpreters from the southern Tyrol. Aside from climatic problems, many of the interpreters were unfamiliar with military terminology. Given that the nature of the campaign did produce lulls in the action, the Italo-German forces were able to come up with a dictionary that contained the most important military terms in both German and Italian, thus making everybody essentially play on the same sheet of music.[87]

During the hard *Crusader* battles, generally the performance of the Italian units was good, albeit somewhat uneven. Some of this was certainly due to a lack of modern equipment, especially antitank guns. This particularly affected the Italian infantry divisions holding the perimeter around Tobruk. On the other hand, Italian artillery and antiaircraft units provided good support to the German Twelfth Oasis Company in its defense of Sidi Omar. One of Rommel's officers gave much of the credit for the successful defense of Halfaya Pass in June 1941 to the Italian infantry. Likewise, Italian armored units, especially the Ariete Armored Division, did well during the *Crusader* battles, and during the retreat to Agedabia, the rear guards of the Italian infantry divisions, aided by German mobile units and favorable terrain, executed a number of excellent delaying actions to successfully stymie the pursuit of the victorious but badly battered British Eighth Army.[88]

In many ways the conduct of the naval war and to a lesser extent the air war in the Mediterranean amounted to a continuation of the idea of parallel war. Certainly there continued to be a fair amount of indecisiveness on the part of the Germans. On 22 August 1941, in a meeting with Hitler at the

Wolfsschanze in East Prussia, Raeder raised the prospect of sending U-boats to the Mediterranean to aid the Italians. Yet the subject barely came up when the Duce visited three days later. All Hitler could bring himself to say was that he was satisfied with the development of the situation in the Mediterranean.[89] As the Axis supply situation worsened during the late summer of 1941, however, Hitler decided to take steps to rectify the situation. On 17 September 1941 he ordered six U-boats, the first of what would ultimately become a commitment of twenty-seven boats, dispatched to the Mediterranean. This was done, however, without any kind of prior planning or coordination with the Italian navy.[90]

The result was that while the fuel crisis for the Axis forces in North Africa reached its apogee in the fall of 1941, the Axis naval forces scored their best successes while waging "parallel war." Although the Royal Navy, aided by *Ultra,* inflicted serious losses on Axis shipping in September 1941, with the two most notable losses being the ocean liners *Neptunia* and *Oceania,* the balance soon shifted to the Axis powers' favor. By November six U-boats had passed the Straits of Gibraltar and were operating in the Mediterranean. The first of these began to show results in October, when the gunboat HMS *Gnat* was torpedoed and heavily damaged by U-79 on 21 October. More serious losses followed in November: U-81 torpedoed and sank the aircraft carrier HMS *Ark Royal* on 13 November, while the battleship *HMS Barham* went down at the hands of U-331 on the twenty-fifth.[91]

In December the Italian navy scored its most notable successes against the British. Given the seriousness of the situation at the time in North Africa, the Italians made a maximum effort to get a convoy through to the desperately needy Axis forces there. Called M42 by the Italians (the German Naval High Command referred to it as Convoy Number 52), it involved a sortie by most of the Italian navy's major units. The British, alerted to the convoy's sailing by *Ultra,* attempted to intercept the convoy with Admiral Sir Philip Vian's Force K, based in Malta. On 17 December Iachino's covering force, which included two battleships, clashed with Force K in the first battle of Sirte. Although no damage was inflicted by either side, Vian was forced to return to Malta to refuel. His second attempt to intercept the convoy ended in disaster when Force K headed into a cleverly laid Italian minefield (including German deepwater mines) off of Tripoli. The cruiser HMS *Neptune* sank after striking four mines, and a similar fate was suffered by the destroyer HMS *Kandahar.* The cruiser HMS *Aurora* and the destroyer HMS *Penelope* were damaged. These losses, plus the revival of Axis air strength in the central Mediterranean, effectively emasculated Force K and compelled its evacuation from Malta.[92]

British discomfiture on the naval side of war in the Mediterranean was completed on 19 December 1941. In perhaps the most daring Italian exploit of the war, Borghese's Tenth Flotilla launched three teams of frogmen from the submarine *Scirè* just outside Alexandria harbor. Penetrating the British defenses in their underwater craft known as "chariots," the daring frogmen attached explosive charges to four ships in the harbor. Although the teams were eventually captured, by the time the smoke cleared the Royal Navy had suffered a disaster. The last two British battleships in the Mediterranean, HMS *Valiant* and *Queen Elizabeth*, went to the bottom of the harbor. Although both would eventually be raised and repaired, they would be out of action for many months. The destroyer HMS *Jervis* was also damaged, and the Norwegian oiler *Sagona* sunk.[93] With Force H effectively neutralized, another convoy, carrying elements of the Littorio Division and German reinforcements, arrived safely in Tripoli.[94] Thus Rommel was able to launch his counterstroke at Agedabia and restore the situation.

The interesting aspect about these Axis successes is the absolute lack of any joint planning on the part of the two navies. The German U-boats sent to the Mediterranean, for example, were based at Salamis in the Aegean. Furthermore, they were under the exclusive operational control of Weichold, as the German admiral in Rome, although eventually an officer would be set up to direct U-boat operations in the Mediterranean.[95] Each navy conducted its operations without reference to the other, although ideally reconnaissance information gathered by both air forces was supposed to be passed to the other. German intelligence, for example, correctly placed the HMS *Valiant* and the HMS *Queen Elizabeth* in the harbor at Alexandria. How and by whom this information was sent to Borghese remains unclear.[96]

There was some cooperation in technical matters between the two navies during this time. The Germans made some forty sonar sets available to the Italians. This investment paid its first dividend on 24 November 1941 when the Italian gunboat *Castore* reported sinking a British submarine. Thereafter several other gunboats were equipped with German sonar equipment. Although not many British submarines were sunk, they respected the threat well enough to keep clear of the Gulf of Taranto, where these ships were employed.[97]

"Parallel war" had its costs as well. The fact that the navies operated separately from each other increased the possibility of fratricide. This became reality on 16 December 1941 when the Italian motor torpedo boat *Orione* rammed and sank U-557, which it mistook for a British submarine.[98]

The final major reason for the reversal of Axis fortunes in the Mediterranean was the revival of Axis air strength there. Axis air strength had declined over the summer of 1941, eroded by losses and German commitments to the Russian front. With the coming of the crisis in the fall, however, and the war in Russia seemingly about to come to a successful conclusion, Hitler and the German High Command shifted their attention to the Mediterranean. Seeing the security of the sea lanes to North Africa as the critical issue, in a 29 October 1941 letter to Mussolini, Hitler offered to send additional Luftwaffe strength to the area. This would provide security for the convoys and, in cooperation with the Italian air force, neutralize Malta. Hitler also promised to send more of the latest versions of German tanks, especially the Pz III and Pz IV, as well as antitank guns. The offer was quickly accepted by Mussolini in his response dated 6 November 1941.[99]

Four days after receiving Mussolini's reply, Hitler ordered the transfer of Luftwaffe units, most notably the II Air Corps, from the eastern front to the Mediterranean. Since there would now be two German air corps operating in the theater, an overarching headquarters would be needed. This appeared in the form of Kesselring's Second Air Fleet, which was also transferred from the east.[100]

In addition to being commander of the Second Air Fleet, Kesselring was given another title, namely, that of *Oberbefehlshaber Süd*, or OB South (literally "Commander-in-Chief South"). The description of his duties is most interesting from the standpoint of coalition warfare. Kesselring's area of direct responsibility was concerned solely with naval and air forces. His assigned mission in regard to North Africa was only to "cooperate" with the Italo-German forces committed in North Africa, although his authority apparently extended over the air forces operating there. In this position Kesselring was subordinate to both OKW and Commando Supremo. His authority over German navy units in the eastern Mediterranean was limited to some degree in that the agreement of the navy was required. The day-to-day liaison activities with Commando Supremo and Mussolini would still be carried out by Rintelen.[101]

The choice of Kesselring would prove in many ways more of a negative than a positive for German fortunes in this theater. Although an able man who spoke Italian rather well, Kesselring was contemptuous of the Italians, an attitude that was clearly communicated to his staff and to the Italians at times.[102] The relationship between Kesselring and Rommel was not much better. They were radically different in both personality and background. A Kriegsakademie graduate and a scion of one of Bavaria's oldest noble families, Kesselring's persona projected a combination of snobbishness and sunny optimism.[103] Rommel was not impressed by the qualities of "Smiling Albert," and the two quickly found themselves at loggerheads. The hard-driving and ambitious

Rommel resented Kesselring's attempts to impinge on what he properly regarded as his sphere, namely, the conduct of ground operations.[104]

Despite the various and sundry personality clashes that beset the respective Axis high commands, the arrival of the Second Air Fleet headquarters and the II Air Corps allowed the Axis powers to restore the situation to their advantage in the winter of 1941–1942. Although apparently still guided by the agreement signed by the two air forces back in August 1941, the air forces sometimes flew missions jointly and effectively neutralized Malta as a British air base.[105] Likewise, both German and Italian aircraft preyed upon Allied shipping in the Mediterranean, although with varying degrees of coordination.[106]

The success of Rommel's January 1942 counterstroke and the revival of Italo-German naval and air strength in the Mediterranean effectively marked the end of the first significant period of coalition warfare as carried out by the two major Axis powers. From the point of view of coalition warfare, several observations can be made.

First, it was actually the Germans who kept the concept of "parallel war" going, even after the Italians had come to regard it as a dead issue. This did vary according to both service and command echelon. At the highest level, both Hitler and Keitel repeatedly stressed to Mussolini and Cavallero throughout the summer of 1941 that Germany regarded the Mediterranean as an Italian theater of war.[107] While the situation on the ground in North Africa demanded some degree of integration, the respective air forces and navies essentially fought their own wars.

This was reflected to some degree in the command arrangements, or lack thereof, made by Germans and Italians in this theater. Without any kind of a mechanism to coordinate the plans and operations of the respective allies, the command situation quickly degenerated into a chaotic free-for-all. Certainly the biggest winner in all this was Rommel, who was generally able to get his way by going through Rintelen to Mussolini, who would usually accede to Rommel's wishes. Halder's proposal to appoint a "commander of German troops in Africa," who would be both Rommel's superior and a buffer between Rommel and the Italians, was turned down by Hitler.[108] The appointment of Kesselring was but a poor substitute, as his purview was limited to air and naval matters as they related to the Axis logistical situation. None of this boded very well for the future.

Another observation deals with the individual services themselves; when it came to conducting coalition warfare, some were simply better than others. In the case of the Mediterranean theater, it would appear that the Luftwaffe was perhaps the best of the three. It was prepared to establish liaison with the Regia Aeronautica almost immediately after Italy's entry into the war, had at least a cadre of officers experienced in working with the Italians, and entered into discussions at the ministerial level involving technology. Later on, with the introduction of the German X Air Corps into the theater, the two air forces were able to reach working agreements on the conduct of the air war over the Mediterranean.[109]

All these efforts, however, produced rather mixed results. To be sure, there were some operational successes, especially after the arrival of the German II Air Corps and the revival of Axis air strength in the central Mediterranean. Providing requested aid to the Italians, as well as reaching agreements regarding technological issues was another matter. Even De La Cerda, no fan of the Italians, noted in his report that when it came to supplies, "the Italians were certainly promised much, but have received only a little."[110]

Of all the German armed forces, the navy was probably the least prepared to conduct coalition warfare in the Mediterranean. Little had been done beyond establishing minimal liaison with the Italians. The navy viewed Hitler's decision to send U-boats into the Mediterranean with dismay, given its focus on the battle of the Atlantic. Finally, the Italians were able to start using German sonar equipment only after both countries had been at war for some twenty months.[111]

In terms of the actual conduct of coalition warfare, probably the most productive event for the Axis allies was the meeting held between Hitler and Mussolini at the *Berghof* from 19 to 21 January 1941. While Knox is correct that it meant the loss of Italy's status as a major power, it also marked the first meeting in which both political and military officials took part, a stark contrast to previous meetings. It also laid the groundwork, however imperfectly, for concerted action of some kind in the near future.[112] Disasters such as those that had overtaken the Italians at the end of 1940 might not have occurred if the *Berghof* meeting, or something like it, had occurred much earlier.

With the situation in the Mediterranean stabilized, Hitler could return his malevolent gaze to where it had been since July 1940, namely, the vast expanses of Soviet Russia that he had always regarded as the future Lebensraum for the German people.[113] Before he could come to grips with Soviet Russian, however, he once again had to rescue his Italian ally in the Balkans.

4

The Balkan Interlude

Hitler always faces me with a *fait accompli*. This time I am going to pay him back in his own coin. He will find out from the papers that I have occupied Greece. In this way equilibrium will be re-established.
Benito Mussolini, 12 October 1940[1]

Italy's advance on Greece from Albania was prepared equally badly both in a political and military way, and therefore led to the well-known failure, which, aside from the military victories for Greece, made it possible for England to establish bases in Greece and on the Greek islands.
Prince Otto Christian von Bismarck, 27 December 1940[2]

In the uniform conduct of this campaign the Führer generally reserved the operational objectives for the allies in relation to the framework of the whole operation.   Lieutenant Colonel Bernhard von Lossberg, 5 May 1941[3]

FOR ADOLF HITLER, as well as the various private empires that functioned collectively as the Nazi regime, southeastern Europe and the Balkans represented a number of things. Economically, the Balkans contained sufficient amounts of raw material, in particular oil, to offset at least partially the denial of such materials by both the Soviet Union and the United States. This made the area an inviting target for Hermann Göring, as part of his program of expanding his influence as the de facto head of the German economy.[4]

The area also possessed untapped racial resources. Both of the principal countries in southeastern Europe, Romania and Hungary, had sizable ethnic German minorities in their populations. Hitler had made it plain early on, at least within the German government, that he wanted these ethnic German minorities to eventually be resettled within the borders of the Reich. This also quickly drew the interest of Reichsführer SS Heinrich Himmler, who along with his chief recruiter, Gottlob Berger, was always on the lookout for new sources of manpower for his burgeoning Schütz Staffel (SS) empire.[5]

Strategically, however, the area was nothing but a seething cauldron of problems that would consistently plague Germany throughout the war. The most notable of these involved Mussolini's desires in the area. The bloodless annexation of Albania in April 1939 had only whetted his appetite for more territorial claims against Greece and Yugoslavia.[6] Equally intractable for Hitler was the long-standing acrimony between Romania and Hungary. That matter, with its important consequences for the prosecution of the war against Soviet Russia, will be discussed in the next chapter.

The most important matter affecting Germany between the fall of France and the invasion of the Soviet Union was the conquest of Yugoslavia and Greece. Mussolini had entertained ideas of expansion into the Aegean for some time. He was not alone in this thinking. The Italian navy had been pressing for action in this regard since the 1930s. In addition, the Duce was being egged on by Ciano and the Italian governor of Albania, Francesco Jacomoni.[7]

With the invasion of the Soviet Union in the offing, Hitler sought above all else to keep this part of the world quiet. While not opposed to an eventual Italian occupation of parts of Greece and Yugoslavia, Hitler feared, quite correctly, that any Italian move against Greece would give the British an opportunity to threaten his southern flank. Therefore, both Hitler and the German high commands (both OKH and OKW) sought to urge their Italian counterparts in the strongest possible terms that no aggressive moves should be made toward either Greece or Yugoslavia.

Hitler tried several approaches to deter Italian aggression in the area. The first was to attempt to persuade or coerce Greece, Yugoslavia, and Bulgaria into joining the Axis. This would result in some success with Bulgaria, a temporary success with Yugoslavia, and no success at all with Greece, which preferred to maintain its policy of neutrality.[8]

The second approach constituted a series of attempts by Hitler personally to dissuade Italy from an aggressive course of action in the Balkans, at least for the time being. During the summer and fall of 1940 Hitler, in a series of meetings with either Ciano or the Italian ambassador Dino Alfieri or in letters to the Duce himself, stressed the importance of keeping the Balkans relatively quiescent. The Führer essentially ignored claims presented by Ciano that the Greek government of General John Metaxas was overtly supporting the British. German diplomats from Ribbentrop down reinforced this view.[9]

The last approach, conducted largely by Hitler and his military advisers, was to tactfully reject Italian requests for German aid in this undertaking. On 9 August 1940 Roatta broached the matter of Greece and Yugoslavia in Rome with Rintelen. Roatta indicated that Mussolini, delicately described in Rintelen's report as "the political leadership," had ordered the Italian General Staff to prepare a plan for an Italian attack against Yugoslavia. While reassuring Rintelen that such an attack would not take place for a year or two if at all, Roatta then inquired whether or not the Germans would be able to provide some assistance. This would be in the form of material aid, including 5,000 trucks, as well as German medical and veterinary personnel.[10]

German response was uniform in substance, but it varied considerably in the tone used publicly as opposed to in private. The public response, delivered via the Foreign Ministry and Rintelen, was to politely suggest that no action be taken against either Greece or Yugoslavia until the matter had been definitively revolved politically. Privately, a number of Germans, including Halder, were incredulous at what they regarded as the latest Italian request for items that were scarce even for German units.[11]

Notwithstanding Germany's objections to an Italian adventure in either Greece or Yugoslavia, preparations went ahead for the attack. During the summer and fall of 1940, in regard to both the invasion of Britain and Italian intentions in the Balkans, both Hitler and Mussolini proved to be masters of disingenuousness and duplicity. For their part, the Germans consistently refused to say anything definitive regarding the cancellation of *Sea Lion*. Although the operation was effectively canceled on 19 September 1940, Hitler did not give Mussolini any real indication of cancellation until the end of September, first through a conversation with Ciano, and then at the 4 October 1940 meeting with the Duce at the Brenner Pass.[12]

For their part, the Italians were quite silent about their intentions regarding Greece and Yugoslavia, at least officially. While admitting to Ribbentrop in a meeting in Rome on 19 September 1940 that he had concentrated 500,000 men on the Yugoslavian border and 200,000 men on the Greek border, Mussolini denied any aggressive intentions for the immediate future, although Italian and German records of the meeting differ considerably on this point.[13] Certainly the Duce rarely, if ever, mentioned the subject in his correspondence with Hitler and did not bring up the matter during the 4 October 1940 Brenner Pass meeting.[14] Likewise, in their military contacts the Italians gave conflicting signals to the Germans. The subject of the Balkans never came up in a 9 October 1940 meeting between Badoglio and the Luftwaffe liaison staff in Rome. On 23 October 1940 Roatta gave Rintelen an absolute denial to the notion that Italy was about to undertake military action against Greece. The next day, however, Badoglio informed Rintelen that Italy had completed preparations for an offensive against Greece. The attack would be predicated on any perceived British violation of Greek neutrality.[15]

Privately, however, the Germans were well aware that the Italians had some sort of plan afoot for military action in the Balkans. Ciano especially distinguished himself with unguarded, vehement verbosity against all things Greek during his late September visit to Berlin.[16] By 18 October 1940 the German ambassador to Italy, Hans Georg von Mackensen, reported that he had received reliable information that Italy would move against Greece in the very near future. Apparently the straw that had broken the camel's back was the dispatching of the German Military Mission to Romania, which Mussolini and his advisers regarded as yet another grievous blow to Italian prestige. Hitler had done this without any prior consultation with his Italian ally, and the German response to Italian complaints was so brusque as to perhaps give even Hitler some regrets about how the matter was handled. Italian embarrassment was only increased when Romania refused to accept the presence of a small Italian force.[17]

Mussolini finally got around to informing Hitler of his intentions to attack Greece in a letter dated 19 October 1940. The timing of the letter was ideally suited to Mussolini's avowed purpose of surprising Hitler, since at that time Hitler was away on a trip to both Spain and France. He only received the letter on 25 October 1940, while he was returning from meetings with Franco and Vichy French leader Marshal Henri Petain. The letter itself might be characterized as an exercise in breezy self-delusion. Mussolini confidently told Hitler that Italy had the ability to strike against Greece and the British in Egypt simultaneously.[18]

Horrified by the contents of Mussolini's letter, Hitler attempted to get back to Italy to personally dissuade the Duce from this course of action, but it was too late. Italy presented a note to the Greek government in Athens at 3:00 A.M. on 28 October 1940. After accusing Greece of permitting the British to use its territorial waters and ports, Italy demanded that Greece surrender strategic points of Greek territory to Italy. Without waiting for the three-hour deadline in the ultimatum to expire, Italy attacked Greece at 5:30 A.M. on 28 October 1940.[19] Poorly prepared and organized, the Italian forces, six divisions with 140,000 men commanded by Visconti Sebastiano Prasca, were expected to eventually occupy all of Greece, a hopelessly unrealistic objective.[20]

The attack, conducted with inadequate forces and even contrary to what was called for by the Regio Excercito's own doctrine, quickly ground to a halt due to a combination of insufficient preparation, atrocious conditions, and stout Greek resistance. Mussolini's sensible proposal for an amphibious landing behind the Greek defenses foundered on the shoals of petty interservice squabbles.[21] Mobilizing all available manpower and taking advantage of both worsening weather and Bulgarian neutrality, the Greek army, commanded by General Alexander Papagos, was eventually able to attain considerable numerical superiority in a couple of sectors on the front. On 14 November 1940 Papagos launched a counterattack.[22]

By Christmas the Italians had been swept out of Greece and back into Albania, where they finally brought a halt to the Greek advance. Italian troops were now faced with the prospect of spending a hard winter in the Balkans. Combined with the disasters suffered at the hands of the British in North Africa, by December 1940 Italy was in a critical situation.

German reaction to the Italian misadventure in Greece again differed publicly and privately. The public reaction might be gauged from the record of Hitler's meeting with Mussolini in Florence on 28 October 1940. Although Italy had attacked Greece that morning, the subject was barely broached in the meeting. All Hitler did was to offer the Duce a German parachute division for a possible operation against Crete. The discussions (mostly a monologue by Hitler) largely revolved around Hitler's recent talks with Pierre Laval, Petain, and Franco.[23]

Private German reaction was another matter. Hitler, not to mention many in the German High Command, were furious with the Italians. Italy's precipitate action now meant an almost certain intrusion into the area by the British. Even then, Hitler was irritated to the point where he considered letting the Italians stew in the mess they made.[24]

The Germans moved quickly to gather information on the developing situation, both politically and militarily. German diplomatic and military officials correctly identified Ciano and Jacomoni as the principal instigators of the fiasco. Rumors of Ciano's impending dismissal were correctly discounted, and Badoglio's firing by Mussolini was greeted with German indifference, as was his replacing of Prasca with General Ubaldo Soddu.[25] It was also quite clear to Hitler and the German High Command, however, much as they might have enjoyed letting the Italians clean up their own mess, that help would have to be given to Italy, and quickly.

German help would be both diplomatic and military. German diplomacy in the late winter and early spring of 1941 would be centered on adding the other countries in the Balkans to the Tripartite Pact, with particular emphasis being placed on Romania and Yugoslavia. In addition, Ribbentrop sent a circular to all German embassies directing them to avoid any comments concerning Italian military reverses. This rare exercise in German diplomatic tact was designed in part to present a united Axis front to the world, and to keep Italian feathers from being ruffled any more than they already were. Hitler also instructed Rintelen to go to Albania and try to exert some influence over the conduct of operations there.[26]

Hitler certainly understood that Italy would require immediate military assistance in the Balkans. The possibility of German intervention in the area appeared in the entry for 1 November 1940 in the OKW war diary. Three days later Halder's diary indicated an estimate of the forces needed for an attack on Greece via Bulgaria. These ideas were eventually formalized into

Operation *Marita*, the broad outlines of which were issued in Hitler's Führer Directive Number 20 on 13 December 1940.[27]

More immediate help would be furnished, as in the Mediterranean, in the form of assistance from the Luftwaffe. Because Germany was not at war with Greece at that time (in fact, diplomatic relations were still in effect between the two countries), the best Hitler could do was to send noncombat aircraft.[28] Consequently, a transport group of Ju-52s was assembled at Foggia in early December 1940. By the middle of the month the unit, designated as the Third Group of the First Special Duty Bomber Wing (III/KG z.b.V. 1), was operating from a base some thirty to thirty-five miles inside Albania. The aircraft were tasked to fly in Italian troops equipped for winter warfare in the mountains and supplies, and to evacuate wounded. From December 1940 through the end of February 1941, the III/KG z.b.V. 1 flew 3,329 sorties, transported 28,871 men and 5,680 tons of material to the Italians, and evacuated 10,740 men, including 7,911 wounded.[29]

The last type of help the Italians requested was a familiar refrain to the Germans, namely, material assistance. Marras led the parade of requests when he went to OKW on 20 November 1940 to ask that Germany send some 3,000 trucks to the Italian forces in Albania via Yugoslavia. Alfieri essentially repeated the request for raw materials during an audience with Hitler on 19 December 1940 in Berlin. With their own preparations for an invasion of Greece and Operation *Barbarossa* looming, not surprisingly Hitler and OKW rejected the Italian requests.[30]

Axis planning as such regarding the Balkans developed during the late fall of 1940. It began with a meeting between Keitel and Badoglio in Innsbruck, which to some degree was more concerned with affairs in Africa. Nonetheless, Badoglio contributed to the campaign in Italy aimed at his dismissal by making a number of indiscreet statements to Keitel over the origins of the Greek fiasco.[31] On 18 November 1940 Ciano met with Hitler and Ribbentrop at the *Berghof*. This was followed by several letters from Hitler to Mussolini.[32] Finally, Hitler, Mussolini, and their respective diplomatic and military advisers met at the *Berghof* on 19–20 January 1941. The last meeting actually might be classified as three different meetings. On the nineteenth Keitel met with Guzzoni, who was standing in for Badoglio's successor, Cavallero, who at that time was in Albania. While they conferred, Hitler and Mussolini met, along with their diplomatic advisers, and covered topics that were largely political and diplomatic. The meeting on the twentieth marked the first time the Axis dictators met with military advisers for both present.[33]

German strategy as it crystallized after the January meetings had both diplomatic and military sides to it. Diplomatically, the Axis powers would try to bring Yugoslavia, Bulgaria, and later Hungary into the Tripartite Pact. Militarily, the Army General Staff initiated planning for an offensive against Greece, with the possibility of undertaking an emergency offensive to prevent an Italian collapse as early as 15 February. An Italian request for the dispatching of German mountain troops to Albania was ultimately rejected.[34] For his part, Mussolini, after a short visit to the front, ordered one more offensive in early March, hoping to garner at least one victory before German intervention. Like all of the other Italian offensives, it, too, failed after a few days. Its only practical result was to send Italian morale plummeting even further.[35]

The diplomatic side of this plan started off successfully enough. Feeling in the end that Soviet Russia was more of a threat than Nazi Germany, Bulgaria ultimately joined the Tripartite Pact on 1 March 1941.[36] A little more than three weeks later Yugoslavia joined the Tripartite Pact on 25 March 1941. Hungary, at Hitler's urging, signed a "treaty of friendship" on 12 December 1940.[37]

Even before these treaties were signed, German military preparations for Greece that would involve some degree of Bulgarian participation went ahead. Hitler himself initiated these preparations when King Boris of Bulgaria visited Hitler at the *Berghof* on 18 November 1940.[38] By 13 December Führer Directive Number 20 clearly indicated that Bulgarian support for Operation *Marita* could be "counted on," but no details were included as to what form this support would take.[39] What the Germans initially needed most was the right of transit through Bulgaria. Once the requisite number of bridges had been built over the Danube River, German forces from Romania would be able to pass through Bulgaria on their way to Greece. The initial request was actually made to Hitler by the army commander in chief, Field Marshal Walter von Brauchitsch, and then passed by Hitler to the German ambassador in Bulgaria, Karl Ritter.[40]

How all this was ultimately carried out depended on the timing of several events and the resolution of some confusion within the German High Command. The Bulgarian government did not want to sign the Tripartite Pact or to order mobilization until after German troops crossed the border. The local German ground commander, Field Marshal Wilhelm List, desired just the opposite as far as mobilization went.[41]

There was also some question regarding who was doing the negotiating for Germany with the Bulgarians. The Bulgarians had originally asked that contact be established between the respective general staffs. Ultimately, Hitler decided that the negotiations would be led for the Germans by List, although the actual talks were conducted by his senior staff officers. Also attending was the military attaché to Sofia, Colonel Hans Bruckmann, while political matters would be left in the hands of Felix Benzler, who had been attached by the Foreign Ministry to List's headquarters. OKW would also have input into this process, which caused Halder some irritation.[42]

The outcome of the negotiations was that the Germans were able to get their way on the issues of mobilization and the construction of bridges, while announcing Bulgaria's signing of the Tripartite Pact on 1 March 1941, with German troops moving into Bulgaria the next day.[43] Bulgaria would be rewarded with some choice pieces of Greek territory, ensuring Bulgaria an outlet to the Aegean Sea.[44]

Yugoslavia turned out to be a much thornier proposition. German diplomacy, through a combination of threats and promises, many of which were delivered personally by Hitler in a 4 March 1941 meeting with Prince Regent Paul, was initially successful. The Yugoslavian Crown Council agreed to sign the Tripartite Pact on 17 March 1941, although Yugoslavia wanted guarantees from Germany as to the country's territorial integrity.[45]

Although the Yugoslavian government was aware that adherence to the Tripartite Pact would be unpopular, it was clearly unprepared for the degree of popular outrage when it was actually announced on 25 March as the signing ceremony took place in Vienna. Nor was the Yugoslavian government alone in this. The German chargé d'affaires in Yugoslavia, Gerhard Feine, assured the Foreign Ministry on 26 March 1941 that "the government is entirely master of the situation."[46]

The mastery of the situation by Prince Regent Paul's government proved most short-lived. Less than twenty-four hours after Feine sent his telegram to Berlin, the regency was overthrown in a coup. The prince regent and his family went to Greece, and seventeen-year-old King Peter II took the throne, while a new government was set up under the former commander of the Yugoslavian air force, General Simovic.[47] The first act of the new government was to renounce the Tripartite Pact.

Furious at the Yugoslavs, Hitler reacted with lightning speed. On 27 March 1941 at 1:00 P.M. he started a conference with Göring, Keitel, Jodl, and several others. Later on the conferees were joined by Brauchitsch, Halder, Ribbentrop, and Rintelen, among others.[48] The result of the conference was the issuing of Führer Directive Number 25, calling for the overrunning of Yugoslavia and the destruction of Belgrade. Given that planning for the attack on Greece was already in hand, all Hitler and his high command did was to essentially append Directive Number 25 to *Marita*.[49] For our purposes the most important part of Directive Number 25 concerned Germany's working with Italy, Hungary, and to a much lesser extent Bulgaria.

While the diplomatic aspects of securing Italian and Bulgarian military cooperation in regard to Yugoslavia presented no great problems, Hungary was another matter. In December 1940 and at German urging, Hungary had signed a treaty of friendship with Yugoslavia.[50] The coup in Yugoslavia certainly meant a change in German policy toward the relationship between Yugoslavia and Hungary. On 27 March 1941 Hitler and Ribbentrop met with Döme Sztójay, the Hungarian minister to Germany. In a fifteen-minute meeting, Hitler laid before Sztójay a thinly veiled demand that Hungary renounce the treaty with Yugoslavia and allow passage for German troops through Hungary for an attack on Yugoslavia. He additionally called for Hungarian participation in the attack.[51]

The government of Admiral Miklos Horthy, fearful of a possible German revocation of the Vienna Awards if Hungary failed to go along with Hitler, quickly acquiesced to his demands.[52] The most notable dissent to this decision was that of Hungarian foreign minister Pál Teleki, who had long felt that any Hungarian military involvement with Germany would result in Hungary becoming embroiled in a war with the West, something to be avoided at all cost. Very much anti-German to begin with and feeling that an abrogation of the friendship treaty would compromise both Hungarian national honor and his own personal honor, on 2 April 1941 Teleki committed suicide in protest of Horthy's decision.[53]

The lining up of Germany's diplomatic ducks presented a new set of challenges to the German armed forces. Bulgaria would not figure very much in the military campaign about to unfold, but both Italy and Hungary would, in that each would have significant ground forces involved. The original OKH directive called for the Hungarian Third Army, commanded by General Gorondy Novak, which would operate under the control of OKH. Its mission would be to advance into the part of the Banat that was under Yugoslav control, with the Danube and Theiss rivers acting as natural borders. No Hungarian movement would be made into the part of the Banat in Yugoslavia that was adjacent to the Romanian border, namely, east of the Theiss River.[54] Hitler, while not really changing the mission, did alter the chain of command when he announced in Führer Directive Number 26 on 3 April 1941 that he would set the "operational objectives" for Hungarians (and the Italians as well), taking these matters out of the hands of the frustrated Halder. Hitler's orders would be transmitted by General Kurt Himer, who would be attached to the Royal Hungarian headquarters.[55]

Working with the Hungarians would not pose many of the type of problems that the Germans would experience working with the Italians, or even the Romanians. According to Bela Király, then a young Hungarian staff officer, one of the requirements for graduation from the Hungarian army's war college was fluency in German, since over half of the books in the school's library were in German, a carryover from the old days of the Austro-Hungarian Empire.[56] Thus the German army would have no trouble with matters such as finding the requisite number of interpreters. In addition, having the Hungarians directly under German control made the issuing of orders much easier. Still, the rapid mounting of the operation meant that the Germans had to scramble a bit to assemble the requisite personnel and material to man and outfit liaison teams that would work with Hungarian units.[57]

The arrangements with the Italians were rather different. First of all, the Italian army had a somewhat larger role to play. Although the Italian Second Army would also be under Hitler's ultimate command, the Italians would have more autonomy in the conduct of operations. The timing of Italian attacks would not necessarily be tied to German operations. To assuage Mussolini's feelings, Hitler would not give orders to the Italians. Instead, as he proposed in a 5 April 1941 letter to Mussolini, he would simply make recommendations and suggestions to the Duce, who would then issue the requisite orders to the Regio Escercito. At the highest levels, liaison duties would be handled by Rintelen. Separate liaison arrangements would be made by each service accordingly. Thus, the Luftwaffe, for example, sent Isenburg, relatively fresh from his experience with the CAI, to establish liaison with the Regia Aeronautica.[58]

The operation opened on 6 April with a massive air raid against Belgrade. Some 500 Luftwaffe aircraft pounded Belgrade for about ninety minutes, causing massive casualties.[59] With Hitler's thirst for vengeance having been slaked, the German Twelfth Army, spearheaded by the XL Panzer Corps, rolled into Yugoslavia. Likewise, the Hungarian forces, after encountering some stiff initial resistance, broke through the Serbian defenses in their designated area of operations. As Yugoslav resistance collapsed quickly with the German advance into the interior of the country, Italy also moved. Italian forces successfully occupied the Dalmatian coast with offensive thrusts north from Albania and south from Italy. The Cuneense Division took some 1,500 prisoners in Yugoslavia, helped by the fact that the Yugoslavians fought "with little conviction."[60]

With Yugoslavia subdued, the Axis offensive rolled on into its original objective, namely, Greece. With the XL Panzer Corps once again acting as the tip of the Twelfth Army's spear, List's troops moved into Greek territory.

By the last day of April the Greek forces had been smashed, British forces sent from Libya had been hurled back off the Greek mainland, and the entire country had been occupied.[61]

Italy contributed very little to this part of the offensive. According to Führer Directive Number 27 of 13 April 1941, Italy was only to attack the Greek forces on the Albanian front with relatively limited forces. The Italians did this, but very slowly, much to Halder's irritation.[62] Hitler sought to further smooth ruffled Italian feathers by ensuring that the surrender of the Greek Epirus Army would not be concluded without Italian participation.[63]

The final act in the Axis conquest of the Balkans was the taking of Crete. The only real Italian involvement was in providing convoy escort to ships that were carrying the seaborne part of the invasion force. The British, warned by *Ultra,* intercepted the convoy on the night of 21–22 May 1941. The convoy's escort was the Italian torpedo boat *Lupo,* under Commander Franceso Mimbelli. Although severely attacked, *Lupo* was able to sufficiently hold off the superior British force of three cruisers and four destroyers so that the majority of the convoy carrying German troops was able to escape back to Greece, as did the torpedo boat itself.[64] Despite this setback, the island was secured by German troops by the end of May.

The Balkan campaign also provided Germany with a slightly different challenge in coalition warfare, namely, how to divide up territory that was overrun. Hitler's overall approach in this matter was based on two major principles. The first was that no matter who occupied a particular area, Germany was to get the benefit of any raw materials that area contained. The Germans were particularly interested in the copper mines at Bor, in the Banat, as well as any coal-producing areas in either Yugoslavia or Greece.[65]

The second guiding principle of Germany policy was to have the other Axis powers provide most of the occupation forces, while at the same time positioning them so that the possibility of further ethnic conflicts in the area could be minimized. Hitler made this quite clear in Führer Directive Number 27, issued 13 April 1941. Germany was to leave only a minimal number of divisions there for occupation duty. The German forces were to be arranged in such a way, however, so that aside from safeguarding German economic interests, the Hungarians would still be separated from the Romanians and the Italians from the Bulgarians.[66] This was further clarified in May as the campaign was in its final stages. As it turned out, Italy would end up providing most of the occupation forces for the area. Thus did Mussolini secure his Mediterranean empire.

The campaign against Greece and Yugoslavia had serious consequences for the Axis, in both the short and long term. For the Germans, the cost of the campaign was relatively light. Although the conquest of Crete was costly in terms of both airborne troops and transport aircraft, the main campaign resulted in only about 5,100 casualties, of which about 1,100 were killed.[67] Nor did the campaign seriously interfere with either the timing or the preparations for the impending invasion of the Soviet Union.[68] For Mussolini, the gains in the Balkans had been dearly bought. Total Italian casualties for the campaign from October 1940 to the end of May 1941 totaled 13,755 killed, 50,874 wounded, and 25,067 missing. In addition, there were some 12,368 casualties from frostbite, plus another 52,108 hospitalized.[69]

In the short term, Hitler had been able to secure a stable southern flank, while also gaining considerably in the realm of territory containing valuable raw materials, including lead, copper, chromium, and coal.[70] In addition, he had been able to do this for comparatively few casualties, as has been noted.

The long-term consequences for the Axis powers were far more serious. Mussolini had redressed the issue of Italy's "mutilated victory" in World War I. Since the vast majority of the German forces were pulled out almost immediately after the conclusion of the campaign, it was now up to the Italians to take their place. Italian forces would have to occupy a good part of Yugoslavia, including the Dalmatian coast, all of Albania, and almost all of Greece. Eventually, the Italian commitment to the Balkans grew to some 500,000 men, who ended up being on the lowest end of the Italian strategic totem pole.[71] Any threat of a later Italian collapse would mean the insertion of more German troops to take the place of the Italians.

The conquest of the Balkans also had major logistical repercussions for the Axis. Mussolini, from a combination of long-standing foreign policy goals and personal jealousy, had essentially brought Italy into a two-front war.[72] Since Italian forces in Albania and Greece would have to be supplied by sea, Italian shipping, already under strain from having to support a war in Africa, would now be stretched even further. This would also apply to the naval forces needed to protect Italian shipping in the Aegean.

All this, however, was in the future. With his southern flank secured, Hitler was now free to return to his original aim, namely, the conquest of the Soviet Union. The world would indeed hold its breath.

1. Field Marshal August von Mackensen, arguably the best German commander in the realm of coalition warfare. This photo was taken in 1934, on the occasion of his eighty-fifth birthday. National Archives.

2. Adolf Hitler and Benito Mussolini in happier times, 1937. National Archives.

3. The uneasy allies. Hitler and Regent Admiral Nikolas Horthy of Hungary, during Horthy's visit to the Kiel shipyards in 1938. National Archives.

4. Dr. Paul Schmidt, Hitler's interpreter. National Archives.

5. Finnish president Risto Ryti,
1941. National Archives.

6. Finnish commander Field
Marshal Karl von Mannerheim,
1942. National Archives.

7. Hitler and his closest ally on the eastern front, Romanian dictator Marshal Ion Antonescu, 1941. Hitler's foreign minister, Joachim von Ribbentrop, is standing behind Antonescu. National Archives.

8. Hitler and Antonescu conferring as the tide turns. This photo probably was taken in 1943, when the two met at Klessheim. National Archives.

9. General (later Field Marshal) Wolfram von Richthofen, 1941. As a commander of the Condor Legion in the Spanish civil war and of air fleets in the area of Army Group South, he gained a great deal of experience in working with both the Italians and the Romanians. National Archives.

10. General Petre Dumitrescu, commander of the Romanian Third Army, 1944. National Archives.

11. Luftwaffe Field Marshal Albert Kesselring, who spent much of his time as *OB* South dealing with the Italians and Rommel. Perhaps the most notable feature of this 1944 photo is that Kesselring is not smiling. National Archives.

12. General Ettore Bastico, Rommel's nominal Italian superior in North Africa. National Archives.

13. Mussolini and Field Marshal Erwin Rommel. This photo was taken during the spring of 1943, after Rommel's recall from Africa. National Archives.

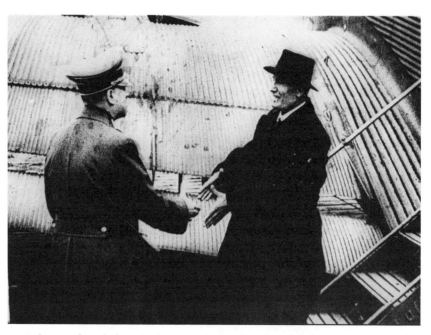

14. What are friends for? A relieved Hitler greets a grateful Mussolini after the Duce's rescue by Otto Skorzeny's commandos. National Archives.

15. The Duce's last crowd scene. The corpses of Mussolini,
his mistress Clara Petacci, and Achille Starace, hung upside
down in Milan, 1945. National Archives.

5

Barbarossa

Preparations and Initial Operations,
September 1940–July 1941

It is apparent from various indications that both Horthy and Antonescu had hints of the plans directly from the *Führer*, which these two gentlemen interpreted as pointing to an imminent German attack on Russia.

General Franz Halder, 4 May 1941[1]

I have decided in these circumstances, as I already mentioned, to put an end to the hypocritical performance of the Kremlin. I assume, that is to say, I am convinced, that Finland, and likewise Romania, will forthwith take part in this conflict.   Adolf Hitler, 21 June 1941[2]

THE CENTERPIECE OF HITLER'S STRATEGY, be it military, economic, or ideological, was always Russia. In the context of the strategic situation of 1941, the conquest of the Soviet Union (at least the area west of the Urals) would complete the isolation of Britain, at least as far as Europe went. That, plus the conquest of Egypt and seizing the Suez Canal, would then allow Germany to carry out preparations for Operation *Sea Lion* at leisure. Economically, the overrunning of the Soviet Union up to the Archangel-Astrakhan Line would mean the achievement of Hitler's economic goal of complete autarky. Finally, and most important, crushing Soviet Russia meant the destruction of the home of "Jewish Bolshevism," in Hitler's eyes the most dangerous enemy of the German race.[3]

For the Wehrmacht, the impending invasion of the Soviet Union created an imposing set of challenges. The most basic of these would be trying to overrun the vast territorial expanse of European Russia while annihilating the Red Army. In the context of this study, *Barbarossa* involved perhaps the most complex set of problems in terms of coalition warfare ever faced by the German military. The operation would involve each branch of the Wehrmacht working with its respective counterpart in Finland, Hungary, Romania, and Italy. Spain would eventually send a division, while the Nazi puppet states of Croatia and Slovakia would also contribute troops.[4]

In the run-up to the invasion, German preparation, both diplomatic and military, would be guided by the principles used by Hitler before 1939 and by the German military throughout the war. Everything would be done essentially on a bilateral basis. At no time did Hitler consider convening a meeting that would include all the leaders of Germany's principal allies. Likewise, OKW made no attempt to create a mechanism to allow for common planning among all the Axis countries.[5]

Politically, militarily, and economically, each of the Axis countries had varying degrees of importance to Germany, and this was critical in determining the role that each country would play in *Barbarossa*. In Europe, the least important member of the Axis was Bulgaria. Although a member of the Tripartite Pact, aside from granting right of transit for German troops, Bulgaria was not asked to contribute much to the invasions of Greece or the Soviet Union. In the case of Greece, given the sizable Italian involvement in the operation and the poor state of Italo-Bulgarian relations, Hitler sought to minimize the potential for friction between those two countries. Aside from transit rights, Hitler wanted full German ownership of the chromium mines at Skoplje. In the actual event, Bulgaria got some minor scraps of land from both Greece and Yugoslavia.[6] In the case of *Barbarossa*, Bulgaria was never considered to be an active player. Given the Russian role in Bulgaria's liberation from Ottoman Turkish rule in 1878, any Russian government, be it czarist or Soviet, enjoyed considerable popularity with the Bulgarian people. Bulgaria would remain neutral until the Soviet Union abrogated its neutrality agreement and declared war in 1944.[7]

Another country with relatively little importance in regard to Operation *Barbarossa* was Japan. Certainly relations between Germany and Japan were not very good at the start of the war owing to the signing of the Nazi-Soviet Pact, a move that clearly surprised and embarrassed the Japanese.[8] By September 1940 relations had been repaired to the extent that Germany and Japan, along with Italy, were able to sign the Tripartite Pact.

The Tripartite Pact, signed on 27 September 1940 in Berlin, was a short document. Written in English, it consisted of only six brief articles, ultimately taking up a little more than one page. Politically, the signatories divided the world between them, with Europe being regarded as the sphere of German and Italian preeminence, while "Greater East Asia" went to the Japanese. All three countries pledged military, political, and economic aid to each other but only if "attacked" (the definition of which was to be determined later) by a third power "at present not involved in the European War or in the Sino-Japanese Conflict."[9]

One of the more interesting aspects of the pact is how different people in Germany, let alone the Axis countries, interpreted it. Hitler regarded the Tripartite Pact as a device that was directed against the United States. The threat posed by the Japanese navy to American interests in the Pacific would ensure that no American intervention would take place after the onset of *Barbarossa*. Japanese aid against the Soviet Union was neither sought nor offered. In fact, according to Warlimont, the attitude at OKW was that the only role the Japanese army would play if it did attack Russia was that of "stripping the corpse." Thus, with the sole exception of a vague proposal or two from the German navy, the idea of conducting some kind of combined planning with the Japanese was never given much thought.[10]

Any number of other people saw it quite differently. Ciano, thinking almost solely in European terms, considered the pact of little value as Japan was too "far away" to render any real assistance to Germany. Ribbentrop told the Italians that the pact was designed to prevent any further Soviet expansion into Europe, while almost simultaneously reassuring the Soviets that it was directed solely against the "democratic (i.e. American) warmongers." Halder considered the pact as something to be used against either the Soviet Union or the United States, depending on the circumstances.[11] The evidence would seem to indicate that even inside the German government and military, there was a considerable degree of confusion over the precise purpose of the Pact. In the end, although Halder expected a Japanese attack against the Soviet Union almost daily by the middle of the summer in 1941, none ever came. The only real cooperation between the powers was confined to the realm of the economic.[12]

Of all the major European members of the Axis, Italy should have played but a minor role in affairs on the eastern front. Italy had no real interests in regard to the Soviet Union. In addition, the Germans had made it quite clear during the run-up to *Barbarossa* that the Mediterranean was preeminently an Italian theater of war.[13]

The Duce, however, was not willing to abide by this. He repeatedly told Ciano that Italy needed to play an active part in any conflict between Germany and the Soviet Union, in order to allow Italy to have its share of the spoils in any postwar settlement.[14] What exactly these spoils would be, however, were never quite apparent. Nevertheless, an offer of assistance to the Germans was almost certainly in order, even if only as a pro forma matter. Given previous German offers of aid and the presence of the DAK in Libya, not to offer assistance would be the height of ingratitude. The only problem was that Mussolini was absolutely serious about the offer and that Hitler would ultimately accept it.

The country that was in the best position in regard to the impending Nazi-Soviet clash was Finland. Attacked by the Red Army in November 1939 after refusing a series of ultimatums from Stalin demanding territorial concessions, Finland had done relatively well. The stout Finnish defense, led by the aged but able Field Marshal Karl von Mannerheim, had earned Finland much sympathy from the international community. After the Russians finally broke through the defenses at Vipurii, Finland made some territorial concessions to the Soviets. The government of President Risto Ryti was understandably interested in regaining these lost territories. In addition, the Finnish government expected some form of aid from Germany in case of renewed hostilities between Finland and the Soviet Union.[15]

For Germany, Finland's only significance was economic. The mines at Petsamo supplied some of the nickel used by the German economy.[16] Other than that, Finland played little if any part in Hitler's plans, at least for the near future.

The fact that Germany's only real interest in Finland was economic placed Finland in perhaps the most advantageous position in regard to Germany of all the minor Axis countries.[17] Not burdened with the baggage of fascist ideology and not being subject to major German pressure, Finland never joined the Tripartite Pact and successfully rebuffed attempts by Hitler to draw Finland into a formal bilateral alliance with Germany. In fact, one could argue that Finland was able to adopt the position that Italy sought to take upon its entry into the war, namely, fighting a "parallel war." Finland would certainly be on the German side in a Nazi-Soviet clash, but on its own terms. Thus, for example, Finland was able to insist that when hostilities began, they would not begin from either Finnish forces or Finnish territory. This extended even to the terminology used by the Ryti government in its public pronouncements. In such cases the Germans were never referred to as "allies." Instead, the term "brothers-in-arms" (*Waffenbruder*) was used, a clear indication of the degree of autonomy that Finland enjoyed even within the Axis orbit.[18]

Romania and Hungary are dealt with together, as their relationship is inextricably linked to Germany's efforts in coalition warfare. As one of the defeated Central powers in World War I, Hungary had to sign a separate treaty with the victorious Entente countries. By the terms of the Treaty of Trianon, Hungary was required to cede about 70 percent of its pre-1914 territory (which was home to about 60 percent of its pre-1914 population), of which the biggest chunk went to Romania. Consequently, the recovery of Transylvania became a major goal of the Hungarian government during the interwar period.[19]

While Hungary sought to reverse the verdict of Trianon, Romania's position was precisely the opposite. Greatly enlarged by Trianon, Romania in
the interwar period tried its level best to preserve the gains made in 1920,
principally by cultivating a close relationship with France. For their part, the
French, seeking collective security through a series of alliances, saw Romania as a critical ally in southeastern Europe.[20] Part of the Franco-Romanian
relationship certainly involved developing contacts between the military establishments of the respective countries.

During the 1930s, however, the rise of both Germany and the Soviet
Union put Romania in a situation where Romania had to gravitate toward
either Germany or the Soviet Union. The Romanian government had made
overtures to Germany as early as 1933, only to be greeted by German suspicion.[21] Economic and political considerations, however, changed this situation. By late 1938 Germany was the major buyer of Romanian oil and a
major supplier of wheat and arms to Romania, a relationship later cemented
by the German-Romanian "Oil Pact" of 27 May 1940. In addition, Romanian governments realized that German support was one of the best guarantees against the demands of a revisionist Hungary.[22]

In the late summer of 1940, however, Romanian politics, always volatile
to begin with, became even more so. The combination of the Soviet annexation of Bessarabia and Northern Bukovina, combined with Hitler's Second
Vienna Award to Hungary and the growing violence and governing incompetence of the Iron Guard, Romania's contribution to the Fascist movement,
brought about the fall of King Carol's government. General Ion Antonescu
became the head of state. Although Carol's son Michael ascended to the
throne, the real power lay with Antonescu, who was also supreme commander of the Romanian army.[23]

Antonescu came to power at a particularly bad time for Romania. Hitler's
Second Vienna Award forced Romania to return roughly half of Transylvania to Hungary. Shortly before that, the Soviet Union, as mentioned in
the previous chapter, had compelled Romania to cede both Bessarabia and
Northern Bukovina to Soviet control. One of those factors that put Antonescu almost immediately in Hitler's good graces was that although he
said that he would seek eventually to reverse the Vienna Award, he was one
of the few leaders in Romania who said he would abide by its terms, at least
for the present.[24]

All these things taken together, plus Antonescu's innate anti-Semitism,
gave the new Romanian leader the feeling that he had more to fear from
Stalin than from Hitler. Thus upon his taking power on 6 September 1940,
Antonescu almost immediately adopted a pro-German foreign policy, fol-

lowed by a request calling for the dispatch of a German military mission to Romania.[25]

The German military forces sent to Romania were under the overall command of the German Military Mission to Romania, commanded initially by army general Erich Hansen and later by Luftwaffe Lieutenant General Wilhelm Speidel. In reality, however, the Germans sent several different missions to Romania. In fact, while the German Military Mission was responsible for the "total mission" of the defense of the Romanian oil fields and associated refining facilities, it had limited authority over the service missions. They "independently" bore responsibility for missions that fell into their areas and could give orders independently of the Military Mission. The chains of command for the service missions actually ran back to their respective service headquarters, not the Military Mission. Given this command structure, it probably made sense to eventually have Speidel act as head of both the Military Mission and the Luftwaffe Mission.[26]

Little need be said of the Navy Mission, although some comment will be devoted to German-Romanian-Italian naval activity on the Black Sea in 1941 later in this chapter. The two principal elements of the German Military Mission were the German Air Force Mission (Deutsches Luftwaffemission in Rümanien, or DLM) and the German Army Mission (Deutsches Heeresmission in Rümanien, or DHM).

The DLM and the DHM had one thing in common in terms of their respective missions, namely, defending Romanian oil fields and facilities. The Soviet annexation of Bessarabia and Northern Bukovina brought the Russians to within easy aerial striking distance of the oil fields at Ploesti, as well as the refining facilities.[27] Thus, the primary mission of both the DLM and the DHM was to guard both Romanian oil fields and refining facilities. The second mission was to prepare the Romania armed forces for their respective roles in *Barbarossa*.[28] The focus, execution, and problems involved in accomplishing both of these missions, however, differed considerably.

The DLM under Speidel had several tasks. The first was to set up antiaircraft defenses around Ploesti. This involved both active measures (fighters and antiaircraft guns) and passive measures (camouflage, damage control, etc.). The second task involved modernizing the Romanian air force and preparing it for its activities in the impending operation against the Soviet Union. Finally, the DLM had to undertake such mundane but important tasks as instructing German troops in differentiating between German, Italian, Russian, Romanian, and Bulgarian aircraft. This was not an easy matter, as the sheer number of makes and models of aircraft, including those of British and French manufacture, could be bewildering.[29]

The record of success for the DLM was a mixed one. Certainly the DLM was able to erect a set of defenses that would make Ploesti one of the most difficult targets to attack in Europe. The DLM was most successful in being able to integrate Romanian and German air defense assets into a common system. The Germans were less successful in attempts to modernize the Romanian air force. The failure here was in many ways due to the Germans themselves. Although the Romanians wanted to buy German aircraft, German aircraft production in 1940–1941 was simply not sufficient to meet the needs of both the Luftwaffe and the Romanian air force. Romanian attempts to purchase licenses to manufacture German aircraft were also refused by the German Air Ministry. Thus the Romanians would have to make due with a mélange of Romanian, German, Italian, French, British, and even Polish aircraft.[30]

The German attitude toward modernizing the Romanian air force may well have been influenced by a couple of factors. In terms of fighters, the Romanian air force had some Hurricanes (which the Germans considered modern), and the standard indigenously produced aircraft, the various forms of the IAR 80, although underpowered and not as well armed as other fighters, enjoyed a rough parity with their principal Soviet counterparts in 1941. Likewise, the two mainstays of the Romanian bomber force, the British Bristol Blenheim and the Italian SM 79 (the Romanian version was the JRS 79), were still serviceable aircraft in 1941.[31] If the campaign was a short one, as the Germans expected, there would be no need to divert resources needed for a serious upgrade of the Romanian air force.

The DHM, commanded initially by General Erich Hansen and later by General Eugen Ritter von Schobert and Major General Wilhelm Hauffe, had its respective tasks to perform. The German army presence in Romania initially was limited to one division but later was expanded to two. The first unit to be committed was the Thirteenth Motorized Infantry Division, commanded by Major General Friedrich-Wilhelm von Rothkirch und Panthen, which arrived in early November 1940. By the end of 1940 it had been reinforced by Major General Hans Valentin Hube's Sixteenth Panzer Division.[32]

These units had two tasks. The first was to support the Romanian forces in Moldavia in their efforts to set up defenses against any new Soviet threat. They also had the task of training the Romanian army to a standard as close as possible to that of the German army. Early on, the Thirteenth Motorized Infantry Division even provided humanitarian assistance, aiding the Romanian civil authorities in the aftermath of an earthquake that struck Romania on the night of 9–10 November 1940.[33]

The activities of all parts of the German Military Mission to Romania had to be severely curtailed in January 1940, as Antonescu had to put down an internal revolt by the Iron Guard. The Iron Guard had been considering some sort of putsch against the monarchy as early as September 1940 and even sought German assistance in this. Hitler, however, regarded Antonescu as a much more reliable alternative. In the end, the Germans pursued a dual-track policy toward Romania on this issue. Germany provided open support for Antonescu when he used the murder of a German officer, as well as some fighting between Romanian units and Iron Guardists, as a pretext to put down the Iron Guard. This support even extended to the use of German army troops in Romania. At the same time, however, Germany provided a safe haven for many members of the Iron Guard, including its leader, Horia Sima, who were fleeing execution or prison.[34]

German training activities were further hindered by the passage through Romania by units of the Twelfth Army on their way to Yugoslavia and Greece. German command arrangements subordinated any units of the German Twelfth Army to the DHM while they were on Romanian territory. In addition, Hansen, as head of the DHM, served as the liaison between the Twelfth Army commander and Romanian headquarters.[35] This posed additional problems, in that although arrangements had been made for the Romanians to pay for the costs of only the two instructional units, this quickly broke down as other German troops moved into or through Romanian territory. Despite attempts by the OKW to restrict or at least regulate the economic activities of German soldiers on Romanian soil, the German presence added considerably to Romania's financial problems. Finally, the winter of 1940–1941 in Romania was severe, which further delayed training for over a month.[36]

As these problems were gradually overcome, the DHM got on with its tasks. The DHM's training activities were conducted at two levels. At the lower level, German instructional units established training centers for five Romanian divisions, the Fifth, Sixth, Thirteenth, Eighteenth, and Twentieth. Training here was in weapons and small-unit tactics. The Germans also tried to convey the principles of German tactical leadership to the Romanians. At the higher level, the DHM instituted a course of instruction for senior officers that would be somewhat like the Kriegsakademie.[37]

As the German buildup for *Barbarossa* proceeded apace and the Germans moved more units into Romania, they were able to broaden their training program. From 19 to 29 May 1941, for example, the III/240th Artillery Regiment, part of the 170th Infantry Division, ran a course of instruction for fifty Romanian officers. A Major Vogt, sent out from the German Artillery Training Center in Romania, conducted the course. The officers of the battalion would act as instructors. The goal was to give Romanian officers instruction in German offensive and defensive artillery techniques at the battery level.[38]

The German effort in training the Romanians was negatively impacted by several factors. First, the scale of German training was almost certainly insufficient for the task at hand. The best evidence of this is that the Germans could set up training centers for only five divisions. In addition, the amount of time available for training came to at best only about four months. Even though more German units became available for such training missions after April, the most they could devote to such tasks was barely one month. Even in the best scenario this was not nearly enough time, considering the position from which the instructional units began.

Matters were almost certainly not helped by a lack of interpreters. It is difficult to determine precisely how many interpreters the DHM and its associated units employed, but it was not many. A list of officers for the Sixteenth Panzer Division headquarters lists only two interpreters, a very small number, given the size of the task assigned to the division in regard to the Romanian army. In some cases, such as the 170th Infantry Division, the Romanian General Staff assigned an officer as interpreter.[39]

Writing his situation report on 7 February 1941, Hube considered the Romanian army to be "worthless" for combat, especially for offensive operations. Although the soldiers were brave and loyal and could be easily led, they were not "active." While the Romanian army provided some semblance of authority in the country, corruption, especially among the officer corps, was both rampant and well-known. The noncommissioned officer (NCO) corps, considered critical by the Germans for superior combat performance, was marked by both corruption and incompetence.[40]

Finally, because of the long period of Franco-Romanian military cooperation, many Romanian senior officers, while having a good theoretical grasp of tactics and operations, had too much of a "French" cast of mind. Having been trained at French schools and in French methods, too many officers were "schematic" in their thinking, in the eyes of Germans, thus reducing their effectiveness in the fluid situations in which German leaders thrived.[41] It would take time for the Germans to effect the kind of changes they wanted in the Romanian army. In May 1941 the DHM considered only small parts of the Romanian army sufficiently trained for defensive operations and, under certain circumstances, limited offensive operations.[42]

The German presence in Romania, even before the buildup for *Barbarossa,* involved the Germans in another touchy area of Romanian politics, namely, the status of the *Volksdeutsche* in Romania. Mainly citizens of Austria-Hungary before World War I, they had been placed in Romania by the territorial stipulations of the Treaty of Trianon. As Romanian citizens they were naturally subject to Romanian law, and even military service.

The German presence in Romania affected this situation in two ways. First, the *Volksdeutsche* represented a potential source of manpower for Himmler's SS and certainly his recruiters made every effort to obtain men for the burgeoning ranks of the SS, not just in Romania but all over Europe.[43] From the Romanian point of view, however, the *Volksdeutsche* who left Romania to join the SS were guilty of a criminal offense, since failure to do compulsory military service was a crime. The German minister to Romania, Manfred Freiherr von Killinger, was able to play a bit on Himmler's psyche in regard to this issue in a message dated 26 February 1941, suggesting that a high level of recruitment of *Volksdeutsche* would be deleterious in the long run. By removing so many young men, the remaining women would have to marry Romanians and thus dilute good German bloodlines.[44]

The other impact was on relations between the German army and the *Volksdeutsche*. Local German newspapers hailed the arrival of the German military in Romania.[45] Before long, local German Gauleiters were coming to local German commanders such as Hube, complaining of mistreatment of *Volksdeutsche* by the Romanian authorities, demanding that the German army protect them and that *Volksdeutsche* living in Romania be given exemptions from service in the Romanian army. A skeptical Hube, after doubtless conferring with his superiors, dismissed one Gauleiter's pleadings about *Volksdeutsche* serving in the Romanian army by advising him that "service in the Romanian Army is also service to the Führer."[46]

As preparations for *Barbarossa* went forward, several other issues regarding Germany and its allies arose. The most obvious was the growing presence of German troops on both Finnish and Romanian soil. In this case OKW had the responsibility for dealing with any matters outside of tactics and operations. Therefore, it was OKW that issued instructions to German troops in these countries regarding their behavior toward their host nations. According to the instructions for German troops in Finland, all German personnel were basically considered exempt from indigenous laws. Finnish police officials could arrest a German soldier only if he was caught in the act of committing a crime, there was no German military authority present, and a report had to be sent up immediately to a German headquarters. Any legal problems in the area of civil law would be adjudicated by a German-Finnish commission. Much of this held true for German troops in Romania. In addition, German troops in both countries were told to act with the utmost honesty and scrupulousness in any economic dealings with the civilian populations.[47]

Another matter that had to be dealt with concerned the allocation of captured material. Germany had already established a record, when it came to filling requests for equipment from allies, of giving them captured material, especially motor vehicles. During the Yugoslavian campaign, the Germans captured enough British aircraft to put together parts sufficient to make three Hurricanes, which were eventually turned over to Romania.[48] It was fully expected, especially in the south, that both German and Romanian forces would come across much abandoned Soviet equipment, as well as capturing it on the battlefield. Eventually the OKH quartermaster came up with the policy that any material captured in small quantities by allied forces could be pressed into service immediately by the allies. In the case of seizures of large stocks of equipment, supplies, and food, the final disposition would be left to the local German army commander.[49]

The three most important matters to be decided in terms of coalition warfare for Germany prior to *Barbarossa* were how the minor Axis forces would be fitted into the plans, the missions they were to be given, and the command arrangements for these forces. As always, such arrangements were made on the basis of a series of bilateral meetings, first with the Finns and the Romanians, and then later on with the Hungarians and Italians. Naturally, the manner in which these issues were decided was directly influenced by the fact that, from the first, Hitler kept the true objective and scope of his intentions secret. Here, as before, we can dispense with the arrangements for Finland first.

The first German-Finnish military contacts occurred at the end of January 1941, when the chief of the Finnish General Staff, General Erik Heinrichs, paid a visit to Halder in Berlin. A few weeks later a couple of senior officers from the army and Luftwaffe staffs, respectively, paid an official visit to Helsinki. While there they cautiously inquired as to what Finland's official military posture would be in the event of a German-Soviet clash.[50] After being told by Heinrichs that Finland would remain neutral, but that if attacked by the USSR it would stand with the Germans, matters lay relatively dormant.

After Hitler laid out on 1 May 1941 how Finland, Hungary, and Romania would fit into *Barbarossa* in broad terms, matters with Finland began to pick up speed, although Halder considered the pace of events far too slow. On 12 May an invitation went to Finland, from OKW via the Foreign Ministry, asking the Finns to send a high-level military delegation to Germany for discussions regarding military cooperation in the event of hostilities between Germany and the Soviet Union.[51] The Ryti government responded by sending a delegation of five officers from the Finnish General Staff headed by Heinrichs personally.

Arriving in Salzburg on 25 May 1941, the Finnish delegation met over the next two days with representatives from both OKW and OKH. Jodl opened the meeting by pointing out that Finland would undoubtedly be caught up in any kind of military clash between Germany and the Soviet Union. He then indicated in a very general form the course that military operations might take, but only in the area covered by Army Group North. Jodl then outlined the areas of Finland where German forces, Finnish forces, or some combination thereof would have to operate, and roughly what their objectives would be. Any Finnish forces operating in northern or central Finland would be under the command of General Nikolaus von Falkenhorst's Army Command Norway. A Finnish corps, preferably the V Corps, would operate with Mountain Corps Norway and the XXXVI Corps. In the south, Field Marshal Mannerheim would command any forces, including German, in the sector that included Lake Ladoga. Liaison duties would be undertaken by an officer of appropriate rank who would be appointed by OKH and posted to Finnish headquarters.[52]

The Finnish response might be described as supportively noncommittal. While agreeing in principle with most of Jodl's proposals, Heinrichs made it quite clear that only an attack against Finland by the Soviet Union would provide a casus belli for the Ryti government. No firm agreement was reached. An OKW offer to have all forces in Finland, both Finnish and German, placed under Mannerheim's command was refused.[53]

The following day at Zossen the Finns met with Halder and representatives of the OKH staff. Halder covered much of what Jodl had the previous day but filled in some details. He also stipulated that the Finns would be responsible for taking Hangö and the Aland Islands. The Finns again agreed to a number of Halder's points but also had stipulations of their own. These again included the idea that Finland would have to be attacked in order to enter the war.

The details of all this were finalized at a conference in Helsinki from 3 to 5 June 1941. In addition, the stated goal of the Finns was simply to recover the territory lost to the Soviets in the Russo-Finnish War. Thus any major Finnish commitment to an advance beyond the 1939 borders, especially across the Svir River in an encirclement operation against Leningrad, was highly unlikely. Finland would undertake a gradual mobilization, beginning on 10 June, set to be completed by the end of the month. The Finns were also able to extract from the Germans a guarantee of Finland's status as an independent state.[54]

These conferences and their outcomes demonstrate the relative advantages that Finland enjoyed in terms of coalition warfare, but also the haphazard manner in which the Germans both planned and ran the war. Although clearly the most militarily able of the Axis allied forces, the Finns were able to place fairly clear limits on the projected employment of their military. In this sense they were able to take advantage of Hitler's orders that as much as possible the allies were to be kept in the dark regarding Germany's intentions.[55] In addition, Finland was the only German ally to whom Hitler had given a clear objective in his initial directive outlining *Barbarossa* in late December 1940.[56] Finally, Mannerheim was able to exercise a sort of veto power over some German proposals. This would happen in 1941 and again in 1942, as we shall see.

Finland also requested material assistance from Germany, especially in terms of aircraft and guns of all kinds. In the end very little was given to Finland. This was partly because the Germans may have considered Finnish resources, especially in antitank defense, sufficient for a short campaign and because Hitler's main priority in this area was Romania.[57]

Matters relating to Hungary in the preinvasion period can also be dealt with relatively quickly. Although the OKW directive of 1 May 1941 clearly indicated that the Hungarians would be involved in *Barbarossa,* very little was done on a practical scale. The Hungarians were told nothing of the impending operation, although there were some very general discussions in Hungary regarding steps the Hungarian army should take in case of a war in the east. In the middle of June 1941 Hitler, through diplomatic channels, urged the Hungarians to strengthen their military presence along the border between Hungary and the Soviet Union.[58] Only well after the start of the operation would serious talks begin between the Germans and the Hungarians on the nature and scope of Hungary's commitment to the war in the east.

The command arrangements for the Romanian part of *Barbarossa* were most complex, as they involved setting up command structures for each of the services of both countries. In this regard, the going-in position for the Germans was that no German unit should be placed under Romanian command.[59] Perhaps the simplest relationships were set up for the Axis naval forces in the Black Sea. The German Navy Mission had command of all German and Romanian units involved in coast defense. This included navy units, army artillery batteries committed to coast defense, and any flak units committed to the defense of the Black Sea ports. Once the campaign began, all Axis naval activity would be under the command of Admiral Black Sea.[60]

Arrangements for the air part of the campaign were quite different. The primary Luftwaffe headquarters in the area was that of Fourth Air Fleet, commanded by General Alexander Löhr. Aside from its associated air corps, the Fourth Air Fleet also exercised command over Speidel's DLM. On 20 June 1941 the DLM assigned a liaison staff, headed by Colonel Walter Bassenge, to the Romanian air force's general staff. Bassenge's task was to secure the agreement of the Romanians regarding the subordination of Romanian air force units to the orders of the Fourth Air Fleet. Tactically, Romanian air force units involved in *Barbarossa* would come under the command of the German IV Air Corps. Issues of cooperation with the army would be handled by the Luftwaffe liaison officer attached to the Eleventh Army (Koluft 11). He would be assisted by a Romanian liaison officer. Romanian air force units conducting close-support missions would do so only in support of Romanian army units. Although the Romanian air force was exclusively responsible for the defense of Romanian territory, including the Ploesti oil fields, the DLM was charged with trying to make the defense system as integrated and coherent as possible, up to and including air-sea rescue operations.[61]

The greatest scale of effort for working with the Romanians was, of course, required by the German army. The Romanians would commit the Third and Fourth Armies to the campaign. Sandwiched between them was Schobert's German Eleventh Army. Although Antonescu would be in nominal command of the Romanian armies, directives for the Romanian forces would come from Army Group South to the Eleventh Army, which would then pass them on to the requisite Romanian headquarters via the liaison staffs that were attached to Romanian units. In effect, at least for the first weeks of the campaign, the Romanian forces would be subordinate to the German Eleventh Army.[62] In addition, individual Romanian divisions would be attached to German corps.

The Germans sent liaison staffs to all Romanian headquarters from those of Antonescu's all the way down to individual brigades. Army liaison staffs tended to vary considerably in size. At army headquarters, a German liaison staff was headed by a general officer, assisted by several special staff officers and their respective staffs. A corps liaison staff would be headed by a colonel (usually a Kriegsakademie graduate), assisted by an intelligence officer and a small staff. The size of a liaison staff seconded to an army or corps headquarters could be anywhere from ten to eighteen men. Liaison staffs posted to divisions or brigades were very small. In most cases such a staff consisted of a major or a captain, assisted by an interpreter and a driver.[63]

Cooperation with the allies presented a variety of problems at different levels of war. At the very top, Hitler proceeded with his standard diplomatic practice, that is, to operate bilaterally. At no time did Hitler host a conference with all the Axis allies in the same room. Rather, he held a series of meetings, mainly with the leaders of the respective countries. In the case of *Barbarossa*, Paul Schmidt was correct in saying that Hitler's closest ally was Antonescu, not Mussolini.[64] Hitler met Antonescu for the first time on 22 November 1940. The Romanian leader, seven years older than Hitler and with distinct military bearing, made a lasting impression, leading the Führer to later speculate about Antonescu's ethnic ancestry in his *Table Talk*. In fact, Antonescu impressed just about every German leader he met with personally, up to and including the not easily impressed Richthofen.[65]

High-level military contacts were also bilateral. In the case of Finland, a high-level military delegation was sent to Berlin for talks, as noted previously. In Hungary's case, Halder paid a visit to Budapest in mid-June, before heading to Bucharest; because extensive Hungarian participation early in the campaign was not envisioned, Halder told the Hungarians nothing of German plans. Talks with the Romanians were normally conducted through the German Military Mission and its associated component headquarters. Military attachés would also be involved in these matters.[66]

As was the standard German practice, at no time was any thought given to the creation of a planning body with representatives from all the powers associated with the Axis.[67] In the context of 1941, however, there may have been some method to the apparent madness on the part of the Germans. Given that the only two participating Axis powers, at least initially, would be Finland and Romania, the Germans may have felt that a combined planning staff would be unnecessary, due to the widely separated sectors of the front in which each ally would be operating.

The titanic struggle that would be the eastern front began on 22 June 1941, with the Germans achieving complete surprise. Especially in the fronts of Army Groups North and Center, rapid progress was made. What is germane to this study is how well or poorly the Germans worked their allies into the course of the campaign.

The role played by the Finns during the entire campaign can be covered in full here. Although Finland had close military involvement with Germany in the run-up to the war, the Germans did not bother to tell the Finns of the onset of *Barbarossa* until the evening of 21 June 1941.[68] The Finnish expectation that the Russians would provide a casus belli was fulfilled rather quickly. Only three hours after the start of the German attack, a handful of Soviet bombers attacked Finnish territory. The Russians answered Finnish protests with a much larger attack on the twenty-fifth, which was directed against several cities, including Helsinki. Thus the Ryti government issued a declaration of war the next day.[69]

Once committed to the struggle, Finland was still able to wage "parallel

war." Despite pressure from Hitler, the Ryti government never broke off relations with the United States, although declarations of war were exchanged
with Britain late in the autumn of 1941. At the operational level Erfurth
pointed out that Mannerheim was willing to comply with German requests,
but only so long as they coincided with Finnish interests.[70]

Operationally, German-Finnish cooperation got off to a good start. Because Hitler's attack against the USSR as well as a Soviet response against
Finland had been anticipated by the Finns, Finland's first steps in the war
had already been choreographed. Finland was able to complete its mobilization and, as planned, attacked on both sides of Lake Ladoga and eventually
secured Hangö in the fall of 1941.[71]

By the end of June, however, there was some question as to whether or
not the Finns would continue operations east of Lake Ladoga to help Army
Group North isolate Leningrad. A German request for the Finns to continue
operations east of Lake Ladoga was made on 27 June. Mannerheim agreed,
although apparently Erfurth raised doubts about the Finnish willingness to
undertake this task, as Halder sent a senior officer from OKH to Finland to
secure Finnish cooperation in this matter. Evidently this turned out not to be
a problem at all, as Halder found out in July, when General Harald Öhquist
returned from Finland. Halder blamed Erfurth for the misunderstanding,
believing that Erfurth probably had a bit too much time on his hands.[72]

This minor contretemps was part of a larger question that concerned Finland in the summer of 1941, namely, war aims. At the onset of *Barbarossa*,
Finland's war aims were clearly understood by everyone both in and outside
of Finland as simply the recovery of the territory lost during the Winter War
of 1939–1940.[73] By late August, the Germans were pressing the Finns to
extend their offensive operations. Encouraged by German victories and not
having reached the old Russo-Finnish border in Karelia, the Finns agreed,
but only to a limited extent. Mannerheim, for example, would undertake
operations into eastern Karelia only if there was the clear prospect of Army
Group North taking Leningrad, and if the Finnish government gave its as-
sent. For the isolation of Leningrad, the Finns would play their part by advancing to the Svir River. Likewise, Mannerheim would consider an attack
to take Hangö only if strong German support was available.[74]

As summer turned into fall, however, and the Finns had been able to reach
the prewar border in Karelia, Finnish enthusiasm for further offensive operations waned considerably. Finnish foreign minister Väinö Tanner publicly
set out Finland's war aims to be as modest as possible in a speech on 14
September 1941. When Keitel relayed in a letter to Mannerheim on 22 September 1941 Hitler's desire for an autumn offensive to cut the Murmansk

railroad, Mannerheim, citing losses and potential economic problems, as well as doubts about what results such an attack might yield, could only promise the limited participation of the Finnish III Corps.[75]

In the actual event, the Finns were able to get their way. An autumn attack by the Finnish III Corps produced a couple of minor encirclements. The Finnish III Corps commander, Major General Hjalmar Siilvasuo, instead of pressing eastward to cut the railroad, decided to liquidate the remaining pockets of Soviet resistance and called off any further offensive operations, much to the annoyance of the German liaison officer.[76] Some students of this aspect of the campaign have suggested that Finnish reluctance to continue the attack to the Murmansk railroad was related to Finland's desire to avoid war with the United States. The United States had warned Finland that there would be serious consequences if the delivery of lend-lease supplies to the USSR was disrupted by the cutting of the Murmansk railroad.[77] Nonetheless, both countries could be satisfied by the end of 1941. Finland had achieved its military objectives, going so far as to demobilize some troops, and the Germans had been able to isolate Leningrad. Hitler pledged his support for Finland in the future and came through with the delivery of 75,000 tons of grain from Germany to help Finland's food situation through the winter, one of the few times German actions matched German promises.[78]

At the lower levels of command, cooperation between the Germans and the Finns was generally good. Because German was normally taught as a second language in the Finnish school system, communication was not a problem. This applied, however, only to ground units. The respective air forces did not exchange liaison officers, so appeals for air support could be made only at the highest levels, thus slowing responses. This resulted in lost opportunities, such as when the German First Air Fleet failed to attack the Soviets retreating by boat across Lake Ladoga before the Finnish advance, much to Mannerheim's irritation.[79]

The Germans were also most impressed by the toughness of the Finns, and by their skill in combat in heavily forested areas and in winter conditions. The most notable example of this was when OKH asked Mannerheim on 24 September 1941 to create a winter warfare school. The school, opened in December at Kankaapää, Finland, was attended by German NCOs and officers, while the Finns provided the instructional staff. During 1942 the curriculum expanded to include forest warfare. Erfurth considered the school to be an outstanding success. The Germans also set up such schools in Army Group North's area, where NCOs could be taught by Finnish instructors sent out from Finland.[80]

As we have seen, Germany's most important ally in *Barbarossa* was Romania. Yet, in German planning for the invasion, no real objective was given to the Romanians. The missions for the Romanians in the operation were outlined by Hitler, first in his meeting with Antonescu in Munich on 11 June 1941. These missions were (1) to defend the oil-producing region of Romania, especially the port facilities at Constanta and the bridges over the Danube there; (2) to gain bridgeheads over the Pruth River; and (3) once the Army Group South advance had made headway, to attack from the Pruth bridgeheads and prevent "an orderly retreat" by the Soviets across the Dniestr River. No specific date was mentioned. Hitler simply indicated that the situation was such that "an explosion might occur at any moment." That was later announced in Hitler's 18 June 1941 letter to Antonescu, in which Hitler informed the Romanian leader that the attack would begin on 22 June 1941.[81]

As with the Finns, some thought was given to the question of timing concerning Romanian participation. In his 11 June 1941 meeting with Hitler, Antonescu expressed his willingness to commit the Romanian army to battle from the first day, having no doubts that the Soviets would commit some hostile act against Romania the moment war broke out between Germany and Russia. Hitler eventually laid out his ideas for Romanian participation in his 18 June 1941 letter to Antonescu, which mirrored the ideas he had presented in the 11 June 1941 meeting.[82]

The details of the campaign are generally well-known and do not bear repeating. Instead, the focus here will be on how well the Germans worked with the Romanians in the 1941 campaign. Unlike in the situation with the Finns, both geography and the size of forces available to the Soviets meant that German-Romanian cooperation was going to have to involve all services.

As noted previously, the German Navy Mission was essentially responsible for the defense of Romania's Black Sea coast ports, especially Constanta. Its principal ally would be the small Romanian navy, which consisted of four destroyers and a variety of light craft, manned by well-trained crews.[83] Soviet naval action taken directly against Constanta was brief. Two Soviet destroyers, *Moskva* and *Kharkov*, bombarded Constanta on 26 June 1941 and inflicted some damage, including blowing up an ammunition train. The success of the two ships was short-lived, however, as they were taken under fire by a German railway battery. While attempting to evade the fire of the 280mm German guns, *Moskva* sailed into a Romanian minefield, striking a mine, with catastrophic results. *Moskva* went down, with only sixty-three survivors.[84]

Another mission the Romanian navy had to carry out was to provide protection against any Soviet navy attempt to interfere with the Romanian crossings of the Pruth River via the delta of the Danube River. Far more common an activity as the Axis advance rolled east was convoy defense. Supply of the forces advancing near the Black Sea coast was best accomplished by convoys from Constanta, proceeding along the coast. These were regularly attacked by Soviet light naval forces and submarines based in Odessa. The effective use of minefields, however, generally kept Soviet naval forces at bay. In addition, arrangements were eventually made between the Romanian air force (through Bassenge's liaison staff), the Fourth Air Fleet, the Romanian navy, the German navy, and, to a lesser extent, the Bulgarian navy, by which aerial and naval escorts were provided for convoy traffic. Under this arrangement the Romanian navy would provide the ships for naval escort (an unavoidable course, since German navy units would not appear in the Black Sea until 1942), while aerial escort would be a joint German-Romanian operation headed by the DLM.[85] Finally, Soviet naval assets were increasingly drawn away from attacks against merchant traffic to help with the supplying of the besieged port of Odessa.

The Romanian air force was heavily engaged from the beginning, as was the DLM. The primary responsibility of the DLM remained as it was initially, namely, the defense of the Romanian oil-producing region and the refining facilities at Ploesti. The DLM was also responsible for the defense of Constanta and the Black Sea. Authority for these missions ultimately rested with Major Trubenbach, commander of Jagd Geschwader 52 (JG 52), who also acted as fighter commander (*Jagd Führer*, or *JaFü*) of the DLM. In that capacity Trubenbach exercised tactical command of all German and Romanian fighter units (in this case a Romanian squadron of British-made Hurricanes) operating in defense of these areas. As *JaFü* for the DLM, Trubenbach worked directly for Speidel. German and Romanian seaplane squadrons flying over the Black Sea, as well as air-sea rescue units, also belonged to the DLM.[86]

Soviet air attacks against targets in Romania began almost immediately upon the outbreak of war. The two major targets were Ploesti and Constanta. Soviet air raids against these two targets began almost immediately after the onset of *Barbarossa* and continued until 15 October 1941. Ploesti was subjected to some thirty-two separate attacks, conducted by 77 aircraft. Soviet losses in these raids were surprisingly light, with a single aircraft shot down by flak and another 4 by fighters. Likewise, the damage they inflicted was light as well. Constanta was attacked some fifty-nine times by a total of 250 aircraft. The defense here was much more successful in destroying the attackers, especially after Speidel deployed JG 52 to the Constanta area. Flak accounted for 21 aircraft, while a further 55 were shot down by fighters.[87]

Aside from actually shooting down Soviet aircraft, Speidel also had to handle another problem created by Soviet air attacks, namely, their reporting. The presence of so many German and Romanian offices resulted in a multiplicity of reports dealing with Soviet air attacks, parachute sightings, and so on. This kind of activity continued even into the middle of July, by which time Speidel had had enough. On 17 July 1941 the angry chief of the German Military Mission sent a stern message to all the separate service missions, to the German Economic Mission, and, through Bassenge, to Romanian headquarters. In rather blunt terms Speidel informed all within earshot that the only authority on German air defense activity in Romania was the DLM. The other missions were to comment on the general situation only as it pertained to their respective areas of expertise. Reports of Soviet air activity over Romania could not be issued without first checking with the DLM for accuracy.[88]

Aside from the defense of the Romanian oil areas, the DLM had also been charged with training part of the Romanian air force for participation in "later combined operations with the Romanian Army forces."[89] That potential mission became a real one as the Romanian army commenced combat operations and moved east.

To support the Romanian army's part in the invasion, the Romanian air force concentrated the majority of its most modern squadrons into the "Air Combat Group," or Gruparea Aeriană de Luptă (GAL) in Romanian. In theory, the GAL was formally subordinated directly to Romanian headquarters, but the reality was more complex. At the outset of the campaign, the DLM (including Bassenge's liaison staff) was subordinated to the Fourth Air Fleet. The Fourth Air Fleet's main German organization for that part of the front was the IV Air Corps. When Löhr sent an order to IV Air Corps, a copy was also sent to Bassenge. Likewise, IV Air Corps would send orders for its units to Bassenge. His job was then to get the Romanians to tailor their plans for the GAL so as to act in accordance with the IV Air Corps. In reality, then, the GAL was in effect subordinate to the IV Air Corps and beyond that to the Fourth Air Fleet, although the process by which orders were transmitted took Romanian sensibilities into account.[90]

The GAL employed a bewildering variety of aircraft. The fighters consisted of German (Me 109E and Hs 112B) and Romanian (IAR 80A) types, while the bombers used were German (He 111), Italian (SM 79B), French (Bloch 210 and Potez 63), Polish (PZL 37B), and Romanian (IAR 37). Romanian IAR 37, 38, and 39 models provided reconnaissance, along with some British Blenheims. Given this, it should not be surprising that serviceability and sortie rates were problematic. On 22 June 1941, for example, the GAL put sixty-five bombers and forty-five fighters into the air against the Soviets. The next day, however, only a handful of Romanian aircraft were able to make sorties.[91]

The GAL spent much of its time during July 1941 flying missions to support the Romanian ground forces either tactically or operationally, apparently achieving enough success to merit favorable mentions in IV Air Corps situation reports.[92] As the summer wore on, however, the focus of the Romanian effort was the port city of Odessa. From mid-August until the completion of the Soviet evacuation on 16 October 1941, the GAL spent most of its time flying missions against Odessa and trying to overcome Soviet air defenses, most notably the Soviet Sixty-ninth Fighter Regiment. Operating at the edge of their effective range, the Romanians did not inflict significant damage, although their losses were about equal to those suffered by their Soviet opponents. By the time Odessa fell, however, the GAL was clearly a spent force.[93]

The primary Romanian service that would be involved with the invasion of the Soviet Union was, of course, the army. Yet it is odd that the ultimate focus of the Romanian army's effort in 1941, the port city of Odessa, was not really included as either an operational or a strategic objective for Rundstedt's Army Group South in the initial plan for *Barbarossa*. Rather, it was to aim for Kiev, the capital of the Ukrainian Soviet Socialist Republic. Yet, as one of the principal students of the Odessa campaign has pointed out, the omission of Odessa was surprising for two reasons. First, as the seventh-largest city in the USSR and the largest port on the Black Sea coast, it was the best possible place from which units of the Soviet Black Sea Fleet could strike against the right flank of Army Group South's advance into the Ukraine. It also had several airfields from which Soviet aircraft could attack Ploesti and Constanta. Second, the capture of Odessa and its port facilities was crucial to sustaining an offensive into the Ukraine logistically. The city's capture would allow the Germans to move supplies via the Black Sea coast, thus taking some pressure off an already strained rail system. In addition, the city could only be taken from the landward side, since the Romanian navy lacked both the strength and the ability to take it by sea, and the Germans had no real naval presence in the Black Sea in 1941.[94]

The immediate mission for the Romanians was to first defend the Pruth River line and eventually cross it, once Army Group South's offensive was well under way. Axis forces in Romania were arranged as follows: the northernmost army along the Soviet-Romanian border was General Petre Dumitrescu's Romanian Third Army; to Dumitrescu's right was Schobert's German Eleventh Army; and then from Schobert's right down to the Black

Sea coast was General Nicolae Ciuperca's Romanian Fourth Army. While in Romania, these formations would be called Army Group Romania and would be placed, nominally at least, under Antonescu's command. This would, as with the command arrangements for the GAL, have the benefit of taking Romanian sensibilities into account.[95]

The Romanians sought to organize both their eggs and the baskets into which they were to be put. Since the first major offensive mission would be undertaken by the Romanian Third Army, that army had assigned to it the majority of Romanian divisions that had undergone German training.[96] The Romanians also sought to simplify their logistical requirements. Because the Romanian army used a variety of weapons types, it tried to standardize as much as it could. Romanian active infantry divisions, for example, were armed with 7.92mm rifles of Czech manufacture, while the reserve units had to use a mix of Russian-, Austrian-, and French-made rifles. The use of Czech rifles in the active divisions was most expedient from the German point of view because Czech rifles could use German ammunition.[97] Despite the best efforts of the Romanians in this regard, these kinds of logistical issues would continue to be a problem.

When the invasion began on 22 June 1941, the Soviets made some small attacks across the Romanian border, but that was all. The Romanians responded with some probes of their own, and the Romanian Guard Division, part of the Romanian V Corps, actually established a bridgehead at Falciu on 22 June. The Guard Division was the only unit in the Romanian Fourth Army that had been extensively trained by the Germans.[98] Farther north, the major effort would be a combined one between the Romanian Third Army and the German Eleventh Army. Just north of Jassy, the main effort would be made by the German XXX Corps. The 198th Infantry Division had the mission to obtain a bridgehead across the Pruth River at Sculeni. They were able to do this against very light Russian resistance on 22 June 1941 and repulsed a Soviet counterattack the next day with heavy losses to the Soviets. The division was then reinforced by the Romanian Sixth Cavalry Brigade and the Romanian Fourteenth Division. By 25 June 1941 the German XXX Corps exercised operational command over two German divisions, the 170th and 198th Infantry, as well as the Romanian Thirteenth and Fourteenth Divisions.[99] Even though the XXX Corps had two Romanian divisions under its control, it had only one officer listed on its headquarters staff as an interpreter, Lieutenant Heinz Dettmann.[100]

With the Sculeni bridgehead secured, on 25 June 1941 the command of the XXX Corps issued a warning order for Operation München. The plan called for the German-Romanian force to attack out of its bridgehead in a northeasterly direction on 26 June 1941. Subsidiary Romanian thrusts would also be made across the Pruth River. Farther south, the Romanian Fourth Army was to launch a concentrated drive across the Pruth toward Kishniev, again moving in a northeasterly direction. The timing of the attack, however, was disrupted by the Soviets, who launched a series of strong counterattacks along the Pruth, in some cases throwing Romanian forces out of their bridgeheads back across the river. It was not until early July, once the Soviet offensive was spent, that the Romanian Fourth Army was ready to go over to the offensive.[101]

Operation *München* turned out to be a somewhat staggered affair. Schobert's German Eleventh Army and Dumitrescu's Romanian Third Army began their respective attacks on 1 July 1941. The Romanian Fourth Army was not supposed to begin its attack until 5 July, but this was moved up to 4 July at Schobert's request. Because this would be taking place on Romanian territory, Antonescu was in nominal command, although in reality Schobert would control both German and Romanian forces.[102] Command arrangements were also somewhat unusual, in that Romanian divisions would occasionally be attached to German corps, and at least one German corps would be operating as part of a Romanian army. Agreements were also reached, apparently on a service-to-service basis, on issues such as the collection and disposition of captured equipment.[103]

Although the objectives of the operation were taken, *München* was hard going for both the German and the Romanian troops. Schobert's force lacked any real armored unit, and the Soviet rear guards were aggressive and well equipped. Although a staff officer of the Romanian First Border Division assured his soldiers that "no single Russian tank can withstand the German 37mm anti-tank gun," actual practice was another matter, especially against the heavier Soviet models. The effectiveness of the antitank guns for the Romanians, such as it was, was also hurt by both scarcity and their being horse-drawn.[104] Matters were not helped by sudden thunderstorms turning the poor roads into bottomless tracks of mud.

The Germans regarded Romanian performance during *München* as generally positive. Liaison officers at division level, while noting the deficiencies of field-grade Romanian command and the lack of a professional NCO corps, praised Romanian soldiers for their bravery and physical endurance. In this regard, performance generally matched the expectations the Germans had for how the Romanians would do. Hitler, in praising the conduct of the Romanian forces in a letter to Mussolini, attributed it to Antonescu's inspiring leadership. Even Halder, a noted skeptic when it came to how the Romanians would fight, confessed pleasant surprise in his diary at the initial

Romanian performance. The liaison staff attached to the Romanian First Border Division was sufficiently impressed to submit a list of thirty-seven names to be considered for receiving German decorations.[105]

With the initial phase of the campaign over, the next mission for the Romanians would be the conquest of the area between the Dniestr and Bug rivers, an area designated as "Trans-Dniestr Land" or, more popularly, "Transnistria."[106] Exactly when Hitler came up with this idea remains a bit of a mystery. In his 12 June 1941 meeting with Antonescu, Hitler assured him that Romania would receive "indemnities," upon which there would be no territorial limitations, but he gave no specifics.[107] On 29 June 1941 Hitler asked Antonescu to place the Romanian Third Army under the command of the German Eleventh Army, a request to which Antonescu acceded immediately. The Romanian Third Army would attack in concert with the German Eleventh Army, break through the Stalin Line, and head towards Vinnitsa. The Romanian Fourth Army, with anticipated Italian assistance, would guard the right flank by clearing southern Bessarabia and seizing Kishniev.[108]

The carrying of the war beyond the borders of Bessarabia into Ukraine would present Germany with a whole new set of challenges in terms of coalition warfare. The next phase of the campaign would see the involvement of all of Germany's major European allies in combat operations. These operations would bring Germany's allies, and Germany itself, to the apex of military success but would also strain them to the breaking point. The next phase of the campaign would also bring Germany's allies into firsthand contact with the grimmest of Nazi Germany's crimes. It is to this part of the campaign that we now turn.

6

Playing "va banque"

Russia, July 1941–January 1942

I therefore thank you, Führer, for having accepted the participation of Italian ground and air forces, in numbers and for a sector yet to be determined by the General Staff.   Benito Mussolini, 23 June 1941[1]

With the fall of Odessa, the war will be practically over for Romania.
Adolf Hitler, 17 October 1941[2]

IN THE INITIAL PHASE OF THE CAMPAIGN, of all Germany's allies, only the Finns and the Romanians had been involved to any degree. Both succeeded in the first weeks of the operation in recovering the territory they had lost to the Soviet Union in 1940. The Finns, as outlined in the previous chapter, went on to advance into Soviet Karelia and aid in a limited way with the encirclement of Leningrad, all in accordance with Finnish interests. The Romanians would now be committed to a much larger undertaking, as part of Army Group South's drive into the Ukraine. This would also involve clearing the north coast of the Black Sea, most notably the port of Odessa. In this endeavor, Army Group South would also employ Hungarian and Italian forces.

The Romanian Third Army did reasonably well and did play a role in Army Group South's successful envelopment of the large parts of the Soviet Sixth and Twelfth Armies at Uman, earning the praise of the Eleventh Army's chief of staff. Likewise the GAL also put in a good effort, at least according to the German IV Air Corps.[3] Although the Romanian Fourth Army was able to close up to the Dniestr River all the way down to the Black Sea without Italian assistance, a new problem arose. As noted previously, very little if any thought had been given to the matter of Odessa. The Romanian Fourth Army, although now closed up to the Dniestr, clearly lacked the strength to effect a crossing, break through the Stalin Line, and take the city. Antonescu therefore asked Hitler to provide German forces to bolster the Romanians. Hitler agreed to provide the LIV Corps, which would control a combination of German and Romanian units.[4]

The next major German target was Kiev. Although Romanian units would not be directly involved in this operation, they would have a supporting role to play. After decorating Antonescu with the Knight's Cross at Berdichev on 7 August 1941, Hitler discussed this question with Antonescu and Rundstedt. One week later Hitler made this plan official, asking Antonescu to have Romanian troops undertake occupation duties between the Dnestr and the Dniepr. The Romanian Third Army, containing the best Romanian units, including the Armored Division, several cavalry brigades, and the Mountain Corps, would operate east of the Dniepr.

The plan to have Romanian troops operate in the Ukraine brought some other issues into consideration. Combat losses suffered by the Romanians so far had to be made good. Since the new campaign required greater mobility, the Romanian Third Army requested that the Germans supply Romanian troops their bread rations. Once across the Bug River, the Romanian field bakeries, drawn by teams of oxen, could not keep up with the pace demanded by operational requirements. The request becomes even more striking when one considers that the German field bakeries were drawn by horses. In addition, slight changes were made in the already existing arrangements concerning the disposal of captured material.[5]

In the course of the late summer and autumn of 1941, Dumitrescu's Romanian Third Army put in a reasonably good performance, acting under the operational control of the German Eleventh Army. Nevertheless, by early October German liaison officer reports were concluding that although a number of units in the Romanian Third Army had fought well, they were exhausted. Thus the majority of the Romanian Third Army took over garrison duty along the Black Sea coast, while just a few units would be involved in the offensive into the Crimean Peninsula. Compared with the Romanian Fourth Army, the Romanian Third Army was able to keep its losses to a reasonable level, ultimately losing a total of 10,172 casualties between the start of the war and the beginning of November 1941.[6]

Antonescu also indicated to Schobert in a letter dated 17 August 1941 that the Romanian Fourth Army would undertake operations against Odessa. The whole of the Black Sea coast up to the Dniepr River would come under Romanian control of one sort or another.[7] Hitler's main reason for offering this territorial plum to Antonescu was that it might prove sufficient compensation for the territory ceded by Romania to Hungary by the Vienna Awards. In addition, the cessation of Romanian operations on the eastern front would leave serious gaps in the line that would have to be covered. Finally, without further operations against the Soviets to occupy them, the Romanian forces could be transferred back to the Hungarian border. Given the tense relationship between the two states, full-scale war between Hungary and Romania over Transylvania could break out at any time, although Hitler had made it clear that the issue would be settled after the war. From Antonescu's point of view, the capture of Odessa would be the crowning achievement of the Romanian forces and would effectively mark the end of their participation in the war. Romania would not only have regained its lost territory, but also become a power in its own right in the "new Europe."[8]

Antonescu's hope was that the Romanian Fourth Army could take Odessa by the end of August. Reality was another matter. By 20 August 1941 the Soviet Independent Coastal Army had more than 34,000 men in fortified positions covering the city, supported by 249 guns.[9] The seaward approaches to the city were defended by coast artillery. German liaison officer reports on the state of the units in the Romanian Fourth Army raised concerns about the state of the army. Heavy losses had been incurred in the battles of July and early August. Also, if Odessa was to be taken quickly, the Romanians would have to abandon their French way of thinking, something the Germans had tried but failed to disabuse them of. In addition, the relative absence of the German Fourth Air Fleet meant that the GAL would have to carry the load in terms of air operations over the city. Although in a somewhat depleted state, the Soviet Sixty-ninth Fighter Regiment would still be able to field enough aircraft to maintain a state of parity in the air. The Soviets could also gain temporary superiority by moving reinforcements into the city by sea.[10]

The Romanian offensive against Odessa began on 18 August 1941. The attack continued for about six days and then, after a short pause, resumed on 28 August, continuing until 5 September 1941. The German Eleventh Army's liaison officer expressed concern to Halder that without the presence of a German headquarters, the attack would run into trouble. The Romanians nevertheless made some progress, although at a heavy cost. The Romanian V Corps penetrated the Soviet defenses north of the city, while the Romanian I and III Corps took some ground west of the city. During this phase of the battle the Romanians took about 7,000 prisoners and destroyed a number of aircraft, most of which were bombers.[11] Nevertheless, by the last week of August it was becoming abundantly clear to the Germans that Antonescu's hope of capturing Odessa before the end of August, or even the beginning of September, was entirely too optimistic. Odessa would remain a problem for some time to come.[12]

A report by Hauffe on the situation in Odessa dated 4 September 1941 led to the assignment of some small German forces to the city, mainly in the form of an engineer regimental staff, four engineer battalions, two infantry battalions, an artillery regimental staff, a heavy artillery battalion of four batteries, two coast artillery battalions, and a signal company. Under the command of Lieutenant General L'Honere de Coubière, who had the title of "Commander of German Units before Odessa," these units would be placed at Antonescu's disposal, although they would be used only for specialized tasks. Any further German help would have to await the conclusion of the battle of Kiev, then in its climactic stage.[13]

Before the arrival of the German forces, however, Antonescu launched another attack that lasted from 11 to 15 September. The left wing of the Soviet Independent Coastal Army was driven out of some positions and retreated from others. The Romanians took some territory south and southwest of the city, as well as 2,000 prisoners. The Soviets, however, were still able to prevent a breakthrough and firmed up their defenses by rushing in the 157th Rifle Division by sea from Novorossisk. A resumption of the Romanian offensive on 17 September, spearheaded in some cases by Coubière's newly arrived infantry and engineer units, achieved little, although one author suggests that the Romanians took some enjoyment at the Germans' initial failure.[14]

The Romanian effort at Odessa received a severe setback when the Soviets, using their naval superiority, were able to mount an attack against the Romanian V Corps, holding the coast north of the city. Using a frontal attack supplemented by an amphibious landing in the Romanian rear and supported by naval gunfire, the Soviets were able to stampede the Romanian V Corps. Although casualties were relatively light, the Romanians lost those positions from which their artillery could bombard Odessa's port facilities.[15]

The debacle suffered by the Romanian V Corps led Antonescu to ask the Germans via Hauffe for substantial help at Odessa. Hitler responded with promises of more artillery and air support, urging Antonescu to concentrate on recapturing the lost artillery positions before undertaking any more major attacks.[16] By mid-October the German help had arrived, although major support from the Luftwaffe would be conditionally timed, given the expectation that major elements of the Fourth Air Fleet would be transferred to the Moscow area relatively soon. A major attack was planned for 23 October 1941.[17]

The attack, however, never came off. The Soviets, sensing that further resistance would be futile, began evacuating Odessa on 1 October 1941. Between 1 and 16 October some 86,000 men and 150,000 civilians, as well as some equipment, were evacuated from Odessa to the Crimea. These soldiers would eventually play a role in the ultimately unsuccessful Soviet defense of the Crimea. On 17 October two divisions from the Romanian I Corps entered the city, followed by other Romanian units, taking some 6,000 prisoners in the process. Antonescu had won his prize, although the port would not be able to accommodate Axis shipping until late December 1941.[18]

The capture of Odessa effectively ended large-scale Romanian participation in the 1941 campaign. Neither the Romanian Third Army nor the Romanian Fourth Army was employed after the fall of Odessa. A Romanian corps fought as part of the German Eleventh Army during its attempt to take the Crimea in the late fall. Some units, such as the Romanian First Infantry Division, were also caught up in the defense against the extended Soviet winter counteroffensive in January 1942. The Romanians did relatively well but were clearly exhausted and had suffered heavy losses in men and equipment.[19]

On a day-to-day basis, cooperation with the Romanians was a hard business for the overworked German liaison staffs. German liaison officers had to keep fully up-to-date on a rapidly changing and fluid situation and communicate this to their Romanian colleagues, a major challenge when communications broke down. Not many German officers or even enlisted men spoke Romanian. The relative dearth of Romanian-speaking German officers often precluded those officers from getting some much needed rest, as their presence with their assigned Romanian units was constantly needed. The overarching German field liaison unit, the German Second Liaison Command, told subordinate liaison staffs that it reserved the right to cancel all leaves for German liaison personnel, and it placed heavy regulations upon their movements as well.[20]

Notably, Hungary was not even mentioned in Führer Directive Number 21, where Hitler gave the broad outlines for *Barbarossa*. German military planners, however, regarded Hungary as important because it provided needed space to allow part of the German army to deploy for the operation.[21] Other than that, however, Hungary would take no part in the operation. During the spring of 1941 Hungarian diplomatic and military intercourse with Germany was concerned with three issues, namely, the impending invasion of Yugoslavia, the status of Transylvania, and the treatment of those *Volksdeutsche* living in Hungary.[22]

Talks between Germany and Hungary in regard to the Soviet Union did not begin, as Hitler had planned, until the end of May 1941. Even then, no real thought was given to the role, if any, that Hungarian forces might play in an invasion of the Soviet Union. Rather, discussions focused on how quickly Hungary could mobilize its armed forces in case of a "military decision" in regard to Germany and the Soviet Union. Even as late as 6 June 1941, Halder was expressing doubts as to whether Hungary would be willing to "be in on it" at all.[23]

Matters stood this way from late May until almost the eve of the invasion. In fact, Himer went on leave for the first twelve days of June 1941, apparently at the suggestion of OKW. The first real clue of German intentions came on 15 June, when Ribbentrop instructed the German minister in Hungary, Otto von Erdmannsdorff, to inform the Hungarian foreign minister that Hitler intended to "clarify" the situation in German-Soviet relations, although the Hungarians were warned that they should "take steps to secure" Hungary's borders. Halder discussed some operational matters with the chief of the Hungarian General Staff, General Henrik Werth, during a short visit to Budapest on 19 June, although Halder claimed that no information on the attack was given to the Hungarians. Then, on 21 June 1941, Hitler sent a letter to Horthy announcing his decision to attack, although the letter would not be delivered to Horthy until 10:35 A.M. on 22 June, well after the attack had begun.[24]

From the start, relations between the Germans and the Hungarians were rather confused about the issue of Hungarian participation in the war. On 22 June 1941 Hitler sent Horthy a handwritten note that, while not demanding that Hungary declare war on the Soviet Union, did hint rather broadly at such a course; nor did Hitler request Hungarian participation in the operation. Likewise, German military thinkers regarded Hungarian military aid to Germany as something that might be nice to have, but also as something that did not require either a demand or even a request on the part of Germany.[25]

Hungarian reaction to both the German attack and Hitler's demand for a declaration of war was rather mixed. The pro-war faction was essentially led by Werth, who although rather annoyed that Germany had informed Finland and Romania of the attack, but not Hungary, feared that any Hungarian failure to participate in the war would endanger further attempts by Hungary to complete its regaining of Transylvania. Horthy, although supportive of the German attack for ideological reasons, considered a declaration of war unnecessary and believed that a simple breaking of diplomatic relations with the Soviet Union would be sufficient.[26]

Matters essentially remained the same until 26 June 1941, when bombs fell on the Hungarian town of Kassa, killing a number of civilians. Exactly who bombed Kassa, the site of an airfield and home of the Hungarian Flying Academy, remains a mystery to this day. Stories quickly circulated that the aircraft that did the bombing had distinctive yellow marking that would be consonant with German aircraft. Salvage crews, however, found an unexploded bomb with Russian markings showing that it had been manufactured at the Putilov Works in Leningrad. In addition, no evidence has ever emerged from extant German records that the attack was deliberately staged by Germany. The most common theory held by informed authorities, that the bombing was done by mistake, remains the most plausible explanation for this affair.[27]

In any case, the Horthy government used the bombing of Kassa as a casus belli, declaring war on the USSR the next day. The declaration proved an unpopular move with the Hungarian people, as the population now operated on the assumption that any major move by the Hungarian government in regard to foreign policy was done in response to German pressure.[28] Nonetheless, Hungary was now committed to the struggle on the eastern front.

The declaration of war on the Soviet Union, punctuated by some Hungarian air raids against Soviet targets, also meant committing some ground forces to operations on the eastern front. This presented the Germans with two problems, namely, where and how to use them. Hungary agreed to commit two major organizations, namely, the grandiloquently named Carpathian Army Group and the Mobile Corps.

The Carpathian Army Group, actually Major General Ferenc Szombathelyi's VIII Corps, consisting of six brigades ranging from infantry to military labor forces, contained more than 90,000 officers and men, supported by more than 21,000 horses and 5,858 motor vehicles. Ideally, they were to attack only after the completed mobilization and deployment of the Mobile Corps.[29] The rapid developments on the eastern front, however, did not allow for this. Thus the Carpathian Group would have to attack to secure the passages through the Carpathian Mountains, from which further deeper advances would be made by the now fully assembled Mobile Corps, while the Carpathian Group would move up to the Dniestr River.

The Carpathian Group started its attack on 28 June 1941 and was able to secure the passes through the Carpathians in three days. Owing to its better mobility, the major Hungarian participant in the war from early July until November 1941 would be the Mobile Corps, with its two motorized brigades and one cavalry brigade.[30]

The employment of the Mobile Corps was complicated by the Romanian presence on the eastern front. Both the Hungarians and the Romanians had made it clear to the Germans that they wanted some sort of buffer unit, be it German or Italian, between them. Likewise, the Germans also thought it wise to keep Hungarian units away from the Slovakian Division. At the time Rundstedt apparently did not see these issues as posing major problems, although he changed his tune after the war.[31] Consequently, the Mobile Corps, commanded by General Béla Miklós, was attached to the German Seventeenth Army.

The activities of the Mobile Corps can be dealt with briefly here. Fighting as part of the German Seventeenth Army under Field Marshal Water von Reichenau and occasionally as part of General Ewald von Kleist's First Panzer Group (later First Panzer Army), the Mobile Corps, about 36,000 strong and equipped with a variety of obsolescent armored vehicles, fought its way across the Ukraine until withdrawn in November 1941. During its period of service it was involved in some of the major battles fought by Army Group South, including Uman and the great encirclement at Kiev in September. It took some 17,000 Soviet prisoners. During this time the Mobile Corps was supported by a small contingent of Hungarian aircraft. Rundstedt thought that the Hungarians were good, although they lacked the "proper enthusiasm."[32]

In terms of practical, day-to-day operations, working with the Hungarians presented relatively few problems, especially in terms of language, as noted previously. The major issues always related to the tense state of affairs between Hungary and Romania, and how the Germans could at times get caught in between. Two examples here will be sufficient to demonstrate the difficulties the Germans faced.

The first concerns the German Eleventh Army. Because the German Eleventh and Seventeenth Armies were often adjacent on the eastern front in 1941, the two headquarters would exchange liaison officers; this held true of the Romanians and Hungarians as well. The Hungarians, however, sent as liaison officer to the German Eleventh Army Colonel Oszkár Baitz. From 1 May 1935 until 1940 Baitz, then a lieutenant colonel, had been the Hungarian military attaché to Romania. Baitz's tour as attaché ended with his being expelled from Romania, presumably for spying. Baitz's mere presence was enough for Antonescu himself to immediately demand that he be removed from the Eleventh Army headquarters.[33] The matter was kicked up to OKW, and mention of the episode was made in the OKW war diary. After several days of bickering, including the involvement of Major General Rudolf Toussaint, the German military attaché in Budapest, Baitz was recalled and eventually replaced by someone less offensive to Antonescu.[34]

The second example concerned a near outbreak of hostilities between elements of Dumitrescu's Romanian Third Army and the Hungarian Mobile Corps. On 12 August 1941 General Gheorghe Manoliu's Romanian Fourth Mountain Brigade began crossing the Bug River at Voznessensk. As it turned out, crossing the river here would bring the Romanians close to the rear of the Hungarian Mobile Corps, operating at that moment as part of the Kleist's First Panzer Group. At 10:00 A.M. Manoliu received a call from a Captain Fulöp from the Hungarian Mobile Corps, essentially demanding that, on the basis of an order from Kleist, the Romanians retreat to the west bank of the Bug.

Manoliu sent word of this back to Dumitrescu and then sent the German liaison officer to the brigade, Captain Kokol, to visit the Hungarian unit to clarify the situation. At 1:00 P.M. Kokol returned with the rather startling announcement by Miklós's chief of staff that if the Romanians continued to cross in this area, the Hungarians would turn around and form a battlefront against them! Although German liaison officers with both the Romanian Third Army and the Hungarian Mobile Corps were able to work out a solution that avoided bloodshed, an angry Dumitrescu complained to Schobert about what he regarded as aggressive Hungarian behavior.[35]

Relations between the Germans and the Hungarians also became somewhat strained, especially toward the end of the summer of 1941. On 8–9 September 1941 Horthy, Minister President Lázsló Bárdossy, and Szombathelyi, who had succeeded Werth as chief of the Hungarian General Staff, visited Hitler's headquarters at Rastenburg in East Prussia. Military discussions, held with Halder and Keitel, centered around the future of the Hungarian Mobile Corps. The Hungarians wanted the Mobile Corps withdrawn for a variety of reasons. Miklós apparently felt that it had "done its bit," and that other Hungarian forces should come up and take their place. Although losses in personnel had not been heavy, losses in equipment were another matter. Szombathelyi wanted the Mobile Corps withdrawn so it could draw replacements and refit so as to be ready for its "Balkan mission," essentially coded language for a showdown with Romania. The Germans rejected this request as selfish, and the discussions became, in Halder's words, "a little warm." Eventually, however, a compromise was reached in which the Mobile Corps would continue operating until the end of the campaign, at which time it would be withdrawn and replaced by another unit. Both sides, however, not very trustful of each other to begin with, had even less trust after this. Halder and Keitel developed a very strong dislike for Szombathelyi, one of the few subjects on which they were in agreement.[36]

The final major German ally on the eastern front to be discussed in an operational sense is Italy. The most interesting thing about the Italian commitment to the eastern front was Mussolini's desire to secure Italian involvement in *Barbarossa,* while the German military authorities sought to keep the Italians out. Even more than with the other allies, Hitler did not let on to the Italians at all about the invasion. The last meeting before *Barbarossa* was a hasty affair called for by Hitler and held at the Brenner Pass on 2 June 1941. The Soviet Union was the only subject *not* discussed. Instead, Hitler engaged in a five-hour rambling monologue covering such subjects as the mysterious flight to England recently undertaken by Rudolf Hess, the progress of the war in the Mediterranean, and raw materials, among other subjects. Cavallero and Keitel discussed matters largely relating to the Middle East and the Mediterranean, up to and including the difficulties involved in mounting an effective intervention in support of pro-Axis forces in Iraq and Syria. Ciano noted in his diary that he could see no reason for why the meeting was called for in the first place.[37]

Nonetheless, the Italians were not entirely in the dark about German intentions. As early as 30 May 1941, Mussolini instructed Cavallero to prepare a corps-sized unit for service in case of a war between Germany and Soviet Russia. Italian suspicions were certainly heightened when Ribbentrop went to Italy to attend a ceremony in Venice on 14 June in which Croatia formally joined the Tripartite Pact. The following day, he cut short a visit with Ciano and returned to Berlin, owing to, in Ciano's words, "an imminent crisis with Russia." On 14 June Marras reported to Mussolini that he had attended a German war game in which the objectives were Leningrad, Moscow, and Odessa. Mussolini evidently instructed Marras to convey the Duce's offer to Hitler for the commitment of a contingent of Italian troops in any invasion of the Soviet Union. Mussolini finally received the definitive word on the invasion in a letter from Hitler (actually delivered to Ciano, who telephoned Mussolini to inform him of its contents) on the eve of the attack.[38]

Once *Barbarossa* was under way, Mussolini strove mightily to insert an Italian force on the eastern front, despite German reservations about such a prospect. These reservations began with Hitler himself. In his 21 June 1941 letter to Mussolini, Hitler expressed at best only halfhearted support for the idea of an Italian contingent on the eastern front. The Führer was far more direct in his urging Mussolini to concentrate Italy's resources and attention on the Mediterranean. Hitler's reservations about having Italians on the eastern front were certainly shared by his chief military advisers.[39]

The Duce, however, would not be deterred. Replying to Hitler's 21 June 1941 letter two days later, Mussolini thanked Hitler for agreeing to the Italian offer of a contingent of ground troops, supported by aircraft. Ciano noted in his diary Mussolini's enthusiasm for sending an Italian force to Russia, although Ciano had also correctly noted Hitler's lack of enthusiasm at such a prospect in his 21 June letter. Although Mussolini was also aware of Hitler's reticence on this point, an attitude shared by some Italian officers, the Duce was more impressed by Cavallero, who predicted an easy German victory.[40]

Hitler, replying to Mussolini on 30 June, cautioned him that deploying Italian forces to the eastern front would take time, owing to the difficult situation with transportation. He suggested that upon its arrival, the Italian force should be attached to the German Eleventh Army. Hitler closed with an invitation for the Duce to meet with him somewhere near the front. Mussolini responded avidly to Hitler's suggestion for a meeting and also informed him that the Italian force of three divisions was ready and would depart for the front as soon as arrangements had been made with the proper authorities.[41]

The force Mussolini decided to commit to the eastern front in 1941 was known as the Corpo di Spedizione in Russe (CSIR). It consisted of two infantry divisions, the Ninth (Pasubio) and the Fifty-second (Torino), as well as the Third Mobile Division (Celere). The two infantry divisions were the so-called binary divisions, that is, divisions with only two infantry regiments instead of the normal three. The Celere Division had a Bersaglieri (elite infantry) regiment and two cavalry regiments. Aside from their core regiments, each division had the usual support units, and the CSIR also had a smattering of corps-level units. It was originally set to be commanded by General Francesco Zingales, but a heart attack put him in a Vienna hospital before the CSIR could even leave for the front. Breaking somewhat with the tradition of seniority in the Regio Esercito, Mussolini appointed General Giovanni Messe commander of the CSIR. Messe already enjoyed a good reputation and turned out to be arguably the best Italian commander in the war.[42]

The CSIR's 62,000 men left Italy in early July 1941, but it took more than a month to get them up to the front owing to transportation issues, as Hitler explained to Mussolini in a letter on 20 July 1941. During the intervening time, however, the German and Italian high commands negotiated terms governing how the CSIR would be employed. Set down in a document dated 4 August 1941 signed by Cavallero and Keitel, the agreement has some interesting features. The CSIR was tactically subordinated to the commander of whatever German army in whose sector the CSIR was operating. In all other cases, however, the CSIR's chain of command ran straight back to Commando Supremo. In addition, deployment and commitment of the divisions was to be left to Messe's judgment. Messe could also refuse an order if he felt that it would place his troops in a position where they could suffer a severe defeat and damage Italian prestige, and buck the decision all the way back to Mussolini. Finally, Messe would also have complete control over all Italian air force units on the eastern front (a total of about eighty-three aircraft, mostly fighters), which were solely committed to the support of the CSIR.[43]

Problems arose almost immediately as the lead unit of the CSIR, the Pasubio Division, reached the front. The CSIR was attached initially to the German Eleventh Army, and Schobert was not very happy with the OKW–

Commando Supremo agreement governing the commitment of the CSIR. He felt that the stipulations in the agreement were too inhibiting. With the CSIR arriving piecemeal, Schobert wanted to push its lead elements, the Pasubio Division and the corps artillery regiment, forward to join the advance on Voznessensk. Schobert furthermore wanted Messe to come forward and take command of the division himself. Supervision of the deployment of the rest of the CSIR could be left to a senior officer on Messe's staff.[44]

Messe demurred at this suggestion when he reported to Schobert on the evening of 6 August 1941. Although he noted that taking command of the forward division was an honorable thing to do, he replied that, for him, it was not practical. As commander of the CSIR, he had three divisions to worry about, not one. Although it is not explicitly mentioned in the message traffic between Schobert and Army Group South, one can infer that Messe argued that Schobert's request violated the agreement just negotiated. In the end, Messe agreed to place the Pasubio Division and the attached artillery at Schobert's disposal, while Messe would bring up the rest of the CSIR. This compromise, however agreed to, was also thought unsatisfactory by Schobert. In the event, the German liaison officer to the division also found much to criticize.[45]

Once committed to action, the CSIR performed reasonably well, despite the limitations under which the Italian troops labored. It was involved in the great encirclement of the Soviet forces at Kiev, taking some 12,000 prisoners. The CSIR also played a significant role in the capture of Stalino in October 1941, earning the praise of the German First Panzer Group's commander, General (later Field Marshal) Ewald von Kleist, and even Hitler himself. That proved to be its last major action, as the CSIR was withdrawn from combat after 12 November 1941, although it remained in Russia.[46]

The Germans had to deal with any number of problems in using the CSIR on the eastern front, some of which were Germany's fault, while others were Italy's. The first issue that arose was a personality clash between Messe and the German liaison officer to the CSIR, a Major Gyldenfeld. In October 1941 Gyldenfeld was replaced by a Major Fellmer, who was "less cold and less German than his predecessor."[47]

Matters were not much better down at the division level. The liaison officer to the Pasubio Division, a Captain Becker, reported that German suggestions and advice were regarded by the Italians as "tiresome and unseemly interference" and were often declined. One can speculate reasonably, however, that some of the attitude on the part of the Italians may have been due to the manner in which Becker communicated suggestions. Another reason for Italian resistance to Becker's advice was that Italian sensibilities were offended by assigning a liaison officer to them of relatively junior rank, something similar to De La Cerda's experience with the Italian air force in North Africa.[48]

The Italians created some problems for themselves by being less than truthful about the capabilities of their divisions. The two Italian infantry divisions were designated as *"autotrasportabile"* (motor transportable), and the reports of the German liaison officer attached to the Pasubio Division referred to it as a "motorized division." In reality, however, the two Italian infantry divisions were at best only partly motorized. Although the CSIR possessed some 62,000 men, it went to Russia with only 7,550 motor vehicles, of which 1,550 were motorcycles with at best a limited carrying capacity. Consequently, Messe often had to strip one or more divisions of motor vehicles in order to fully motorize a division and get it into action. This meant that, at best, the CSIR could operate only in segments, and with service elements strung out behind the lead formations over long distances.[49]

One other aspect of the CSIR's presence in the Soviet Union that caused both German and Italian military leaders considerable concern was the prospect of its expansion. Almost immediately after dispatching the CSIR to the eastern front, Mussolini sought to enlarge the Italian forces operating in the Soviet Union. Almost immediately after *Barbarossa*'s onset he told Fascist Party leader Giuseppe Bottai that "for the moment we will send three divisions." Mussolini apparently felt that if Italy was to remain a major power in Europe, the Italian force on the eastern front had to be at least as large as those committed by Hungary and Romania.[50]

The meeting offered by Hitler and eagerly sought by Mussolini was delayed for about two months. On 24 July 1941 Mussolini suggested postponing the meeting until after 10 August, by which time it was expected that the CSIR would be in action on the eastern front. A further delay was imposed on 7 August, when the Duce's favorite son, Bruno, was killed in a crash while test flying an Italian experimental four-engine bomber, the notoriously unreliable P-108B. Consequently, it was a deeply devastated Mussolini who went to visit Hitler at the Führer's gloomy headquarters at Rastenburg in East Prussia on 25 August 1941.[51]

The meeting between Hitler and Mussolini lasted for five days. Major discussions covering military issues on 25 and 27 August were interspersed with a trip to Army Group South's headquarters at Uman, where Hitler and Mussolini inspected some units of the Torino Division in something of a makeshift review. The return trip to Rastenburg was marked by Mussolini taking over the controls of the Focke-Wulf Condor for a while (he was a licensed pilot), as terrified German and Italian officials looked on.

Not surprisingly, it was the last airplane trip Hitler and Mussolini ever took together.[52]

In his letter of 24 July 1941 Mussolini had informed Hitler that he was readying a second corps-sized unit to join the CSIR and would be willing to send a third corps if necessary. Hitler, while thanking Mussolini for the offer, also politely declined it, citing the usual difficulties in transportation and logistics. Hitler then said that he would give the proposal further study. Hitler's initial attitude was reinforced two days after Mussolini departed Rastenburg when Keitel met with Cavallero. Keitel argued that the sending of further Italian forces to Russia was impractical given the limitations of transport. In addition, a second corps could be sent to the east only if it met three stipulations, namely, that it would be completely motorized, that it would be able to stay on for occupation duties, and that it would not be injurious to Italian forces in Italy's primary theater, the Mediterranean. Keitel stated flatly that he did not believe a second Italian corps could meet these conditions, a statement Cavallero effectively agreed with when he said that a second Italian corps would be no more motorized than the CSIR.[53]

The Duce let the matter rest until November 1941. On 22 November he instructed Ciano before Ciano left for Berlin that he was to raise again with Hitler the prospect of sending more Italian divisions to the eastern front. Ciano did just that when he met Hitler in Berlin on 26 November 1941. Hitler again cited the transportation problems involved in such a move but then, perhaps as a sop to Mussolini, mentioned that Italian troops might be useful for operations in the Caucasus. Hitler strongly emphasized, however, the need for Italy to maintain its hold on North Africa.[54] The matter of expanding the CSIR would ultimately be decided in 1942.

Aside from operational matters, the Axis powers on the eastern front were involved, to a greater or lesser degree, with the conduct of occupation policies. This brought them in contact, conflict, or collaboration with German occupation police in Russia, and with the Holocaust as well. It should be recognized here that both Finland and Romania would, to some extent, be reclaiming territory that had been taken from them by the Soviet Union during the winter of 1939–1940. Once beyond the pre-1939 borders, Romanian forces especially could be considered as occupying territory. Both reclaimed and occupied territory, again in Romania in particular, were subject to policies aimed at implementing what would be called "the Final Solution."

Given the perceived economic importance of all the territory to be taken in the Soviet Union, the Germans clearly sought to ensure that they would derive the maximum advantage economically from such areas, regardless of who occupied them. This was clearly outlined in a 20 June 1941 memo signed by General Georg Thomas, the head of Wirtschaft Rüstungs Amt (WiRüAmt; Economics and Armaments Office), which reflected the thinking of both Hitler and Keitel on this issue.[55]

In terms of occupation policies and atrocities, the German ally that was least effected was Finland. Because the Finns were able to enter the war on their own terms, the Ryti government did not have to go along with Germany's planned war of annihilation against the Soviets. Jews served in the Finnish army, and the government was able to successfully rebuff several attempts by high-ranking Nazi officials, up to and including Heinrich Himmler, to get Finland to embrace the savage Nazi occupation policies and the murderous concepts on which they were based. The initial offensive in that area would be aimed at recovering Finnish territory that had been taken by the Soviets during the Winter War of 1939–1940. Because those areas would revert to Finnish control, German units operating there would still be bound by the OKW directive that regulated their behavior while on Finnish soil.[56]

In stark contrast to Finland, Romania was the Axis ally that was easily the most involved in both occupation policies and atrocities in the Soviet Union. As noted earlier, after the recovery of Bessarabia and Northern Bukovina, Hitler, in his 14 August 1941 letter to Antonescu, offered in somewhat vaguely defined terms the area between the Bug and the Dniestr. The proposal was generally approved by Antonescu, although with some reservations. A rapid round of German-Romanian negotiations followed in Tighina. The agreement formally creating Transnistria was signed on 30 August 1941 and promptly disseminated by Army Group South to its subordinate units. The precise border of the territory, however, especially in the north, was not formalized until 20 September 1941.[57]

Hitler offered Antonescu this plum, even to the point of allowing Romania to economically exploit Transnistria, for several reasons. First, having a relatively substantial area as that garrisoned by Romanian troops would free up German troops from having to do such duty. Second, Hitler apparently hoped that this sop would serve to divert Romanian attention from the quest to reverse the Second Vienna Award, a hope that turned out to be forlorn. Finally, even if Romania still remained focused on its problems with Hungary, the sheer size of the force required to occupy Transnistria, namely, one army headquarters in Odessa, two or three corps headquarters in Transnistria, plus one more east of the Bug River, commanding a total of seven infantry divisions and two cavalry brigades, would not be available for war against Hungary.[58]

Some of the details are worth examining. Romania would be responsible for the security of both Transnistria and the area between the Bug and the

Dniepr rivers. The Romanian occupation forces would be under the tactical control of Army Group South. Although responsible for the security of both areas, the Romanians would only be allowed to exploit Transnistria for economic purposes. The area between the Bug and the Dniepr, containing such vital economic sites as the iron mines at Krivoi Rog and the giant Dniepostroi dam, were regarded as critical to the German war economy. This was also in keeping with Thomas's previously noted memorandum of 20 June 1941. It was clearly assumed, however, that after the end of the war the region between the Bug and the Dniepr would revert to German administration, as this was land clearly earmarked for habitation by German colonists and perhaps some non-German "Nordic" races as well.[59]

The transportation facilities in Transnistria, especially the rail net and the port facilities in Odessa, would be run by German military authorities, although a Romanian liaison staff would be present. Roads and bridges were left under Romanian control, although the DHM was tasked to provide technical help in the form of engineers to aid in rebuilding destroyed bridges. Likewise, telephone communications were left to the Romanians, although communications centers critical to the conduct of the war would be under German control.[60]

Aside from the Romanians, the Hungarians were also given a sector to occupy, bordering on the eastern edge of the General Government (occupied Poland) and extending eastward into the rear area of Army Group South. As always, there would be a buffer between the Hungarian sector and Transnistria. Unlike the arrangements with the Romanians, the Hungarians were tasked solely with providing security. Any kind of exploitation, economic or otherwise, would be left to the Germans. The area would eventually be turned over completely to German administration.[61] The CSIR had only a sector on the front, with no real rear area responsibilities.

Romanian, Hungarian, and Italian troops on the eastern front came face-to-face with one of the ugliest aspects of World War II, namely, German occupation policies and their connection to the Holocaust. Behavior here was sharply split between the Hungarians and Italians, on one side, and the Romanians, on the other. Horthy himself was to a degree anti-Semitic, as was reflected in his comments in his memoirs about the abortive Communist revolution launched by Bela Kun in 1919. Nonetheless, Horthy was on good terms with a number of leading members of the Jewish community in Hungary. Thus, while Horthy might not have cared for Jews in general, he was not given to the kind of virulent anti-Semitism that flourished in Germany. In addition, his nineteenth-century aristocratic background and breeding were sufficient to prevent him from ever countenancing even the thought of genocide.[62] This attitude was ultimately reflected in Hungarian behavior both in Hungary and in Russia. Although Hungarian troops did have an unfortunate propensity to loot, no massacres occurred in their sector of the front. When such instances did occur, as in the part of Yugoslavia occupied by Hungary in April 1941, the individuals responsible were arrested, tried, convicted, and imprisoned, although they were released by the Nazis in 1944. In Hungary, the population often gave aid and comfort to Jews seeking escape from slave labor gangs in southern Poland, much to the irritation of German authorities.[63]

The behavior of the Romanians was another matter. Right from the start, Romanian troops engaged in atrocities against Jews. Those Jews living in Bessarabia and Northern Bukovina were rounded up and sent to a makeshift concentration camp at Targu-Jiu and eventually moved eastward into Transnistria. Once the Jews reached Transnistria, the Romanian authorities there sought to drive them farther east, into areas where SS Einsatzgruppe D was known to be operating. This brought German complaints, although these were more in regard to how poorly these moves were organized and conducted rather than mere humanitarian concerns. Romanian occupation authorities promised humane and decent conduct to the Ukrainian inhabitants of Transnistria, while at the same time urging them to abandon any loyalty to the Soviet government because it was nothing more than a "Jewish gang." Reality, however, was another matter, as both Ukrainians and *Volksdeutsche* were subjected to looting by Romanian troops, with numerous instances of rape. For their part, Romanian authorities complained of high-handed behavior by German police agents toward Romanian officers in Transnistria.[64]

Undoubtedly the most notable Romanian atrocity in the 1941 campaign was the dreadful Odessa massacre. Odessa still had a large Jewish population when the Romanians entered the city on 16 October 1941. According to the German liaison officer with the Romanian Intelligence Service, large piles of explosives, detonators, and other such material were left out in the open near the port and were poorly guarded. In addition, beneath the city was an extensive network of catacombs with at least 160 known entry points, facilitating traffic by Soviet partisans. On 22 October they struck, detonating a large bomb beneath the Romanian headquarters (previously home to the Soviet Secret Police, the NKVD) on Engels Street. Because two previous warnings of possible danger by the Romanian Intelligence Service had not materialized, a third warning was ignored. The blast destroyed the headquarters, killing the commander of the Romanian Tenth Infantry Division, General Ioan Glogianu, along with his entire staff. A number of senior German officers were also killed.

Romanian vengeance was swift. Antonescu, who had already put orders in place calling for the execution of 200 communist hostages for every Romanian officer killed by partisans, sanctioned further executions. On 23 October 1941 some 19,000 Jews were shot near the harbor, the corpses doused with gasoline and then burned. A further 40,000 Jews were rounded up, driven out of the city to another location, and then shot.[65] In November, Antonescu's government made it clear to the Germans that the fate of Romania's Jewish population would ultimately be left in German hands. In the actual event, however, a number of Romanians were able to save Jews for a variety of reasons, ranging from principle to sheer venality. Nonetheless, probably more than 200,000 Jews perished, either at Romanian hands or after being turned over by the Romanians to the Germans. Whereas Horthy received only a short prison term after the war, and no Finnish or Italian leaders were punished for such crimes, Antonescu, his brother (and foreign minister) Mihail, and the Romanian administrator in Transnistria, Georghe Alexianu, were executed by the Soviets after the war.[66] Thus did Romania play its part in the Holocaust.

All of Germany's major allies in Europe had played roles of varying degrees of significance in the invasion of the Soviet Union. Clearly the two most important were Finland and Romania. Finland had rendered some assistance to the Germans in providing General Eduard Dietl's Mountain Corps a staging area for their offensive operations to protect Petsamo and against Murmansk. In addition, the Finnish threat to Leningrad via Vyborg and the Finnish advance into Karelia forced the Soviets to keep or even divert troops there, forces desperately needed to stave off Army Group North's thrust though the Baltic States toward Leningrad.[67]

The Romanian contribution to *Barbarossa* was also considerable. The two Romanian armies committed served to tie down Soviet forces that could have been employed elsewhere. Likewise, the Romanian occupation of Transnistria certainly saved the Germans from having to employ troops there for occupation duties, while the Romanians could be counted on to do their part in carrying out the genocidal policies that were so much of a part of Nazi Germany's war of annihilation against Soviet Russia. From this standpoint, Hitler had every reason for satisfaction with Antonescu.[68]

From the standpoint of coalition warfare, the arrangements made by the Germans for the 1941 campaign were logical, given the premise on which the Garman plan was based. The level of equipment employed by the

Romanian, Hungarian, Italian, and Finnish forces, while not near the level of modernity employed by the Germans or the Russians, was sufficient for the 1941 campaign.[69]

The command arrangements made by the Germans for incorporating their allied forces made sense to a degree. Perhaps the most dubious was the inclusion, at Mussolini's insistence, of the CSIR on the eastern front, a force that, for all it actually did accomplish, drew needed supplies away from the Italian forces in Italy's primary theater, North Africa.[70] It also brought a number of Italian officers, such as Messe, into close proximity with the barbarities of German occupation policy, thus serving to further undermine in many Italian minds the value of Germany as an ally.

The greatest problem the Germans created for themselves was in the very premise upon which *Barbarossa* was based, namely, that the Soviet Union could be knocked out in a relatively short campaign that would be successfully concluded by the end of 1941. The falsity of that premise was definitively shown on 5 December 1941, when the Soviet counterattack at Moscow brought the last German lunge at the Soviet capital to a halt, and even threw Army Group Center back some distance.

Although the Germans would eventually master the winter crisis by February 1942, the German High Command had no clear ideas about what to do next. The one thing they were certain about was that although major successes had been achieved, the cost was high. Between 22 June 1941 and 20 March 1942, the German army had suffered more than 1 million casualties. Massive losses in equipment of all types had also been incurred. More than 260,000 horses had been lost, as well as 3,100 armored vehicles, 115,000 motor vehicles of all kinds, and 10,400 artillery pieces. By 20 March 1942, the Luftwaffe possessed fewer aircraft in total than it had in September 1939.[71]

Germany's allies on the eastern front were in somewhat similar states. Finland had suffered the least in absolute numbers, with 22,000 killed if one counts both the Winter War of 1939–1940 and Finnish participation in *Barbarossa* up to the end of October 1941. Given Finland's relatively small population, however, this was still a significant percentage. In addition, perhaps as many as 250,000 men needed to be released from the Finnish Army, at least in the short term, to restore a functioning economy in Finland.[72] This would certainly raise questions about how much of a part the Finns would play, or be willing to play, in 1942.

Romania was likewise in a situation approaching exhaustion by the end of 1941. Many Germans, ranging from Hitler down to the lowest-level liaison officers, recognized that most Romanians regarded the war, at least for them, as being over once Odessa was taken.[73] Although liaison officer reports were generally positive about the Romanian army, all noted the degree of exhaustion that was evident. Losses, especially around Odessa, had sapped the spirit of the army. Combat had severely damaged the lower echelons of the officer corps, and the kind of NCO corps required to fill the gaps created in the campaign did not exist in the Romanian army. Likewise, the Germans felt that Romanian commanders needed to get out of the "French mind-set," which they had acquired during the interwar period. These were not insurmountable obstacles, but they would take time (most likely years) to correct. All this should have called into question the ability of the Romanians to participate in a second campaign to a major degree, but apparently it did not. The DHM's report on its activities from its arrival in Romania until the end of 1941 stated that the Romanians would be able to participate effectively in a summer campaign in 1942.[74]

For the Hungarians, casualties were not prohibitive, but losses in equipment were another matter. The Mobile Corps had lost a great deal of equipment, including several thousand motor vehicles. Hungary lacked the industrial capacity to replace these losses on its own, and the only power it could turn to for assistance was Germany. The losses suffered by Germany, however, in the 1941 campaign easily outran German production. Problems of insufficient material also beset German-Hungarian cooperation in the area of aircraft production.[75] Such facts again should have called into question the ability of Hungary to play a major role on the eastern front in 1942.

Even more important, the conclusion of the 1941 campaign represented a critical junction for Germany and its Axis allies. The three principal Axis allies on the eastern front, Romania, Hungary, and Finland, all had compelling territorial reasons for participating in *Barbarossa*, reasons that would have been evident to any private soldier in those armies. By the end of 1941, however, those compelling territorial objectives had been met. Thus, while Hitler would certainly be willing to pursue another campaign in the Soviet Union in the spring of 1942, whether or not that willingness would extend to Finland, Romania, and Hungary, and, more important, to the common soldiers of those armies, was another matter.

Although a major part of European Russia had been seized in the summer of 1941, Germany's best effort had failed to knock out the Soviet Union. Hitler would try again in the summer of 1942, and the result would be the end of the Axis as a military alliance.

7

Disaster at Stalingrad

> I say this in our common interest, because the preservation of the fighting power of Romanian units operating under German control lies not only in Romania's interest, but in Germany's interest as well.
>
> Marshal Ion Antonescu, 15 January 1942[1]

> Like everybody else who has had anything to do with the Germans, he [Messe] hates them, and says that the only way of dealing with them would be to punch them in the stomach. Galeazzo Ciano, 4 June 1942[2]

> It must be well understood, however, that in other positions the Romanian troops retreated without any resistance and thus fell prey to destruction by pursuing tanks. Colonel General Hermann Hoth, 3 January 1943[3]

THE UNSUCCESSFUL CONCLUSION of the 1941 campaign, capped initially by the Soviet counterattack at Moscow, eventually by a general winter counteroffensive in January 1942, left the Germans in a difficult situation, to say the least. Although the Germans had conquered huge swaths of territory, they had failed to knock out the Soviet Union. While casualties during the summer campaign were heavier than anticipated, numbering about 743,000 by 26 November 1941, they were manageable.[4] The winter crisis, however, made a difficult situation far worse in any number of ways. The Soviet counteroffensive (aided by the harshest winter in a century) generated a huge number of casualties. In the period 1 December 1941 to 10 February 1942, the Germans suffered just more than 200,000 casualties in combat. Aside from combat losses, the German army suffered numerous casualties from frostbite and other maladies resulting from exposure.[5]

The late fall and winter campaign also generated huge losses of equipment. By 21 December 1941 the Tenth Panzer Division, for example, had a total of 25 operational tanks out of a normal complement of 120. In November 1941 alone the German army lost almost 6,000 trucks, more than twice the number of trucks produced by Germany that month.[6] Heavy losses were also suffered in guns and other forms of heavy equipment.

The failure of *Barbarossa* also left the Germans with a set of unappealing alternatives for how to proceed, even after mastering the winter crisis.

Clearly a resumption of the offensive over the entire front was out of the question. Halder supposedly suggested that major operations be suspended for a year. Instead, Army Group Center would undertake some minor operations to eliminate several salients in its front created by the Soviet winter offensive. The German army would take advantage of the lull to refit and recover in order to resume full-scale operations in 1943. Some officers even advocated withdrawals to varying degrees. None of this found favor with Hitler, who sought some type of decisive action against the Soviets, clearly indicating this in letters to Mussolini, Antonescu, and Horthy on 29 December 1941.[7]

Ultimately, Hitler pressed for a couple of offensive operations. One would be the proposed reduction of Leningrad. This would require the movement of the German Eleventh Army from the Crimea after the capture of Sevastopol, as well as Finnish cooperation. That would then be followed up by a German-Finnish attack to cut the Murmansk railroad.[8]

Since Finland ended up playing only a very minor role in the 1942 campaign, Hitler wanted Finnish assistance for the reduction of Leningrad. Mannerheim, however, concerned about Finland's long-term manpower situation and skeptical of an ultimate German victory, would have none of it. Therefore, Mannerheim, in a letter of 3 February 1942 to Keitel, suggested that Leningrad had to be taken as a prerequisite for any further attack against the Murmansk railroad, and that the city be taken by the Germans alone. A personal visit by Hitler to congratulate Mannerheim on his seventy-fifth birthday failed to make any further impression on the marshal, as the Finns informed Keitel the next day that there would be no large-scale attack in the summer of 1942.[9]

In the end, the state of affairs around Leningrad remained relatively static. Although Field Marshal Erich von Manstein's German Eleventh Army was transferred to the Leningrad sector after its capture of Sevastopol, German plans were disrupted by a Soviet offensive aimed at the high ground around Siniavino, the seizure of which would break the German siege of Leningrad. Although the Germans were eventually able to stymie the Soviet attack, stopping it absorbed the combat power of Manstein's divisions. Thus the Finns played little part in operations in 1942, aside from the Finnish III Corps mounting a stout defense against a Soviet attack in Karelia. In addition, German and Finnish authorities worked to improve supply facilities for Dietl's troops in Finland.[10]

The more ambitious of the offensives would be in the south. After three preliminary operations against the Russian positions in the Crimea and at Sevastopol, the Russian bulge around Izyum, and the area west of the Donetz River, the main offensive would begin. Army Group South, now under the command of Field Marshal Fedor von Bock, would cross the Donetz. It would then be divided into Army Groups A and B. Army Group A, commanded by Field Marshal Wilhelm List, would take Rostov and then move south toward the Caucasus oil fields.

Army Group B, with Bock in command, would seize Voronezh and then move south along the Don River, trapping the Soviet forces in the large area between the Don and Donetz rivers. It would extend its front along the Don River, to include what was described in Hitler's directive as the "Stalingrad strip." By these operations, Hitler expected to deprive Soviet Russia of its primary source of oil, while securing it for Germany. These gains, even if they did not knock out the Soviets completely, would at least deprive the Red Army of the lifeblood it required to mount major operations.[11]

These operations, especially those of Army Group B, would require a high level of participation on the part of the Romanians and the Hungarians at the very least. It was not until early 1942, however, that the Germans made preliminary inquiries of the Romanians and Hungarians regarding their level of participation for a 1942 summer campaign. To assist German operations in the area between the Bug and the Dniepr rivers and in the Crimea, on 15 January 1942 Antonescu placed at the disposal of Army Group South forces consisting of three mountain brigades, three cavalry brigades, and four infantry divisions, plus several battalions of artillery. On 10–11 February 1942 Antonescu visited Hitler's headquarters at Rastenburg to discuss the prospect of the level of Romanian commitment in a second Russian campaign. The details were worked out a little later, during Keitel's trip to Bucharest.[12]

In many ways, Romania's position in 1942 was somewhat analogous to that of Austria-Hungary at the end of 1917, in that all its territorial ambitions, save one, had been achieved. Antonescu was willing to increase Romanian participation, but only if Hungarian participation was increased. As usual, Transylvania was a significant factor in Antonescu's decision making. As in 1941, Antonescu was concerned that a major deployment of the Romanian army to the eastern front, combined with the troops needed for occupation duties in Transnistria, would leave Romania's position in Transylvania vulnerable to Hungarian ambitions. The German military attaché in Budapest essentially confirmed that Antonescu's concerns were justified. Ultimately, however, the Romanians would put almost 500,000 men in the field both for the 1942 summer campaign and to maintain the occupation of Transnistria.[13]

The Hungarians were also pressed to provide more troops for the eastern front in 1942. Horthy was not at all enthusiastic about this. In his 15 January 1942 reply to Hitler's letter of 29 December 1941, Horthy did not mention Russia at all, but rather Hungary's overall political situation, especially regarding Romania. In January 1942, however, Keitel visited Budapest with a demand disguised as a request that Hungary provide an army composed of three corps for the eastern front. Fearful that Germany would support Romania in its dispute with Hungary if the Hungarians did nothing, the Horthy government agreed to commit some 250,000 men to the prospective 1942 summer campaign. The combat forces would amount to about 200,000 men in the Hungarian Second Army, while a further 50,000 men would do occupation duty.[14]

The continued bad blood between the Romanians and the Hungarians was a considerable source of concern for Hitler, who sought to reassure Antonescu in their February 1942 meeting about Hungary. As in 1941, Hitler enlisted Mussolini's aid in an attempt to find a solution to the problem. Both dictators agreed in their meeting at Klessheim on 29 April 1942 to have Ribbentrop and Ciano try to defuse the situation. This would ultimately turn into a special Italo-German commission in the summer of 1942 that would try to deal with the situation. As in 1941, however, Hitler's attempts to calm the tension between his two allies would come to naught.[15]

The final German ally with a large presence on the eastern front was Italy. To some degree, Mussolini was trying to hedge his bets. In the spring of 1942, he urged Hitler to reach a separate peace with Stalin. Yet as in 1941, Mussolini also believed that a major Italian presence on the eastern front was essential if Italy was to have a significant place in a German-dominated Europe after the war. Thus as early as August 1941 Mussolini was planning on the commitment of at least a second Italian corps on the eastern front. The Duce's plans were even more grandiose than that. Ultimately he wanted to have a fully equipped army fighting on the eastern front.[16] Although Hitler turned down Mussolini's first offer in August 1941, Mussolini had Ciano repeat the offer on 25 October 1941, only to be refused again. Mussolini, however, was not to be denied. He had Ciano make the offer yet again a month later. This time Hitler, faced with mounting German casualties as the winter crisis loomed, accepted the offer.[17]

Italy's expanded commitment to the eastern front would ultimately take the form of the Italian Eighth Army. Moving to the front in May 1942, at its peak the Italian Eighth Army had 229,000 men, 16,700 motor vehicles, 946 artillery pieces, 90 heavy antitank guns, and 25,000 horses.[18] It would mark Italy's maximum contribution to the Axis war effort.

While Hitler was willing to have more Italian troops on the eastern front, he was less willing to give Mussolini latitude in naming a commander for the

Italian Eighth Army. Mussolini's choice to command the army was Crown Prince Umberto. Hitler, being the supreme antimonarchist, however, would not hear of it. The logical choice should have been Messe, given his experience with the CSIR and his proven ability as a combat commander. Returning to the tradition of rule by seniority in the Regio Esercito, however, Mussolini's second choice was the most senior general available, namely, Italo Gariboldi. Although he did have seniority, Gariboldi had compiled a record in North Africa that revealed him to be almost completely unfit for the position. A furious Messe tried to argue with Mussolini both about Gariboldi's appointment and about the wisdom of making a major commitment to the eastern front, but to no avail.[19]

The large-scale commitment of Italian, Romanian, and Hungarian forces to the eastern front posed a variety of problems for the Germans. The prime of these was the issue of logistics. The weapons used by Germany's allies in the 1941 were sufficient, though already obsolescent. The antitank weapons used by the Romanians, Hungarians, and Italians in 1941, for example, could be used with success against the older Soviet tanks. By 1942, however, the Soviet Commissariat of Tank Production had essentially (and wisely) reduced the types of tanks used by the Soviet armored forces to the T-34/76 and the KV-1.[20] These machines were almost impervious to the lighter types of antitank guns.

Naturally, Germany's allies all requested large numbers of German heavy antitank guns, especially the 75mm antitank gun, which was certainly capable of taking on the heavier Soviet tanks successfully. Tanks and other motor vehicles were requested as well. Antonescu, for example, expected the Germans to supply and to some extent equip, especially with artillery, the units he had placed at the disposal of the Germans in January 1942. As expected, Romania was to deliver oil both to Germany and directly to the German armed forces. Further, the DHM would undertake the training of additional divisions raised by the Romanians. It would also continue to provide training and education for senior Romanian officers.[21] Likewise, the Hungarians desired large amounts of German weapons and equipment. The Italians also requested raw materials from the Germans, as stipulated in an agreement signed by a German-Italian military commission on 14 March 1942.[22]

Here again, as in 1941, Germany's promises far exceeded its deliveries. The Hungarians, for example, were able to get only twenty-two German Panzer IVs by May 1942, not nearly enough for the Hungarian Second Army's needs. The vehicles and antitank guns provided by the Germans came from captured stocks of obsolete French and Belgian equipment, leading the

Hungarians to accuse the Germans of giving better material to the Romanians. In reality, the majority of Romanian divisions committed to the 1942 summer campaign were woefully short of equipment, a fact of which the Germans were well aware. Antitank guns available to the Romanians were still of the 37mm, 47mm, and 50mm variety, and in short supply in any case. Vehicles in particular were in lacking, so much so that antitank guns had to be drawn by horses. Radios likewise were lacking. Although the Italian Eighth Army was lavishly equipped by Italian standards, it had only a handful of German heavy antitank guns.[23]

The result of these efforts was that the Germans were going into the 1942 summer campaign with a group of allied armies that were sadly deficient in material. Moreover, the Germans were well aware of this. Liaison commands to every major Romanian formation, for example, compiled a number of reports on the condition of various Romanian army units, and on the army in general, and sent them to the DHM. Only six of the Romanian divisions, namely, the Sixth, Seventh, Thirteenth, and Fourteenth Infantry Divisions and the Second and Third Mountain Divisions, were rated as being worthy of independent missions or capable of heavy combat.[24]

Aside from simply equipping its own forces and those of its allies, the German army faced the difficult problem of operational logistics. Because the German plan called for a massive expansion of the front in the south, the rail system needed to support such an advance would be severely strained. Aside from having to keep the German Sixth, Seventeenth, First Panzer, and Fourth Panzer Armies, the German rail system would also have to maintain the Italian, Hungarian, and Romanian forces as well.

To be sure, the Germans did put plans in place to keep the Italian Eighth Army, for example, supplied and paid in an orderly fashion. An agreement was reached between OKW and Commando Supremo on 14 March 1942 governing such matters. It was formalized in a written agreement between the two staffs on 16 June 1942 and then converted by OKH into a directive issued to the appropriate German army commands ten days later.[25] Whether or not such agreements could be executed as stipulated under the strain of a major campaign, however, would be another matter.

The course of the 1942 summer campaign is too well-known to be related again here. Instead, this study will examine the problems the Germans faced in conducting coalition warfare in the three media (air, sea, and land) and how well or poorly they coped with these challenges.

The efforts of the Axis air forces, other than the Luftwaffe, were rather less in 1942 than in 1941. The Italian Eighth Army and the Hungarian Second Army were supported by only a handful of aircraft from their respective air forces.[26] The largest of the aerial contingents, as in 1941, would be the Romanian GAL. The most notable improvement in the GAL was that by 1942 it was composed almost exclusively of Romanian aircraft. While this eased problems with maintenance, the main issue for Romanian aircraft was age. Although the GAL was equipped with the IAR 80 and IAR 81, the most modern Romanian-made aircraft in the inventory, the new aircraft being introduced by the Soviets in 1942 were rendering these aircraft obsolescent. Romania lacked the capability to keep up, especially when it came to the development of aircraft engines. The inventory of the Romanian air force in general still contained too many different types of aircraft of foreign manufacture, including hopelessly obsolete Polish, British, French, and Italian models, along with some German aircraft.[27]

The command arrangements for the employment of the GAL remained convoluted, since, at least according to Richthofen, neither the Luftwaffe High Command nor OKW was willing to make a decision on the matter. Equally problematic was the status of the DLM relative to the German Fourth Air Fleet. In August 1941 the DLM was subordinated to the German Fourth Air Fleet.[28] As the campaign (and the German Fourth Air Fleet) moved farther east, these arrangements made less and less sense.

The issue was finally discussed on 12 August 1942, in a meeting at Richthofen's headquarters, when the campaign was well under way. The conferees included Richthofen, Gerstenberg, who as head of the DLM also represented Antonescu, and Bassenge, described by Richthofen now as "completely Balkanized."[29] Eventually these questions were resolved, with the GAL supporting the Romanian Third and Fourth Armies, although individual squadrons occasionally operated under the German VIII Air Corps. Consequently, the contributions of the GAL to the land campaign were relatively limited, although information on the Romanian participation in this part of the campaign, as one student of the campaign notes, is rather scarce. The DLM was also made independent of the German Fourth Air Fleet.[30]

Somewhat more successful were the Axis naval efforts on the Black Sea. The 1942 campaign presented the Axis naval forces on the Black Sea with two missions, one defensive and the other offensive. As the German offensive rolled first east and then south, Axis naval forces were expected to provide protection for the sea lines of communication as they extended along the northern coast of the Black Sea. Concomitant with this was the task of keeping at bay the Soviet naval forces based on the eastern coast of the Black Sea. These questions were discussed even while the Soviet counteroffensive was going on in January 1942. The German navy would send a number of small craft by land to the Black Sea ports it controlled. This would allow the Germans to create the forces needed for transport as well as protection against submarines. They could not be used operationally for some time, however, because the ports of Nikolaev, Ostashkhov, and Odessa were all blocked by ice.[31]

Here again the Germans would be calling the shots, although there would be limits as to what the Germans could demand of their allies. Romanian naval and coast artillery units would be trained by German navy personnel under the command of the German navy commander on the Black Sea, Vice Admiral Friedrich Götting. He would report to the German navy commander south, Admiral Wilhelm Marschall. The Romanians would also be under the effective operational control of the Germans, much to the annoyance of the Romanians.[32] This would, however, facilitate operations against the Soviet Black Sea Fleet by providing the Axis naval forces with unity of command, at least theoretically.

In February 1942 Navy Group South sent its request to Antonescu that outlined the size and scope of the Romanian naval commitment. Marschall's view was that Romania should send most of its navy to the Black Sea, and in point of fact, the preponderance of Axis naval forces on the Black Sea would be provided by Romania. These forces would be used for missions such as coastal convoy escort, mine clearing, and coastal security operations in the Bosporus and the rear areas of land forces. The biggest ships in the navy, several modern destroyers, might also be used for operations against Soviet bases. In any case, the Germans would equip the Romanian ships with German sonar sets.

Antonescu's response was to agree with most of the German proposals, but with reservations. He was particularly concerned about conducting naval operations off of Sevastopol, which he regarded as being of little importance strategically. Antonescu also did not want to risk the Romanian destroyers on offensive operations, and he regarded convoy defense as the primary mission for the Romanian forces. Finally, instead of offensive mine-laying operations off the Crimean coast, Antonescu preferred to use the mines to strengthen the defenses of Odessa.[33]

The other Axis naval presence on the Black Sea would be that of Italy. Given that the primary Soviet threat would be from submarines, and that the Italian navy's major commitments were in the Mediterranean, in February 1942 the Germans sensibly sought only light forces from the Italians. The first Italian craft to arrive were four MAS torpedo boats, which reached Galatz, Romania, on 29 April 1942. These would be reinforced by six small submarines and four other torpedo boats and placed under the command of Mimbelli, whose earlier actions as commander of the *Lupo* had earned him a considerable degree of respect from the Germans.[34]

In the actual course of events, Axis activity on the Black Sea proved fairly successful, in terms of both interservice relations and coalition operations. Both services realized that success would require very close cooperation. In one of his better personnel choices, Göring chose Colonel Wolfgang von Wild for the post of commander of *Fliegerführer Süd* (air commander south), whose area of operations encompassed the Crimea and the Black Sea. OKM, for its part, instructed Navy Group South to undertake a series of steps to ensure that closer cooperation would take place between the services, including the exchange of liaison officers, the full sharing of information, and training to help Luftwaffe pilots identify Axis ship types and navy personnel to identify Luftwaffe aircraft. Although communication between various types of Axis ships and aircraft was problematic, Navy Group South seemed to have enough interpreters on hand to facilitate communication between ships, as the available records indicated no major problems owing to a shortage of interpreters.[35]

For coalition operations, the Germans came up with arrangements that took the capabilities of their allies into consideration. Since the preponderance of the merchant shipping used on the Black Sea supply routes would be Romanian, the Romanian forces involved would be used for convoy defense and the laying of defensive minefields. This would coincide with both Marschall's view of Romanian capabilities and Antonescu's view of Romania's naval priorities. The Italian and German forces would be committed to more offensive actions against the Soviet naval forces.[36]

The first mission Axis naval forces had to accomplish was to sever Soviet sea lines of communications, first to the Crimea and then to Sevastopol. These operations would be conducted, theoretically at least, in concert with the offensive by Colonel General Erich von Manstein's German Eleventh Army, which had several Romanian divisions attached to it.

In the actual event, the activity of the Axis land and naval forces was somewhat staggered. Manstein's offensive began on 8 May 1942. Because the Axis naval forces were still in the process of arriving, naval activity was essentially confined to convoy defense. Some success was achieved in this, as from 20 April to 20 May 1942, Axis shipping was able to move some 57,000 tons of supplies from Romania to Black Sea ports. Soviet naval activity was also relatively free from any Axis naval threat, although the German Fourth Air Fleet put in a strenuous effort to interdict Soviet seaborne supply efforts.[37]

With the Crimea secured, the next major objective was the port of Sevastopol. Once again the Axis naval forces had the dual tasks of protecting their own sea lines of communication while mounting an effective blockade of Sevastopol's harbor. The Italo-German forces were able to effectively blockade the harbor once the German-Romanian ground offensive started on 7 June, and especially after the aircraft of *Fliegerführer Süd* had sunk or severely damaged two of the heavier warships in the Black Sea Fleet. Once that had been accomplished, the light Italo-German forces made life very difficult for the Soviet submarines that were still used to bring in limited supplies to Sevastopol. Italian forces were equally successful in fending off Soviet submarine attacks against Axis shipping, sinking three during the period 15–19 June 1942.[38] Indeed, the activity of the Italo-German naval forces on the Black Sea during the Crimean campaign and the ensuing siege and conquest of Sevastopol probably ranks as the high point of German coalition operations in any theater in World War II.

With the fall of Sevastopol, the campaign on the Black Sea now moved into a new phase. The German, Romanian, and Italian naval forces would continue to escort convoys to the ports along the northern coast of the Black Sea. The Romanians would continue to devote their resources to convoy defense, as Antonescu was reluctant to commit naval forces whose loss might endanger Romania's postwar position vis-à-vis Hungary. Axis naval forces would be supported in their endeavors by German and Romanian seaplanes.[39] The Axis naval forces would also support the advance of elements of the German Seventeenth Army across the Kerch Strait into the Taman Peninsula. Although the army did succeed in capturing the Soviet naval base of Novorossisk, that marked the extent of the German advance.

Since the Dardanelles could be closed at any time, the German Navy High Command decided to undertake the construction of a fleet at the Nikolaev shipyards. Although the details regarding the size and composition of a fleet remained sketchy, the navy felt that this would be a better alternative, at least in terms of transporting light craft overland to the Black Sea ports with operating rail communications. These efforts, along with construction programs at various Danube shipyards, gave the Germans a capable force, at least in terms of light craft, by the start of 1943.[40]

With the campaign going the Germans' way during the summer of 1942, the German navy began to look toward the day when it would have to operate on the Caspian Sea. From the standpoint of Germany's opinion of its allies, it is worth noting that in its long-range planning, the first element the navy wanted to introduce on the Caspian Sea was a squadron of Italian light craft. This high opinion was also reflected in meetings between Hitler and the Navy High Command. Consequently, on 18 July 1942 the navy asked Supermarina (the Italian Navy High Command) to authorize the assignment of Italian MAS boats, submarines, and small motorboats to the Caspian Sea. Supermarina formally agreed two weeks later.[41]

The Axis naval forces on the Black Sea were still able to keep the Soviets at bay, even as the tide of war turned against Germany and its allies. The development of subsequent events would place the German naval forces on the Black Sea in a difficult situation.[42] How that situation was handled will be dealt with in a later chapter.

It was in the area of land warfare that Germany made its greatest effort in coalition warfare, and where the German army failed completely. The first area where the German army was overwhelmed by the scale of the efforts of its allies was in the number of interpreters. The expansion of the Romanian and Italian presence on the eastern front brought forth the need for interpreters in large numbers. Thus German liaison staffs remained so small that some had only one interpreter, although the Germans complained, with some justice, that the Romanians were not doing nearly enough to supply their share of interpreters. In their reports on the status of the various Romanian army, corps, and division headquarters, the Germans noted which commanders and chiefs of staff spoke German, and how well.[43] In addition, for this campaign the Germans also needed interpreters to deal with the various and sundry indigenous peoples into whose areas the Germans intended to advance.[44]

The command arrangements for the campaign were somewhat less convoluted than in 1941. Although there were cases, such as the Romanian VI Corps in the Crimea and the Romanian Corps at the Izyum bulge, that fought as part of German armies, these were rarities. Instead, the Romanian forces would be concentrated into the Romanian Third Army. Once Army Group South was divided into Army Groups A and B by Hitler's Directive Number 45, the Romanian Third Army would be under the command of Army Group A. Several individual Romanian corps, such as the Romanian VI Corps, would be attached to individual German armies. The Hungarian Second Army and the Italian Eighth Army would be assigned to Army Group B. This would achieve the twin objectives of having all the Axis allied units under German command and keeping the Romanians and Hungarians away from each other.[45]

One month after issuing Directive Number 45, Hitler decided on an additional change in command arrangements. With the battle for Stalingrad itself beginning, and with the departure of the Eleventh Army for the Leningrad sector, Hitler proposed the creation of a new army group. Army Group Don

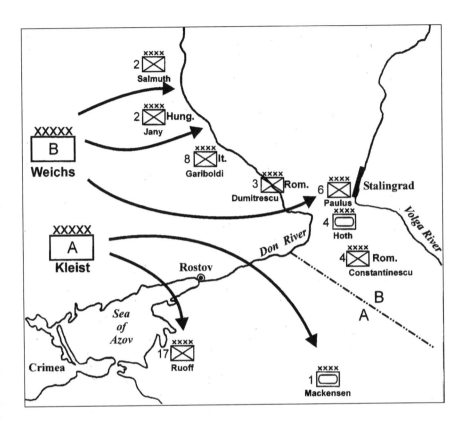

The Drive to Stalingrad, Summer 1942

would be composed of the Romanian Third Army, the re-forming Romanian Fourth Army, and the German Sixth Army. Command of this group would be given to Antonescu for two reasons. First, in terms of the eastern front, Hitler clearly considered Antonescu as his most important ally and continued to hold him in high personal regard. Hitler also apparently thought that naming Antonescu to the position would draw a greater effort from the Romanians.[46]

This proposal never came to fruition. Although Antonescu was willing to accept (apparently with some misgivings) the position, and a "Staff Don" was created in an embryonic fashion, the contingencies on which the proposal was made were never achieved. The position depended both on Stalingrad being secured and on successful follow-on operations being conducted. In addition, no real thought was ever given to command relationships and other sticky matters. Finally, Antonescu's illness made it impossible for him to assume the position at the time.[47] In the actual event, the organization that Antonescu was supposed to have taken over went instead to Manstein, brought in to save the situation after the crisis broke.

As the Axis forces advanced in diverging directions toward the Caucasus and the Volga, all the deficiencies in the Romanian, Hungarian, and Italian divisions—defects that were well known to the Germans before June 1942—became glaringly apparent. All the Axis forces were greatly affected by the shoestring nature of German logistics. As in 1941, the advance far outstripped the ability of German railroad repair units to keep pace. Consequently, the constant shortage of rail and truck space for supplies forced the Germans to make hard choices in terms of priorities, which they invariably did in their favor.

This certainly did not sit well with the Romanians, Hungarians, and Italians. Antonescu had raised this issue indirectly with the Germans as early as July 1942. Later on the Romanians compiled a list of grievances they had suffered over time at the hands of the Germans; their complaints included the violation of the agreed allocation of space to get more fodder to horses used by the Germans. In the increasingly hard conditions of the late Russian fall and early winter, this practice led to considerable losses in horses in the Romanian armies. Equally grating was the fact that hospitalized German patients received larger rations than Romanian patients.[48]

Even without such grievances, the nature of the Axis advance over the late summer and early fall of 1942 led to the nearly complete breakdown of Axis logistics as the struggle in Stalingrad neared its climax. The two trains per day allocated to the Italian army, for example, proved utterly inadequate to the task of keeping a force as large as the Italian Eighth Army supplied.[49] The Italian authorities themselves did not help. The War Ministry, for example, rejected requests from units in the Italian Eighth Army for felt boots. Italian soldiers had to struggle through the Russian winter with hobnailed alpine boots, which while suitable for a mountainous region, ended up simply being excellent conductors of cold on the Russian steppes. The result was high frostbite casualties. Gariboldi's command acted in a somewhat delusional fashion as well. By the beginning of November 1942 the Italian Eighth Army was still reporting the majority of its divisions as capable of offensive operations, while at the same time the German general at Gariboldi's headquarters reported that 40 percent of the army's motor vehicles were immobilized because of a lack of diesel fuel. Veterinary equipment was also in short supply.[50]

Logistical failure contributed to the primary problem of morale. This was more of a problem for the Hungarian and Italian forces on the eastern front.

Soldiers in both of these armies had little motivation to fight the Soviets. Officers and soldiers alike were also appalled at the barbarity of German behavior in the Soviet Union, and indeed all over Europe. For them the war in Russia would be a German affair.[51]

Consequently, as the Axis advance rolled eastward toward the Don and the Volga, the morale of the Hungarian and Italian troops steadily sank. Although the Hungarians had done well in antipartisan operations, they could also commit atrocities.[52] When it came to major operations, Hungarian performance was mixed. The Hungarian Second Army, much to Halder's annoyance, allowed the Soviets to establish a bridgehead across the Don at Uryv, a position that the Red Army would hold against a German attempt to crush it.[53] Even during the period of the Axis offensive, Bela Király noted that officers often told troops "don't be a hero," and that their most important mission was to get back to Hungary alive. Even while on the Don, the Hungarians still regarded Romanians, not the Soviets, as the real enemy.[54]

The Soviet counteroffensive, which began on 18 November 1942, deliberately exploited the vulnerabilities of these units, especially the lack of antitank weapons. The Soviets also unintentionally exploited German deficiencies in conducting coalition warfare. Nowhere was this better illustrated than in the Soviet attack on the Romanian Third Army and its mobile reserve, the German XLVIII Panzer Corps.

As the German summer offensive slowed down and the German Sixth Army was sucked into the vortex of Stalingrad, two important decisions were made. The first was essentially made by the German Sixth Army's commander, General Friedrich Paulus. The army's transport was based largely on its horses, some 90,000 as of July. With the army occupying a static position for an extended period, local supplies exhausted, and the rail system unable to keep the army fully supplied, Paulus sent the majority of the horses out of the city. Thus the German Sixth Army had effectively immobilized itself operationally by the end of October 1942.[55]

With the German Sixth Army effectively stuck in Stalingrad, its flanks, especially its left flank following the course of the Don River, became a crucial sector. This was entrusted to Dumitrescu's Romanian Third Army, via the DHM, which had a mobile staff traveling with Dumitrescu's headquarters. As the summer turned into fall, the Romanian Third Army had to take up the line of the Don, which it did not reach until late September and did not occupy fully until early October. In addition, the Romanian Third Army had to extend its line north to relieve some units of the neighboring Italian Eighth Army. To accomplish this, Dumitrescu had to use up all his tactical reserves. Attempts to create tactical reserves were frustrated by the fact that the Romanians had to fend off several Soviet attacks in late October.[56] Even if reserves could be created, the lack of mobility of these units effectively confined them to acting simply in local areas. The Romanian Ninth Infantry Division, for example, lacked about 26 percent of its trucks. The remaining trucks, a mélange of various types, were too heavily laden, contributing to wear and wastage. Further, about one-third of its horses were light Russian *panje* horses, unsuited to hauling heavy equipment. Consequently, the frontage held by Romanian divisions was grossly overextended. In many cases individual divisions were holding fronts of more than ten miles.[57]

To be sure, the Romanians sounded the alarm bells on a number of issues related to the Romanian Third Army's position. On 20 October 1942 the chief of the Romanian General Staff, General Ilie Steflea, wrote to Hauffe, the head of the DHM, about the Romanian Third Army's position. Steflea noted the lack of field fortifications and the absence of material needed to construct them. In addition, the Romanians lacked the tanks, antitank guns, and artillery needed to create effective forces capable of launching counterattacks. Although the army had been able to stop Soviet attacks, the losses inflicted on the Romanians (about 6,000 men) could not be replaced. In view of this, Steflea asked Hauffe to get Army Group B to rescind the order to extend its front northward. Two days later Antonescu himself wrote to Hauffe. In addition to Steflea's arguments, Antonescu noted the long frontage assigned to the Romanians and the lack of mobility on the part of inadequate reserves the Romanians did have. Antonescu concluded with a plea that the sacrifice shown by Romania's soldiers so far not be thrown away by mistakes in the leadership. In the end, all Hitler could do was to have OKH promise delivery of material for field fortifications, and that the Romanian First Panzer Division would be equipped with modern German tanks.[58]

By mid-November 1942 the Romanian position had not improved but rather deteriorated. The material for constructing field fortifications had not been delivered in large amounts, and what had been delivered had been used in building large bunkers for command posts. The majority of antitank guns were of the obsolescent 37mm and 47mm variety, and each division had no more than six 75mm German antitank guns, a situation that aroused even Hitler's concern. In any case, the vast majority of these were horse drawn, and thus lacked mobility. The constant Soviet probing attacks made it impossible to stockpile ammunition in amounts sufficient for a major battle. Radios were also in short supply.[59]

Army Group B decided to remedy the lack of mobile reserves by inserting General Ferdinand Heim's XLVIII Panzer Corps behind the front of the Romanian Third Army. The corps was to be composed of the Twenty-second

Panzer Division, elements of the Fourteenth Panzer Division, and the Romanian First Panzer Division. Although this may have looked like an impressive force on paper, reality was another matter. The corps was a virtually new formation, as none of the formations had been in it before. The Twenty-second Panzer Division had just been brought down from the area behind the Italian Eighth Army, the Romanian First Panzer Division had only just completed its formation in July 1942 and had been assigned to the corps on 10 November 1942, and the Fourteenth Panzer Division was still in action in Stalingrad.[60] The tank situation for the corps was also not good. The Twenty-second Panzer Division had only 40 tanks, including 5 Czech-made Pz 38Ts. Although the Romanian First Panzer Division had 108 tanks, 87 of these were Czech Pz 38Ts or Romanian-made R-2 tanks. The German tanks promised to Antonescu by Hitler had not appeared in any real numbers. To redress this, OKH planned to bring in the fresh Sixth Panzer Division from France, but that division would arrive too late. To familiarize himself with the corps, Dumitrescu planned on making an inspection visit to the unit on 17 November.[61]

On 19 November 1942 the storm finally broke over the Romanian Third Army. The Soviets had carefully planned a phased attack on the Romanian units covering the flanks of the now-immobilized German Sixth Army in Stalingrad, starting with Dumitrescu's forces. Romanian reaction to the initial Soviet attacks was mixed. In some cases, Romanian infantry retreated quickly, especially when they lacked an effective means of antitank defense. The most notable example of stout defense was provided by the Romanian Fifth, Sixth, and Fifteenth Infantry Divisions, commanded by General Mihail Lascar of the Romanian Sixth Infantry Division (Group Lascar), which held its position against several major Soviet attacks, even while surrounded. In an attempt to rectify the situation, General Maximilian Freiherr von Weichs, the commander of Army Group B, issued orders to Army Group Don calling for officers to round up retreating Romanian soldiers, supply them, and then turn them over to the nearest Romanian headquarters to get them back into combat.[62]

At the onset of the initial Soviet attacks, Army Group B placed the Romanian II Corps under the command of General Karl Hollidt, also commander of the German XVII Corps, to shore up the left flank of the Romanian Third Army. Weichs also directed Heim to commit the XLVIII Panzer Corps in a counterattack to relieve Lascar's troops. The attempt miscarried from the start. The elements of the Fourteenth Panzer Division assigned to the corps were still in the Stalingrad area, and thus too far away to bring any help. Matters were made worse when at 3:00 A.M. on 20 November, a Soviet

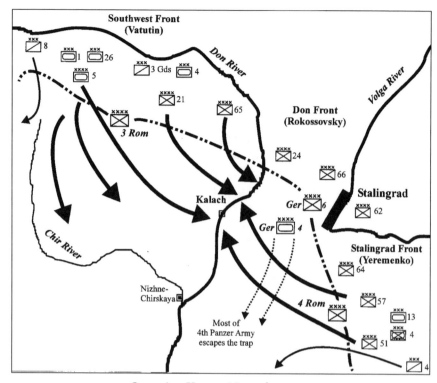

Operation *Uranus,* November 1942

attack overran the German signals unit with the Romanian First Panzer Division. The German liaison staff to the division was also overrun, and the German liaison officer, a Major Klingspor, was wounded. Consequently, Heim lost contact with the division for more than a day, as contact between the XLVIII Panzer Corps and the Romanian First Panzer Division was not reestablished until 10:50 A.M. on 21 November. Nor did Army Group B help matters by issuing contradictory orders to the XLVIII Panzer Corps, first ordering it to Lascar's aid and then ordering it to move toward another Soviet breakthrough at Blinov.[63]

Consequently, Heim's attempts to restore the situation quickly unraveled. The Twenty-second Panzer Division and the Romanian First Panzer Division fought a series of unsuccessful and uncoordinated actions in a futile attempt to stem the Soviet tide. By 28 November 1942 the corps' war diary stated that the combat strength of the corps presented "a shocking picture." The Twenty-second Panzer Division could field only 600 infantry and thirteen tanks, while the Romanian First Panzer Division had been reduced to 400 infantry and three tanks.[64] Attempts to halt the Soviets with all available German and Romanian aircraft were hampered by a combination of bad weather and low numbers of operational aircraft. With the available reserves spent, there was little to stop the Soviet Fifth Tank Army from heading for Kalach and the rear of the German Sixth Army. The battered Romanian Third Army withdrew to the Chir River.[65]

Farther south, the Soviet Fifty-first Army of the Stalingrad Front launched an equally successful attack on the Romanian Fourth Army, beginning on 20 November. Here again, the reaction was much like that of the Romanian Third Army. The only difference was that while the Romanian Third Army was able to largely escape the Soviet onslaught, the units covering the Romanian Fourth Army's left flank, the Romanian First Cavalry and Twentieth Infantry Divisions, totaling about 12,600 men, ended up retreating into Stalingrad. The rest of the Fourth Army that could escape retreated west, eventually establishing a connection with elements of the German Fourth Panzer Army on its left.

With the German Sixth Army, along with some elements of the German Fourth Panzer and Romanian Fourth Armies, now trapped in Stalingrad, Hitler sought to find a way to mount a drive to relieve Paulus's besieged forces. Manstein, now in command of Army Group Don, assembled a relief force based on General Herman Hoth's German Fourth Panzer Army. Reinforced with panzer divisions rushed from France and other sectors on the eastern front, the relief attempt would be spearheaded by the LVII Corps, while the German Sixth Army would be kept supplied by airlift. For the plan to work, however, the Romanian, Italian, and Hungarian armies and their German "corset stays" would have to hold their positions against further Soviet attacks.[66]

Manstein's relief attempt, launched on 12 December 1942, met with some initial success, driving Soviet forces across the Aksay River and approaching the Stalingrad pocket from the southwest. By 18 December 1942, however, Manstein's attack had stalled at the Myshkova River. As Manstein struggled to restart the offensive and persuade Hitler (unsuccessfully) to give Paulus an order permitting the German Sixth Army to mount a breakout, the Soviets sought to further isolate the Stalingrad pocket by launching a new series of offensives.[67]

During the period from late December 1942 through the middle of January 1943, the Soviets conducted a series of attacks along the front from Kantemirovka in the north to Sovietnoye in the south. As before, these attacks were launched with strong tank support. Weakened by losses, still lacking effective antitank weapons and warm clothing, and with poor morale, as well as still having to hold overextended positions with insufficient reserves, in many places the Romanian, Italian, and Hungarian soldiers collapsed immediately. One German liaison officer report noted that the soldiers of the Romanian First Infantry Division, for example, were simply incapable of confronting a strong enemy. The men were poorly clothed and equipped, a fact even harshly critical German liaison reports recognized. They were physically weak and, most important, lacked an effective means of dealing with Soviet tanks. One report noted that Romanian 75mm antitank guns failed to knock out T-34s even at close range. This led to an absolute fear of tanks among the soldiers, who would retreat at the very sight of them. This also applied to many of the Italian and Hungarian units.[68] Although some units, such as the Italian Alpini and the Romanian VII Corps, conducted themselves superbly, it was not enough. As in the November attacks, attempts to stop the Soviets with German and Romanian aircraft ran afoul of cumulative attrition, bad weather, low rates of serviceability, and the loss of forward airfields.[69] All this effectively served to doom the German Sixth Army in Stalingrad.

By the end of January 1943, the Romanian, Hungarian, and Italian forces on the eastern front were in tatters. The Italian Eighth Army had suffered anywhere from 75,000 to 80,000 dead and missing, but these figures do not reveal the full extent of the disaster. According to an Italian officer in the Pasubio Division, of the 30,000 Italian troops in the XXXV Corps at the start of the Soviet offensive, only 4,000 were able to make it back to the German lines by 15 January 1943. Of the 4,000 survivors, more than 3,000 were afflicted with frostbite and other injuries.[70]

Much the same could be said for the Romanian and Hungarian forces. The most recent estimate of Romanian casualties holds that of the 250,000 men Antonescu committed to the campaign, some 140,000 were killed, wounded, or captured. Total Hungarian casualties from the end of April 1942 until the beginning of March 1943 were a staggering 176,971. The winter battles alone cost the Hungarians close to 100,000 casualties.[71] Naturally, just about all the vehicles and equipment with the Romanian, Hungarian, and Italian forces were lost as well.

Given the circumstances, and with the German lines now very much shorter than they had been, the Romanian, Hungarian, and Italian forces were mostly sent home. The Romanians were the first to go. Hauffe and Antonescu had an extended discussion on the state of affairs on 28 December 1942. Antonescu clearly indicated that any attempt to refit the Romanian Third and Fourth Armies near the front was out of the question. Thus, on 27 January 1943 Hauffe informed Steflea that the remnants of the Romanian Third and Fourth Armies would be withdrawn to Transnistria. Their transportation and resupply would be arranged by Army Group Don and the German military authorities in Ukrainian territory.[72] The Italians had initially hoped to maintain a corps-sized formation on the eastern front, but this proved impossible. Consequently, all the Italian forces were withdrawn in the spring of 1943. The Hungarian presence on the eastern front would continue in a limited sense until the summer of 1943.[73]

Not surprisingly, during the crisis, relations between the Germans and their allies were severely strained at every level. At the lower levels, this strain was exacerbated by the Germans' habit of stealing equipment from their allies. Although German liaison officers tried to stop this practice, their efforts were largely ignored. German soldiers often regarded their Romanian, Hungarian, and Italian allies as "too soft" for the eastern front, while the Romanians, Hungarians, and Italians considered German soldiers of all ranks to be selfish and arrogant.[74]

The farther one went up the chain of command, the more bitter the recriminations became. Romanian, Italian, and Hungarian commanders pointed to factors such as overextended frontages and the lack of equipment, especially antitank guns, and were resentful of German criticism. German officers considered these explanations nothing more than excuses. Liaison officer reports invariably pointed out examples where Romanian, Hungarian, and Italian soldiers fled from Soviet tanks, even when they had the means to fight. Generals such as Hoth and Richthofen considered their allies as lacking the needed ideological commitment and will to successfully withstand Soviet attacks.[75]

The greatest repercussions were, naturally, at the top. Because Italy's disaster on the eastern front coincided with the defeats in North Africa, the combined effects of these for Germany will be discussed in the next chapter. For the Finns, Romanians, and Hungarians, Stalingrad had immediate effects. The Finns were particularly annoyed when the Germans sought to conceal the extent of the Stalingrad disaster from them. Once the Ryti government obtained some information, as early as December 1942 the Finns, with Swedish urging, began looking for a way out of the war, a fact of which the Germans were well aware.[76]

German relations with the Romanians and the Hungarians, always tense, were now severely strained. To be sure, on 24 November 1942, Steflea urged the commanders of the Romanian Third and Fourth Armies to avoid looking for scapegoats and to concentrate on the emergency at hand. Fingerpointing, however, could not be avoided. Hitler himself started this somewhat indirectly when he admitted to Ciano in an 18 December 1942 conference

(Mussolini was ill) that the Soviet attack against the Romanian Third Army had been "completely successful," but avoided any discussion of blame.[77]

Matters quickly deteriorated from there. Antonescu, whose government was now endangered by the disaster, demanded the scalps of several German commanders, including Heim and Hollidt, for abandoning Romanian soldiers in order to save German units. He also complained of abuse of Romanian soldiers at the hands of the Germans. Finally, Antonescu noted cases where German soldiers retreated or fled as well as Romanians. At the same time, to partly mollify the Germans, some promises were made to investigate cases where Romanian divisions had conducted themselves poorly.[78]

The Germans took a dual approach to the Romanians. Manstein played the role of the heavy, demanding in a letter to Antonescu that the Romanian leader furnish "incontrovertible proof" of misconduct by German commanders before Manstein would even consider relieving them. He likewise demanded the same standard of proof for charges of German mistreatment of Romanian soldiers before he would take disciplinary action. Hitler played the softer part, satisfying Antonescu to a degree by relieving Heim, going so far as to condemn him to death, although the sentence was not carried out. Hitler also took pains to award Lascar (by then a Soviet prisoner) the Knight's Cross, something Antonescu used to buck up his soldiers.[79]

Hitler felt no such compunction when it came to dealing with Horthy. When Hitler met Horthy at Klessheim in April 1943, Hitler wasted no time in accusing Hungarian troops of having fought badly in the recent winter battles. Horthy countered that the high losses suffered by the Hungarians testified to the bravery of the troops. Hitler also wanted Horthy to dismiss Premier Miklos Kállay for being insufficiently anti-Jewish. Horthy, reflecting Hungarian popular sentiment about both Germany and the war, refused.[80] Relations between Germany and its allies could only deteriorate from there.

The Stalingrad campaign marked the complete failure of Germany in terms of coalition warfare. Only in the area of the Black Sea were the Germans able to effectively harness the assets of the available Italian and Romanian forces and keep a materially superior, if rather cautiously commanded, Soviet Black Sea Fleet at bay.

The bulk of the Axis military commitment in 1942 was on land, and it was here where the German failure was total. From a strategic standpoint, the most egregious failure was that of Mussolini. His decision to commit the bulk of Italy's war-making capability to the eastern front was about as bad as any he made during the war. More will be said about this in the discussion of the 1942 North African campaign in the next chapter.

The Stalingrad campaign exposed in sharp relief all the shortcomings of the German military establishment and its ability, or lack thereof, to wage coalition warfare. Germany's failure to produce the requisite amounts of vehicles, weapons, and equipment meant that its Romanian and Hungarian allies would be going into a major campaign woefully underequipped against a well-armed and well-equipped opponent. Furthermore, the Germans were well aware of these deficiencies at every level from Hitler down and at every critical stage of the campaign.[81]

The dispatching of liaison staffs down to the division level meant that German liaison officers were spread very thinly indeed, so much so that the death or disabling of individual officers, such as Major Klingspor with the Romanian First Panzer Division, could have very negative consequences.[82] Finally, no account was taken of the moral factors so important in motivating men to fight. While Antonescu, Horthy, and Mussolini each had their reasons for committing large forces to the 1942 campaign, none of this reached as far down as the common soldier or NCO of these armies. This helped magnify the hardships caused by lack of material, while sapping the majority of the fighting spirit of these units, with some exceptions.

Stalingrad may or may not have been the turning point for the war in Europe, but it certainly marked the effective end of the Axis as something that even pretended to be a military coalition. Germany might still claim Romania, Hungary, and Finland as allies, but after Stalingrad it stopped being a question of if these could ever cease being Germany's allies and instead became a matter of when.[83]

Hitler's longest-standing ally, Italy, had probably suffered the worst of all his allies in the late fall and early winter of 1942–1943. For Italian arms suffered disaster not only in the east but in North Africa as well, a result that put Mussolini's government in a position that would make it the first Axis ally to topple. It is to the course of events in North Africa that we now turn.

8

Desert Sands II

The Mediterranean and North Africa, February 1942–May 1943

Tobruk has fallen and the British have left us with 25,000 prisoners. This is a great success for us and opens new developments.

Galeazzo Ciano, 21 June 1942[1]

As to your troops, you can show them no other road than that to victory or death.   Adolf Hitler, 3 November 1942[2]

AFTER ADMITTING DEFEAT in the bloody *Crusader* battles of November and December 1941, Rommel was able to successfully conduct a withdrawal from Tobruk back to Agedabia. Aided by the resurgence of Axis air activity against Malta, the effective neutralization of British naval forces in the central Mediterranean at the first battle of Sirté, and the successful attack against the British battleships in Alexandria harbor, Axis supplies flowed unimpeded into Tripoli. His supply lines to Italy restored, Rommel launched a counterattack in late January that came as something of a surprise to the British, bringing in 1,000 prisoners and much booty. Encouraged by this, Rommel sought, with Mussolini's support, to extend his offensive with the aim of retaking Cyrenaica. This was accomplished by the middle of February. Both sides then consolidated their positions along a line west of Tobruk from the coast south down to Bir Hacheim.[3]

With active operations now at a halt for the foreseeable future, both sides began to consider their respective strategies. For the Axis powers, strategy revolved around two issues, namely, the coming fight with the British for control of the Gazala position and eventually Tobruk, and then Malta. Although the Italians had already indicated to Rintelen support for these operations, to hash out these issues formally, on 22 April 1942 Hitler invited Mussolini to come to Salzburg on 28 or 29 April for a meeting.[4]

The Italian delegation arrived on 29 April 1942. This time the meetings were held not at the *Berghof* but rather at nearby Klessheim castle and lasted two days. In fact, one could divide the conference into two separate meetings, a political one on the twenty-ninth and a military one on the thirtieth. On the twenty-ninth Mussolini, in a rare moment of being able to get a word in, assured Hitler that while the winter had been a hard one for Italy, the morale of the Italian people was still good and the Duce's government in complete control of the situation. Mussolini also promised Hitler that he would take measures against the older generals in the Italian army who were insufficiently imbued with Fascist ideology. Ciano and Ribbentrop also met separately, but the subjects discussed did not differ much from what passed between Hitler and Mussolini.[5]

The meeting on 30 April dealt with the thorny military problems. The principal issue was what course to pursue in North Africa. The most serious issue was Malta. The most fervent supporter for taking the island was Kesselring, except that he noted the lack of suitable places for using airborne forces. This would place the onus for the operation on the Italian navy. The ultimate decision was that an operation against Malta should be undertaken. Hitler, however, added the caveat that no concrete plans regarding Malta be discussed until Rommel's supply lines were secured, and the best way to do that was by taking Tobruk. This may have accounted for his angry response at Luftwaffe general Kurt Student when he brought up the idea of an airborne assault against Malta on 20 May, as Rommel's offensive was not due to begin until 26 May. The Führer was also very skeptical of the Italian navy's ability to keep any force invading Malta adequately supplied by sea. During the meeting on 30 April Hitler, as usual, did most of the talking, including one lunchtime monologue that lasted, according to Ciano, for an hour and forty minutes that "omitted absolutely no argument."[6] Nonetheless, everyone was relatively satisfied with the outcome of the meeting. Rommel, although he groused in his post–campaign memoir about a lack of support, essentially got his way, in that his upcoming Gazala offensive received priority. Hitler, while committed to Rommel's offensive, emerged with enough maneuvering room to avoid having to go ahead with an amphibious or airborne operation against Malta. For his part Mussolini, as was usually the case after meeting Hitler, left Klessheim with renewed confidence over the projected course of operation.[7]

While decisions of broad strategic import were being finalized at Klessheim, Rommel was concerning himself with more operational and tactical matters. The lull in the campaign during the late winter and early spring of 1942 gave him the relative luxury of time during which he instituted a rigorous training program for all his troops. He was able to raise the level of proficiency of his troops and all aspects of warfare, and especially those aspects unique to war in the desert.[8]

As the time drew near for Rommel's offensive to begin, planning began to encompass some of the ancillary aspects of the operation. On 12 May 1942, for example, Rommel's headquarters conducted a planning exercise with the commanders of the DAK, the Italian X and XX Corps, and the German Ninetieth Light Division. The theme of the exercise was an attack on Tobruk. Rommel also issued orders dealing with the disposition and salvage of captured material, making sure that all captured material ended up in German hands.[9]

While Rommel was completing his preparations for the coming attack on the Gazala line, the naval and air war in the Mediterranean continued apace. As before, Malta remained the focus of German and Italian aerial efforts. Throughout the period January–April 1942, Malta was heavily attacked by Axis aircraft, with the German II Air Corps taking most of the load. During February 1942 alone, the Germans flew 2,299 sorties against Malta, while the Regia Aeronautica flew only 24. The attacks against Malta reached their peak in April and May 1942, with a total of 1,077 Italian sorties and 11,161 German sorties against the island. All these attacks, plus the losses inflicted on the island's fighter defenses, served to effectively neutralize Malta as an aerial threat to Axis supply lines for the near future.[10]

The most notable event at sea was the Second Battle of Sirté, fought on 24 March 1942. Iachino's force, based on the battleship *Littorio,* three cruisers, and eight destroyers, attempted to intercept a convoy bound for Malta, escorted by seven destroyers and the antiaircraft cruiser HMS *Carlisle* and covered by Vian's reconstituted Force K of three cruisers and seven destroyers. Aided by *Ultra,* Vian was able to intercept Iachino's force as it attempted to attack the convoy, which had already been attacked unsuccessfully by both Italian and German aircraft from Sicily. The following battle resulted in some damage to both sides and imposed a critical delay on the convoy's arrival at Malta. This allowed Axis aircraft and submarines to successfully attack and destroy most of the merchant ships in the convoy.[11]

Aside from the major action of Second Sirté, the Axis naval and air forces also engaged in other activities. The Italian Tenth Flotilla divided its time between ships still in Malta's Valletta harbor and attacking British merchant ships in Gibraltar. Meanwhile, Italian convoy escorts and British submarines based at Malta continued their attritional struggle. During the period January–June 1942, British submarines sank nine Italian and one German merchant ship. In April, however, Axis air and naval forces took a serious toll of British and Allied submarines, sinking or damaging six. The effective neutralization of Malta as an air and naval base, plus continued heavy Italian escort for Axis convoys (despite fuel shortages), allowed Rommel to build up the requisite logistical support for his coming attack.[12]

Executing his daring plan to outflank the British position from the south, Rommel fought a series of confused, bloody, and ultimately victorious actions, destroying a number of the British Eighth Army's brigades and a good many of its tanks.[13] During these battles Rommel was able to get some good performances from his Italian units. Although not as tactically proficient as his German units, the Italian divisions, especially the Ariete and Trieste Divisions, put in good service. The Ariete, for example, helped the Twenty-first Panzer Division overrun and smash the Indian Third Motorized Brigade. It then launched a brave but futile direct assault on Bir Hacheim, strongly held by the Free French 150th Brigade. It then slipped around Bir Hacheim to the north, helping to encircle it and take a covering position against any British relief attempts.[14]

In its covering position along Aslagh Ridge, the Ariete gave some ground but was still able to hold its position against the British XXX Corps on 5–6 June 1942, actually deflecting the British Twenty-second Armored Brigade away from the ridge right into a mobile counterattack force from the Fifteenth Panzer Division. The Ariete's performance was all the more impressive because of the lack of air support. This gave Rommel the time he needed to complete the destruction of the Free French position at Bir Hacheim with the German Ninetieth Light and Trieste Divisions.[15]

Having broken the Gazala line and defeated British attacks to restore the position at Knightsbridge, Rommel was able to turn his attention to the prize that had eluded him in 1941, namely, Tobruk. Using the Italian marching infantry to encircle the port, he massed his mobile divisions for a concentrated attack against Tobruk's defenses from the east. Once a breach in Tobruk's no longer formidable defenses had been created, the Ariete and Trieste Divisions were able to hold open the shoulders of the breakthrough, while the German Fifteenth and Twenty-first Panzer Divisions exploited the gap. The attack, opening at 5:40 A.M. on 21 June 1942, moved with almost clocklike precision. By 6:30 A.M. the antitank ditches of the outer defenses had been overrun. By 7:00 P.M. the port was in Rommel's hands, along with 33,000 prisoners and a great deal of booty. Equally critical was the fact that the port facilities were captured apparently without much damage.[16] The capture of Tobruk probably marked the high point of Italo-German cooperation in terms of land warfare in North Africa.

With Tobruk in Axis hands, the question of Malta and its physical conquest once again came to the fore. Mussolini, in a letter prepared by Cavallero, urged that the invasion of Malta (Operation *Hercules*) proceed, but on the condition that the Italian navy receive some 40,000 tons of oil. Without such a delivery, Mussolini warned, the operation would have to be postponed, perhaps indefinitely. Rommel, heady with victory and newly promoted field marshal, reflected his parochial view and asked Mussolini to lift the restriction on Panzer Army Africa that limited it to advancing no farther than the Egyptian frontier. Rommel also put his case to Hitler most effectively by sending an aide of his, Dr. Ingemar Berndt, a close friend of Joseph Goebbels, to Germany to urge an immediate pursuit into Egypt.[17]

Warned by Student that an airborne operation could not be successful without a concomitant seaborne invasion, and distrustful of the Italian navy's ability to support such an operation, Hitler decided to eschew *Hercules.* He told Mussolini by letter on 23 June 1942 that Rommel's victories had created a unique opportunity that needed to be exploited without delay. The giddy Führer urged an immediate advance into Egypt and decided to drop the assault on Malta. The decision to continue the movement into Egypt was confirmed on 25 June in a meeting at Derna, attended by Kesselring, Cavallero, Bastico, and Weichold, among others. Since Rommel was still, technically at least, Bastico's subordinate, Mussolini issued the appropriate orders via Commando Supremo on 27 June 1942. Malta would be postponed until September.[18] In the meantime, German airpower in Italy would be reinforced to keep up the pressure against Malta. Rintelen was directed by OKW to get the Regia Aeronautica to commit the same number of Italian bombers and fighters to the continuing assault on Malta.[19]

The decision to opt for the immediate pursuit into Egypt and to put off Malta has long been held as a fatal blunder on the part of Hitler. Yet it is worth the exercise to ponder what might have happened had the Axis decided to attempt the operation. To be sure, given the state of Malta's air defenses by the early summer of 1942, it is difficult to envision the island's garrison being able to hold off a determined assault by an Italo-German force. The cost, however, would not have been light. Given the experience of Crete, one can safely assume that losses in transport aircraft would have been heavy, even under the most favorable circumstances.

In addition, even if Malta were taken, it would not solve the long-term problems facing the Axis powers in the area. To be sure, taking the island would have made the immediate problem of securing Rommel's supply lines a much simpler proposition. There were, however, some long-term issues that would be ultimately insoluble. The first was the fuel situation facing the Italian navy, which was already experiencing some shortages as early as March 1942.[20] Even if the Germans came across with the 40,000 tons of oil Mussolini requested in order to undertake *Hercules,* the Italian navy would still have been facing the same fuel shortages that eventually immobilized much of it later in the summer of 1942.

The taking of Malta also would have considerably eased the air situation for the Axis powers in the summer of 1942. Nonetheless, the taking of the island would have involved aircraft losses of all types. In addition, having taken Malta, the Axis would then have to station land, naval, and air forces there, supplying them as well. It is difficult to see how this could have been sustained over the long run. It is also hard to envision how the Germans could have maintained air forces on Malta for any length of time. Given the growing Allied aerial superiority, declining German operational readiness rates, and the demands of other fronts on Luftwaffe resources, it is frankly impossible to see how a credible aerial threat could have been mounted over any length of time. Shorn of its naval and air defenses, Malta's Axis garrison would be effectively isolated, and could thus be bypassed, much like the Japanese garrison at Rabaul in the southwest Pacific.

Taking Malta would have complicated Allied logistics as well, closing off the Mediterranean route for convoys going to Egypt. Nevertheless, with the longer route around Africa to the Red Sea and the Suez Canal still available, the British could still complete a buildup of their forces in Egypt. In addition, they could do this relatively undisturbed, as Rommel would have had to stop at the Egyptian border for several months while *Hercules* went through its final planning stages and then execution. Ultimately, the taking of Malta would have spared the Germans and Italians problems of a short-term nature. To be sure, Malta's seizure would have allowed the Axis the possibility of extending the war in North Africa later into 1943, and thus delaying the invasion of Sicily. This might well have set the invasion of Italy back into early 1944, thus delaying the concomitant defection of Italy. Delay, however, would have been the best that the Axis could have hoped for. Ultimately, capturing Malta would have done little to solve the long-term problems facing the Axis in the Mediterranean.[21]

Having gotten his way, Rommel pressed ahead, ordering his units into Egypt. According to the directive issued by Commando Supremo, the Panzer Army was to take Mersa Matruh and then advance to a line between the Arabian Gulf and the Qatara Depression. This would serve as the jumping-off point for the next bound forward, which would carry Rommel's forces all the way to Cairo, Alexandria, and the Suez Canal. Anxious to gain his share of the glory, Mussolini insisted that when Rommel's forces reached the Suez Canal, German and Italian troops be present in equal numbers. The Duce then headed to Africa at the end of June, to be able to enter Cairo riding a white horse. He would return after a month, with only broken health to show for his trouble.[22]

On 25 June 1942, aided by a poorly organized British defense, Rommel was able to inflict yet another stinging defeat on the numerically superior

British at Mersa Matruh with his leading elements, taking the position on the twenty-ninth. At the beginning of July, Rommel again urged his forces eastward, toward the line indicated by the directive he had received from Commando Supremo. By 15 July 1942, however, Rommel's advance had ground to a halt, checked by Auchinleck's defenses at Deir al Shein near El Alamein. Mussolini wrote to Hitler a week later that the halt was needed because of the exhaustion of the troops. This particularly applied to the Italian infantry, who, lacking motor transport, had marched hundreds of miles along the coast road. Likewise, the equipment situation of Rommel's forces was equally poor. By the middle of July 1942, all his armored divisions, be they German or Italian, were down to a mere handful of tanks each. The OKW war diary noted that the Panzer Army now needed a respite of just over a month, and the period could not include any new combat losses and demanded the stable maintenance of a seaborne supply line.[23]

Aside from equipment, the units were short of various types of personnel. The Fifteenth Panzer Division, for example, felt the acute need for interpreters. By the beginning of August 1942, because of combat losses, the division had only two English interpreters and eight Italian interpreters. It therefore requested the assignment of fifteen Egyptian-Arabic, fifteen English, thirty Italian, and ten French interpreters. This request most likely went unfulfilled, since by the end of August 1942 the division was still noting in its activity report the need for high-quality interpreters, who were regarded as critical for cooperation with the Italians.[24]

The Germans also began to run into problems regarding their available airpower. To keep Malta sufficiently neutralized required almost constant attention from the German and Italian air forces. They could not, however, both do this and support Rommel's advance into Egypt at the same time. As the first battle of El Alamein was reaching its climax in mid-July, Rommel's force found itself operating under conditions of air inferiority, while at the same time German and Italian aircraft were heavily attacking Malta, then already recognized as a growing threat.[25]

Far more ominous for both Germany and Italy was the pull exerted by the needs of the eastern front. On 4 August 1942 Hitler, responding to Mussolini's letter of 22 July 1942, noted the importance of air transport in solving the problems in North Africa. At the same time, however, Hitler also stated that creating a strong air transport group for North Africa would weaken the air transport situation in Russia, thus negatively impacting the advances in the Caucasus and the Don Bend. Likewise the combat power of the Luftwaffe in the Mediterranean was steadily reduced by combat losses and transfers to both the eastern front and Germany.[26]

The difficulties in the air situation were reflected in other ways as well. The Italian navy, for example, wanted to use an MAS boat flotilla to secure local coastal convoy traffic. It would only do so, however, if sufficient numbers of Italian and German aircraft were available, an impossibility by the late summer of 1942.[27]

The primacy of the eastern front also exerted a baleful influence on the state of the Italian forces in North Africa. Italy was capable of devoting her full resources to either Russia or North Africa, but not both. Consequently, the relatively lavish amount of equipment bestowed on the Italian Eighth Army meant that the bulk of the Italian infantry divisions in North Africa had to go without adequate motor transport. This greatly reduced their operational mobility, a fatal flaw in the conditions of the North African desert. In addition, in the spring of 1942 Italy still had the requisite shipping and port capacity to be able to satisfy the equipment needs of its infantry divisions in North Africa.[28]

Aside from not being able to get around the problems imposed by the British presence on Malta, the Germans and Italians had additional problems of their own making to deal with. These largely concerned the port of Tobruk. The port had been captured on 21 June, along with considerable stocks of food, fuel, and ammunition, all of which Rommel put to his own use. The port facilities, although apparently not heavily damaged, would require some work to get in a state to receive ships. On 7 July 1942 the OKW war diary noted that the work needed to get Tobruk up to its full capacity was still only in its early stages. Consequently, the bulk of Axis supplies had to be delivered to Benghazi or, even worse, to Tripoli, by that time some 1,300 miles from the front. Even after Tobruk had been brought up to a daily receiving capacity of 2,000 tons (about 1,500 tons of that total by coastal convoy from Benghazi and Tripoli), it was not until 27 August 1942 that the German and Italian authorities reached an agreement on how the available port facilities in Tobruk would be shared. The importance of this agreement was increased by the fact that Germans and Italians were still maintaining separate supply services.[29]

Consequently, as is well-known, the Axis supply situation steadily deteriorated during the late summer and early fall of 1942. The Italian navy, which had already faced fuel shortages in the spring, was now effectively crippled by a lack of fuel shortages.[30] Aided by *Ultra*, the revived British air strength on Malta and some submarines took a steady toll of tankers trying to get fuel to Rommel's forces. August was a particularly bad month, and sinkings were compounded by tactical failure as Rommel's last attempt to reach Suez foundered on the British defenses, again aided by *Ultra*, at Alam Halfa.

Attempts to use air transport as a substitute for seaborne transport came up short for a couple of reasons. First, as noted previously, German airpower was being negatively affected both by losses suffered in the theater and by the demands of other fronts. In addition, the mounting of an effective air transport system depended on the delivery of the requisite amount of fuel to Crete. This could only be done by ship, thus subtracting the tonnage from the major supply routes to North Africa, as well as the tonnage needed to bring supplies to the Italian troops then garrisoning Greece and Albania. Thus, by the middle of September 1942, Rommel's army was facing a logistical crisis. The best idea Hitler could come up with, conveyed to Mussolini by Göring on the eve of the British offensive, was that Italian submarines be used to carry supplies. He also added, rather obviously, that Malta remained "a complex problem."[31]

Aside from the supply problem, by the late summer of 1942 the Italian troops in North Africa faced the identical problem that confronted their compatriots in Russia, namely, inadequate weaponry, especially in the realm of antitank warfare. The standard Italian 47mm antitank gun, despite such defects as a lack of an armored shield, could at least deal successfully with British tanks such as the Crusader. By the late summer of 1942, however, British Eighth Army's 1,100 tanks included 210 American Grant and 270 Sherman tanks. Although very susceptible to German antitank weapons, the Grant and the Sherman could easily overmatch Italian antitank guns. This would severely affect the Italian infantry divisions. These units would have been greatly helped by being equipped with German antitank guns, but the German guns the Italians did have were mostly located with the Italian Eighth Army on the eastern front.[32]

The critical deficiencies of the Italian troops were noted by Rommel in a long letter to OKW and OKH on 22 September 1942. After rather unfairly blaming Commando Supremo for not getting sufficient fuel and ammunition to his forces, Rommel turned to the present state of his own forces. While expressing confidence in the superiority of his German troops, Rommel had considerable doubts about his Italian troops. While noting the inferior rations of the Italian soldiers, and his opinion that the Italian soldier "does not have the nerve" to stop British tanks that have broken through, his greatest concern was the state of the equipment of the Italian forces. What contributed most to the Italian soldier's feeling of inferiority, according to Rommel, was the lack of effective armor-piercing weapons. Tanks were obsolescent, and motor transport was insufficient. All this made it unlikely that his force could stop a British offensive, which he thought might begin in October.[33]

Before heading for Germany on sick leave, Rommel deployed his forces, trying to maximize the ability of his units. Holding his front line with his less mobile infantry and extensive minefields, Rommel backed them up with his armored formations, pairing the Twenty-first Panzer Division with the Ariete and the Fifteenth Panzer Division with the Littorio. He also received some reinforcements in the form of units such as the Folgore Parachute Division that had been previously earmarked for the invasion of Malta.[34]

Much like the *Crusader* battles in November and December 1941, the performance of the Italian units was better than the Germans expected or the British would care to admit. Despite their antiquated equipment and weapons, the efforts of the Italian infantry, especially in the Trento and Bologna Divisions, must have been considerable, given the hard time the British, now led by General (later Field Marshal) Bernard Law Montgomery, had in finally penetrating the Axis positions. Likewise, the performance of the Italian mobile divisions gave no cause for German dissatisfaction. The Fifteenth Panzer Division, for example, had no complaints at all about the conduct of the Littorio Division. Likewise, for all his grumbling Rommel, in commenting on the loss of the Ariete Division, said that "we lost our oldest Italian comrades, from whom we had probably always demanded more than they, with their poor armament, had been capable of performing." Hans von Luck, an officer with the Twenty-first Panzer Division, recorded in his memoirs how the Ariete, Littorio, and Trieste Divisions fought with "death defying courage."[35]

With British airpower savaging his supply lines and Montgomery's superiority beginning to tell at El Alamein, Rommel sought to conduct a retreat to Fuka, about sixty miles to the west. Hitler refused, however, only to reverse himself twenty-four hours later.[36] The delay, however, was fatal, especially for the Italian infantry. While Rommel could successfully extricate his motorized German elements because of their mobility, the Italian infantry divisions, chronically short of transport, were left to the mercy of their fully motorized British opponents.

The first person to recognize the strategic implications of El Alamein and the deteriorating situation on the eastern front was Mussolini. Even one day before the onset of Operation *Torch*, the Duce suggested to Rintelen that a separate peace be made with the Soviet Union. Mussolini also informed Rintelen that he would suggest this to Hitler at a meeting at the end of November.[37]

Matters were made more complex by the landing of an Anglo-American force in French Northwest Africa. With Rommel's forces now retreating as rapidly as possible across Libya, and with American and British forces

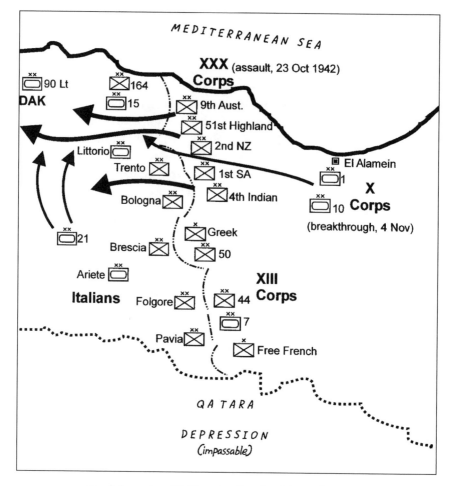

Breakthrough at El Alamein, October–November 1942

beginning to advance eastward from Morocco, a fundamental strategic decision had to be made. Mussolini and Ciano were asked to come to Germany
for an urgent conference. Ciano ended up going, as Mussolini was still in
ill health. Also attending was Pierre Laval, the Vichy French premier. While
Laval sat outside the conference room, Hitler informed Ciano that he had
decided to invade Vichy France. Reinforcements would be sent to Tunisia
to build up a bridgehead there to thwart the soon-to-be-advancing Anglo-
American invasion force.[38]

The effort to shore up the position in Tunisia would have to be a largely
German one. On 20 November 1942 Rintelen reported on the state of the

Italian army. Of the nine Italian divisions composing the X, XX, and XXI Corps at El Alamein, eight had been completely destroyed, while the one surviving division (Pistoia) had been "severely battered." For immediate service in North Africa, the Superga and Livorno Divisions, both "tolerably equipped and armed," were being sent. Beyond that, there was not much available. Some divisions could be moved from Greece to Italy, but these units had not had a refit since the spring of 1941 and were short of all kinds of equipment. The bulk of the Regio Esercito was in the Italian Eighth Army in Russia.[39] In effect, Italy's cupboard was bare.

By the end of November 1942, it had become increasingly clear that holding two different fronts would be impossible. Although Mussolini and Hitler issued a joint "stand fast" order to Rommel to hold the Mersa El Brega position as a possible jumping-off point for a new offensive, this was a fantasy. In some ways the issuance of the order reflected the dysfunctional command system that continued even during this crisis. Rommel received the order from Pohl on 12 November, who was sent by Cavallero to convey it. Although Cavallero was in North Africa at the time on a three-day trip, at no time did he attempt to personally consult with Rommel, who also claimed that his requests to meet with Cavallero were ignored. Once the order was received, Rommel responded with a frank message outlining the terrible state of his forces. On 24 November Rommel reiterated this in a long-overdue meeting with Cavallero and Kesselring. The official response was yet another hold-the-line message by Mussolini.[40]

Appalled at this, Rommel then decided to fly to Hitler's headquarters in Rastenburg. Arriving on 28 November, Rommel was admitted into Hitler's presence at 5:00 P.M. Rommel urged the evacuation of North Africa, seeing that in the long run it could not be held. Hitler, deeply distracted by the now breaking Stalingrad crisis, told Rommel that the political situation demanded the retention of a Tunisian bridgehead. He airily promised Rommel lots of guns and tanks before dismissing him. One thing Rommel may have gotten across to Hitler was the state of affairs in Tripoli. Hitler promptly dispatched a telegram to Mussolini complaining that Tripoli was blocked by ship traffic leaving the port for two weeks, so that a ship with supplies for Rommel would not be able to be unloaded until 4 December. Under those conditions, Tripoli could not be held.[41]

As for Tunisia itself, the initial Axis move into the area went better than expected. Kesselring was able to move the Tenth Panzer Division and elements of the 334th Infantry Division into Tunisia. Later major elements of the Hermann Göring Panzer Parachute Division (a Luftwaffe formation) and the Italian Centauro Division were brought in. Enough airpower was

concentrated so that Kesserling was able to secure air superiority tempo-
rarily over Tunisia. This allowed the Germans to make an administrative
parachute jump into Tunisia as well. The port of Gabes was secured, thus
easing Rommel's supply problems somewhat. The initial American advance
into the area from the west was checked, so that by the end of 1942 the Axis
bridgehead in Tunisia was relatively secure.[42]

With crises now breaking both in North Africa and on the eastern front,
it was high time for a reconsideration of Germany's strategic options. On
6 December 1942 Hitler invited Mussolini, via German ambassador Hans
Georg von Mackensen, to come to Rastenburg later in the month to discuss
the situation. The Duce, still ill from his fruitless sojourn to Africa, could
only send Ciano and Cavallero to represent him. Arriving in Rastenburg on
18 December, Ciano conveyed Mussolini's suggestion that at the very least,
Hitler should seek a separate peace with Stalin. In doing this, of course,
Mussolini was clearly implying that the situation in the Mediterranean was
a greater immediate threat to Italy (or at least his government) than the
situation at Stalingrad was to Germany. The Duce was also hinting, rather
broadly, that any successful defense of the Axis position in the Mediterranean would require a major infusion of German help. Hitler, however, would
have none of it.[43]

As more German and Italian forces entered Tunisia, new command arrangements were required, for by the end of January 1943 the command
setup was utterly dysfunctional. The German forces being sent into Tunisia
were eventually designated the Fifth Panzer Army, commanded by General
Hans-Jürgen von Arnim. Theoretically Kesselring, as OB South, should have
exercised command over the two armies, but, given his other responsibilities,
he did not. Thus the two armies conducted their operations independently of
each other and were to cooperate when necessary. This certainly contributed
to Rommel's failure to get more out of his moderately successful attack on
the American II Corps at Kasserine Pass than he actually did.[44]

In a classic case of being a day late and a dollar short, only in the final
stages of the campaign in North Africa, for the first time in the war, were the
Germans and Italians able to create a combined command structure. Overall command in Tunisia now lay in Army Group Africa (later Army Group
Tunisia), a position held by Arnim (Rommel had been recalled to Germany).
Arnim had an Italian chief of staff, who worked directly for Commando
Supremo. Like a German chief of staff, he had the duty to express his views
to the army group commander and was responsible for the liaison between
that commander and the subordinate armies. In addition, the chief of staff
had to transmit orders to all subordinate Italian units. In doing so, he had

the authority to make suitable changes in the text of the orders to make them more understandable in Italian. Panzer Army Africa was redesignated as the Italian First Army, and command was given to Messe. Under him was a German chief of staff, with responsibilities similar to those of Arnim's chief of staff.[45]

These structural changes were concomitant with several major personnel changes. The first to go was Cavallero, who was regarded by many in Italy as too pro-German. Mussolini replaced him with General Vittorio Ambrosio, whose anti-German propensities were well-known. The Germans regarded Cavallero's departure with mixed feelings. Rommel thought him a weak "office chair soldier." Kesselring felt that Cavallero had been subjected to some unfair criticism by his Italian colleagues but offered no real opinion on him in his memoirs. Rintelen thought Cavallero's departure unfortunate, both at the time and afterward.[46]

The next to go was Ciano, who was caught up in a general purge of Mussolini's cabinet. Other victims included Giuseppe Bottai and Raffaello Riccardi. Mussolini, already holding five different government posts, decided to take over Ciano's position as well.[47]

The last to go was Rommel. Still not well from his physical illnesses contracted in Africa and very much depressed mentally by the course of events, Rommel had long seen Africa as hopeless. Regarded now by Hitler as a defeatist, but still a major figure in the pantheon of heroes extolled by the Nazi propaganda machine, and thus too important to lose, Rommel was recalled to Germany. After a dispiriting 10 March 1943 audience with Hitler at his headquarters in Russia, Rommel was given extended leave. Kesselring stayed on as OB South, although he also regarded North Africa as lost. Mussolini, however, sought to reassure Kesselring of his support.[48]

All these changes availed little help for the Axis forces in North Africa. Both Hitler and Mussolini agreed on the need to maintain the position in Tunisia. When the two dictators met at Klessheim on 7–8 April 1943, although Hitler boasted to Mussolini that the Axis troops in North Africa would "turn Tunisia into the Verdun of the Mediterranean," much more of that meeting was devoted to the defense of Italy and Greece.[49] With Axis supply lines being savaged by the combination of submarine, aircraft, and *Ultra,* the end was certain. When the Allies launched their final offensive in late April 1943, the Axis forces initially fought stoutly, but after the first positions were taken, the defenses collapsed quickly. Although Messe had promised Mussolini to fight on to the end, Mussolini ordered him to surrender. The Allies ended up taking some 275,000 prisoners, most of them Italians. Mussolini's attempt to recreate the Roman Empire was over.[50]

Both Germany and Italy reaped the full fruits of a series of bad decisions made in 1941 and 1942 regarding the conduct of the war, both in general and in the Mediterranean in particular. For Germany, the 1942 campaign proved to be a classic example of mismatching ends and means. With Germany already committed to a major offensive on the eastern front, the decision to mount an attack on the Gazala position and take Tobruk was understandable, but to go farther in North Africa was simply insupportable in the long run. Even if Malta were taken, the logistical difficulties involved, given Italy's situation, would have precluded any successful advance past the Egyptian border. This had particularly serious consequences for the Luftwaffe, especially in regard to its air transport and fighter arms. The Luftwaffe simply did not have the assets to adequately meet the needs of both operations.[51]

For Italy, the effects of the bad decisions made in 1940 and 1941 manifested themselves fully in 1942 and were combined with some equally bad decisions on Mussolini's part in 1942. The consequences of the decision to invade Greece in October 1940 became readily apparent. The large Italian occupation force in Greece, Yugoslavia, and Albania could be supplied only by sea. This served to be a drain on both Italian merchant shipping and light forces needed for escort duty, as well as the Italian navy's already difficult fuel situation. Even then, it proved to be inadequate, as by April 1943 Ambrosio recognized that the situation required the dispatching of three more Italian divisions to Greece, Crete, and the Dodecanese, units that Commando Supremo simply did not have.[52]

A far more serious mistake by Mussolini that now became apparent was the decision to commit the bulk of Italy's forces to the eastern front in 1942. While the campaign in the east did not take a very heavy toll on Italian air assets, a vast amount of equipment (by Italian standards) was sent to the Eighth Army over the summer of 1942, which proved inadequate. Just a portion of this material would have improved the capabilities of the Italian infantry divisions considerably, especially in the area of mobility, given the scale of the forces involved.[53] Instead, the Italian forces in Russia were poorly equipped relative to their opponents, while those in North Africa were simply underequipped.

Mussolini's decision to go to North Africa and then spend about a full month there must also be regarded as a poor choice. While there, he did not even bother to go to the front to get a more accurate picture of the state of affairs there. In addition, the trip only served to ruin his health, leaving him unable to attend conferences at critical times because of his illness.

The dysfunctional command system and clashing personalities also contributed to the disaster that overtook the Axis forces in North Africa. On the German side Kesselring and Rommel were often at loggerheads. Kesselring thought Rommel too narrow in his perspective, while Rommel thought Kesselring too parochial, often more interested in the Luftwaffe's situation than in the conditions facing the ground troops.[54] Hitler's promotion of Rommel to field marshal, while deserved for his superb performance in the battles around Gazala and Tobruk, served only to further muddy the command arrangements. As a field marshal, Rommel had right of direct access to Hitler, thus giving him the ability to go around his nominal superior Kesselring.

Command relations with the Italians were little better. Both countries maintained separate chains of command, resulting in a slow decision-making process. A classic example of this was the slow progress made in how to make the best use of Tobruk's port facilities. Both sides made complaints about the other, some justified and many not. Rommel, for example, accused the Italians of not doing enough to keep his forces supplied, overlooking the sacrifices made by the Italian merchant marine to keep material flowing to North Africa. Cooperation at the lower levels was somewhat better, and Rommel's use of his Italian troops at Tobruk was excellent.[55]

As the Axis position in North Africa collapsed, there was a good deal of acrimonious finger-pointing. Such a reaction, while understandable on the part of both the Italians and the Germans, was also beside the point. Mussolini's cherished dream of a new Roman Empire was over. It was his very political existence, and that of his government, that was now in mortal danger, along with the southern flank Hitler had long worried about.

9

All Fall Down
The Collapse of the Axis

Japan must reckon that one day, she is to be attacked by Russia. This preemptive attack with sufficient forces would be advantageous, but action by weaker forces would not lead to success. . . . Since we know too little of Japan's circumstances, we can offer no advice.   Wilhelm Keitel, 30 July 1943[1]

The *Führer* anticipated Italian treason as something absolutely certain.
Joseph Goebbels, 10 September 1943[2]

Some 250 Romanians who collaborated with us, including Marshal Antonescu, have been brought before a special tribunal.
Joseph Goebbels, 21 March 1945[3]

THE TWIN DISASTERS IN Stalingrad and North Africa effectively destroyed the Axis as a military alliance, such as it was. It now remains to tell the story of the eventual collapse of Germany's allies. Although Italian and Romanian light naval forces still operated on the Black Sea, land forces were another matter. By the middle of 1943, Romanian, Hungarian, and Italian forces (or what was left of them) had all been withdrawn from combat on the eastern front. Of the Hungarians, only two divisions were left in the east for occupation duty. As for the Romanians, nine divisions were left on the eastern front, and the occupation forces in Transnistria remained. The remnant of the Italian Eighth Army was completely withdrawn.[4]

Politically, the disasters served to create dangerous situations for all the Axis governments. Stalingrad greatly threatened Antonescu's position, which encouraged pro-English sympathies in the army and brought him into conflict with the Romanian royal family. In addition, large segments of the populations of both Romania and Hungary were still more interested in fighting each other. Optimistic reports were still coming from German offices in Italy and from Kesselring, so much so that even Hitler doubted their veracity, and with good reason. By June 1943 Mussolini's government was deeply unpopular. Finally, the Stalingrad debacle convinced the Finnish government to begin looking for a way out of the war.[5]

That Italy was the first of Germany's allies to fall by the wayside was expected. The collapse of the Axis position in North Africa left Italy in an extremely vulnerable condition. The Germans and their Italians had to consider the next move by the Allies. The most obvious question was whether the next target was Sicily, Sardinia, or the Balkans. German attention to a considerable degree was focused on Sardinia, thanks to a successful deception operation on the part of British intelligence, Operation *Mincemeat*.[6] The main part of Hitler's attention, however, was devoted to the upcoming offensive on the eastern front against the Soviet salient around Kursk.

The situation in the Balkans was also of concern to both the Germans and the Italians. The Germans were well aware of the poor state of Italian forces in the Balkans, which had not had a refit since the spring of 1941. With the turn of the tide against the Axis, the condition of these units became a matter for worry as the Balkans became a possible target. To be sure, the Germans did pass on to the Italians such lessons as those that were learned from the repulse of the Dieppe raid in August 1942.[7] The state of both Italian and German forces in the Balkans, however, became an issue critical enough to consume a good deal of time at a meeting between Keitel and Ambrosio at Klessheim on 9 April 1943. The outcome was a further draining of equipment and supplies from critical theaters to the Balkans throughout the summer of 1943. During August 1943, for example, some 34 ships delivered 38,133 tons of supplies, 473 vehicles, 168 guns, and several thousand men to the Greek mainland and the Greek isles, especially Crete and Rhodes.[8]

Although German attention was diverted to Sardinia and the Balkans, Sicily was not entirely forgotten. The problem, however, was that the Germans and the Italians now fell back into the bad habits that had bedeviled them earlier. During the final stages of the North Africa campaign, the Germans and Italians were finally able to create a unified command structure. For Sicily, however, both countries slid back virtually to the days of parallel war. After the disasters in North Africa and Russia, the level of mistrust between the Germans and the Italians was fairly high, and this was reflected in the command arrangements. Although the German XIV Panzer Corps, commanded by the one-armed Hans Valentin Hube, was theoretically under the command of the head of the Italian Sixth Army, General Alfredo Guzzoni, in reality Hube worked directly for Kesselring. Hube could therefore disregard any orders from Guzzoni that he considered incorrect or contrary to German interests. This created a difficult situation for the German liaison officer at Guzzoni's headquarters, General Fridolin von Senger und Etterlin. Nonetheless, the devoutly Catholic Bavarian Senger was a good choice for the post. Matters were made worse by the recrudescence of service parochialism in both Germany and Italy. Kesselring was often at odds with both Rommel, now exercising command in northern Italy, and Richthofen, busy with reinforcing Sardinia. On the Italian side, relations between the army and navy were so poor that at least one Italian admiral referred to Commando Supremo in sneering terms.[9]

The equipment situation for both German and Italian forces on Sicily was rather poor. Of the two German divisions rebuilding on the island at the start of the invasion, only the Hermann Göring Panzer Parachute Division was being re-created as a panzer division. The other, the Fifteenth Panzer Grenadier Division, was the successor to the Fifteenth Panzer Division of Afrika Corps fame and was being reconstituted as a panzer grenadier division because of equipment shortages, especially tanks.[10] The Italian situation, of course, was far worse. Although Fiat was producing a high-quality assault gun by this time, it was available in only limited numbers. Attempts to have Fiat produce German tanks failed, apparently because of Italian intransigence, even though Hitler was willing to offer "designs, patents, and even machine tools." Attempts to use Italian aircraft factories to produce some German models failed, owing to overly complicated contract stipulations and excessive strain on Italian facilities in northern Italy. Some Italian airframes, when mated with German aircraft engines, made excellent fighters. For example, the Macchi 205 combined a modified Macchi 202 airframe with a German Daimler Benz 605 engine, giving it the appearance of an Me 109. They were never produced in sufficient numbers or were made too late to make a difference.[11]

During the course of the campaign many of the Italian units, especially the poorly trained and miserably equipped coast defense divisions, collapsed immediately. Other Italian units, despite casualties, performed reasonably well, although as the Axis forces withdrew from the island and more German forces were brought in, by the latter half of July the defense lines were almost entirely held by Germans. This allowed Hube, with strong backing from Rommel, to wrest the conduct of the defense of Sicily from Guzzoni's hands. It also gave the Germans cause to resort to old habits, such as stealing vehicles from Italian units.[12]

The brightest spot in the conduct of the campaign for the Axis was the evacuation. Interestingly, the Germans and Italians took the decision to remove their respective forces from the island separately. Hitler decided to order plans for the evacuation after Mussolini was deposed. The command to evacuate Italian troops was given by Guzzoni, independent of both the Germans and the new Italian government, headed by Badoglio.[13] Although the German navy was initially opposed to the operation, it proved to be one of the rare occasions marked by good interservice and interallied cooperation. Hube's forces, with some minor assistance from the Italians, were able to successfully conduct a phased withdrawal to Messina. The Luftwaffe, aided to an extent by the Italian army, was able to erect one of the most formidable concentrations of antiaircraft guns of the entire war. The German and Italian navies were able to run effective ferry services across the Straits of Messina, helped by a series of clever active and passive defense measures to protect craft conducting the evacuation. Thus the Germans were able to take almost 40,000 troops, 15,000 wounded, 51 tanks, and 163 guns off of Sicily, while the Italians brought 59,000 troops, 227 vehicles, and 41 guns across the Straits to the Italian mainland. In fact, the last troops to leave Sicily were a small Italian patrol, ferried to the mainland by a German E-boat.[14]

The Sicilian campaign had far more profound consequences for Germany in a strategic and political sense. Strategically, the invasion caused Hitler to call off the offensive at Kursk, which had been in progress since 5 July 1943 with mixed results for the Germans. The initiative on the eastern front would now pass permanently into Soviet hands.[15]

The failure of Kursk and the invasion of Sicily also led OKW to pursue one of its more bizarre ideas, namely, that Japan should now be urged to launch an attack on the Soviet Union. The idea was first broached as early as July 1942 by Ribbentrop, who approached Japanese ambassador General Ōshima Hiroshi with this in a somewhat offhanded way, and apparently ignorant of the results of the battle of Midway. Ribbentropp revisited this subject in the spring of 1943 with Ōshima, who, although sympathetic, transmitted his government's refusal.[16] The Germans returned to the idea in late July 1943, only to be given a firm refusal by the Japanese. Keitel, notably, confessed to knowing "too little of Japan's circumstances" and not much about the state of affairs in the Pacific generally. By the end of September 1943 this notion was clearly dead.[17]

Politically, the invasion of Sicily meant the end of Mussolini's government. Although as late as 30 June 1943 reports from Italy still presented a somewhat optimistic picture, reality quickly set in after the Allies landed in Sicily. On 19 July 1943 Hitler flew to Treviso to meet with Mussolini at San Fermo. Over the course of the meeting Hitler, as usual, did almost all of the talking, trying to shore up the plainly listless and apathetic Duce. He also apparently urged Mussolini to concentrate all power in his hands and to depose the Italian royal family, although accounts differ on this. Mussolini, when able to get a word in, apparently once again urged Hitler to make a separate peace with Stalin, depending on which description of the meeting one believes. Matters were made worse still for the ailing Mussolini when word arrived during the meeting that Rome was suffering a heavy air raid.[18]

Still depressed and apathetic, Mussolini went back to Rome and convened the first meeting of the Fascist Grand Council since the start of the war. Meeting over the night of 24–25 July 1943, the council, chaired by Dino Grandi, voted to have Mussolini removed as prime minister. On the twenty-fifth, Mussolini informed Vittorio Emmanuaele of the vote, and the king, in a rare spasm of personal courage, dismissed Mussolini and appointed Badoglio in his place. Mussolini was then placed under arrest and taken to the island of Ponza.[19]

Hitler was outraged at Mussolini's removal. With the situation still unclear, rumors made the rounds that Mussolini had been executed, although that was eventually cleared up. Hitler and OKW were also in agreement that Italy would be less trustworthy than ever, especially with Badoglio, "our grimmest enemy," in charge.[20] Thus Hitler almost immediately had plans put in hand for the rapid invasion and securing of Italy, and some troops were moved in right away without informing the Italians. In addition, the defense of Greece was now placed in German hands, and Italian units there would now be backstopped by German units, although the value of units such as the Eleventh Luftwaffe Field Division was dubious at best.[21]

The overthrow of Mussolini served to raise the level of mistrust between the Germans and the Italians to new levels. This was clearly reflected in the 6 August 1943 meeting at Tarviso, conducted from 3:00 to 5:30 P.M., with six principal participants. The Germans were represented by Keitel, Rintelen, and Warlimont, while the main Italian conferees were Ambrosio, his deputy, Major General Carlo Rossi, and Marras. Keitel opened by making no apologies for moving of troops into Italy without informing the Italians, saying that the "dangerous situation" required it. The Germans also demanded that all the antiaircraft defenses in Sicily, with the evacuation about to begin, needed to be placed in German hands. In addition, the Germans declared that the defense of the alpine passes was now a German task. Unstated was the fact that this would facilitate any major move by German forces into Italy in case of an Italian defection, an eventuality that Hitler now considered a certainty.[22]

Hitler's expectation became reality on 9 September 1943. The Allies launched the invasion of Italy on the night of 8–9 September 1943. Although there were some anxious moments for the American forces at Salerno, the landing was successful. The British had a much easier time crossing the Straits of Messina and rapidly began to advance north. Much as Hitler anticipated, the invasion was accompanied by an Italian defection. Badoglio's representative had signed an agreement with the Allies on 3 September, but Badoglio waited until the invasion to make his move. After sending a telegram to Hitler announcing the armistice, Badoglio, the king, and several other members of the government fled by ship for Malta as the Allies came ashore. Badoglio and the king would be accompanied by the rest of the Italian fleet, which had sallied from LaSpezia, and was also headed for Malta. Both the government and the fleet made it to safety, although a German air attack sank the battleship *Roma*.[23]

Once the Allied invasion and Italy's defection became facts, the Germans put into action the plans already devised for just this eventuality. Units quickly rolled into Italy. Although Hitler had considered a withdrawal into the Apennines, he quickly came around to Kesselring's view, which called for establishing defense lines south of Rome. In addition, on 12 September 1943 Mussolini was rescued by an SS commando team in a daring operation led by Otto Skorzeny.[24]

The German occupation of Italy left several problems to solve. The first of these was what to do with the millions of Italian troops still under arms either in Italy or in the Balkans. As something of a formality, Mussolini announced to all Italian soldiers, via OKW, that the "King's treason" had released Italian soldiers from their oath to him. Italian soldiers would then be offered a choice. Individually, they could swear an oath to "defend the Italian Fatherland," if they were posted in German-held areas. Large units would have the oath administered by Mussolini.[25] Very few Italians took Mussolini up on the offer. Consequently, the Germans disarmed and imprisoned some 1.7 million Italians from all services. The positions guarded by the Italians, such as Greek islands, were then taken over by the Germans. Sizable stocks of fuel, supplies, and equipment were also seized by the Germans. In some cases, such as the crews of Italian submarines in Constanta, the few who took the oath were integrated into German ships, while Italian ships were turned over to the Romanians.[26]

The second problem for the Germans was what to do with Mussolini, now that he had been rescued. Mussolini decided to try to re-create his old regime, with German support, in the form of the Republic of Salò. From the German standpoint, having a friendly administration in northern Italy was clearly desirable, at least according to Kesselring. The problem was that in the same message, "smiling Albert" also noted that German soldiers considered Italy "occupied territory" and treated it accordingly.[27]

In the end, the attempt to create a rump Fascist regime in the north fell apart. Most Germans, outside of Hitler's devoted circle, who saw Mussolini in this period agreed that he was a broken reed. To a majority of both Germans and Italians, Mussolini was clearly, to use Gerhard Schreiber's words, "Berlin's useful idiot." Italians were further alienated by German behavior in Italy, and by German attempts to round up Jews in Italy for deportation, measures that often met with passive resistance on the part of the Italian population.[28]

Equally pathetic was the attempt to create a military force for Mussolini's new government. Mussolini had proposed to Hitler the creation of a new 500,000-man Italian army, fired by Fascist ideology. Hitler sensibly cut the number down to a total of four divisions, which were to be fully equipped by 1 April 1944 and ready for combat by late summer of 1944. Even this modest goal was unattainable. The equipment was slow in coming, and German officers responsible for training the Italians were arrogant and condescending, and lacked interpreters in any case. When the units did appear, German headquarters in whose areas they were operating were happy to be rid of them, as indicated in marginalia. When the Fourteenth Army was informed by SS commander and police chief in Italy that the army was no longer responsible for the Italian Blackshirt units in its area, "good riddance!" was written in the margin of the document.[29]

Consequently, all Mussolini could do was to sit in his Potemkin republic and play at governing. He engaged in activities such as taking revenge on those enemies and opponents of his who had not fled to Allied lines, including Ciano, arrested and eventually executed on 11 January 1944. The much-reduced Duce would also occasionally give OKW or Hitler his analysis of the military situation as the Italian campaign ran its course.[30] Caught up in the final collapse of the German forces in Italy, Mussolini tried to escape disguised as a German soldier, but to no avail. Caught and executed on 28 April 1945 by Italian communist partisans, the Duce was taken to his last crowd scene, as his corpse and that of his mistress, Clara Petacci, were hung upside down from some scaffolding in the great square of Milan.[31]

The fates of Germany's major allies on the eastern front in some ways were reflective of their respective relationships with Germany. Finland can be dealt with first. As noted earlier, Finland, with some urging from Sweden and later the United States, had been looking for a way out of the war as early as December 1942, something of which the Germans were well aware.[32] Given that German attention was largely devoted to the southern end of the front from the spring of 1942 until the summer of 1944, the Finns were able to exercise a fair amount of autonomy as to what they would and would not do. The winter warfare school continued to operate during the winter of

1942–1943. On the other hand, Mannerheim objected strenuously enough to the raising of a Finnish SS battalion that it was disbanded in July 1943.[33]

Mounting any kind of major operation against the Soviets was another matter. The inactivity continued on the Finnish front throughout 1943. The Finns, anxious to withdraw from the war, wanted to avoid further moves against the Soviets, as this would make reaching an agreement with Stalin difficult. In addition, a new offensive against the Soviets could bring about a declaration of war against Finland by the United States, the best possible agency by which Finland could make peace with the Soviet Union.[34] Thus Finland refused to undertake any move, even with German support, against the Murmansk railway in 1943, even though the Germans and Finns had twice as many men on that sector of the front and the offensive, at least according to Erfurth, had a good chance of cutting the railway and thereby isolating Murmansk.[35]

By the summer of 1944, Finland was at the end of its tether. Although its armed forces were strong numerically, with 420,000 men and 26,000 women serving, these numbers failed to cover much underlying weakness. The size of the armed forces (about 12 percent of the nation's population) in itself was a problem. The demands of the front drained much needed labor from the Finnish economy, which was still agriculturally based. Thus Finland could not even take advantage of the territory it had recaptured. Lack of spare equipment and weapons forced the Finns to press captured Soviet material into service. Thus, by 1944 standardization of equipment was a problem.[36]

The Finnish government had been trying to put out peace feelers to the Soviets during the winter of 1942–1943. Hitler promptly demanded that Finland halt these contacts. He and Ribbentrop then demanded that Finland sign a pact that would signify the abandonment of its previous position of waging parallel war. In Finnish government councils Mannerheim strongly warned against such a course, and his immense prestige and common sense carried the day. In addition, although Hitler and Ribbentrop could make threats against Finland for trying to make a separate peace, they had few available means to carry out such punishments as they threatened. Ultimately, Hitler had to be satisfied with a public statement by Prime Minister Edwin Linkomies that Finland would fight on. For their part, the Germans would maintain economic aid to Finland.[37]

By the summer of 1944, there could be no doubt about the outcome for the Finns. With the German siege of Leningrad now lifted, the Soviets were ready to launch an offensive into Karelia and Finland proper. The hope was to knock Finland out of the war, thus freeing up troops for employment on other sectors of the front.[38] Beginning on 10 June 1944, the Soviet Leningrad and Karelian Fronts attacked on both sides of Lake Ladoga. By 21 June the Finns had been driven back to the Vyborg area. After a short pause, Soviet operations resumed, and by 15 July Vyborg had been secured.[39]

Faced with the prospect of a possible Soviet drive on Helsinki, the Finns drew the inevitable conclusions. Ryti resigned as president and was replaced by Mannerheim. The aged Marshall urged the Finnish Parliament to accept the proffered Soviet terms, although they were regarded as excessively harsh. Mannerheim's prestige, however, once again carried the day. A cease-fire was agreed to on 4 September 1944, and an armistice was signed by a Finnish delegation in Moscow on the seventh, although the agreement was not fully accepted by the Finnish government until 19 September 1944.[40]

Aside from some territorial concessions to the Soviets, the armistice also required the Finns to sever relations with Germany. This left the German Twentieth Mountain Army in a difficult situation. Hitler's initial reaction was to order the army to hold on to the nickel mines at Petsamo, but he quickly changed his mind. On 6 September 1944 he formally ordered the German Twentieth Mountain Army to withdraw into Norway. Since the army's area of operations was fairly large, the Finns were able to give the Germans a wide berth to conduct their withdrawal, although in some cases shots were traded. All materials that could not be evacuated were to be destroyed to prevent their falling into Finnish or Soviet hands.[41] By the start of November, the German Twentieth Mountain Army had completed its move back into Norway.[42]

After meeting Mussolini at Klessheim on 8–9 April 1943, Hitler then entertained Antonescu and Horthy at Klessheim over the next two weeks. Antonescu arrived shortly after Mussolini's departure. At their conference Antonescu took a tack similar to Mussolini, but with the priorities reversed. While Mussolini had urged Hitler to seek a separate peace with Stalin, Antonescu suggested that Hitler find some sort of accommodation with the West, in order to continue the war against the Soviets.[43] Antonescu got no further with his recommendation to Hitler than Mussolini did.

Horthy's visit with Hitler from 16 to 18 April at Klessheim was far more acrimonious than Hitler's meeting with Antonescu. An angry Führer accused the Hungarians of fighting badly, if at all, during the recent Stalingrad disaster. For his part, Horthy pointed the finger right back at Hitler, reproving the Germans for promising a great deal of armored vehicles and guns but rarely, if ever, delivering on them. Hitler then demanded that Horthy dismiss Kállay as prime minister for putting out peace feelers to the Anglo-Allies and, more ominously, for being insufficiently harsh toward Hungary's Jews.[44]

Neither bucking up Antonescu nor tongue-lashing Horthy changed the situation. In regard to Romania and Hungary, Germany still faced the same set of intractable problems. The armies of both countries were in a shambles, and what was left of the field forces committed to the 1942 summer offensive had been withdrawn by the spring of 1943.[45] Neither of these forces could be built back up very quickly. Matters were not helped by the constant poaching of Romanian manpower by Gottlob Berger's SS recruiters. The effort, spearheaded initially by Artur Phleps, eventually brought about 60,000 Romanian *Volksdeutsche* into the SS, much to the irritation of the Romanians.[46]

About the only positive thing for the Germans in regard to their allies was that, as the battle line moved back toward them, the Romanian and Hungarian governments realized that they needed to worry more about the Soviets than about each other. Popular opinion on this question, however, remained as obdurate as ever.[47]

Matters were not helped by the Germans. Deliveries of German equipment to Romania could best be described as a trickle. Between November 1943 and mid-August 1944, Germany delivered only 130 Panzer IVs and 108 assault guns. This would leave the rebuilding Romanian First and Second Panzer Divisions badly understrength, especially in tanks and armored reconnaissance vehicles.[48]

Indigenous Hungarian and Romanian capabilities were also wasted. Both Hungary and Romania had industrial facilities that could produce German tanks, such as the Panzer IV. For this to happen, however, the German army had to sell the patents for the vehicles to the Romanians and Hungarians. When the Germans did offer the patents, it was at a price far higher than the Romanians and Hungarians could afford. The Luftwaffe also did this with Hungarian attempts to purchase German aircraft, or sold the Hungarians obsolete German or French models. An attempt to have the Hungarian firm Manfred Weiss produce some German models failed to bring about the desired results for a variety reasons, including a lack of machine tools and constantly changing requirements on the part of the Germans.[49]

As the Allied air offensive against Germany gained momentum, it was plainly apparent that, given its importance to the German war economy, Ploesti would become a major target. During his 23 September 1942 meeting with Hitler, Antonescu made plain his desire to obtain German radar equipment and fighters for Ploesti.[50] Thus, the Romanian air force enjoyed a higher-priority status in terms of equipment and readiness. During 1943 Gerstenberg, now head of the DLM, received enough material to make Ploesti one of the most heavily defended localities in Europe. Romanian crews manned the German-made antiaircraft guns and flew a sizable percentage of the German-made fighters dedicated to the defense of Ploesti. Gerstenberg also deployed the German Passive Air Defense Brigade, while the Romanians deployed the Marshal Antonescu Passive Air Defense Regiment. These units became expert at procedures such as smoke generation, camouflage, constructing dummies, and extinguishing fires.[51]

The German-Romanian defenses of Ploesti performed fairly well. Gerstenberg was a superb choice to succeed Speidel as head of the DLM. Fluent in Romanian, Gerstenberg cultivated excellent relations with his Romanian counterparts. In addition, German promises of equipment were matched by German delivery, so that by 1 August 1943, when American bombers made their first visit to Ploesti, the city and its associated oil production and refining facilities were ringed by fifteen heavy and twelve light antiaircraft batteries, plus a large number of fighters. The result was the infliction of heavy losses on the raiding force.[52] The Luftwaffe continued to pour resources into Ploesti after the 1 August 1943 raid, so that even as Allied efforts against Ploesti increased, the defenses, both active and passive, continued to perform well right up until the Romanian collapse.[53]

For all the achievements of the DLM, however, both the Germans and the Romanians made a great many avoidable mistakes. In the case of the Luftwaffe, these usually revolved around sharing technology. In early July 1943, for example, the Romanians reached an agreement with Sweden by which Romania would send Sweden oil in return for machine tools, which would go to the IAR aircraft works. The German Aviation Ministry, however, objected, saying that such an agreement required the approval of the German Economic Ministry. Although the deal was affirmed by the Germans, it was only approved after a time lag of more than three weeks, an unconscionable delay at a time when every moment counted.[54] On the Romanian side, given a choice of German aircraft to manufacture, the Romanian Ministry of Aviation decided to build the FW 189. Although the FW 189 was a good aircraft for reconnaissance and ground attack, given the state of the Romanian army, fighters may have been a better choice. In that regard, some factories in Romania were already producing Me 109s on license, but that effort had only begun in 1943.[55]

The Romanian army saw very little action over the course of 1943 and early 1944. Six infantry divisions were involved in the defense of the Taman Peninsula in the Kuban and subsequently retreated into the Crimea. As the Soviet tide rolled inexorably west, Hitler had to ask Antonescu once again to commit troops to the eastern front, to what would hopefully be quiet sectors like the Crimea. The Soviet offensive moved past the northern edge of

the Crimea at the end of October 1943. Trapped in the Crimea was General
Erwin Jaenecke's German Seventeenth Army. Included in the German Seventeenth Army's order of battle was the Romanian I Mountain Corps, with the
Romanian First, Second, and Third Mountain Divisions, the Romanian Cavalry Corps with the Romanian Second, Sixth, and Ninth Cavalry Divisions,
as well as the Romanian Tenth and Nineteenth Infantry Divisions. Altogether
about 130,000 German and 70,000 Romanian troops were cut off.[56]

As long as Odessa remained in German and Romanian hands, however,
keeping the forces in the Crimea supplied by sea using the short hop from
Odessa to Sevastopol was a reasonable possibility. Even before the stranding
of Jaenecke's forces in the Crimea, Hitler had forbidden their evacuation, as
the loss of the Crimea would place Romania's oil industry under the threat
of Soviet air attack. Although Antonescu had urged Hitler in the strongest
possible terms in February 1944 to abandon the Crimea, Hitler would not
budge. It is worth noting that as early as the fall of 1943 OKW had begun
planning for the occupation of both Romania and Hungary, in anticipation
of either or both defecting, although the plan for Romania's occupation was
eventually shelved.[57]

Once a Soviet thrust along the northern coast of the Black Sea pushed the
Axis forces out of Odessa, as well as most of Transnistria, the Crimea could
be supplied only by ship from Constanza. In addition, Antonescu renewed
his call for the evacuation of the Crimea, feeling that the troops presently
trapped might be better used along the line of the Dniestr. Antonescu was
joined in his call for evacuation by Jaenecke, who actually flew to Hitler's
headquarters to urge this course of action. An outraged Hitler fired Jaenecke
and replaced him with General Kurt Allmendinger.[58]

Changing generals availed no help for Hitler. By the end of April 1944 the
Axis positions in the Crimea had been forced back to the Sevastopol area.
The final Soviet attack to clear the peninsula began on 5 May 1944. Disaster
loomed almost immediately for the German Seventeenth Army. On 9 May
Hitler finally ordered the evacuation, but as was normally the case now, it
was too late. Because previously Hitler had forbidden any evacuation, no advance planning had been done for just that contingency. With Hitler's sudden
change of mind, however, German Navy Group South now had to hurriedly
cobble together an evacuation operation. Although the available German
and Romanian naval forces performed admirably under the circumstances,
and the Luftwaffe mounted yet another airlift operation, accomplishments
were limited. Figures vary considerably among sources, but the most reliable
estimate is that slightly fewer than 40,000 German and Romanian troops
were removed from the Crimea between the middle of April and 11 May

1944. The rest of the German Seventeenth Army was lost, with more than 31,000 German and 25,000 Romanian casualties, plus another 20,000 men missing.[59]

As the Germans were forced back across the Dniestr toward the Pruth River, Romanian field forces had to be integrated into the German defense. Army Group South was now divided into, rather optimistically, Army Group North Ukraine and Army Group South Ukraine. Hungarian forces were incorporated into Field Marshal Walter Model's Army Group North Ukraine, while in Romania the Romanian Third and Fourth Armies were subordinated to Field Marshal Ferdinand Schörner's Army Group South Ukraine.[60]

The Germans had to accomplish three tasks in regard to the Romanian forces involved in Romania's defense. The first was to help get the Romanian forces as well equipped as possible, the second was to train them, and the third was to use them as effectively as possible. As to equipping the Romanian forces now taking the field, the Germans clearly failed. As noted previously, by August 1944 the Romanian forces were badly underequipped, particularly in tanks and reconnaissance vehicles. Radios were also in short supply. The Germans did not help matters by attempting at times to deprive the Romanians of the equipment they did give them.[61]

Training also remained problematic. General Otto Wöhler, commander of an ad hoc unit called Army Group Wöhler, visited the Romanian First Panzer Division on 13 June 1944 to observe a training exercise in which the division would attack a newly won bridgehead and make a river crossing to establish a bridgehead. Wöhler's biggest criticism was the lack of an opposing force, which to his mind made the entire exercise unrealistic. Also noted was the lack of initiative on the part of NCOs and junior officers, a long-standing criticism of the Romanian army going back to early days of the DHM.[62]

Relations with the Romanians on the part of the army began to matter once again. The behavior of German units in Romania upon their retreat into Romania in May 1944 was initially harsh, not surprising given how inured German troops had become to brutality over the past four years. Angry Romanian protests did have an effect. On 5 June 1944 Wöhler visited the German Twenty-fourth Panzer Division, the Romanian Fourth Army headquarters, and the Romanian VII Corps. Wöhler emphasized to his German troops that relations with the Romanians must remain good. It was the duty of the German troops to be friendly. Thereafter, relations improved, and at times Romanian civilians would provide intelligence to German units on Soviet activities, such as an attempt to insert agents behind the German lines.[63]

The Romanian armies were positioned to hold their lines along rivers. The Romanian Fourth Army's line was along the Pruth River, while the Romanian Third Army guarded the line of the Dniestr down to the Black Sea. Between them was the rebuilt German Sixth Army, commanded by General Maximilian Fretter-Pico, while to the Romanian Fourth Army's left was Wöhler's German Eighth Army. As usual, the command arrangements were needlessly complex. Friessner was subordinate to OKH, while the DHM, which still exercised authority over some German units in Romania, answered to OKW.[64]

The front remained relatively quiet during the latter part of May, lasting through June and much of July 1944. Soviet attention was focused to a degree on Army Group North Ukraine, to draw German reserves to that area. The primary focus of Soviet operations in the early summer of 1944 was directed toward Army Group Center. As Operation *Bagration* proceeded to destroy Army Group Center and drive the German line back toward Poland, German resources were drawn from both Army Group North Ukraine and South Ukraine to shore up the crumbling German situation in Poland. As *Bagration* wound down, the Soviets began to shift their resources to the southern sectors of the front. By early August 1944, the Soviets were ready to launch a massive offensive aimed at destroying the Romanian armies and the German Sixth Army, followed by a drive on Ploesti and Bucharest.[65]

Throughout July, the Romanians had been putting out peace feelers to the Soviets, an activity of which the Germans were well aware. With his paranoia rising to new levels, especially after the failed assassination plot of 20 July 1944, Hitler summoned Antonescu to what would be their last meeting at Rastenburg on 6 August 1944. Present also were Keitel and Heinz Guderian, the chief of the Army General Staff. During the acrimonious encounter, marked by Antonescu and Guderian conversing in French, Hitler demanded a pledge from Antonescu to fight on at Germany's side until the end. For his part, Antonescu demanded more German resources to defend Romania, rather bluntly reminding Hitler that his previous promises in such cases as the Crimea had proved worthless. Antonescu also suggested a withdrawal to better defensive positions in the Carpathian Mountains. In light of Germany's inability to guarantee Romania's territorial integrity to any meaningful degree, Antonescu now felt that he had the legal grounds on which to base a break with Germany, if the moment presented itself. For his part, Hitler interpreted Antonescu's proposed withdrawal as a prelude to some sort of Romanian treachery.[66]

This possibility very quickly became a reality. The Soviets launched their offensive on 20 August 1944 and scored a major breakthrough against the

Romanians at Jassy. Antonescu, whose political position had been weakened by the Stalingrad disaster, was further endangered by his relationship with the Romanian royal family, which had deteriorated steadily from the summer of 1943 on, and by rising anti-German sentiment in the Romanian officer corps. On 23 August 1944 Antonescu's enemies struck. King Michael dismissed Antonescu and had him arrested, along with two of his ministers. Romania was now out of the Axis; it was only a matter of time before the new Romanian government would side with the Allies.[67] Germany's most important ally in its war against the Soviet Union and in its carrying out the Holocaust, as well as its principal source of oil, had been knocked out of the war.

The last German ally to be dealt with is Hungary. The war, never entirely popular in Hungary, became extremely unpopular there after Stalingrad. German reports toward the conduct of the Romanians were generally negative, but those dealing with the Hungarians were positively scathing. This extended all the way to Hitler, who made his disgust with the Hungarians plain during his meeting with Horthy on 18 April 1943.[68]

The Hungarians began rebuilding their armed forces after the completion of the withdrawal by the remnants of the Hungarian Second Army in early 1943. It was slow going, however, in every respect. The projected reorganization, which called for the light divisions to become regular infantry divisions, proceeded slowly, as did the manning of these units. By October 1943 only four divisions had been brought back to full strength. Given these problems, it is not surprising that when Hitler asked for several Hungarian divisions to go to the Balkans after Italy's defection, Horthy refused.[69]

The equipment situation was every bit as bad as the manpower situation. The Stalingrad campaign had resulted in huge losses of equipment, which were not easily replaced. By 6 June 1944 the Hungarian army possessed a mere 336,000 rifles, and 397 light and heavy artillery pieces. The hopelessly obsolete Pz 38 was still in service, although in small numbers. Hungary remained dependent on Germany for deliveries of requisite arms and equipment. According to an agreement reached between the respective general staffs in June 1944, the Germans would provide Hungary with up to 900 light and heavy machine guns, 35 antitank guns (75mm), and 25 tank destroyers per month. As usual, however, actual delivery of these items was another matter. The totals often fell short or were diverted into German hands.[70] Thus, as the Soviet tide began to lap against the borders of both Romania and Hungary, the Hungarian army was hardly in a condition to keep the Soviets out.

Relations between the two governments were in about the same state as the Hungarian army. Stung by Italy's defection and aware of Hungarian peace feelers to the west, Hitler summoned Horthy to Klessheim yet again on 18 March 1944. In a stormy meeting, Hitler immediately accused Hungary of trying to make a separate peace and told Horthy of his plan to send troops into Hungary immediately. Horthy's refusal brought forth a threat against his family, a move that prompted him to storm out of the room, declaring that he would resign. Hitler entreated Horthy to return and eventually successfully bullied him into installing a new government that contained members of Hungary's fascist movement, Ferenc Szalasi's Arrow Cross Party. Kállay was replaced as prime minister by the more ideologically compatible Döme Sztójay. While this was going on, orders went out for the waiting German forces to occupy Hungary. By the end of 19 March 1944, Hungary was occupied by the Germans.[71]

Politically, the occupation of Hungary marked the end of Hungary as a member of the Axis. Thereafter Horthy and his family remained virtual prisoners of the Germans, who effectively controlled the Sztójay government. By 15 October 1944 Horthy was able, despite the German presence, to get an agreement with the Soviets by which Hungary would leave the war. After Horthy dropped this news on the German ambassador, Edmund Veesenmeyer, Hitler struck back immediately by having Otto Skozeny abduct Horthy's son Niklas and send him to Mauthausen. The admiral himself was arrested, and a puppet government under Szalasi was installed in Budapest.[72]

The occupation of Hungary also resulted in one of the most tragic episodes of the Holocaust, namely, the destruction of Hungarian Jewry. Hungarian treatment of Jews had long been irksome to the Germans, as was Horthy's refusal to undertake harsher measures against Hungary's Jews.[73] As the course of events pointed toward a German occupation of Hungary, the Germans cast a murderous eye toward Hungary's Jews. Even before entering Hungary, German officers were instructed to make absolutely clear to Hungarians how great a "danger" the Jews were. Once the Germans effectively seized Hungary, the fate of Hungarian Jewry, marked by the infamous activities of Adolf Eichmann, was sealed. That oft-told and tragic tale, however, is beyond the scope of the present work.[74]

During the period from the spring of 1944 until the end of the war, the Germans worked with Hungarian forces. The cooperation, however, was not very successful. Theoretically, the Hungarian army could field fifteen divisions and two brigades, plus a number of army-level artillery battalions. Reality was quite different. Equipment stocks were low, and Hungarian ammunition production capacity was limited. Matters were not helped by the fact that, as noted previously, the Germans took equipment intended for Hungary. The Germans also took a healthy percentage of some types of

Hungarian ammunition production, such as 88mm and 40mm shells. To make the best possible use of Hungarian manpower, the Germans demanded that once the Hungarian army had mobilized its fifteen divisions, no further units be created. Instead, the available manpower would be used to furnish the existing divisions with a steady supply of personnel. German commanders would have considerable influence in the appointment of officers.[75]

In the end, none of this mattered. Hungarian units were no match for the overwhelming superiority of the Red Army. Morale, not good to begin with after the German occupation of March 1944, collapsed after the 15 October 1944 coup. By 10 November 1944 the commander of Army Group South, General Johannes Friessner, reported that the Hungarian army was neither able nor willing to fight. Although some Hungarian units would be involved in the siege of Budapest, by that time Hungary's membership in the Axis was long over.[76]

The period between May 1943 and November 1944 exposed all the flaws inherent in Germany's conduct of coalition warfare. Hitler's decision to reinforce the Tunisian bridgehead in North Africa served ultimately to deprive the Axis of both German and Italian assets that would have been much better employed in the defense of Sicily and the Italian mainland. Germany also suffered the long consequences of Mussolini's disastrous invasion of Greece, as the Italian collapse forced Germany to devote scarce resources to replace Italian forces in the Balkans.

Germany's failure in regard to Italy, Romania, and Hungary in this period was largely technological and economic. The service ministries, the controlling agencies regarding manufacturing patents, would only part with patents that would allow Italian, Romanian, and Hungarian plants to make German equipment at prices they could not afford.[77] This proved a critical waste of productive capacity and served only to increase the strain on German industry, already incapable of meeting the needs of the Wehrmacht.

Strategically, all of Hitler's allies saw the situation more clearly than Hitler did, but at the same time many of them also misjudged the situation. Only Finland was able to come close to getting out of the war on terms that could be described as relatively benign. The Ryti government's earlier ability to evade full membership in the Axis allowed Mannerheim the maneuvering room to withdraw from the war without any major reactions from the Germans, who lacked the ability to undertake retaliatory measures anyway.

The Italians, Romanians, and Hungarians did not have that same luxury. The Hungarians were caught in a particularly unfortunate situation. Of all the participants on the Axis side, the Hungarians were the most unwilling. Consistent Hungarian opposition to German barbarity in the Soviet Union and the Balkans only earned German suspicion, and at the instant of Italy's defection, German planning began almost immediately for an occupation of Hungary.[78]

Although both Mussolini and Antonescu urged Hitler to make peace, their urging was for a peace that would be only to their benefit. Mussolini urged a separate peace with Stalin, which would allow Germany to concentrate against the Anglo-Americans, while Antonescu wanted a peace with the Anglo-Americans, thus freeing up German resources against the Soviets.[79] These pleas by both Antonescu and Mussolini, however, had a degree of naïveté about them. Both seemed oblivious to the Allied policy of unconditional surrender, announced at the Casablanca meeting of January 1943. In addition, both ought to have realized that a separate peace would be unlikely, given the catalog of barbarity compiled by the Germans (and the Romanians), especially in the Soviet Union during their occupation of Soviet territory. Finally, Mussolini and Antonescu generally thought more in terms of standard international power politics rather than the kind of nihilistic ideological and racial struggle envisioned and practiced by Hitler.

Benjamin Franklin once cautioned his fellow leaders during the American Revolution that if they did not hang together, surely they would all hang separately. Militarily, the Axis was in effect hanged together during the period from November 1942 to May 1943. After that, politically they all hung separately (in one case literally), one dictator at a time. The Axis was dead.

10

Germany and Coalition Warfare
Some Concluding Remarks

In a coalition war it comes to learn objectively about the people and the instrument of war of the allies and to create a *basis of trust* from this. We cannot repeat the mistakes we made in 1914/18 in regard to our former ally, Austria-Hungary.   DHM Handbook, 23 September 1942[1]

The German command expected the Italian divisions to perform the same as German divisions. They equated division for division. This did not take into account the fact that Italian divisions were much smaller, poorly armed and equipped, poorly trained and poorly led.   Enno von Rintelen, 1952[2]

IN A POSTWAR MANUSCRIPT, Burkhardt Müller-Hillebrand asserted that at least in terms of liaison with the armies of its allies, Germany waged coalition warfare effectively. Jürgen Förster, on the other end of the spectrum, argued that the Axis was "hardly a coalition at all."[3] Anyone who has read the preceding pages with even minimal care would correctly conclude that this study sides much more with Förster's argument than with Müller-Hillebrand's.

Nevertheless, several questions remain unresolved. That the German military establishment was ultimately ineffective in waging coalition warfare is beyond dispute, but the preceding examination leads to a slightly more nuanced conclusion. That would be that each service conducted coalition warfare a little differently from its sister services.

The Luftwaffe was able to cooperate effectively to a degree with its Italian and Romanian counterparts in an operational sense. In the Mediterranean, the Luftwaffe and the Regia Aeronautica reached reasonable agreements to divide up the airspace over the theater. The two air forces did at times fly joint strikes against Malta and undertook convoy escort as well. They were able to do this despite the self-imposed limitation of a lack of a unified command structure.[4] The DLM in Romania worked well enough with the Romanian air force to turn Ploesti into one of the toughest targets in Europe, employing a variety of active and passive measures that served to take a heavy toll of attacking aircraft while minimizing the extent of damage suffered.[5]

Where the Luftwaffe failed miserably was in the sharing of technology, particularly in the case of aircraft in general, and especially aircraft engines. In the case of the Italians, the failure to develop a suitable engine for a dive-bomber effectively wrecked the ability of the Regia Aeronautica to field an adequate dive-bomber. Although German-manufactured engines might have solved the problem, the practice of mating German engines with Italian airframes did not even begin in a serious way until 1943, much too late in the war to make a difference. When it came to selling German aircraft to Italy, often older models were sold, especially early in the war. In the fall of 1940, when the German Air Ministry sold Ju 87 dive-bombers to the Italians, they sold only the Ju 87B, at that time an older model that was being phased out of the German inventory. The idea of selling modern aircraft to the Italians came up only in 1943, and by then German production could not keep pace even with German losses, let alone Italian, Romanian, or Hungarian needs. One Luftwaffe liaison officer certainly hit the mark when he said, "The Italians were certainly promised much, but have received only a little."[6] Likewise, the Germans were equally parsimonious with radar equipment, at least as far as the Italians were concerned. It was probably due only to the vital importance of Ploesti that the Luftwaffe was more willing to dispatch radar equipment to Romania, although that material was under the control of the DLM.[7]

Of all the German services, the navy was probably the most successful in its endeavors regarding coalition warfare. To be sure, the cooperation between German and Italian submarines was not nearly as effective as it could have been, although, as pointed out earlier, even a limited contribution by the Italian forces in the Caribbean furthered Dönitz's strategy. For antisubmarine warfare in both the Mediterranean and the Black Sea, the German navy's willingness to equip Italian MAS boats with German sonar made both bodies of water very dangerous for British and Soviet submarines. The worth of these craft was shown in the German navy's desire to introduce them to the Caspian Sea first once the coast had been reached.[8]

The army clearly took the prize when it came to failure in coalition warfare. The War Ministry mirrored the practices of the Air Ministry when it came to either providing equipment to Germany's allies or providing them licenses needed to manufacture the equipment on their own. The constant promises of equipment made by Hitler and his top subordinates to Germany's allies rarely matched actual deliveries. The extortive practices of the War Ministry when it came to selling patents and licenses virtually ensured that the Romanian, Hungarian, Italian, and Finnish armies would remain hopelessly outclassed in terms of weapons and equipment against their Soviet opponents.[9]

In dealing with their allies in an operational or tactical setting, German liaison officers often came across as arrogant, and their advice frequently was regarded as unwanted interference. Allied armies were often subjected to discrimination at the hands of the German supply services, even when times were relatively good. In times of crisis, German troops often stole equipment from their allies or diverted equipment and weapons meant for their allies into German hands.[10]

The employment of the allied armies by the Germans for Operation *Barbarossa* was appropriate to their capabilities and limitations but was based on the expectation that the campaign would be a short one. In 1941 the Finns, Romanians, and even the Hungarians had compelling reasons to participate in the war against the Soviet Union. The failure of the invasion left the Germans in a difficult situation with regard to their allies. Although the Romanians, Finns, Hungarians, and Italians had performed reasonably well in 1941, losses had been heavy in both men and equipment. While the Finns were able to avoid having to commit large forces to combat in 1942, the Italians sent large forces thanks to a foolish decision by Mussolini. The Hungarians and Romanians ended up having to play a major role in the campaign from the start. The forces that Romania and Hungary committed to the eastern front in 1942 had significant deficiencies in men, morale, and equipment, difficulties of which the Germans were well aware. All these factors came back to haunt the Germans during the Soviet winter offensive at Stalingrad.[11]

Perhaps the only bright spot in the German army's conduct of coalition warfare was Rommel's campaigns in North Africa. The circumstances that obtained in North Africa often produced lengthy lulls between operations, which allowed Rommel to undertake a fair amount of training for both his German and his Italian units. Measures such as the creation of a German-Italian military dictionary promoted better communication. Finally, the scale of the forces there did not produce a demand for interpreters that simply overwhelmed the ability of the German army to supply them.[12] This, however, was much more the exception than the rule. In the end Rommel, perhaps the most successful of Germany's field commanders in coalition warfare, did not come close to being the equal of a Mackensen.

Germany's conduct of coalition warfare was clearly the worst at the strategic level. To be sure, Hitler did have to deal with some situations that the Allies never faced. The tension between Romania and Hungary, for example, always threatening to break out into full-scale war, remained a problem for Hitler that defied any simple long-term solution. The only thing that eventually quelled the deadly squabbling between Romania and Hungary was the prospect of a Soviet invasion, which appeared as a distinct possibility initially in October 1943.[13]

Far more of Germany's problems in conducting coalition warfare at the strategic level were of its own making. Hitler and his military chiefs repeated the mistake made by the German military in World War I, namely, the failure to create some kind of unified command organization that would involve all the services and the military establishments of Germany's allies. There was no Axis equivalent to the Allied Combined Chiefs of Staff. Nor was there an Axis equivalent to a Teheran or Yalta meeting. Hitler's conduct of the war proceeded along the same course as his prewar foreign policy, namely, as a series of bilateral relationships.[14]

The lack of a unified command system virtually ensured that Germany and its allies would often work at cross-purposes. The best example of this was clearly the "parallel war" conducted by Germany and Italy through-out much of 1940 and 1941. A unified command organization might have prevented disasters such as those suffered by the Italians in North Africa and Greece in the late fall and early winter of 1940–1941. As it existed, the Axis command setup guaranteed a situation where lines of command would be needlessly confused and complex. Hitler made it even more so when he promoted Rommel to field marshal, thus giving Rommel the means to circumvent Kesselring when he saw fit. The only time in the war when the Germans and Italians were able to create a functional command system was in North Africa, but far too late in the campaign to make any difference. Once the Axis forces in North Africa were destroyed, the Germans and Italians immediately went back to the old, inefficient way of doing things.[15]

The command system in the east was marred as well by necessary complexity. The Romanians, Hungarians, Italians, and Finns all had their own separate chains of command. The Finns, in particular, because of their position, were able to really conduct parallel war. In addition, the Germans' practice of selling various types of foreign equipment to their allies, plus their own procurement practices, ensured a lack of standardization sufficient to make logistics an even worse nightmare than it already was. As complicated as the command system was in 1941, it was relatively effective. A slightly simplified command arrangement in 1942 proved far less efficient, especially as the Axis armies advanced in diverging directions.

The general differences in the nature of strategic goals between Germany and its allies also created problems. Germany's goals in fighting the war were clearly set by Hitler's ideology more than anything else. Hitler embarked on the invasion of the Soviet Union for ideological reasons as much as for economic, military, and political purposes. The war of annihilation against

Bolshevism was certainly regarded as a "crusade" by Hitler and his lieuten-
ants. His allies, however, went to war for reasons related much more to standard power politics rather than ideology. Mussolini, Antonescu, Horthy, and
Ryti were all far more interested in obtaining territorial adjustments than
in eradicating whole races. This was clearly illustrated when Mussolini and
Antonescu, respectively, pleaded with Hitler to make a separate peace, and
when Hitler rejected these suggestions. Perhaps the only ally that cooperated
closely with Germany in its policies in the east was Romania. Italian and
Hungarian troops especially were utterly appalled by German behavior in
the Soviet Union. German attempts to indoctrinate the soldiers of their allies
failed completely.[16]

German strategic thinking, such as it was, was generally based on wars
being short. This was certainly the case in *Barbarossa*. In 1941, the Romanian, Hungarian, and Finnish armies possessed equipment of sufficient
modernity to allow them to fight against the Soviets on close but not quite
equal terms. By late 1942, however, this disparity had grown to such proportions that the Romanians, Hungarians, and Italians were all at a hopeless
disadvantage against the Soviets. Given that the Germans were well aware
of this at every level, to include Hitler, any realistic assessment of the state
of the Romanian, Hungarian, and Italian forces should have forced Hitler
and the German General Staff to recast their strategic plans to objectives that
were much less grandiose.[17]

To be sure, Hitler was not alone in poor strategic decision making. Mussolini's record in this realm of warfare was equally abysmal, especially his insistence on committing the bulk of Italy's forces to the eastern front in 1942.
While the men there could make little if any difference in the outcome of
the campaign, the lavish degree of equipment, by Italian standards, ensured
that the majority of the Italian forces in North Africa would be fighting with
gross shortages of transport, a crucial element in desert warfare.[18]

That Germany compiled a poor record in conducting coalition warfare at
the strategic level over two world wars, and especially in the Second World
War, is indisputable. It is also clear that—for a number of reasons—the
individual services themselves were wildly uneven in their interactions with
their respective Romanian, Hungarian, Italian, and Finnish counterparts.

The German military, especially during Hans von Seeckt's tenure as chief
of the Reichswehr, devoted a great deal of time to the study of World War
I in its various facets. One of these was not, apparently, coalition warfare.
This was especially odd, considering Seeckt's experience with the Austro-
Hungarian army in World War I. This lack of interest was manifested in the

relative absence of articles on the subject in German professional military periodicals between the wars, with the exception of those by Georg Wetzell.

German professional military education failed to fill this gap as well. The curriculum of the Kriegsakademie was focused entirely at the tactical and operational levels of war. Coalition warfare, and even joint operations, would have been covered in the curriculum of the Wehrmachtakademie, an institution created for the education of senior officers. The school, however, beset by bureaucratic opposition particularly on the part of Göring and Hitler, and the death of its chief supporter, Luftwaffe general Walter Wever, proved a stillborn experiment.[19]

Another important aspect of this question revolves around Hitler and the German military leadership. One thing that Hitler and his principal military advisers shared was that they were all veterans of the western front in World War I. Hitler spent his entire service in the war in France, as did Keitel. Alfred Jodl and Halder did do short tours in the east but served the rest of the time on the western front. Only Jodl worked with any of Germany's allies in World War I, and that was only for a short time.[20] In short, none of these men had much experience in having to deal with allies.

Germany's failure to deal successfully with its allies was also reflective of another defect, namely, the inability of the services to deal with each other. In both world wars the German record in being able to mount successful joint operations could only be described as abysmal. The individual services were often at odds with each other, in both peace and war. The kind of strategic culture within the Wehrmacht may well have promoted Germany's failure in coalition warfare.[21]

Ultimately, the German failure in coalition warfare in World War II was illustrative of Germany's conduct of the war in general. At the lower levels of warfare, the German military continued to perform with skill throughout the war. At the higher levels of war, however, especially strategy, where coalition warfare can play such an important part, Germany's military and political leadership failed utterly. In World War II Hitler and his military leaders were able to repeat almost every mistake made by their Wilhelmine predecessors, in some cases for the same reasons. For that, we should be grateful.

NOTES

Introduction

1. Daniel J. Hughes, ed., *Moltke on the Art of War: Selected Writings* (Novato, Calif.: Presidio Press, 1993), pp. 36–37.

2. For an interesting collection of essays on this subject, see George J. Andreopoulous and Harold E. Selesky, eds., *The Aftermath of Defeat: Societies, Armed Forces and the Challenge of Recovery* (New Haven, Conn.: Yale University Press, 1994). For a perceptive general work on military failure, see Eliot A. Cohen and John Gooch, *Military Misfortunes: The Anatomy of Failure in War* (New York: Vintage Books, 1990).

3. Mark Axworthy, Cornel Scafes, and Craciunoiu, *Third Axis/Fourth Ally: Romanian Armed Forces in the European War, 1941–1945* (London: Arms and Armour, 1995).

4. James J. Sadkovich, "German Military Incompetence through Italian Eyes," *War in History* 1, no. 1 (March 1994): 39–62; Brian R. Sullivan, "The Italian Armed Forces, 1918–1940," in *Military Effectiveness,* ed. Allen R. Millett and Williamson Murray (Boston: Allen and Unwin, 1988), vol. 2, pp. 169–217; MacGregor Knox, *Mussolini Unleashed, 1939–1941: Politics and Strategy in Fascist Italy's Last War* (New York: Cambridge University Press, 1982); and Lucio Ceva, *Le forze armate* (Torino: UTET, 1981).

5. Earl F. Ziemke, *Stalingrad to Berlin: The German Defeat in the East* (Washington, D.C.: U.S. Army, 1968), p. 59; Richard L. DiNardo, "The Dysfunctional Coalition: The Axis Powers and the Eastern Front in World War II," *Journal of Military History* 60, no. 4 (October 1996): 721–722; and Richard L. DiNardo and Daniel J. Hughes, "Germany and Coalition Warfare in the World Wars: A Comparative Study," *War in History* 8, no. 2 (April 2001): 166–190.

6. The best study is Gerhard L. Weinberg, *The Foreign Policy of Hitler's Germany,* 2 vols. (Chicago: University of Chicago Press, 1970–1980). Where necessary, diplomacy is also covered in Weinberg, *A World at Arms: A Global History of World War II* (New York: Cambridge University Press, 1994); and Norman J. W. Goda, *Tomorrow the World: Hitler, Northwest Africa and the Path toward America* (College Station: Texas A&M University Press, 1998). See also Norman Rich, *Hitler's War Aims,* 2 vols. (New York: Norton, 1973–1974).

7. The best study of the Blue Division is still Gerald R. Kleinfeld and Lewis A. Tambs, *Hitler's Spanish Legion: The Blue Division in Russia* (Carbondale: Southern Illinois University Press, 1979).

8. See, for example, United States State Department, *Documents on German Foreign Policy 1918–1945* (Washington, D.C.: Government Printing Office, 1949–1956), series D, vol. 12, no. 660, pp. 1066–1069 (hereafter cited as *DGFP;* unless otherwise noted, all references to *DGFP* will be from series D).

9. See, for examples, the German 13th Liaison Headquarters, Final Report of the German 13th Liaison Headquarters, 29 October 1941, National Archives

Records Administration Microfilm Series T-501, roll 275, frame 000706 (hereafter cited as NARA T-501/275/000706); and German Liaison Officer to the Italian Fifth Air Fleet in North Africa and to the Commanding General of the X Air Corps, 19 May 1941, File RL 2 II/38, Bundesarchiv-Militärarchiv, Freiburg-im-Breisgau, Germany (hereafter cited as BA-MA RL 2 II/38).

10. There has been a veritable explosion of literature on this subject. Some recent works include James S. Corum, *The Roots of Blitzkrieg: Hans von Seeckt and German Military Reform* (Lawrence: University Press of Kansas, 1992), pp. 122–143; Williamson Murray, *The Change in the European Balance of Power, 1938–1939: The Path to Ruin* (Princeton, N.J.: Princeton University Press, 1984), pp. 32–45; Richard L. DiNardo, "German Armor Doctrine: Correcting the Myths," *War in History* 3 (November 1996): 384–397; and James S. Corum, *The Luftwaffe: Creating the Operational Air War, 1918–1940* (Lawrence: University Press of Kansas, 1997), pp. 15–48, 124–154.

1. Prussia, Germany, and Coalition War

1. Carl von Clausewitz, *On War*, ed. and trans. Michael Howard and Peter Paret (Princeton, N.J.: Princeton University Press, 1984), p. 603.

2. Field Marshal Helmuth Graf von Moltke, *Ausgewählte Werke*, ed. F. von Schmerfeld (Berlin: Reimar Hobbing, 1925), vol. 1, p. 44.

3. Karl Graf von Kaganeck Diary, 4 August 1914, BA-MA MSg 1/1914.

4. Hans von Seeckt, Report on the KuK Army with Organizational Plans for the KuK Armies, ca. December 1917, Nachlass Seeckt, BA-MA N 247/32.

5. Christopher Duffy, *The Military Life of Frederick the Great* (New York: Hippocrene Books, 1986), p. 83.

6. Christopher Duffy, *The Army of Frederick the Great* (New York: Hippocrene Books, 1974), p. 188; Duffy, *Military Life of Frederick the Great*, p. 191; and Dennis E. Showalter, *The Wars of Frederick the Great* (New York: Longman's, 1996), p. 250.

7. Jay Luvaas, ed. and trans., *Frederick the Great on the Art of War* (New York: Free Press, 1966), p. 11.

8. Gunther E. Rothenberg, *The Art of Warfare in the Age of Napoleon* (Bloomington: Indiana University Press, 1978), p. 47.

9. A dated, if still reasonably good, study of the Jena campaign is F. Loraine Petre, *Napoleon's Conquest of Prussia—1806* (1907; repr., New York: Hippocrene Books, 1977).

10. Michael V. Leggiere, *Napoleon and Berlin: The Franco-Prussian War in North Germany, 1813* (Norman: University of Oklahoma Press, 2002), p. 41; and Rothenberg, *Art of Warfare in the Age of Napoleon*, p. 55.

11. Leggiere, *Napoleon and Berlin*, p. 51.

12. Rothenberg, *Art of Warfare in the Age of Napoleon*, p. 56; and Leggiere, *Napoleon and Berlin*, pp. 127–129.

13. See F. Loraine Petre, *Napoleon's Last Campaign in Germany—1813* (1912; repr., New York: Hippocrene Books, 1974). Some interesting details are provided in Gordon A. Craig, "Problems of Coalition Warfare: The Military Alliance against Napoleon, 1813–1814," in *The Harmon Memorial Lectures in Military History*

1959–1987, ed. Lieutenant Colonel Harry R. Borowski (Washington, D.C.: Office of Air Force History, 1988), pp. 325–346.

14. Geoffrey Wawro, *The Austro-Prussian War: Austria's War with Prussia and Italy in 1866* (New York: Cambridge University Press, 1996), p. 92.

15. Emperor Friedrich III, *Das Kriegstagebuch von 1870–1871,* ed. Heinrich O. Meissner (Berlin: K. S. Kohler, 1926), p. 111; and Dennis E. Showalter, *The Wars of German Unification* (London: Arnold, 2004), p. 254.

16. General Georg Wetzell, "Der Bündniskrieg," *Militär Wochenblatt* 122, no. 14 (2 October 1937): 840; and Graydon A. Tunstall Jr., *Planning for War against Russia and Serbia* (Boulder, Colo.: Social Science Monographs, 1993), p. 31.

17. Gunther E. Rothenberg, "Moltke, Schlieffen, and the Doctrine of Strategic Envelopment," in *Makers of Modern Strategy,* ed. Peter Paret (Princeton, N.J.: Princeton University Press, 1986), p. 308. See also Eberhard Kessel, *Moltke* (Stuttgart: K. F. Koehler, 1957), pp. 703–729.

18. In 1888 Waldersee urged a preemptive war against Russia, which Bismarck opposed. Gerhard Ritter, *The Schlieffen Plan: Critique of a Myth* (New York: Praeger, 1958), pp. 21–22.

19. Compare Antoine Henri Baron Jomini, *The Art of War* (Philadelphia: Lippincott, 1862), pp. 51–54, and Clausewitz, *On War,* pp. 80–81. See also Showalter, *Wars of German Unification,* pp. 199–200; Wetzell, "Der Bündniskrieg," p. 840; and Tunstall, *Planning for War against Russia and Serbia,* p. 28.

20. Gerhard Ritter, *The Sword and the Scepter: The Problem of Militarism in Germany* (Coral Gables, Fla.: University of Miami Press, 1968–1972), vol. 2, p. 239.

21. Dennis E. Showalter, *Tannenberg: Clash of Empires, 1914* (Dulles, Va.: Brassey's, 2004), pp. 34–35; and Arden Bucholz, *Moltke, Schlieffen, and Prussian War Planning* (Oxford: Berg, 1993), pp. 192–195.

22. Holger H. Herwig, *The First World War: Germany and Austria-Hungary 1914–1918* (London: Arnold, 1997), p. 50; Gunther E. Rothenberg, *The Army of Francis Joseph* (West Lafayette, Ind.: Purdue University Press, 1976), p. 175; Tunstall, *Planning for War against Russia and Serbia,* p. 46; DiNardo and Hughes, "Germany and Coalition Warfare in the World Wars," p. 168; Ritter, *Sword and the Scepter,* vol. 2, p. 240; and Annika Mombauer, *Helmuth von Moltke and the Origins of the First World War* (New York: Cambridge University Press, 2001), p. 82. See also Lothar Höbelt, "Schlieffen, Beck, Potiorek und das Ende der gemeinsam deutsch-österreichisch-ungarischen Aufmarschpläne im Osten," *Militärgeschichtliche Mitteilungen,* no. 36 (February 1984): 7–30. A rather revisionist view of Schlieffen's ideas is debated in Terence Zuber, "The Schlieffen Plan Reconsidered," *War in History* 6, no. 3 (July 1999): 262–305; and Terence M. Holmes, "The Reluctant March on Paris: A Reply to Terence Zuber's 'The Schlieffen Plan Reconsidered,'" *War in History* 8, no. 2 (April 2001): 208–232. Zuber's ideas are more fully developed in Zuber, *Inventing the Schlieffen Plan: German War Planning, 1871–1914* (Oxford: Oxford University Press, 2002).

23. Colonel General Helmuth von Moltke, *Erinnerungen-Briefe-Dokumente 1877–1916,* ed. Eliza von Moltke (Stuttgart: Der Kommende Tag, 1922), p. 252; and Mombauer, *Helmuth von Moltke and the Origins of the First World War,* p. 113.

24. Ritter, *Sword and the Scepter*, vol. 2, p. 243. Moltke did suggest to the Austrians that it might be wise for them to postpone any major action against Serbia until the Russian threat had been eliminated. Field Marshal Franz Baron Conrad von Hötzendorf, *Aus Meiner Dienstzeit 1906–1918*, 6th ed. (Vienna: Rikola Verlag, 1921–1925), vol. 1, pp. 404–405; and Lawrence Sondhaus, *Franz Conrad von Hötzendorf: Architect of the Apocalypse* (Boston: Humanities Press, 2000), p. 100.

25. Tunstall, *Planning for War against Russia and Serbia*, p. 106; Sondhaus, *Franz Conrad von Hötzendorf*, p. 125; and Istvan Deak, *Beyond Nationalism: A Social and Political History of the Habsburg Officer Corps* (New York: Oxford University Press, 1990), pp. 144–145.

26. Conrad, *Aus Meiner Dienstzeit*, vol. 3, p. 368. The emperor was also extensively involved in the cover-up of Redl's activities. Deak, *Beyond Nationalism*, p. 145. See also Tunstall, *Planning for War against Russia and Serbia*, p. 106; and Herwig, *First World War*, pp. 65, 74. The most comprehensive study of the Redl affair is Georg Markus, *Der Fall Redl* (Vienna: Amalthea Verlag, 1984).

27. Ritter, *Sword and the Scepter*, vol. 2, pp. 245–246; Tunstall, *Planning for War against Russia and Serbia*, p. 86; and Gerhard Seyfert, *Die militärischen Beziehungen und Vereinbarungen zwischen dem deutschen und dem österreichischen Generalstab vor und bei Beginn des Weltkrieges* (Leipzig: J. Moltzen, 1934), pp. 53–61. See also Conrad, *Aus Meiner Dienstzeit*, vol. 1, pp. 379–393, 403–404, 631–634; and Hew Strachan, *The First World War*, vol. 1, *To Arms* (Oxford: Oxford University Press, 2001), p. 290.

28. Kessel, *Moltke*, p. 704; and Wetzell, "Der Bündniskrieg," p. 840.

29. Bucholz, *Moltke, Schlieffen, and Prussian War Planning*, p. 107; and Moltke, *Erinnerungen-Briefe-Dokumente*, p. 8.

30. Ritter, *Schlieffen Plan*, p. 170; and Holger Herwig, "Strategic Uncertainties of a Nation-State: Prussia-Germany, 1871–1918," in *The Making of Strategy: Rulers, States, and War*, ed. Williamson Murray, MacGregor Knox, and Alvin Bernstein (New York: Cambridge University Press, 1994), p. 263.

31. Brian R. Sullivan, "The Strategy of the Decisive Weight: Italy, 1882–1922," in *Making of Strategy*, pp. 322, 329. For German reaction to Pollio's death, see Gunther Kronenbitter, "Die Macht der Illusionen. Julikrise und Kriegsausbruch 1914 aus der Sicht des deutschen Militärattachés in Wien," *Militärgeschichtliche Mitteilungen* 57, no. 2 (1998): 519, 534. For a slightly different view, see Mombauer, *Helmuth von Moltke and the Origins of the First World War*, pp. 169–170.

32. Conrad, *Aus Meiner Dienstzeit*, vol. 4, pp. 193–194; Moltke, *Erinnerungen-Briefe-Dokumente*, p. 9; and Showalter, *Tannenberg*, pp. 67–68.

33. Showalter, *Tannenberg*, p. 68; Conrad, *Aus Meiner Dienstzeit*, vol. 3, pp. 669–670. Kaganeck assured Conrad that the prospect of French neutrality in the crisis was quite "out of the question." Kronenbitter, "Die Macht der Illusionen," p. 538.

34. Kronenbitter, "Die Macht der Illusionen," p. 542; and Kaganeck Diary, 4 August 1914, BA-MA MSg 1/1914.

35. Count Josef von Stürgkh, *Im deutschen Grossen Hauptquartier* (Leipzig: Paul List Verlag, 1921), p. 14.

36. Kaganeck Diary, 6 August 1914, BA-MA MSg 1/1914. For the Austrian side of the 1914 campaign, see Norman Stone, *The Eastern Front 1914–1917* (New York:

Scribner's, 1975), pp. 70–91; Herwig, *First World War,* pp. 87–96; Rothenberg, *Army of Francis Joseph,* pp. 172–181; Sondhaus, *Franz Conrad von Hötzendorf,* pp. 145–147; and Gary W. Shanafelt, *The Secret Enemy: Austria-Hungary and the German Alliance, 1914–1918* (Boulder, Colo.: East European Monographs, 1985), pp. 42–43. Kaganeck was also rather surprised by the fact that the Austrians allowed the Russian ambassador to stay in Vienna for several days after war was declared. Kaganeck Diary, 4 August 1914, BA-MA MSg 1/1914.

37. Conrad later claimed that he thought a unified command unnecessary. Conrad, *Aus Meiner Dienstzeit,* vol. 4, p. 259.

38. Stürgkh, *Im deutschen Grossen Hauptquartier,* p. 40; and Holger Afflerbach, *Falkenhayn: Politisches Denken und Handeln im Kaiserreich* (Munich: R. Oldenbourg, 1996), p. 250.

39. August von Cramon, *Unser Österreichisch-Ungarischer Bundesgenosse im Weltkrieg. Erinnerungen aus meiner vierjahrigen Tatigkeit als bevollmachtiger deutscher General beim KuK Armeeoberkommando* (Berlin: E. S. Mittler und Sohn, 1922), pp. 13–14; General Erich von Falkenhayn, *The German General Staff and Its Decisions 1914–1916* (New York: Dodd, Mead, 1922), p. 96; Rothenberg, *Army of Francis Joseph,* p. 186; and Stone, *Eastern Front,* p. 128.

40. Mackensen owed his selection to the position to some close back-channel cooperation between Falkenhayn and Seeckt, who then became Mackensen's chief of staff. Theo Schwarzmüller, *Zwischen Kaiser und Führer. Generalfeldmarschall August von Mackensen: Eine Politische Biographie* (Paderborn: Ferdinand Schöningh, 1996), pp. 120–122. See also Lieutenant Colonel Wolfgang Foerster, ed., *Mackensen: Briefe und Aufzeichnungen des Generalfeldmarschalls aus Krieg und Frieden* (Leipzig: Bibliographisches Institut, 1938), p. 146; and August von Cramon and Paul Fleck, *Deutschlands Schicksalsbund mit Österreich-Ungarn: Von Conrad von Hötzendorf zu Kaiser Karl* (Berlin: Verlag für Kulturpolitik, 1932), p. 102.

41. German Eleventh Army, Army Order, 4 May 1915 and 6 May 1915, Nachlass Seeckt, BA-MA N 247/24; Herwig, *First World War,* pp. 142–144; Charles de Gaulle, *The Enemy's House Divided,* trans. Robert Eden (Chapel Hill: University of North Carolina Press, 2002), p. 70; and Foerster, *Mackensen,* p. 153.

42. Cramon and Fleck, *Deutschlands Schicksalsbund mit Österreich-Ungarn,* p. 111; and Arthur J. May, *The Passing of the Habsburg Monarchy 1914–1918* (Philadelphia: University of Pennsylvania Press, 1966), vol. 1, p. 427.

43. Army Group von Mackensen, "The Dobrudja Campaign," pts. 1 and 2, ca. December 1916, BA-MA PH 5I/18; and Herwig, *First World War,* pp. 219–222.

44. Rothenberg, *Army of Francis Joseph,* p. 186.

45. Stürgkh, *Im deutschen Grossen Hauptquartier,* p. 134.

46. Corum, *Roots of Blitzkrieg,* pp. 26–28; and Seeckt, Report on the KuK Army with Organizational Plans for the KuK Army, ca. December 1917, Nachlass Seeckt, BA-MA N 247/32.

47. Conrad, *Aus Meiner Dienstzeit,* vol. 3, pp. 809–810; and DiNardo and Hughes, "Germany and Coalition Warfare in the World Wars," p. 169.

48. Kaganeck Diary, 8 August 1914, BA-MA MSg 1/1914; and Stürgkh, *Im deutschen Grossen Hauptquartier,* pp. 14, 43, 64.

49. Herwig, *First World War,* pp. 106–107; Stürgkh, *Im deutschen Grossen Hauptquartier,* p. 23; and Strachan, *First World War,* vol. 1, p. 319.

50. Conrad, *Aus Meiner Dienstzeit,* vol. 5, p. 655; Lamar Cecil, *Wilhelm II* (Chapel Hill: University of North Carolina Press, 1996), vol. 2, p. 217.

51. Falkenhayn, *German General Staff and Its Decisions,* pp. 86–88; and Afflerbach, *Falkenhayn,* p. 260.

52. Stürgkh, *Im deutschen Grossen Hauptquartier,* pp. 103; and Sondhaus, *Franz Conrad von Hötzendorf,* p. 167.

53. Sondhaus, *Franz Conrad von Hötzendorf,* p. 167.

54. Afflerbach, *Falkenhayn,* pp. 256–257; and Sondhaus, *Franz Conrad von Hötzendorf,* p. 169.

55. Afflerbach, *Falkenhayn,* pp. 341–350; and Stürgkh, *Im deutschen Grossen Hauptquartier,* pp. 133–134.

56. Cramon, *Unser Österreichisch-Ungarischer Bundesgenosse im Weltkrieg,* pp. 36–45.

57. Falkenhayn's critics held him responsible for the Austrian disaster, although it is difficult to see how he could have prevented Conrad from pursuing the course he did. For this view, see General George Wetzell, *Von Falkenhayn zu Hindenburg-Ludendorff: Der Wechsel in der deutschen Obersten Heeresleitung im herbst 1916 und der rümanische Feldzug* (Berlin: E. S. Mittler und Sohn, 1921), p. 4; and de Gaulle, *Enemy's House Divided,* p. 78. See also Herwig, *First World War,* p. 186; Rothenberg, *Army of Francis Joseph,* p. 194; and Kaganeck Diary, 27 April 1916, BA-MA MSg 1/2517/2.

58. Cramon, *Unser Österreichisch-Ungarischer Bundesgenosse im Weltkrieg,* pp. 69–70; and Ritter, *Sword and the Scepter,* vol. 3, p. 93.

59. Rudolf Kiszling, "Bündniskrieg und Koalitionskriegführung am Beispiel der Mittelmächte im Ersten Weltkrieg," *Wehrwissenschaftliche Rundschau* 10 , no. 12 (1960): 638; Foerster, *Mackensen,* pp. 288–290; Cramon, *Unser Österreichisch-Ungarischer Bundesgenosse im Weltkrieg,* pp. 72–73; and Army Group von Mackensen, "The Dobrudja Campaign," ca. December 1916, BA-MA PH 5I/18.

60. DiNardo and Hughes, "Germany and Coalition Warfare in the World Wars," p. 179. See also Shanafelt, *Secret Enemy,* p. 105.

61. Fritz Fischer, *Germany's War Aims in the First World War* (New York: Norton, 1967), p. 139; and Kaganeck Diary, 6 August 1914, BA-MA MSg 1/1914.

62. Ludendorff to Moltke, 17 May 1915, Nachlass Ludendorff, BA-MA N 77/2.

63. Fischer, *Germany's War Aims in the First World War,* p. 210; and Ritter, *Sword and the Scepter,* vol. 3, p. 107.

64. Ludendorff to Moltke, 1 April 1915, Nachlass Ludendorff, BA-MA N 77/2; Fischer, *Germany's War Aims in the First World War,* p. 205; and Afflerbach, *Falkenhayn,* p. 251. Ludendorff's low regard for the Austrians is scarcely concealed in his memoirs. See, for example, Erich Ludendorff, *Meine Kriegserinnerungen 1914–1918* (Berlin: E. S. Mittler und Sohn, 1919), pp. 69–70, 162, 177.

65. Conrad, *Aus Meiner Dienstzeit,* vol. 4, p. 252; and Stürgkh, *Im deutschen Grossen Hauptquartier,* p. 60.

66. Ritter, *Sword and the Scepter,* vol. 3, p. 60; John R. Schindler, *Isonzo: The Forgotten Sacrifice of the Great War* (Westport, Conn.: Praeger, 2001), p. 24; Sondhaus, *Franz Conrad von Hötzendorf,* p. 176; and Afflerbach, *Falkenhayn,* pp. 266–267.

67. Ludendorff to Moltke, 17 May 1915, Nachlass Ludendorff, BA-MA N 77/2.

68. Falkenhayn, *German General Staff and Its Decisions,* pp. 106–107. Much closer to the truth is Afflerbach, *Falkenhayn,* pp. 249–250, 285.

69. Afflerbach, *Falkenhayn,* pp. 284–285, 355; Deak, *Beyond Nationalism,* p. 192; and Schindler, *Isonzo,* p. 48.

70. Herwig, *First World War,* p. 243; and Schindler, *Isonzo,* p. 200. Sondhaus claims that Conrad and Ludendorff enjoyed a good personal relationship, both during and after the war. Ludendorff did back some of Conrad's proposals, but he almost certainly did so partly from self-interest and partly from his personal struggle against Falkenhayn. While Ludendorff's postwar writings on Conrad may have been complimentary to some degree, one gets no sense of that from reading Ludendorff's private letters to Moltke in 1915. Compare, for example, Ludendorff, *Meine Kriegserinnerungen,* pp. 58, 63–164, with Ludendorff to Moltke, 9 January 1915, Nachlass Ludendorff, BA-MA N 77/2. See also Sondhaus, *Franz Conrad von Hötzendorff,* p. 168.

71. Partly as payback for the German failure to declare war on Italy in 1915, Austria-Hungary refused to declare war on the United States in 1917. Shanafelt, *Secret Enemy,* pp. 116–117, 175.

72. Stürgkh, *Im Deutschen Grossen Hauptquartier,* p. 60. See also Shanafelt, *Secret Enemy,* pp. 195–196.

73. Herwig, *First World War,* pp. 336–337; Rothenberg, *Army of Francis Joseph,* p. 212; Ritter, *Sword and the Scepter,* pp. 206–225; and Schindler, *Isonzo,* p. 281.

74. Jonathan Grant, "The Sword of the Sultan: Ottoman Arms Imports, 1854–1914," *Journal of Military History* 66, no. 1 (January 2002): 22; Alan Moorehead, *Gallipoli* (New York: Harper, 1956), p. 22; and Otto Liman von Sanders, *Five Years in Turkey* (Annapolis, Md.: Naval Institute Press, 1927), pp. 1–2.

75. Moorehead, *Gallipoli,* p. 23.

76. In this case, Sanders was able to get the decision reversed. Liman, *Five Years in Turkey,* p. 9.

77. Hans Kannengiesser, *The Campaign in Gallipoli* (London: Hutchinson, 1927), pp. 21, 129; and Liman, *Five Years in Turkey,* p. 19.

78. Moorehead, *Gallipoli,* p. 290; and Edward J. Erickson, "Strength against Weakness: Ottoman Military Effectiveness at Gallipoli, 1915," *Journal of Military History* 65, no. 4 (October 2001): 998–1001.

79. Grant, "Sword of the Sultan," p. 22.

80. Karl Dönitz, *Memoirs: Ten Years and Twenty Days* (1958; repr., Annapolis, Md.: Naval Institute Press, 1980), p. 145; and Liman, *Five Years in Turkey,* p. 133.

81. Ritter, *Sword and the Scepter,* vol. 3, p. 198.

82. Holger Herwig, "Generals versus Admirals: The War Aims of the Imperial German Navy, 1914–1918," *Central European History* 5, no. 3 (September 1972): 233.

83. Stürgkh, *Im deutschen Grossen Hauptquartier,* p. 134.

84. Cecil, *Wilhelm II,* vol. 2, p. 176; and John C. G. Röhl, *The Kaiser and His Court* (Cambridge: Cambridge University Press, 1994), p. 199.

85. Geoffrey G. Field, *Evangelist of Race: The Germanic Vision of Houston Stewart Chamberlain* (New York: Columbia University Press, 1981), p. 254.

86. Walter Görlitz, *The History of the German General Staff* (New York: Praeger, 1957), p. 116.

87. Herwig, "Strategic Uncertainties of a Nation-State," p. 253. See also Schwarzmüller, *Zwischen Kaiser und Führer,* p. 417.

88. Bucholz, *Moltke, Schlieffen, and Prussian War Planning,* p. 219; and Moltke, *Erinnerungen-Briefe-Dokumente,* p. 374.

89. Conrad, *Aus Meiner Dienstzeit,* vol. 3, pp. 146–147.

90. Tunstall, *Planning for War against Russia and Serbia,* p. 100; Conrad, *Aus Meiner Dienstzeit,* vol. 3, p. 149; Kronenbitter, "Die Macht der Illusionen," p. 530; Foerster, *Mackensen,* p. 34; and Schwarzmüller, *Zwischen Kaiser und Führer,* p. 116. Deak points out that Conrad's only solution to Austria-Hungary's Serbia problem was to invade, conquer, and annex Serbia, thus considerably enlarging the empire's Slavic population. Deak, *Beyond Nationalism,* p. 73.

91. Kaganeck Diary, 21 September 1914, BA-MA MSg 1/1914.

92. Ludendorff to Moltke, 1 April 1915, and Ludendorff to Moltke, 5 April 1915, Nachlass Ludendorff, BA-MA N 77/2; and Ritter, *Sword and the Scepter,* vol. 3, p. 99.

93. Seeckt, Report on the KuK Army with Organizational Plans for the KuK Army, ca. December 1917, Nachlass Seeckt, BA-MA N 247/32; and Lundendorff to Moltke, 17 May 1915, Nachlass Ludendorff, BA-MA N 77/2. Never the most stable individual, Ludendorff exhibited extreme thinking after the war, when he came under the influence of his second wife, Mathilde Kemnitz, who was an ardent Nazi. This manifested itself most strongly in Ludendorff's last major (if very strange) work, *Der totale Krieg.* For examples of this, see Erich Ludendorff, *Der totale Krieg* (Munich: Lundendorffs Verlag, 1936), pp. 13, 17. See also D. J. Goodspeed, *Ludendorff: Soldier, Dictator and Revolutionary* (London: Rupert Hart-Davis, 1966), pp. 235–236; and Ian Kershaw, *Hitler 1889–1936: Hubris* (New York: Norton, 1999), p. 269. Some interesting information on Jews in the Austro-Hungarian officer corps can be found in Deak, *Beyond Nationalism,* p. 196.

94. See Dominick Graham and Shelford Bidwell, *Coalitions, Politicians and Generals: Some Aspects of Command in the Two World Wars* (London: Brassey's, 1993), pp. 58–78; and Jehuda L. Wallach, *Uneasy Coalition: The Entente Experience in World War I* (Westport, Conn.: Greenwood Press, 1993).

95. Eugenia C. Kiesling, *Arming against Hitler: France and the Limits of Military Planning* (Lawrence: University Press of Kansas, 1996), p. 53.

96. Ludendorff, *Meine Kriegserinnerungen,* p. 172; and Ludendorff, *Der totale Krieg,* pp. 107–108.

97. Wetzell, "Der Bündniskrieg," *Militär Wochenblatt* 122, no. 18 (29 October 1937): 1094.

98. See, for example, Lieutenant Colonel Wolfgang Foerster, "Generalfeldmarschall von Mackensen 90 Jahren alt," *Militärwissenschaftliche Rundschau* 4, nos. 5 and 6 (December 1939): 597–604; and Fritz Hartung, "Die geschichtliche Bedeutung des Weltkriegs," *Militärwissenschaftliche Rundschau* 4, no. 4 (November 1939): 443–455.

99. Captain Albert C. Wedemeyer, "German General Staff School" (Berlin: U.S. Embassy, July 1938). Many thanks to Colonel William R. Kellner, USMC, for furnishing me with a copy of this document. See also General Albert C. Wedemeyer,

Wedemeyer Reports! (New York: Holt, 1958), pp. 49–54, for some very perceptive comments.

100. Horst Boog, *Die Deutsche Luftwaffenführung 1935–1945: Führungsprobleme, Spitzengliederung, Generalstabsausbildung* (Stuttgart: Deutsche Verlags Anstalt, 1982), p. 405; and Corum, *Luftwaffe,* pp. 253–254. See also Geoffrey P. Megargee, *Inside Hitler's High Command* (Lawrence: University Press of Kansas, 2000), pp. 34–35.

101. Wehrmachtakademie, Presentation on How the Lack of a Joint Commander of the Different Armed Services Effected the Central Powers and the Entente in the World War, Berlin, May 1936, NARA T-78/385/6351132.

102. Boog, *Die Deutsche Luftwaffenführung,* pp. 407–409.

103. Corum, *Luftwaffe,* p. 254. It is impossible to tell if the school simply died a "natural death" or someone (with Göring the most likely suspect) went out of his way to have it shut down. Boog suggests that Hitler was also perfectly happy to see the school fall by the wayside. Boog, *Die Deutsche Luftwaffenführung,* p. 409.

104. Wehrkreis III Foreign Language Examinations (Oral) 1932, Berlin, 7 October 1932, Nachlass Freytag von Loringhoven, BA-MA N 362/1; and DiNardo, "Dysfunctional Coalition," p. 716.

105. Corum, *Luftwaffe,* p. 253.

106. Brian R. Sullivan, "From Little Brother to Senior Partner: Fascist Italian Perceptions of the Nazis and Hitler's Regime, 1930–1938," *Intelligence and National Security* 13, no. 1 (Spring 1998): 92.

107. Enno von Rintelen, Remarks on the Selection and Training of German Officers for Service as Military Attachés, 1951, Nachlass Rintelen, BA-MA N 433/23.

2. Hitler, Diplomacy, and Coalition Warfare

1. Adolf Hitler, *Mein Kampf,* trans. Ralph Manheim (Boston: Houghton Mifflin, 1971), p. 681.

2. Quoted in Pietro Badoglio, *Italy in the Second World War* (1948; repr., Westport, Conn.: Greenwood Press, 1976), p. 2.

3. Quoted in Brian R. Sullivan, "The Impatient Cat: Assessments of Military Power in Fascist Italy, 1936–1940," in *Calculations: Net Assessment and the Coming of World War II,* ed. Alan R. Millett and Williamson Murray (New York: Free Press, 1992), p. 97.

4. Field Marshal Albert Kesselring, *The Memoirs of Field Marshal Kesselring* (1953; repr., London: Greenhill Books, 1977), p. 78.

5. This, of course, does not include Hitler's war service in France and Belgium. Kershaw, *Hitler 1889–1936,* p. 510; and Alan Bullock, *Hitler: A Study in Tyranny,* rev. ed. (New York: Harper and Row, 1964), p. 297. See also Weinberg, *Foreign Policy of Hitler's Germany,* vol. 1, p. 10.

6. Adolf Hitler, *Hitler's Second Book,* ed. Gerhard L. Weinberg, trans. Krista Smith (New York: Enigma Books, 2003), pp. 16–19. Also compare Bullock, *Hitler,* p. 320, and Weinberg, *Foreign Policy of Hitler's Germany,* vol. 1, p. 3. Bullock later modified his opinion somewhat in Alan Bullock, *Hitler and Stalin: Parallel Lives* (New York: Knopf, 1992), pp. 143–145. This work will not go into an extended study of Hitler's foreign policy, which has already been delved into at great length

by some of the scholars noted here, with Weinberg in particular being the leading expert.

7. Hitler, *Hitler's Second Book,* pp. 175–223; and R. J. B. Bosworth, *Mussolini* (London: Arnold, 2002), p. 267.

8. Weinberg, *Foreign Policy of Hitler's Germany,* vol. 1, p. 8.

9. Adolf Hitler, *Hitler's Table Talk 1941–1944,* trans. Norman Cameron and R. H. Stevens (1953; repr., New York: Enigma Books, 2000), pp. 10, 49, 121.

10. Hitler, *Mein Kampf,* p. 681; and Hitler, *Hitler's Table Talk,* pp. 9–10.

11. Being an inveterate antimonarchist, Hitler had no love for the Hohenzollern dynasty either. See, for example, Hitler, *Mein Kampf,* pp. 237–239; and Hitler, *Hitler's Table Talk,* pp. 35–36.

12. Hitler, *Mein Kampf,* p. 577. The quoted statement was italicized in the book.

13. See, for example, ibid., p. 659. See also Kershaw, *Hitler 1889–1936,* pp. 247–248.

14. Denis Mack Smith, *Mussolini: A Biography* (New York: Knopf, 1982), pp. 190–191; Sullivan, "Italian Armed Forces, 1918–1940," p. 170; and MacGregor Knox, *Common Destiny: Dictatorship, Foreign Policy and War in Fascist Italy and Nazi Germany* (Cambridge: Cambridge University Press, 2000), pp. 61–66.

15. MacGregor Knox, "Expansionist Zeal, Fighting Power, and Staying Power in the Italian and German Dictatorships," in *Fascist Italy and Nazi Germany: Comparisons and Contrasts,* ed. Richard Bessel (New York: Cambridge University Press, 1996), pp. 124–126.

16. Bullock, *Hitler,* p. 297; Philip V. Cannistraro and Brian R. Sullivan, *Il Duce's Other Woman* (New York: Morrow, 1993), pp. 450–452; and Santi Corvaja, *Hitler and Mussolini: The Secret Meetings* (New York: Enigma Books, 2001), pp. 32–34.

17. It was Mussolini who informed Dollfuss's widow personally of his murder at the hands of Austrian Nazis. Even after the crisis had cooled, the Italian press, reflecting the position of the Italian government that controlled it, engaged in bitter attacks on the German government. Weinberg, *Foreign Policy of Hitler's Germany,* vol. 1, pp. 102–105.

18. Badoglio, *Italy in the Second World War,* p. 2; and Cannistraro and Sullivan, *Il Duce's Other Woman,* p. 510.

19. Sullivan, "From Little Brother to Senior Partner," pp. 86–87.

20. Cannistraro and Sullivan, *Il Duce's Other Woman,* p. 512; and Manfred Messerschmidt, "Der Weg in der Krieg 1936–1938," in Militärgeschichtlichen Forschungsamt, *Das Deutsche Reich und der Zweite Weltkrieg* (Stuttgart: Deutsche Verlags Anstalt, 1974–1998), vol. 1, pp. 620–621. For a different view, see Mack Smith, *Mussolini,* pp. 183, 186; and Bosworth, *Mussolini,* p. 272. The question of an ideological comparison and contrast between Italian Fascism and Nazism is a fascinating one, but it lies beyond the scope of the present work.

21. Knox, *Mussolini Unleashed,* pp. 12–13; and Sullivan, "From Little Brother to Senior Partner," p. 87.

22. Count Galeazzo Ciano, *Diary 1937–1943,* ed. Robert L. Miller and Stanislao Pugliese, trans. Robert L. Miller (New York: Enigma Books, 2002), pp. 54, 58, 69–70; Weinberg, *Foreign Policy of Hitler's Germany,* vol. 1, p. 268; Sullivan, "From Little Brother to Senior Partner," p. 87; and Bosworth, *Mussolini,* p. 326.

23. Ciano, *Diary*, p. 28; Sullivan, "From Little Brother to Senior Partner," p. 88; Joachim C. Fest, *Hitler* (New York: Harcourt, Brace and Jovanovich, 1974), p. 502; and Messerschmidt, "Der Weg in der Krieg," p. 621.

24. Mussolini was apparently very much impressed by the infamous Joad Resolution, when the Oxford University Debating Society passed a resolution stating that under no circumstances would they fight for "King and country." Mussolini took this as representing the whole of English society. Mack Smith, *Mussolini*, pp. 194–195.

25. Weinberg, *Foreign Policy of Hitler's Germany*, vol. 1, p. 269; and Knox, *Mussolini Unleashed*, p. 34. For a somewhat benign view of the Ethiopian War, see Luigi Villari, *Italian Foreign Policy under Mussolini* (New York: Devin-Adair, 1956), pp. 123–163.

26. Messerschmidt, "Der Weg in der Krieg," p. 621.

27. Weinberg, *Foreign Policy of Hitler's Germany*, vol. 1, pp. 35–36, 49–50.

28. Corum, *Roots of Blitzkrieg*, p. 170. See also Yuri Dyakov and Tatyana Bushuyeva, eds., *The Red Army and the Wehrmacht* (Amherst, N.Y.: Prometheus Books, 1995).

29. R. J. Overy, *War and Economy in the Third Reich* (Oxford: Oxford University Press, 1994), pp. 144–174.

30. Göring and Balbo remained on close personal terms even after Balbo's virtual exile by Mussolini to North Africa until Balbo's death in 1940. Sullivan, "From Little Brother to Senior Partner," p. 92. See also R. J. Overy, *Göring: The "Iron Man"* (London: Routledge and Kegan Paul, 1984), p. 32.

31. Major General Heinz Guderian, *Achtung—Panzer!*, trans. Christopher Duffy (London: Arms and Armor, 1992), pp. 209–210. See also James S. Corum, "The Spanish Civil War: Lessons Learned and Not Learned by the Great Powers," *Journal of Military History* 62, no. 2 (April 1998): 313–334.

32. *DGFP*, vol. 3, no. 2, p. 4; Corum, *Luftwaffe*, pp. 183–185.

33. Weinberg, *Foreign Policy of Hitler's Germany*, vol. 1, p. 290; and Robert Whealey, *Hitler and Spain: The Nazi Role in the Spanish Civil War* (Lexington: University Press of Kentucky, 1989), pp. 72–94.

34. *DGFP*, vol. 3, no. 297, p. 320. Franco was not entirely happy with the manner in which the Germans and Italians came to his aid, but he realized that he had to accept it nonetheless. Brian Crozier, *Franco* (Boston: Little, Brown, 1967), p. 226; and Raymond L. Proctor, *Hitler's Luftwaffe in the Spanish Civil War* (Westport, Conn.: Greenwood Press, 1983), p. 57.

35. *DGFP*, vol. 2, no. 199, p. 222. Franco's irritation with the Italians over the size of the CTV is in John F. Coverdale, *Italian Intervention in the Spanish Civil War* (Princeton, N.J.: Princeton University Press, 1975), p. 215. See also Crozier, *Franco*, p. 300.

36. Knox, *Mussolini Unleashed*, p. 6; Sullivan, "Italian Armed Forces," p. 170; *DGFP*, vol. 3, no. 489, p. 533; and Bosworth, *Mussolini*, p. 317.

37. Corum, *Luftwaffe*, p. 192.

38. Edward B. Westermann, *Flak: German Anti-aircraft Defenses, 1914–1945* (Lawrence: University Press of Kansas, 2001), pp. 74–75.

39. *DGFP*, vol. 3, no. 488, p. 533; and Corum, *Luftwaffe*, p. 187.

40. The German chargé d'affairs in Spain, Wilhelm Faupel, suggested that the former German adviser to the Chilean General Staff, Colonel Knauer, head the staff.

DGFP, vol. 3, no. 214, p. 236; Corum, *Luftwaffe*, pp. 216–217; and Crozier, *Franco*, p. 226.

41. Whealey, *Hitler and Spain*, pp. 44–45.

42. Proctor, *Hitler's Luftwaffe in the Spanish Civil War*, p. 66.

43. *DGFP*, vol. 3, nos. 317–320, pp. 335–340. Mussolini wanted the war to continue so that Italy could win back some of the prestige lost in the defeats suffered during 1937, especially at Guadalajara. Weinberg, *Foreign Policy of Hitler's Germany*, vol. 2, p. 149; and Coverdale, *Italian Intervention in the Spanish Civil War*, pp. 263–264.

44. General Wolfram von Richthofen, Report of 3 February 1937, Nachlass Richthofen, BA-MA N 671/1; Corum, *Luftwaffe*, p. 214.

45. Ciano, *Diary*, p. 181.

46. Bosworth, *Mussolini*, pp. 317–318; and Ciano, *Diary*, p. 55.

47. *DGFP*, vol. 3, no. 551, p. 626; Coverdale, *Italian Intervention in the Spanish Civil War*, p. 349; Corum, *Luftwaffe*, p. 211; and Richthofen Report, 13 March 1937, Nachlass Richthofen, BA-MA N 671/1.

48. Weinberg, *Foreign Policy of Hitler's Germany*, vol. 2, p. 654. The question as to whether Hitler would have profited more from going to war in 1938 has been vigorously debated by historians. For a contrary view to Weinberg, see Murray, *Change in the European Balance of Power*, pp. 225–229.

49. *DGFP*, vol. 7, nos. 212, 246, 329, pp. 224, 260, 334; and Johanna Menzel Meskill, *Hitler and Japan: The Hollow Alliance* (New York: Atherton Press, 1966), p. 10.

50. H. P. Willmott, *Empires in the Balance* (Annapolis, Md.: Naval Institute Press, 1982), p. 57; and Bernd Martin, "Das deutsch-japanische Bündnis im Zweiten Weltkrieg," in *Der Zweite Weltkrieg*, ed. Wolfgang Michalka (Munich: Piper, 1989), pp. 126–127.

51. Manfred Messerschmidt, "Der Ausgangssituation 1939," in *Das Deutsche Reich und der Zweite Weltkrieg*, vol. 1, pp. 696–697. The story of German-Soviet relations from 23 August 1939 to 22 June 1941 is an interesting one, but it is outside the scope of this study. An older work on the subject is Trumbull Higgins, *Hitler and Russia: The Third Reich in a Two Front War 1937–1943* (New York: Macmillan, 1966), pp. 35–130. For more recent scholarship, see Jürgen Förster, "Hitlers Entscheidung für den Kreig gegen die Sowjetunion," in *Das Deutsche Reich und der Zweite Weltkrieg*, vol. 4, pp. 29–37; Joachim Hoffman, "Die Sowjetunion bis zum Vorabend des deutschen Angriffs," in *Das Deutsche Reich und der Zweite Weltkrieg*, vol. 4, pp. 76–97; Gerd R. Ueberschär, "Hitlers Entscheidung zum Krieg gegen die Sowjetunion und die Präventivkriegsdiskussion in der neuern Literatur," in *22 Juni 1941: Der Überfall auf die Sowjetunion*, ed. Hans Schafranek and Robert Streibel (Vienna: Picus Verlag, 1991), pp. 13–22; Manfred Zeidler, "German-Soviet Economic Relations during the Hitler-Stalin Pact," in *From Peace to War: Germany, Soviet Russia and the World, 1939–1941*, ed. Bernd Wegner (Oxford: Berghahn Books, 1997), pp. 95–111; and Ueberschär, "Der Pakt mit dem Satan, und den Teufel auszutreiben: Der deutsche-sowjetische Nichtsangriffsvertrag und Hitlers Kriegsabsicht gegen die UdSSR," in *Der Zweite Weltkrieg*, pp. 568–585.

52. Mack Smith, *Mussolini*, p. 240; *DGFP*, vol. 7, nos. 307, 535, pp. 314, 509–510. Ciano used the term "neutrality." Ciano, *Diary*, p. 271; and Corvaja, *Hitler and Mussolini*, p. 115.

53. Knox, *Mussolini Unleashed*, p. 30; and Ciano, *Diary*, p. 320.

54. Badoglio, *Italy in the Second World War*, p. 12; and Ciano, *Diary*, p. 320. See also Sullivan, "Impatient Cat," p. 123.

55. Intelligence Section, Command Staff, Commander-in-Chief of the Luftwaffe, Orientation Booklet on Italy, 1 April 1940, NARA T-321/245/000299; and Navy High Command (OKM), Report on Italy and Her Navy, 1 October 1939, NARA T-82/92/064361.

56. Brian Sullivan, "The Strategy of the Decisive Weight: Italy 1882–1922," in *Making of Strategy*, pp. 307–351. Knox argues that Mussolini effectively abandoned this strategy with his 1937 visit to Berlin. Knox, *Mussolini Unleashed*, p. 35. See also Sullivan, "From Little Brother to Senior Partner," pp. 105–106. Mussolini's most recent biographer suggests that Mussolini watched the progress of events in 1939–1940 much more carefully than Salandra's government observed the course of affairs in 1914–1915 before taking the plunge into war. Bosworth, *Mussolini*, p. 370.

57. Walter Warlimont, *Im Hauptquartier der deutschen Wehrmacht 1939–1945* (Frankfurt am Main: Bernard und Graefe Verlag für Wehrwesen, 1962), p. 78; and *DGFP*, vol. 7, nos. 341, 364, pp. 346–347, 367.

58. Intelligence Section, Command Staff, Commander-in-Chief of the Luftwaffe, Orientation Booklet on Italy, 1 April 1940, NARA T-321/245/000299; and OKM, Report on Italy and Her Navy, 1 October 1939, NARA T-82/92/064361. See also Unsigned, "Der Angriff im italienischen Heer," *Militärwissenschaftliche Rundschau* 4, no. 1 (January 1939): 125–137; and *DGFP*, vol. 8, no. 236, p. 263.

59. *DGFP*, vol. 7, no. 301, pp. 309–310; Ciano, *Diary*, p. 265; and Gerhard Schreiber, "Mussolinis 'non belligeranza,'" in *Das Deutsche Reich und der Zweite Weltkrieg*, vol. 3, pp. 32–33.

60. *DGFP*, vol. 7, no. 301, p. 314; and Ciano, *Diary*, p. 265.

61. Field Marshal Fedor von Bock, *The War Diary 1939–1943*, ed. Klaus Gerbet (Atglen, Pa.: Schiffer Military History, 1996), p. 37; and Wilhelm Keitel, *Generalfeldmarschall Keitel: Verbrecher oder Offizier?*, ed. Walter Görlitz (Berlin: Musterschmidt Verlag, 1961), p. 235.

62. General Franz Halder, *The Halder Diaries* (Washington, D.C.: Infantry Journal, 1950), vol. 2, p. 27.

63. Ciano, *Diary*, pp. 300–301.

64. Knox, *Mussolini Unleashed*, p. 135; and Ciano, *Diary*, p. 367.

65. Knox, *Mussolini Unleashed*, p. 17.

66. Wawro, *Austro-Prussian War*, p. 92; John Gooch, "Italy during the First World War," in *Military Effectiveness*, vol. 1, p. 166; Ciano, *Diary*, p. 329; and Goda, *Tomorrow the World*, p. 5.

67. Knox, *Mussolini Unleashed*, p. 55; and Ciano, *Diary*, p. 288.

68. Badoglio, *Italy in the Second World War*, p. 4; Knox, *Mussolini Unleashed*, pp. 25–30; and Ciano, *Diary*, p. 307. See also Sullivan, "Italian Armed Forces," pp. 196–197; and Halder, *Halder Diaries*, vol. 3, p. 151.

69. Knox, *Mussolini Unleashed*, pp. 23–24; Sullivan, "Italian Armed Forces," p. 199; and General Hellmuth Felmy, "Die Deutsche Luftwaffe auf dem Mittelmeer-Kriegschauplatz," 1956, Karlsruhe Collection, United States Air Force Historical Research Agency, Maxwell AFB, Alabama (hereafter cited as USAFHRA). For a slightly

different interpretation, see Karl Gundelach, *Die Deutsche Luftwaffe im Mittelmeer 1940–1945* (Frankfurt am Main: Peter D. Lang, 1981), vol. 1, p. 20.

70. Peter C. Smith, *Into the Assault* (Seattle: University of Washington Press, 1985), pp. 63–65; and James S. Corum, "The *Luftwaffe* and Its Allied Air Forces in World War II: Parallel War and the Failure of Strategic and Economic Cooperation," *Air Power History* 51, no. 2 (Summer 2004): 9.

71. Liaison Staff to the Italian Air Force to Lieutenant Colonel Schmid of the General Staff, Luftwaffe Command Staff, 19 June 1940, BA-MA RL 9/52/1.

72. Villari, *Italian Foreign Policy under Mussolini,* p. 247.

73. *DGFP,* vol. 9, no. 1, p. 9; Knox, *Mussolini Unleashed,* p. 80; Gundelach, *Die Deutsche Luftwaffe im Mittelmeer,* vol. 1, pp. 16–17; and Schreiber, "Mussolinis 'non belligeranza,'" p. 33.

74. *DGFP,* vol. 8, no. 663, p. 880; and Ciano, *Diary,* p. 328.

75. Paul Schmidt, *Hitler's Interpreter* (New York: Macmillan, 1951), p. 172; and *DGFP,* vol. 9, no. 1, pp. 1–16. Mussolini had a decent knowledge of German, which he exaggerated, as he did not understand the nuances of the language. He may also have known French, plus a little Spanish and even English. Schmidt, *Hitler's Interpreter,* p. 64; Cannistraro and Sullivan, *Il Duce's Other Woman,* p. 81; Corvaja, *Hitler and Mussolini,* pp. 34–35; Bosworth, *Mussolini,* p. 281; and Ciano, *Diary,* p. 332.

76. *DGFP,* vol. 9, no. 1, p. 9.

77. Bullock, *Hitler,* p. 581; Schmidt, *Hitler's Interpreter,* p. 172; and *DGFP,* vol. 9, no. 1, p. 13.

78. *DGFP,* vol. 9, no. 46, p. 76.

79. *DGFP,* vol. 9, nos. 1, 92, pp. 12, 132.

80. Ciano, *Diary,* pp. 340–341; and *DGFP,* vol. 9, no. 68, p. 106.

81. *DGFP,* vol. 9, nos. 212, 239, 272, pp. 299–300, 333–335, 374–375. See also Weinberg, *World at Arms,* p. 132.

82. Ciano, *Diary,* p. 351; and *DGFP,* vol. 9, no. 276, p. 379.

83. Badoglio, *Italy in the Second World War,* pp. 14–15; Ciano, *Diary,* pp. 356–357; *DGFP,* vol. 9, nos. 356, 357, 373, pp. 483, 485, 505; and Knox, *Mussolini Unleashed,* p. 118.

84. OKM, Report on Italy and Her Navy, 1 October 1939, NARA T-82/92/064361, *DGFP,* vol. 9, no. 597, p. 1005; Hans Umbreit, "Die Herstellung der deutschen Hegemonie über Westeuropa," in *Das Deutsche Reich und der Zweite Weltkrieg,* vol. 2, p. 310; Schreiber, "Mussolinis 'non belligeranza,'" p. 77; and Halder, *Halder Diaries,* vol. 3, p. 20.

85. *DGFP,* vol. 9, no. 357, pp. 484–486.

86. Intelligence Section, Command Staff, Commander-in-Chief of the Luftwaffe, Orientation Booklet on Italy, 1 April 1940, NARA T-321/245/000299; *DGFP,* vol. 10, no. 129, p. 154; Anthony Martienssen, ed., *Führer Conferences on Naval Affairs 1939–1945* (Annapolis, Md.: Naval Institute Press, 1990), p. 79; and *DGFP,* vol. 9, no. 420, 538, pp. 556–557, 912.

87. *DGFP,* vol. 9, no. 421, p. 558.

88. *DGFP,* vol. 10, nos. 166, 185, pp. 209, 242; and Liaison Staff to the Italian Air Force to Lieutenant Colonel Schmid of the General Staff, Luftwaffe Command Staff, 19 June 1940, BA-MA RL 9/52/1.

89. Gundelach, *Die Deutsche Luftwaffe im Mittelmeer,* vol. 1, p. 30.

90. Percy Ernst Schramm, ed., *Kriegstagebuch des Oberkommando der Wehrmacht 1940–1945* (Frankfurt am Main: Bernard und Graefe Verlag für Wehrwesen, 1965), entry for 2 August 1940, vol. 1, p. 6 (hereafter cited as *KTB/OKW*).

91. Ceva, *Le forze armate,* p. 342; Knox, *Mussolini Unleashed,* pp. 88–89; and Gerhard Schreiber, "Der Kriegseintritt Italiens," in *Das Deutsche Reich und der Zweite Weltkrieg,* vol. 3, p. 87.

92. Warlimont, *Im Hauptquartier der deutschen Wehrmacht,* p. 80; Keitel, *Generalfeldmarschall Keitel,* p. 235; and Rintelen, "Operational Command in the German-Italian Coalition," 19 February 1948, Nachlass Rintelen, BA-MA N 433/5.

93. Fred Taylor, ed. and trans., *The Goebbels Diaries 1939–1941* (New York: Putnam's, 1983), p. 135. Goebbels thought that Farinacci was a "fine fellow and a sincere Fascist." Taylor, *Goebbels Diaries,* p. 129.

94. *KTB/OKW,* 30 September 1940, vol. 1, p. 95; Warlimont, *Im Hauptquartier der deutschen Wehrmacht,* p. 81; *DGFP,* vol. 9, no. 387, p. 519; and Rintelen to Chief of Attaché Section, OKH, 15 June 1940, NARA T-78/365/6327182. See, for example, Rintelen to OKW, 19 April 1941, NARA T-78/359/6319326.

95. Rintelen, "Operational Command in the German-Italian Coalition," 19 February 1948, Nachlass Rintelen, BA-MA N 433/5; *DGFP,* vol. 10, no. 407, pp. 566–570; and Lucia Ceva, *La condotta italiana della Guerra: Cavallero e il Commando supremo 1941/1942* (Milan: Feltrinelli Editore, 1975), p. 34.

96. Luftwaffe High Command Quartermaster to Luftgaukommando VII, 11 June 1940, BA-MA RL 9/52/1; and Felmy, "Die Deutsche Luftwaffe auf dem Mittelmeer-Kriegschauplatz," Karlsruhe Collection, USAFHRA.

97. Liaison Staff to Italian Air Force to Lieutenant Colonel Schmid of the General Staff, Luftwaffe Command Staff, 19 June 1940, BA-MA RL 9/52/1. See also Gundelach, *Die Deutsche Luftwaffe im Mittelmeer,* vol. 1, p. 30.

98. Martienssen, *Führer Conferences on Naval Affairs,* pp. 78–79; and David Alvarez, "Axis Sigint Collaboration: A Limited Partnership," *Intelligence and National Security* 14, no. 1 (Spring 1999): 5–6.

99. Gerhard Schreiber, "Das strategische Dilemma im Sommer und Herbst 1940," in *Das Deutsche Reich und der Zweite Weltkrieg,* vol. 3, p. 226; and Rintelen, "German-Italian Military Cooperation in the Second World War," 1952, Nachlass Rintelen, BA-MA N 433/6.

100. Halder, *Halder Diaries,* vol. 4, p. 92; Hans Umbreit, "Kriegseintritt Italiens," in *Das Deutsche Reich und der Zweite Weltkrieg,* vol. 2, p. 312; Badoglio, *Italy in the Second World War,* p. 22; and Knox, *Mussolini Unleashed,* p. 129.

101. Halder, *Halder Diaries,* vol. 4, pp. 92–93.

102. Goda, *Tomorrow the World,* pp. 14–15.

103. *DGFP,* vol. 10, no. 166, p. 211; and Ciano, *Diary,* p. 371.

104. *DGFP,* vol. 10, no. 185, p. 242; and Martienssen, *Führer Conferences on Naval Affairs,* pp. 120–121.

105. Dönitz, *Memoirs,* pp. 144–145.

106. *KTB/OKW,* 12 August 1940, vol. 1, p. 24; and Bernd Stegemann, "Der U-Boot-Krieg," in *Das Deutsche Reich und der Zweite Weltkrieg,* vol. 2, p. 347.

107. Martienssen, *Führer Conferences on Naval Affairs,* p. 133; *KTB/OKW,* 5 Sep-

tember 1940, vol. 1, p. 65; and Commander Marc Antonio Bragadin, *The Italian Navy in World War II* (Annapolis. Md.: United States Naval Institute, 1957), p. 297.

108. Dönitz, *Memoirs,* p. 145.

109. Leoni sank the tanker *British Fame* on 12 August 1940, Boris damaged the tanker *Hermes* on the twenty-first and sank the merchantman *Ilvington Court* on the twenty-sixth, while Ghiglieri damaged the *Aguila* on the nineteenth. Jürgen Rohwer, *Axis Submarine Successes, 1939–1945* (Annapolis, Md.: Naval Institute Press, 1983), pp. 25–26; and Stegemann, "Der U-Boot-Krieg," p. 347.

110. Dönitz, *Memoirs,* p. 146; and Rohwer, *Axis Submarine Successes,* pp. 31–32, 35.

111. Dönitz, *Memoirs,* pp. 146–147; Stegemann, "Der U-Boot-Krieg," p. 347; James J. Sadkovich, *The Italian Navy in World War II* (Westport, Conn.: Greenwood Press, 1994), p. 21; and Jack Greene and Alessandro Massignani, *The Naval War in the Mediterranean 1940–1943* (London: Chatham, 1998), p. 270.

112. Dönitz, *Memoirs,* p. 148; and Rohwer, *Axis Submarine Successes,* p. 41.

113. Dönitz, *Memoirs,* p. 149.

114. Stegemann, "Der U-Boot-Krieg," p. 347; Dönitz, *Memoirs,* p. 149; Gaylord T. M. Kelshall, *The U-Boat War in the Caribbean* (Annapolis, Md.: Naval Institute Press, 1994), p. 175; and Sadkovich, *Italian Navy in World War II,* p. 51.

115. *DGFP*, vol. 10, no. 185, p. 242; and *KTB/OKW,* 12 August 1940, vol. 1, pp. 23–24. See also Ciano, *Diary,* p. 376.

116. Quartermaster of Luftgaukommando for Belgium/Northern France, Preparations for the Installation of an Italian Air Division, 31 August 1940, BA-MA RL 18/4.

117. Liaison Staff to the Italian Air Force to Luftwaffe Command Staff Operations Officer, Conversation with Marshal Badoglio on 9 October 1940, BA-MA RL 9/52/2; and *KTB/OKW,* 10 October 1940, vol. 1, p. 119.

118. Kesselring, *Memoirs of Field Marshal Kesselring,* p. 78; and Keitel, *Generalfeldmarschall Keitel,* p. 242.

119. Luftgaukommando for Belgium/Northern France, Liaison Staff to the Italian Air Force, 10 September 1940, BA-MA RL 18/4.

120. Luftgaukommando for Belgium/Northern France, Transport of the *CAI,* 24 September 1940, BA-MA RL 18/4. It took some twenty-four trains to transport the CAI from Italy to Belgium. Gundelach, *Die Deutsche Luftwaffe im Mittelmeer,* vol. 1, p. 37.

121. Some logistical help was expected from Field Marshal Hugo Sperrle's Third Air Fleet. Liaison Staff to Royal Italian Air Force in Belgium to Quartermaster of the Third Air Fleet, 5 October 1940, and Liaison Staff to the Royal Italian Air Force, Report on the Exercises of the Italian 56th Fighter Wing, 25 October 1940, BA-MA RL 18/4; and Derek Wood and Derek Dempster, *The Narrow Margin: The Battle of Britain and the Rise of Air Power 1930–1940* (New York: McGraw-Hill, 1961), p. 401.

122. Liaison Staff to the Royal Italian Air Force, Report on the Exercises of the Italian 56th Fighter Wing, 25 October 1940, BA-MA RL 18/4; and MacGregor Knox, "The Italian Armed Forces, 1940–3," in *Military Effectiveness,* vol. 3, p. 169. For a somewhat contrary opinion, see Sadkovich, *Italian Navy in World War II,* p. 75.

123. Wood and Dempster, *Narrow Margin,* p. 404; *KTB/OKW,* 31 October 1940, vol. 1, p. 340; and Kesselring, *Memoirs of Field Marshal Kesselring,* p. 78.

124. *KTB/OKW,* 6 November 1940, vol. 1, p. 153.

125. Wood and Dempster, *Narrow Margin,* pp. 404, 451–452; and *KTB/OKW,* 12 November 1940, vol. 1, p. 169.

126. Second Air Fleet, Instructions for Blind Flying Training of Italian Pilots, 14 November 1940, BA-MA RL 18/4.

127. *KTB/OKW,* 14 December 1940, vol. 1, p. 210.

128. Second Air Fleet to Luftgaukommando for Belgium/Northern France, 19 January 1940, BA-MA RL 18/4.

129. Liaison Staff to Italian Air Force to Lieutenant Colonel Schmid of the General Staff, Luftwaffe Command Staff, 19 June 1940, BA-MA RL 9/52/1; and Smith, *Into the Assault,* pp. 64–67.

130. Dönitz, *Memoirs,* p. 150; and Peter Padfield, *Dönitz: The Last Führer* (New York: Harper and Row, 1984), p. 241.

131. This is not to suggest that Dönitz's strategy was correct. It is to suggest that his employment of the Italians and the successes they achieved, however they might be characterized, fit well into his strategic conception.

132. Luftwaffe High Command Quartermaster to Luftgaukommando VII, 11 June 1940, BA-MA RL 9/52/1.

133. The most notable example of this, as we shall see, was the decision by Mussolini to commit the bulk of Italy's forces to Russia in 1942.

134. Gundelach, *Die Deutsche Luftwaffe im Mittelmeer,* vol. 1, p. 30; and German Liaison Staff to Italian Air Force Headquarters in Rome, Agreement on the Action of Italian and German Air Forces in the Central and Eastern Mediterranean and Surrounding Areas, 31 August 1941, BA-MA RL 2 II/38.

3. Desert Sands I

1. Unsigned, "Der Angriff im italienischen Heer," 125.

2. Ciano, *Diary,* p. 377.

3. *DGFP,* vol. 11, no. 597, p. 1008.

4. Commander *Panzerarmee Afrika,* Battle Report of *Panzerarmee Afrika,* 18 November 1941–6 February 1942, February 1942, BA-MA RH 27-15/7.

5. Gundelach, *Die Deutsche Luftwaffe im Mittelmeer,* vol. 1, p. 17.

6. Weinberg, *World at Arms,* p. 324.

7. See, for example, Klaus Schmider, "The Mediterranean in 1940–1941: Crossroads of Lost Opportunities?" *War and Society* 15, no. 2 (October 1997): 20–21.

8. *DGFP,* vol. 10, nos. 129, 166, pp. 147–155, 209–211. See also Peter Hoffman, "The Gulf Region in German Strategic Projections, 1940–1942," *Militärgeschichtliche Mitteilungen,* no. 44 (February 1988): 61–62.

9. *KTB/OKW,* 7 August 1940, vol. 1, p. 11; and Halder, *Halder Diaries,* vol. 4, pp. 170, 174.

10. Gundelach, *Die Deutsche Luftwaffe im Mittelmeer,* vol. 1, p. 30.

11. Smith, *Into the Assault,* p. 67.

12. Peter C. Smith, *The Stuka at War* (New York: Arco, 1971), pp. 67–69; and Smith, *Into the Assault,* p. 67.

13. Rintelen, "Operational Command in the German-Italian Coalition," 19 February 1948, Nachlass Rintelen, BA-MA N 433/5; and Schreiber, "Der Kriegseintritt Italiens," pp. 83–84.

14. Sullivan, "Italian Armed Forces," pp. 178–179.

15. Halder, *Halder Diaries,* vol. 4, pp. 179, 195; and *KTB/OKW,* 14 September 1940, vol. 1, p. 77.

16. Martienssen, *Führer Conferences on Naval Affairs,* pp. 135, 141–142. A full discussion of this issue is in Goda, *Tomorrow the World,* pp. 71–93.

17. *KTB/OKW,* 20 September 1940, vol. 1, p. 83.

18. Schreiber, "Das strategische Dilemma im Sommer und Herbst 1940," pp. 243–249; and Knox, *Mussolini Unleashed,* p. 198.

19. See, for example, *DGFP,* vol. 11, no. 107, p. 186. An excellent discussion of this meeting in regard to the subject of Northwest Africa is in Goda, *Tomorrow the World,* pp. 97–101.

20. *DGFP,* vol. 11, no. 149, pp. 256–257; Goda, *Tomorrow the World,* p. 99; and Ciano, *Diary,* p. 387.

21. *DGFP,* vol. 11, no. 149, p. 245; Rintelen, "Operational Command in the German-Italian Coalition," 19 February 1948, Nachlass Rintelen, BA-MA N 433/5.

22. *KTB/OKW,* 10 October 1940, vol. 1, p. 118; and Chief of Liaison Staff to the Italian Air Force to Luftwaffe Command Staff Ic, Conversation with Marshal Badoglio on 9 October 1940, 9 October 1940, BA-MA RL 9/52/2.

23. *KTB/OKW,* 14 October 1940, vol. 1, p. 121; and Schreiber, "Das strategische Dilemma im Sommer und Herbst 1940," p. 249.

24. Halder, *Halder Diaries,* vol. 4, p. 223.

25. *KTB/OKW,* 23 October 1940, vol. 1, p. 124; Halder, *Halder Diaries,* vol. 4, pp. 240–241; Christian Hartmann, *Halder: Generalstabschef Hitlers 1938–1942* (Paderborn: Ferdinand Schöningh, 1991), pp. 221–222; Schreiber, "Das strategische Dilemma im Sommer und Herbst 1940," pp. 204–205; and Martienssen, *Führer Conferences on Naval Affairs,* p. 146.

26. Goda, *Tomorrow the World,* pp. 103–105. See also John Weitz, *Hitler's Diplomat: The Life and Times of Joachim von Ribbentrop* (New York: Ticknor and Fields, 1992), p. 253. Although the story of German-Spanish relations is a most interesting one, it is beyond the scope of this study.

27. *DGFP,* vol. 11, no. 149, p. 256; and Chief of Liaison Staff to the Italian Air Force to Luftwaffe Command Staff Ic, Conversation with Marshal Badoglio on 9 October 1940, 9 October 1940, BA-MA RL 9/52/2.

28. Ciano, *Diary,* p. 390; Knox, *Mussolini Unleashed,* pp. 198–199; Badoglio, *Italy in the Second World War,* pp. 23–24; and *DGFP,* vol. 11, no. 199, p. 333. Oddly enough, in his rather cryptic diary Halder seemed to be more understanding of Graziani's delay. Halder, *Halder Diaries,* vol. 4, p. 247.

29. *KTB/OKW,* 24 October 1940, vol. 1, p. 126.

30. Halder, *Halder Diaries,* vol. 4, pp. 246–247; and *KTB/OKW,* 28 October 1940, vol. 1, p. 132.

31. The outcome of the meeting is summarized in *KTB/OKW,* 13 November 1940, vol. 1, pp. 171–172. The entry for 19 November 1940, however, notes that the meeting took place at Inn.sbruck on 14–15 November 1940. Apparently the diarist (probably Percy Ernst Schramm) added material dealing with the meeting afterward, but with the incorrect date. See also *DGFP,* vol. 11, no. 400, p. 709; Goda, *Tomorrow the World,* p. 140; Halder, *Halder Diaries,* vol. 5, p. 28; and Rintelen, "Op-

erational Command in the German-Italian Coalition," 19 February 1948, Nachlass Rintelen, BA-MA N 433/5.

32. *DGFP,* vol. 11, no. 353, pp. 606–610.

33. *DGFP,* vol. 11, no. 369, pp. 642–643.

34. Ciano, *Diary,* p. 403; *DGFP,* vol. 11, nos. 383, 487, pp. 672, 835–836; and *KTB/OKW,* 2 December 1940, vol. 1, p. 194.

35. Gerhard Schreiber, "Mussolinis Überfall auf Greichenland oder der Anfang vom Ende der italienischen Grossemachtstellung," in *Das Deutsche Reich und der Zweite Weltkrieg,* vol. 3, p. 408; *DGFP,* vol. 11, nos. 352, 369, 383, pp. 606–610, 639–643, 671–672; Halder, *Halder Diaries,* vol. 5, pp. 21–28; and *KTB/OKW,* 12–14 November 1940, vol. 1, pp. 169–173.

36. Most strident in this is Sadkovich, *Italian Navy in World War II,* p. 93. More balanced are Knox, *Mussolini Unleashed,* p. 239; and Schreiber, "Mussolinis Überfall auf Greichenland oder der Anfang vom Ende der italienischen Grossemachtstellung," pp. 408–409. A standard British account of the raid is Donald Macintyre, *The Battle for the Mediterranean* (New York: Norton, 1965), pp. 36–38.

37. Knox, *Mussolini Unleashed,* pp. 252–253.

38. Weinberg, *World at Arms,* pp. 210–211.

39. Correlli Barnett, *The Desert Generals,* new and enlarged edition (Bloomington: Indiana University Press, 1982), pp. 37–38; and Barrie Pitt, *Western Desert 1941* (London: Jonathan Cape, 1980), pp. 101–108.

40. Barnett, *Desert Generals,* pp. 39–40.

41. Bernd Stegemann, "Die italienisch-deutsche Kriegführung im Mittelmeer und in Afrika," in *Das Deutsche Reich und der Zweite Weltkrieg,* vol. 3, p. 598; Ceva, *Le forze armate,* pp. 295–296; and Pitt, *Western Desert,* p. 190. Knox puts Italian losses as slightly lower. Knox, *Mussolini Unleashed,* p. 256.

42. Ciano, *Diary,* pp. 403–404.

43. Knox, *Mussolini Unleashed,* p. 254; and Ciano, *Diary,* p. 404.

44. Weinberg, *World at Arms,* p. 211.

45. Badoglio, *Italy in the Second World War,* p. 24; Ciano, *Diary,* p. 403.

46. Knox, *Mussolini Unleashed,* p. 256. Mussolini initially wanted to court-martial Graziani but ultimately did not. Instead, a court of inquiry investigated Graziani's conduct and issued a report very critical of him on 28 February 1942. Badoglio, *Italy in the Second World War,* p. 25.

47. Ciano, *Diary,* pp. 398–399; and Knox, *Mussolini Unleashed,* pp. 243–248. Rintelen reported that many Italian officers considered Badoglio's removal unfair. *KTB/OKW,* 18 December 1940, vol. 1, p. 234.

48. Knox, *Mussolini Unleashed,* pp. 247–248; Ciano, *Diary,* pp. 399–400; Corvaja, *Hitler and Mussolini,* p. 192; and Ugo Cavallero, *Diario 1940–1943,* ed Giuseppe Bucciante (Rome: Ciarrapico Editore, 1984), p. 5. Notably, Halder made no mention of the change in his diary. The first mention of it in the OKW diary is on 11 December 1940, when Rintelen reported on his first meeting with Cavallero. *KTB/OKW,* 11 December 1940, vol. 1, p. 225.

49. Ceva, *La condotta italiana della guerra,* pp. 34–35. Rintelen complained on 2 January 1941 that he had yet to see a situation map of either Libya or Albania. Compare *DGFP,* vol. 11, no. 597, p. 1009; and Rintelen, "Operational Command

in the German-Italian Coalition," 19 February 1948, Nachlass Rintelen, BA-MA N 433/5.

50. Gundelach, *Die Deutsche Luftwaffe im Mittelmeer,* vol. 1, pp. 93–94; and *DGFP,* vol. 11, no. 487, pp. 835–836.

51. *DGFP,* vol. 11, nos. 586, 642, pp. 993–994, 1073–1075; *KTB/OKW,* 11 January 1941, vol. 1, p. 261; and Martienssen, *Führer Conferences on Naval Affairs,* pp. 169–170.

52. *DGFP,* vol. 11, no. 589, pp. 996–999; Pitt, *Western Desert,* p. 137; Ciano, *Diary,* p. 409; and *KTB/OKW,* 4 January 1941, vol. 1, pp. 245–246.

53. *DGFP,* vol. 11, no. 679, p. 1145; *KTB/OKW,* 22 January 1941, vol. 1, pp. 272–276; Ciano, *Diary,* pp. 414–415; and Cavallero, *Diario,* pp. 69–71.

54. Goda, *Tomorrow the World,* p. 158; Ciano, *Diary,* p. 415; *DGFP,* vol. 11, nos. 679, 683, pp. 1148, 1158–1159; *KTB/OKW,* 22 January 1941, vol. 1, pp. 272–274; Rintelen, "Operational Command in the German-Italian Coalition," 19 February 1948, Nachlass Rintelen, BA-MA N 433/5; and Corvaja, *Hitler and Mussolini,* p. 202.

55. Goda, *Tomorrow the World,* p. 162.

56. *DGFP,* vol. 11, no. 597, pp. 1009–1010; *KTB/OKW,* 26 January 1941, vol. 1, p. 281; and Rintelen to OKW, 29 January 1941, NARA T-78/359/6319227. On 18 February 1941 Hitler decided to send a full panzer division (the Fifteenth) to North Africa after the Fifth Light Division (later Twenty-first Panzer) completed its deployment. OKW to Rintelen, 19 February 1941, NARA T-313/476/8774527.

57. *DGFP,* vol. 12, no. 24, p. 45; Rintelen to OKW, 9 February 1941, 1030 Hours, NARA T-78/359/6319246; and Rintelen to OKW, 9 February 1941, 1930 Hours, NARA T-78/359/6319240. Graziani's relief was first mentioned in the OKW war diary on 27 February 1941. *KTB/OKW,* 27 February 1941, vol. 1, p. 337.

58. David Irving, *The Trail of the Fox* (New York: Avon Books, 1977), pp. 41–69; and *DGFP,* vol. 12, no. 17, pp. 29–30.

59. Rommel's offensive was aided by Churchill's foolish decision to essentially shut down Wavell's offensive in favor of diverting men and material to aid Greece.

60. Memoirs and studies on this abound. A good collection of works from all sides is Larry H. Addington, "Operation *Sunflower*: Rommel versus the General Staff," *Military Affairs* 31, no. 3 (Fall 1967): 120–130; Pitt, *Western Desert,* pp. 241–284; Irving, *Trail of the Fox,* pp. 80–136; David Fraser, *Knight's Cross: A Life of Field Marshal Erwin Rommel* (New York: HarperCollins, 1993), pp. 213–270; Volkmar Kühn, *Mit Rommel in der Wüste* (Stuttgart: Motorbuch Verlag, 1987), pp. 13–53; Stegemann, "Die italienisch-deutsche Kriegführung im Mittlemeer und in Afrika," pp. 615–630; and Ceva, *Le forze armate,* pp. 303–305.

61. Hartmann, *Halder,* p. 260; Addington, "Operation *Sunflower*," p. 121; and *KTB/OKW,* 13 February 1941, vol. 1, p. 321. Initially, the German force in Africa was designated as Korps Rommel. On 19 February 1941 the title was officially changed to the Deutsches Afrika Korps. OKW to Rintelen, 19 February 1941, NARA T-313/476/8774527.

62. Megargee, *Inside Hitler's High Command,* pp. 96–97. As noted earlier, Rintelen reported directly back to OKW, but copies of his messages also went to OKH. See, for example, Rintelen to OKW, 29 January 1941, NARA T-78/359/6319227.

63. Cavallero, *Diario,* p. 26; Rintelen to OKH, 24 March 1941, NARA T-78/359/6319308. Mussolini had told Hitler in a 22 February 1941 letter that he had already ordered all mobile forces to be placed under Rommel's command "in order to achieve unity of action." *DGFP,* vol. 12, no. 76, p. 137. Halder initially thought a major thrust toward Tobruk was the optimal course of action for Rommel, but he changed his mind about a week later. Halder, *Halder Diaries,* vol. 6, pp. 23, 32.

64. B. H. Liddell-Hart, ed., *The Rommel Papers* (New York: Harcourt, Brace, 1953), p. 111; Megargee, *Inside Hitler's High Command,* p. 97; and Hartmann, *Halder,* pp. 260–262.

65. OKW to Luftwaffe High Command, German Africa Corps, 20 May 1941, BA-MA RL 2 II/38.

66. Halder, *Halder Diaries,* vol. 6, p. 150.

67. OKW, Discussion Points between the Chief of OKW and General Cavallero, 29 August 1941, BA-MA RL 2 II/38. Rommel complained that such a command should have gotten him a promotion to colonel general. Fraser, *Knight's Cross,* p. 272; and Liddell-Hart, *Rommel Papers,* p. 149.

68. *KTB/OKW,* 28 February 1941, vol. 1, p. 340. The arrangement was formalized in May 1941. OKW to Luftwaffe High Command, German Africa Corps, 20 May 1941, BA-MA RL 2 II/38. See also Gundelach, *Die Deutsche Luftwaffe im Mittelmeer,* vol. 1, pp. 126–127. Fröhliche had a very poor relationship with Rommel. In late 1941 he was replaced as *Fliegerführer Afrika* by General Hoffmann von Waldau, who enjoyed a much better relationship with Rommel. Kenneth Macksey, *Kesselring: German Master Strategist of the Second World War* (London: Greenhill Books, 1996), p. 112; and Commander, *Panzerarmee Afrika,* Battle Report of *Panzerarmee Afrika,* 18 November 1941–6 February 1942, February 1942, BA-MA RH 27-15/7.

69. German Liaison Officer to Italian Fifth Air Fleet, Report of Liaison Officer to Italian Fifth Air Fleet in North Africa to Commanding General X Air Corps, 19 May 1941, BA-MA RL 2 II/38. On the other hand, the subordination of flak to the Italian army was fortunate in some situations, such as in the assistance it provided to the German Twelfth Oasis Company in its defense of Sidi Omar in November 1941. Report of the Twelfth Oasis Company on the Battle of Sidi Omar, December 1941, NARA T-314/2/000017.

70. The German sector was further subdivided into a X Air Corps sector and one for the Luftwaffe units operating out of Greece and Crete over the Aegean. German Liaison Staff to Italian Air Force, Agreement on the Action of the Italian and German Air Forces in the Central and Eastern Mediterranean and Surrounding Areas, 31 August 1941, BA-MA RL 2 II/38. The areas outlined can be visualized from the map in Stegemann, "Die italienisch-deutsche Kriegführung im Mittelmeer und in Afrika," vol. 3, pp. 604–605.

71. Sadkovich, *Italian Navy in World War II,* pp. 34–35; and Corvaja, *Hitler and Mussolini,* p. 142. Sadkovich, in trying to alibi somewhat for that Italians, notes correctly that Germany left a good part of its merchant tonnage to be interned in foreign ports in 1939. Germany, however, did not necessarily need a large merchant marine, given its continental position, nor did Germany possess the kind of navy required to adequately protect a large merchant fleet. In addition, Germany was able to at least partially cover the shortfall by confiscating merchant ships from the conquered

countries or by chartering ships from neutrals. Martienssen, *Führer Conferences on Naval Affairs,* p. 226.

72. Corum, "The *Luftwaffe* and Its Allied Air Forces in World War II," p. 10; John Winton, *Ultra at Sea: How Breaking the Nazi Code Affected Allied Naval Strategy during World War II* (New York: Morrow, 1988), p. 164; Stegemann, "Die italienisch-deutsche Kriegführung im Mittelmeer und in Afrika," p. 606; and Sadkovich, *Italian Navy in World War II,* pp. 134–136.

73. *KTB/OKW,* 18 February 1941, vol. 1, p. 330.

74. *KTB/OKW,* 27 February 1941, vol. 1, p. 338.

75. Winton, *Ultra at Sea,* pp. 165–166; and Sadkovich, *Italian Navy in World War II,* p. 126. Hitler's low opinion of the Italian royal family is well laid out in Hitler, *Hitler's Table Talk,* p. 218.

76. Rintelen to OKH, 24 March 1941, NARA T-78/359/6319308; Rintelen to OKW, 2 April 1941, NARA T-78/359/6319326; and Hartmann, *Halder,* pp. 259–260.

77. Winton, *Ultra at Sea,* pp. 16–17; and Stegemann, "Die italienisch-deutsche Kriegführung im Mittelmeer und in Afrika," p. 608.

78. J. Valerio Borghese, *Sea Devils* (Chicago: Henry Regnery, 1954), pp. 80–82; Rohwer, *Axis Submarine Successes;* and Stegemann, "Die italienisch-deutsche Kriegführung im Mittelmeer und in Afrika," p. 609.

79. A standard British view of Cape Matapan would be Winton, *Ultra at Sea,* p. 21. See also Greene and Massignani, *Naval War in the Mediterranean,* p. 160. Interpretations of the battle as only a "temporary setback" are Sadkovich, *Italian Navy in World War II,* p. 133; and Knox, *Mussolini Unleashed,* p. 283.

80. Martienssen, *Führer Conferences on Naval Affairs,* p. 192.

81. Winton, *Ultra at Sea,* p. 165. For the Italian side, see Bragadin, *Italian Navy in World War II,* pp. 69–70; and Sadkovich, *Italian Navy in World War II,* pp. 139–141. The Italians had requested some 574,000 tons of oil of various types in February 1941, of which the Germans could provide only limited quantities. *DGFP,* vol. 12, no. 19, p. 33; and *DGFP,* vol. 12, no. 27, p. 49. By the summer of 1941 the major units of the Italian navy that had been damaged at Cape Matapan had been repaired but were still inactive, this time owing to lack of fuel. Halder, *Halder Diaries,* vol. 6, p. 134; and Sadkovich, *Italian Navy in World War II,* p. 150.

82. For two radically different interpretations of roughly the same set of figures, compare Sadkovich, *Italian Navy in World War II,* pp. 344–345, with Stegemann, "Die italienisch-deutsche Kriegführung im Mittelmeer und in Afrika," pp. 646–650.

83. Naval High Command, Overview of the Situation in the Mediterranean, Aegean and Black Seas from 15–31 October 1941, BA-MA RM 7/115.

84. As an example of how serious the equipment losses were for Rommel's forces, on 18 November 1941 the Twenty-first Panzer Division had 35 Pz II, 68 Pz III, and 17 Pz IV ready for action. By 3 December 1941, the division had only 5 Pz III and 2 Pz IV operational. Fifth Panzer Regiment, Records for Historian of the *DAK,* 18 February 1942, NARA T-315/786/000316. *Crusader,* especially the fighting around Sidi Rezegh, has always been a favorite subject for students of the North African campaign. A sampling of the literature on this includes Barnett, *Desert Generals,* pp. 94–118; Pitt, *Western Desert,* pp. 353–481; Major General F. W. von Mellen-

thin, *Panzer Battles* (repr., New York: Ballantine Books, 1971), pp. 66–106; Colonel Rainer Kriebel, *Inside the Africa Corps: The Crusader Battles, 1941–1942*, ed. Bruce I. Gudmundsson (London: Greenhill Books, 1999); Ceva, *Le forze armate*, pp. 308–313; and Stegemann, "Die italienisch-deutsche Kriegführung im Mittelmeer und in Afrika," pp. 658–682.

85. Irving, *Trail of the Fox*, p. 185.

86. During the period of the *Crusader* battles, the Fifteenth Panzer Division listed four interpreters on its staff. By comparison, the XXX Corps, operating in Romania during the opening phase of *Barbarossa* with up to three Romanian divisions attached to it, had only one officer assigned to interpreting duties. List of Command Staff of Fifteenth Panzer Division, 19 November 1941–15 February 1942, NARA T-315/664/000776; and List of Command Staff of XXX Corps, 1 July 1941, NARA T-314/824/000463.

87. Lieutenant Colonel John Hixson and Benjamin Franklin Cooling, *Combined Operations in Peace and War* (Carlisle Barracks, Pa.: U.S. Army War College, 1982), p. 207; Corum, *Roots of Blitzkrieg*, p. 132; and Rintelen, "German-Italian Military Cooperation in the Second World War," 1952, Nachlass Rintelen, BA-MA N 433/6.

88. Report of the Twelfth Oasis Company on the Battle of Sidi Omar, December 1941, NARA T-314/2/000017; Pitt, *Western Desert*, p. 440; United States Army Military History Institute, Manuscript no. D-024, Major General Hans Henning von Holtzendorf, "Grunde für Rommels Erfolge in Afrika 1941/1942," 27 March 1947, p. 10 (hereafter cited as USAMHI, MSS no. D-024); Kriebel, *Inside the Afrika Corps*, pp. 141, 257; Cavallero, *Diario*, pp. 216, 218; and MacGregor Knox, *Hitler's Italian Allies: Royal Armed Forces, Fascist Regime, and the War of 1940–1943* (Cambridge: Cambridge University Press, 2000), pp. 153–154.

89. Martienssen, *Führer Conferences on Naval Affairs*, pp. 225–229; and *DGFP*, vol. 13, no. 242, p. 387.

90. While Dönitz was not necessarily supportive of the move, he considered it an "unavoidable" one at the time. Dönitz, *Memoirs*, pp. 158–159; and Martienssen, *Führer Conferences on Naval Affairs*, p. 235.

91. Rohwer, *Axis Submarine Successes*, p. 227; and Stegemann, "Die italienisch-deutsche Kriegführung im Mittelmeer und in Afrika," p. 652; and Naval High Command, Overview of the Situation in the Mediterranean, Aegean and Black Seas from 1–15 November 1941, BA-MA RM 7/115.

92. Macintyre, *Battle for the Mediterranean*, pp. 119–120; Greene and Massignani, *Naval War in the Mediterranean*, p. 203; Stegemann, "Die italienisch-deutsche Kriegführung im Mittelmeer und in Afrika," p. 654; Sadkovich, *Italian Navy in World War II*, pp. 212–218; and Knox, *Hitler's Italian Allies*, p. 134. The convoy took 1,400 British prisoners back to Italy. Naval High Command, Overview of the Situation in the Mediterranean, Aegean and Black Seas from 16–31 December 1941, BA-MA RM 7/115.

93. Stegemann, "Die italienisch-deutsche Kriegführung im Mittelmeer und in Afrika," p. 656; Greene and Massignani, *Naval War in the Mediterranean*, pp. 202–204; Sadkovich, *Italian Navy in World War II*, p. 217; Bragadin, *Italian Navy in World War II*, p. 151; Borghese, *Sea Devils*, pp. 131–157; and Macintyre, *Battle for the Mediterranean*, pp. 121–123.

94. Ceva, *Le forze armate,* p. 311.

95. Naval High Command, Overview of the Situation in the Mediterranean, Aegean and Black Seas from 15–31 October 1941 and from 1–15 December 1941, BA-MA RM 7/115; and Martienssen, *Führer Conferences on Naval Affairs,* p. 240.

96. Naval High Command, Overview of the Situation in the Mediterranean, Aegean and Black Seas from 16–31 December 1941, BA-MA RM 7/115; German Air Liaison Staff, Agreement on the Action of Italian and German Air Forces in the Central and Eastern Mediterranean and Its Surrounding Areas, 31 August 1941, BA-MA RL 2 II/38; and Borghese, *Sea Devils,* p. 138. The British were somewhat forewarned by *Ultra* of the impending operation. As a result, the commander of the naval base, Rear Admiral G. H. Creswell, who was responsible for the security of the ships, was relieved by Cunningham. Winton, *Ultra at Sea,* pp. 173–174; and Greene and Massignani, *Naval War in the Mediterranean,* p. 204.

97. Naval High Command, Overview of the Situation in the Mediterranean, Aegean and Black Seas from 16–30 November 1941, BA-MA RM 7/115; and Greene and Massignani, *Naval War in the Mediterranean,* p. 269.

98. Naval High Command, Overview of the Situation in the Mediterranean, Aegean and Black Seas from 16–31 December 1941, BA-MA RM 7/115; and Greene and Massignani, *Naval War in the Mediterranean,* p. 197.

99. *DGFP,* vol. 13, nos. 433, 454, pp. 714–715, 752–753.

100. Gundelach, *Die Deutsche Luftwaffe im Mittelmeer,* vol. 1, p. 339; and Macksey, *Kesselring,* p. 102.

101. *DGFP,* vol. 13, no. 535, pp. 938–939; OKW, Memorandum on OB South, December 1941, NARA T-313/476/8774563; and Macksey, *Kesselring,* p. 107. It is worth noting that while Ciano never even mentions Kesselring's appointment in his diary, Rintelen's name still appears rather often. Ciano, *Diary,* pp. 461–471.

102. Macksey, *Kesselring,* p. 102. In a postwar manuscript, Kesselring derided the Italians as being interested only in "coffee, cigarettes and women." USAMHI, MSS no. C-015, Field Marshal Albert Kesselring, "Italy as a Military Ally," July 1948, p. 5. The most common view of Kesselring is that he got along well with the Italians. See, for example, Shelford Bidwell, "Kesselring," in *Hitler's Generals,* ed. Correlli Barnett (New York: Grove Weidenfeld, 1989), pp. 276–277; and Macksey, *Kesselring,* pp. 114–115. A rather different impression can be gained from Ciano, *Diary,* p. 487.

103. Macksey, *Kesselring,* p. 112.

104. Liddell-Hart, *Rommel Papers,* p. 182; Macksey, *Kesselring,* pp. 112–113.

105. Most missions against Malta were flown by the II Air Corps, which was based in Sicily. Since the II Air Corps was lacking in fighter strength, the Regia Aeronautica had to divert fighters to fly escort on some missions. Sadkovich, *Italian Navy in World War II,* pp. 220–221. There were also occasions during the summer of 1941 when German and Italian Stuka units flew strikes jointly against targets in the Sollum area, escorted by German fighters. Smith, *Into the Assault,* pp. 76–78. Otherwise, as noted previously, the airspace in the Mediterranean was divided into German and Italian zones. German Air Liaison Staff, Agreement on the Action of the Italian and German Air Forces in the Central and Eastern Mediterranean and Surrounding Areas, 31 August 1941, BA-MA RL 2 II/38.

106. Naval High Command, Overview of the Situation in the Mediterranean, Aegean and Black Seas from 1–15 December 1941, BA-MA RM 7/115.

107. *DGFP*, vol. 11, no. 679, p. 1148; Halder, *Halder Diaries*, vol. 6, p. 172; Cavallero, *Diario*, p. 225; and OKW, Discussion Points between the Chief of OKW and General Cavallero, 29 August 1941, BA-MA RL 2 II/38.

108. Rintelen to OKW, 24 March 1941, NARA T-78/359/6319308; *DGFP*, vol. 12, no. 76, p. 137; and Rintelen to OKW, 8 December 1941, NARA T-313/476/8774569; Liddell-Hart *Rommel Papers*, p.182; and Hartmann, *Halder*, p. 262.

109. Luftwaffe High Command Quartermaster to Luftgaukommando VII, 11 June 1940, BA-MA RL 9/52/1; German Liaison Staff to the Italian Air Force to Luftwaffe High Command Ic, Conversation with Marshal Badoglio, 9 October 1940, BA-MA RL 9/52/2; Pohl to General Hans Jeschonnek, 26 September 1941, BA-MA RL 2 II/38; and Agreement on the Employment of the Italian and German Air Forces in the Central and Eastern Mediterranean and Surrounding Areas, 31 August 1941, BA-MA RL 2 II/38.

110. German Liaison Officer to the Italian Fifth Air Fleet, Report of the Liaison Officer to the Italian Fifth Air Fleet in North Africa to the Commanding General of the X Air Corps, 19 May 1941, BA-MA RL 2 II/38.

111. Stegemann, "Die italienisch-deutsche Kriegführung im Mittelmeer und in Afrika," p. 681; and Greene and Massignani, *Naval War in the Mediterranean*, p. 269.

112. Knox, *Mussolini Unleashed*, p. 279; and *DGFP*, vol. 11, nos. 679, 683, pp. 1145–1151, 1158–1159.

113. Hitler, *Mein Kampf*, p. 654.

4. The Balkan Interlude

1. Ciano, *Diary*, p. 388.

2. *DGFP*, vol. 11, no. 583, p. 985.

3. Lieutenant Colonel Bernhard von Lossberg, OKW National Defense Section, "Operations in the Southeast," 5 May 1941, NARA T-77/792/5520954.

4. Weinberg, *Foreign Policy of Hitler's Germany*, vol. 2, p. 233; *DGFP*, vol. 5, no. 304, p. 403; Reichamt für wehrwirtschaftliche Planung, "Die rohstoffwirtschaftliche Bedeutung des Südostraums für die deutsche Wehrwirtschaft," March 1939, NARA T-84/80/1367770; Overy, *War and Economy in the Third Reich*, p. 159; and Rich, *Hitler's War Aims*, vol. 2, p. 240.

5. International Military Tribunal, *Trial of the Major War Criminals* (Nuremberg: U.S. Government, 1947–1949), vol. 26, Doc. 686-PS, p. 256 (hereafter cited as IMT, *TTMWC*); Office of the Reichsführer SS, Circular for SS Officers on SS Volunteers from the Ethnic German Group in Romania, ca. October 1943, NARA T-175/474/2996144; and George H. Stein, *The Waffen SS: Hitler's Elite Guard at War* (Ithaca, N.Y.: Cornell University Press, 1966), pp. 168–169.

6. Mussolini had been considering, albeit in a vacillating fashion, attacking either Greece or Yugoslavia in August 1939. Mario Cervi, *The Hollow Legions: Mussolini's Blunder in Greece, 1940–1941* (Garden City, N.Y.: Doubleday, 1971), p. 9.

7. Robert Mallett, *The Italian Navy and Fascist Expansionism 1935–1940* (London: Frank Cass, 1998), p. 138; and Ciano, *Diary*, pp. 388–389. Jacomoni was also Cavallero's son-in-law. Cervi, *Hollow Legions*, p. 34.

8. Charles Cruikshank, *Greece 1940–1941* (Newark: University of Delaware Press, 1976), p. 16.

9. *DGFP,* vol. 10, nos. 129, 166, 407, pp. 153–154, 209–211, 569. See also Gerhard Schreiber, "Die deutsch-italienische Politik gegenüber den südosteuropäischen Staaten," in *Das Deutsche Reich und der Zweite Weltkrieg,* vol. 3, pp. 366–367; and Ciano, *Diary,* pp. 272–274.

10. *DGFP,* vol. 10, no. 343, p. 482. For Italian planning in regard to Yugoslavia and Greece in the summer of 1940, see Ceva, *La condotta italiana della guerra,* p. 47.

11. *DGFP,* vol. 10, no. 353, pp. 497–498; Halder, *Halder Diaries,* vol. 4, pp. 160, 170; and Schreiber, "Die deutsch-italienische Politik gegenüber den südosteuropäischen Staaten," p. 362.

12. Ciano, *Diary,* pp. 385, 387; *DGFP,* vol. 11, no. 149, p. 247; and Martienssen, *Führer Conferences on Naval Affairs,* p. 139. It is interesting to note that while Hitler was mildly hinting at the prospect of canceling *Sea Lion* in a 17 September 1940 letter to Mussolini, Ribbentrop was still assuring Ciano that the only thing needed for the invasion to commence was a period of good weather. Ciano, *Diary,* p. 383; and *DGFP,* vol. 11, no. 68, p. 103.

13. *DGFP,* vol. 11, no. 73, p. 121. A careful comparison of the Italian and German records of this meeting is in Schreiber, "Mussolinis Überfall auf Griechenland oder der Anfang vom Ende der italienischen Grossmachtstellung," pp. 369–370.

14. *DGFP,* vol. 10, no. 388, pp. 538–539; *DGFP,* vol. 11, no. 149, pp. 245–259; and Mack Smith, *Mussolini,* p. 257.

15. Liaison Staff to the Italian Air Force to *Luftwaffe* Command Staff Ic, Conversation with Marshal Badoglio, 9 October 1940, BA-MA RL 9/52/2. A copy of this message went to OKW on request. *DGFP,* vol. 11, no. 252, p. 427.

16. *DGFP,* vol. 11, nos. 107, 135, pp. 186, 229; and Halder, *Halder Diaries,* vol. 4, p. 245. Ciano did not make any comments about Greece either in his meeting with Hitler on 29 September 1940 or in his diary. *DGFP,* vol. 11, no. 124, pp. 214; and Ciano, *Diary,* p. 385.

17. *DGFP,* vol. 11, no. 191, pp. 322–323; Ciano, *Diary,* p. 388; Schreiber, "Mussolinis Überfall auf Greichenland oder der Anfang vom Ende der italienischen Grossmachtstellung," 374; and Knox, *Mussolini Unleashed,* p. 229.

18. *DGFP,* vol. 11, no. 199, pp. 331–334; and Knox, *Mussolini Unleashed,* pp. 224–225.

19. *DGFP,* vol. 11, nos. 247, 252, pp. 422–423, 427–428.

20. The original plan called for the occupation of northern Greece, but it was quickly expanded. The evolution of Italian planning is detailed in Schreiber, "Mussolinis Überfall auf Greichenland oder der Anfang vom Ende der italienischen Grossmachtstellung," pp. 385–390.

21. Italian offensive doctrine at the time called for the execution of concentrated attacks at several places, with large forces available to conduct pursuit. In no sector of the Greek front was this the case. Unsigned, "Der Angriff im italienischen Heer," 125–129; *DGFP,* vol. 11, no. 252, p. 428; *KTB/OKW,* 9 November 1940, vol. 1, p. 162; Schreiber, "Mussolinis Überfall auf Greichenland oder der Anfang vom Ende der italienischen Grossmachtstellung," p. 398; Ceva, *Le forze armate,* p. 290; Cavallero, *Diario,* p. 19; Cruickshank, *Greece,* pp. 41–43; and Knox, *Mussolini Unleashed,* p. 234. An accurate, if somewhat snide, contemporaneous German analysis is Lieutenant Colonel Bernhard von Lossberg, OKW National Defense Section,

"Operations in the Southeast," NARA T-77/792/5520954. Cervi remains the classic account of the Italian side of the campaign.

22. Schreiber, "Mussolinis Überfall auf Greichenland oder der Anfang vom Ende der italienischen Grossmachtstellung," p. 410.

23. *DGFP*, vol. 11, no. 246, p. 411; and Halder, *Halder Diaries,* vol. 5, p. 2. Ciano and Ribbentrop were also present at the meeting. Ciano apparently edited out any major comments about this conference in his diary, since the entire Greek affair, something he had long advocated, turned into a major Italian embarrassment. Ciano, *Diary,* p. 391; and Knox, *Mussolini Unleashed,* p. 291. A perceptive analysis of Hitler's talks with Petain, Laval, and Franco is in Goda, *Tomorrow the World,* pp. 103–112.

24. Halder, *Halder Diaries,* vol. 5, p. 4; *KTB/OKW,* 1 November 1940, vol. 1, p. 144; Corvaja, *Hitler and Mussolini,* p. 180; and Ian Kershaw, *Hitler 1936–1945: Nemesis* (New York: Norton, 2000), p. 331. Peter Padfield's suggestion that Hitler's anger at Mussolini and the Italians over the Greek affair was feigned is not supported by the available evidence. Peter Padfield, *Himmler: Reichsführer-SS* (New York: Henry Holt, 1990), p. 314.

25. Halder, *Halder Diaries,* vol. 5, p. 28; *DGFP*, vol. 11, nos. 505, 519, 589, pp. 859–860, 876–877, 999; and Keitel, *Generalfeldmarschall Keitel,* p. 248. Soddu was eventually dismissed as well, with Cavallero taking over command in Albania. This change in command did not even rate a mention in the OKW war diary. Knox, *Mussolini Unleashed,* pp. 257–258; and *KTB/OKW,* 18 December 1940, vol. 1, p. 234.

26. *DGFP*, vol. 11, nos. 452, 498, 499, pp. 790, 850–851; and Halder, *Halder Diaries,* vol. 5, p. 63.

27. *KTB/OKW,* 1 November 1940, vol. 1, p. 143; Halder, *Halder Diaries,* vol. 5, p. 7; *DGFP*, vol. 11, no. 511, pp. 867–869; and Detlef Vogel, "Die deutsche Balkanpolitik im Herbst 1940 und Früjahr 1941," in *Das Deutsche Reich und der Zweite Weltkrieg,* vol. 3, p. 421.

28. *DGFP*, vol. 11, no. 487, p. 836.

29. Gundelach, *Die Deutsche Luftwaffe im Mittelmeer,* vol. 1, pp. 90–91. Lossberg inflated the figures only slightly. Lieutenant Colonel Bernhard von Lossberg, OKW National Defense Section, "Operations in the Southeast," 5 May 1941, NARA T-77/792/5520954.

30. *KTB/OKW,* 20 November 1940, vol. 1, p. 183; Halder, *Halder Diaries,* vol. 5, p. 34; and *DGFP*, vol. 11, no. 538, pp. 911–914.

31. Keitel, *Generalfeldmarschall Keitel,* p. 241; Rintelen, "Operational Command in the German-Italian Coalition," 19 February 1948, Nachlass Rintelen, BA-MA N 433/5; *KTB/OKW,* 13 November 1940, vol. 1, p. 171 (since the conference did not take place until 14–15 November 1940, it would seem fairly obvious that the diary entry was made well after the conference and in the wrong place); Badoglio, *Italy in the Second World War,* p. 31; and Knox, *Mussolini Unleashed,* p. 244.

32. *DGFP*, vol. 11, no. 353, pp. 610; Ciano, *Diary,* p. 396; *DGFP*, vol. 11, nos. 369, 452, 586, pp. 639–643, 789–791, 990–994.

33. *KTB/OKW,* 22 January 1941, vol. 1, p. 272; and *DGFP*, vol. 11, nos. 672, 679, pp. 1127–1133, 1145–1151.

34. Rintelen to *OKW,* 2115 Hours, 29 January 1941, NARA T-78/359/6319227; Halder, *Halder Diaries,* vol. 5, p. 198; Rich, *Hitler's War Aims,* vol. 2, p. 240; and

George E. Blau, *The German Campaign in the Balkans (Spring 1941)* (Washington, D.C.: Department of the Army, 1953), p. 15.

35. Rintelen to OKW, 3 March 1941, NARA T-78/359/6319295; Cavallero, *Diario,* pp. 107–111; Cervi, *Hollow Legions,* p. 234; and Rintelen to OKW, 5 April 1941, NARA T-78/359/6319329.

36. Weinberg, *World at Arms,* p. 219. The course of negotiations between Germany and Bulgaria can be followed through the documents published in *DGFP,* vol. 11.

37. *DGFP,* vol. 11, no. 514, p. 872; and Weinberg, *World at Arms,* p. 216.

38. *DGFP,* vol. 11, no. 378, p. 652; and Vogel, "Die deutsche Balkanpolitik im Herbst 1940 und Frühjahr 1941," pp. 428–429.

39. *DGFP,* vol. 11, no. 511, p. 867.

40. *DGFP,* vol. 11, no. 644, p. 1076.

41. *DGFP,* vol. 11, no. 649, pp. 1081–1085; and Halder, *Halder Diaries,* vol. 5, p. 113.

42. *DGFP,* vol. 11, nos. 656, 662, pp. 1101–1103, 1113; Blau, *German Campaign in the Balkans,* p. 16; and Halder, *Halder Diaries,* vol. 5, p. 112. For a slightly different perspective on OKW's involvement, see Warlimont, *Im Hauptquartier der deutschen Wehrmacht,* p. 143.

43. *DGFP,* vol. 11, nos. 704, 738, pp. 1185, 1237; *DGFP,* vol. 12, nos. 54, 86, 98, pp. 104, 160, 181; and Halder, *Halder Diaries,* vol. 6, p. 11.

44. *DGFP,* vol. 12, no. 114, p. 203.

45. *DGFP,* vol. 12, nos. 130, 131, 156, 165, 173, pp. 230–232, 281–282, 291–294, 303–304.

46. *DGFP,* vol. 12, no. 211, p. 264.

47. Blau, *German Campaign in the Balkans,* p. 21; and *DGFP,* vol. 12, no. 214, p. 368.

48. *DGFP,* vol. 12, no. 217, pp. 372–375; Detlef Vogel, "Von Umsturz im Jugoslawien bis zum Kriegsausbruch am 6 April 1941," in *Das Deutsche Reich und der Zweite Weltkrieg,* vol. 3, p. 444; and Hartmann, *Halder,* p. 254.

49. *DGFP,* vol. 12, no. 223, pp. 395–396; OKH, Deployment Directive for "*Operation 25*" as Well as Supplemental Directive for "*Marita,*" 30 March 1941, NARA T-78/329/6285875; and Lieutenant Colonel Bernhard von Lossberg, OKW National Defense Section, "Operations in the Southeast," 5 May 1941, NARA T-77/792/5520954.

50. Weinberg, *World at Arms,* p. 221.

51. *DGFP,* vol. 12, no. 215, pp. 369–371.

52. The Vienna Awards were Hungary's means of regaining the territory lost in World War I, effective through the vehicle of German expansion. In the First Vienna Award in 1938, Hitler gave Hungary back the territory lost to Czechoslovakia, as part of his dismemberment of the Czech state after the Munich Agreement. In the Second Vienna Award in 1940, Hitler forced Romania to cede to Hungary part of the territory lost to Romania in the Treaty of Trianon after World War I.

53. *DGFP,* vol. 12, no. 261, p. 447; Carlile A. Macartney, *A History of Hungary 1929–1945* (New York: Praeger, 1956), vol. 1, p. 489; and Cecil D. Eby, *Hungary at War* (University Park: Pennsylvania State University Press, 1998), p. 15.

54. Originally the Hungarian Second Army under Lieutenant General Gusztáv Jany was to play a major role in the operation, but in the event most of the forces that were initially allocated to Jany went instead to the Hungarian Third Army. *DGFP*, vol. 12, no. 223, pp. 395–396; OKH, Deployment Directive for *"Operation 25"* as Well as Supplemental Directive for *Marita*, 30 March 1941, NARA T-78/329/6285875; and Leo W. G. Niehorster, *The Royal Hungarian Army, 1920–1945* (Bayside, N.Y.: Axis Europa Books, 1998), p. 64.

55. OKH, Deployment Directive for *"Operation 25,"* as Well as Supplemental Directive for *"Marita,"* 30 March 1941, NARA T-78/329/6285875; *DGFP*, vol. 12, no. 256, p. 441; *KTB*/German General at the Headquarters of the Royal Hungarian Armed Forces, 1 April 1941, BA-MA RH 31 V/1; and Halder, *Halder Diaries*, vol. 6, p. 47. Less critical in this regard is Megargee, *Inside Hitler's High Command*, pp. 100–101. In his report, of course, Lossberg wrote that Hitler's essential exercising of command over the Italians and Hungarians was simply the mark of brilliance on the part of the Führer, the ultimate combination of both "strategist and statesman." Lieutenant Colonel Bernhard von Lossberg, OKW National Defense Section, "Operations in the Southeast," 5 May 1941, NARA T-77/792/5520954.

56. Telephone interview with Bela Király, 20 December 1993. Professor Király was one of my professors in graduate school.

57. *KTB*/German General at the Headquarters of the Royal Hungarian Armed Forces, 3 April 1941, BA-MA RH 31 V/1.

58. *DGFP*, vol. 12, nos. 256, 281, pp. 441, 477–478; and Rintelen to OKW, 5 April 1941, NARS T-78/359/6319329.

59. There is considerable debate on how many casualties resulted from the raid. Numbers range from 1,500 to 30,000 killed. The truth probably comes closer to the larger number. Detlef Vogel, "Der deutsche Überfall auf Jugoslawien und Greichenland," in *Das Deutsche Reich und der Zweite Weltkrieg*, vol. 3, pp. 458–459; Weinberg, *World at Arms*, p. 220; and Blau, *German Campaign in the Balkans*, 49.

60. *KTB*/German General at the Headquarters of the Royal Hungarian Armed Forces, 12 April 1941, BA-MA RH 31 V/1; and Cervi, *Hollow Legions*, p. 278.

61. Blau, *German Campaign in the Balkans*, p. 111; and Vogel, "Der deutsche Überfall auf Jugoslawien und Greichenland," p. 475.

62. *DGFP*, vol. 12, no. 335, p. 539; Halder, *Halder Diaries*, vol. 6, pp. 76–78; and Blau, *German Campaign in the Balkans*, p. 118.

63. *DGFP*, vol. 12, nos. 379, 409, pp. 600, 644–647; and Halder, *Halder Diaries*, vol. 6, p. 78.

64. Sadkovich, *Italian Navy in World War II*, p. 152; Charles W. Koburger Jr., *Naval Warfare in the Eastern Mediterranean 1940–1945* (Westport, Conn.: Praeger, 1993), pp. 94–95; and Franz Kurowski, *Der Kampf um Kreta* (Herford: Maximilian Verlag, 1965), p. 117. Bragadin overstates the losses to the convoy. Bragadin, *Italian Navy in World War II*, pp. 108–109. Ciano makes no mention of the incident. Ciano, *Diary*, pp. 427–430.

65. IMT, *TTMWC*, vol. 27, Doc. 1195-PS, pp. 60–62.

66. *DGFP*, vol. 12, no. 335, pp. 539–540; OKH to Second and Twelfth Armies, 20 May 1941, NARA T-78/329/6285773; and Halder, *Halder Diaries*, vol. 6, p. 89.

67. Blau, *German Campaign in the Balkans,* p. 112.

68. Most serious scholars agree that *Barbarossa* could not have started any ear-lier than it did. See, for examples, Blau, *German Campaign in the Balkans,* p. 150; Higgins, *Hitler and Russia,* pp. 109–110; and Vogel, "Der deutsche Überfall auf Jugoslawien und Greichenland," p. 483.

69. Cervi, *Hollow Legions,* p. 308.

70. Lieutenant Colonel Bernhard von Lossberg, OKW National Defense Section, "Operations in the Southeast," 5 May 1941, NARA T-77/792/5520954, *DGFP,* vol. 12, no. 385, p. 607; and IMT, *TTMWC,* vol. 27, Doc. 1195-PS, pp. 60–62.

71. Mack Smith, *Mussolini,* p. 266. A German summary report on the state of the Italian army dated 20 November 1942 noted that the divisions in the Balkans had not received any new equipment or men since the spring of 1941. German General at Italian Armed Forces Headquarters, Report on the Status of the Italian Army, 20 November 1942, NARA T-78/343/6300382.

72. Sadkovich's contention that Hitler's interfering with Italy's sphere of influence in the Balkans, as well as Berlin's unresponsiveness to Italian requests for raw materi-als and weapons, led Mussolini to attack Greece does have an element of truth to it. Sadkovich, "German Military Incompetence through Italian Eyes," pp. 48–49. What he overlooks, however, is that both Mussolini and his political and military advis-ers had long-standing plans to expand into the area. In addition, with the demands for *Barbarossa* taking priority, German military leaders considered Italian requests excessive, to say the least. This attitude extended back to before the war, as well as after the miscarrying of the attack on Greece. Mallett, *Italian Navy and Fascist Expansionism,* p. 138; Ciano, *Diary,* p. 376; Mack Smith, *Mussolini,* p. 231; *DGFP,* vol. 7, no. 301, pp. 309–310; Ciano, *Diary,* p. 265; *DGFP,* vol. 10, no. 129, p. 154; Rintelen to OKW, 20 December 1940, NARA T-77/590/1771374; and Halder, *Hal-der Diaries,* vol. 5, p. 80.

5. Barbarossa

1. Halder, *Halder Diaries,* vol. 6, p. 97.

2. *DGFP,* vol. 12, no. 660, p. 1068.

3. *DGFP,* vol. 12, no. 660, p. 1066; IMT, *TTMWC,* Doc. 1456-PS, vol. 27, pp. 220–221; Hans Umbreit, "Die besetzten Gebiete as Teil des deutschen Macht-bereichs," in *Das Deutsche Reich und der Zweite Weltkrieg,* vol. 5/2, p. 38; and Jürgen Förster, "Wehrmacht, Krieg und Holocaust," in *Die Wehrmacht: Mythos und Realität,* ed. Rolf-Dieter Müller and Hans-Erich Volkmann (Munich: R. Oldenbourg, 1999), p. 953.

4. This chapter will discuss the respective parts played by the Finnish, Roma-nian, Hungarian, and Italian forces. The best study of the Blue Division's activities in Russia is still Kleinfeld and Tambs, *Hitler's Spanish Legion.* Slovakia's part in the war is discussed in Jürgen Förster, "Die Entscheidungen der 'Dreierpaktstaaten,'" in *Das Deutsche Reich und der Zweite Weltkrieg,* vol. 4, pp. 894–897. Croatia sent enough volunteers to form a reinforced regiment. *DGFP,* vol. 13, no. 46, p. 52; and Peter Gosztony, *Hitlers Fremde Heere: Das Schicksal der nichtdeutschen Armeen im Ostfeldzug* (Düsseldorf: Econ Verlag, 1976), pp. 130–133.

5. Weinberg, *Foreign Policy of Hitler's Germany*, vol. 1, p. 8; Warlimont, *Im Hauptquartier der deutschen Wehrmacht*, p. 160; and Rintelen, "Operational Command in the German-Italian Coalition," 19 February 1948, Nachlass Rintelen, BA-MA N 433/5.

6. *DGFP*, vol. 12, nos. 114, 223, 393, 605, pp. 203, 396, 623, 983; and Weinberg, *World at Arms*, p. 221.

7. Förster, "Die Entscheidungen der 'Dreierpaktstaaten,'" p. 901.

8. *DGFP*, vol. 7, nos. 212, 246, 329, pp. 224, 260, 334; Martin, "Das deutsch-japanische Bündnis im Zweiten Weltkrieg," p. 125; Meskill, *Hitler and Japan*, p. 10; and Weinberg, *Foreign Policy of Hitler's Germany*, vol. 2, p. 630.

9. The text is in *DGFP*, vol. 11, no. 118, pp. 204–205. A picturesque description of the scene in the Reich Chancery is in Schmidt, *Hitler's Interpreter*, p. 191.

10. Weinberg, *World at Arms*, p. 182; Meskill, *Hitler and Japan*, p. 27; and Warlimont, *Im Hauptquartier der deutschen Wehrmacht*, p. 160.

11. Ciano, *Diary*, p. 385; Michael Bloch, *Ribbentrop: A Biography* (New York: Crown, 1992), p. 306; *DGFP*, vol. 11, nos. 73, 109, 152, pp. 115–116, 188, 261; and Halder, *Halder Diaries*, vol. 4, p. 211.

12. Meskill, *Hitler and Japan*, pp. 151–153; and Rolf-Dieter Müller, "Rahmenbedingungen und zivile Faktoren der Kriegsproduktion," in *Das Deutsche Reich und der Zweite Weltkrieg*, vol. 5/2, pp. 540–544.

13. *DGFP*, vol. 12, no. 660, p. 1068; OKW to Luftwaffe High Command, German Africa Corps, 20 May 1941, BA-MA RL 2 II/38; and DiNardo and Hughes, "Germany and Coalition Warfare in the World Wars," p. 182.

14. Mack Smith, *Mussolini*, p. 269; Knox, *Hitler's Italian Allies*, pp. 81–82; and Ciano, *Diary*, p. 440.

15. *DGFP*, vol. 12, no. 250, pp. 434–435; Gerd Ueberschär, "Die Einbeziehung Skandinaviens in die Planung 'Barbarossa,'" in *Das Deutsche Reich und der Zweite Weltkrieg*, vol. 4, p. 365; Oliver Warner, *Marshal Mannerheim and the Finns* (Helsinki: Otava, 1967), p. 183; and Olli Vehviläinen, *Finland in the Second World War: Between Germany and Russia* (New York: Palgrave, 2002), p. 89.

16. Transportation problems made it impossible for the Germans to exploit the resources at Petsamo as much as they would have liked. Hitler's worries in this regard were heightened by the fact that the routes from the Petsamo mines could be easily blocked by the Soviets. Rich, *Hitler's War Aims*, vol. 1, p. 206; and John Perkins, "Coins for Conflict: Nickel and the Axis, 1933–1945," *Historian* 55, no. 1 (Autumn 1992): 98. Greece was another major supplier of nickel to Germany. I. G. Farben, "Der deutsche Rohstoffbezug aus der UdSSR und Südosteuropa," ca. 1939, NARA T-84/80/1367891.

17. To be sure, Finland was a target (one of many) for SS recruiters, a topic about which more will be said later.

18. Chief of the General Staff of Army Command Norway, Results of German-Finnish Conference in Helsinki, 3–5 June 1941, 7 June 1941, NARA T-312/994/9187113; Waldemar Erfurth, *Der Finnische Krieg, 1941–1944* (Revised and expanded edition) (Wiesbaden: Limes Verlag, 1977), p. 37; John H. Wuorinen, ed., *Finland and World War II 1939–1944* (1948; repr., Westport, Conn.: Greenwood Press, 1983), p. 115; and Vehviläinen, *Finland in the Second World War*, p. 91.

19. Tibor Hajdú and Zsuzsa L. Nagy, "Revolution, Counterrevolution, Consolidation," in *A History of Hungary,* ed. Peter F. Sugar and Péter Hanák (Bloomington: Indiana University Press, 1994), p. 314; and Axworthy, Scafes, and Craciunoiu, *Third Axis/Fourth Ally,* p. 12.

20. Axworthy, Scafes, and Craciunoiu, *Third Axis/Fourth Ally,* p. 13.

21. Weinberg, *Foreign Policy of Hitler's Germany,* vol. 1, p. 118.

22. Maurice Pearton, *Oil and the Romanian State* (New York: Oxford University Press, 1971), p. 251; Rebecca Haynes, *Romanian Policy towards Germany, 1936–1940* (New York: St. Martin's Press, 2000), p. 22; and Weinberg, *Foreign Policy of Hitler's Germany,* vol. 2, pp. 237–238. Time does not permit here a recitation of the tortuous path followed by Romanian politics during the 1930s.

23. *DGFP,* vol. 11, no. 19, p. 24; and Axworthy, Scafes, and Craciunoiu, *Third Axis/Fourth Ally,* p. 23.

24. *DGFP,* vol. 11, no. 19, p. 24; and Halder, *Halder Diaries,* vol. 5, p. 40.

25. *DGFP,* vol. 11, no. 75, p. 127; *KTB/OKW,* 18 September 1940, vol. 1, p. 81; Halder, *Halder Diaries,* vol. 4, p. 202; Haynes, *Romanian Policy toward Germany,* p. 153; and Radu Ioanid, *The Sword of the Archangel: Fascist Ideology in Romania* (Boulder, Colo.: East European Monographs, 1990), p. 193.

26. OKW, Defense of Constanza and the Oil Area, 20 February 1941, BA-MA RL 2 II/271; and Halder, *Halder Diaries,* vol. 6, p. 102.

27. Prior to May 1940, Britain provided the biggest concern for the Germans in regard to the safety of the Romanian oil fields. *DGFP,* vol. 9, no. 116, p. 165; Rich, *Hitler's War Aims,* vol. 2, p. 241; and Jürgen Förster, "Die Gewinnung von Verbündeten in Südosteuropa," in *Das Deutsche Reich und der Zweite Weltkrieg,* vol. 4, p. 333.

28. *DGFP,* vol. 11, no. 84, pp. 144–145.

29. Command Staff, Luftwaffe High Command to Fourth Air Fleet, 18 January 1941, BA-MA RL 2 II/271, 239th Infantry Division, Identification of Aircraft in the Southeast Area, 12 April 1941, NARA T-315/1713/000845; Förster, "Die Gewinnung von Verbündeten in Südosteuropa," p. 337; and Axworthy, Scafes, and Craciunoiu, *Third Axis/Fourth Ally,* p. 278.

30. Corum, "*Luftwaffe* and Its Allied Air Forces in World War II," p. 12; and Axworthy, Scafes, and Craciunoiu, *Third Axis/Fourth Ally,* pp. 278–280.

31. DLM to Luftwaffe High Command, Yugoslavian Booty for Romania, 5 July 1941, NARA T405/49/4888254. The characteristics of these aircraft are discussed in Axworthy, Scafes, and Craciunoiu, *Third Axis/Fourth Ally,* pp. 253–269; and Corum, "*Luftwaffe* and Its Allied Air Forces in World War II," p. 12.

32. *DGFP,* vol. 11, no. 80, p. 136. Schobert took over after his arrival in Bucharest on 23 May 1941; *DGFP,* vol. 12, no. 544, p. 864. After both Schobert and Hansen left Romania in command of the Eleventh Army and LIV Corps, respectively, Hauffe took over as head of the DHM. DHM, Build-up and Action of the Romanian Army since the Start of the German Army Mission, 18 January 1942, NARA T-501/269/000069; and Förster, "Die Gewinnung von Verbündeten in Südosteuropa," p. 337.

33. DHM, Build-up and Action of the Romanian Army since the Start of the German Army Mission, 18 January 1942, NARA T-501/269/000069; *DGFP,* vol. 11, no. 84, p. 145; and DHM, Order of the Day No. 4, 12 November 1940, NARA T-501/272/000418.

34. *DGFP*, vol. 11, nos. 9, 691, p. 11, 1169; and Förster, "Die Gewinnung von Verbündeten in Südosteuropa," p. 339.

35. OKH, Instructions on Command Relationships in Romania, 28 December 1940, BA-MA RL 2 II/271.

36. OKW, Instructions for the Behavior of German Soldiers in Romania, 11 January 1941, NARA T-501/281/000230; Förster, "Die Gewinnung von Verbündeten in Südosteuropa," p. 338; and DHM, Build-up and Action of the Romanian Army since the Start of the German Army Mission, 18 January 1942, NARA T-501/269/000069.

37. DHM, Build-up and Action of the Romanian Army since the Start of the German Army Mission, 18 January 1942, NARA T-501/269/000069; and Chief of the General Staff of the DHM, Training of General Officers, 1 February 1941, NARA T-501/281/000216.

38. DHM, Course of Instruction for Romanian Artillery Officers, 12 May 1941, NARA T-315/1516/000402.

39. 16th Panzer Division, List of Officers for the Staff of the 16th Panzer Division from 1 November–11 December 1940, 11 December 1940, NARA T-315/680/000013; and DHM, Course of Instruction for Romanian Artillery Officers, 12 May 1941, NARA T-315/1516/000402.

40. Commander of Training Staff II of the DHM in Romania, Situation Report, 7 February 1941, NARA T-315/680/000134.

41. DHM, Build-up and Action of the Romanian Army since the Start of the German Army Mission, 18 January 1942, NARA T-501/269/000069; DHM, Report and Map Annexes of the German 2nd Liaison Command on the Campaign of the Romanian Fourth Army, 25 October 1941, NARA T-501/275/000605; and German 13th Liaison Command, Final Report of the German 13th Liaison Command, 29 October 1941, NARA T-501/275/000706.

42. DHM, Build-up and Action of the Romanian Army since the Start of the German Army Mission, 18 January 2002, NARA T-501/269/000069.

43. Stein, *Waffen SS,* p. 169. For details of *SS* recruiting efforts in Finland, see Berger to Himmler, 3 December 1940, NARA T-175/127/2652259; and Gerd Ueberschär, "Freiwillige aus Nordeuropa zu Beginn des Krieges gegen die Sowjetunion," in *Das Deutsche Reich und der Zweite Weltkrieg,* vol. 4, pp. 926–930.

44. Killinger to Himmler, 26 February 1941, NARA T-175/128/2653688.

45. See, for example, article from *Banater Deutsche Zeitung,* 14 December 1940, NARA T-315/680/000045. The file that contains that particular article has a number of articles from various German-language papers published in Romania.

46. 16th Panzer Division, Partial Record of Conversation between *Gauleiter* Fromm and Hube, 28 January 1941, NARA T-315/680/000088.

47. OKW, Instructions for the Behavior of German Soldiers in Romania, 11 January 1941, NARA T-501/281/000230; OKW, Special Instructions for German Units Staying on Finnish Sovereign Territory, 10 June 1941, NARA T-77/488/1652397; and 239th Infantry Division, Basic Instructions for German Units in Romania, 3 April 1941, NARA T-315/1713/000835.

48. IMT, *TTMWC,* Doc. 2353-PS, vol. 30, p. 279; USAMHI, MSS no. P-108, Part I, Major General Burkhard Müller-Hillebrand, "Germany and Her Allies in World War II," 1953, p. 109; and DLM to Luftwaffe High Command, Chief of Procurement, Yugoslavian Booty for Romania, 5 July 1941, NARA T-405/49/4888254.

49. Seventeenth Army Quartermaster, Incorporation of Captured Material, 11 August 1941, NARA T-312/664/8297707. See also General for Captured Air Material, Conference with General Ionescu of the Romanian Air Force, Major Bindner and Captain Pesalken, Commanders of the 16th and 5th Air Material Staffs, Collection of Captured Material in the Joint Operations of German and Romanian Troops in Bacau on 28 June 1941, 30 June 1941, NARA T-405/49/4887887.

50. Halder, *Halder Diaries*, vol. 5, p. 99; and *DGFP*, vol. 12, no. 69, p. 125.

51. *DGFP*, vol. 12, nos. 431, 501, pp. 685, 787; and Halder, *Halder Diaries*, vol. 6, p. 115.

52. This was General Waldemar Erfurth, who arrived for duty at Mannerheim's headquarters on 13 June 1941. Erfurth, *Der Finnische Krieg*, p. 36.

53. *DGFP*, vol. 12, no. 554, pp. 879–885; Warlimont, *Im Hauptquartier der deutschen Wehrmacht*, p. 158; and Marshal Carl Mannerheim, *The Memoirs of Marshal Mannerheim* (London: Cassell, 1953), p. 406.

54. Albert Seaton, *The Russo-German War 1941–45* (New York: Praeger, 1970), p. 68; Ueberschär, "Die Einbeziehung Skandinaviens in die Plannung 'Barbarossa,'" p. 392; Erfurth, *Der Finnische Krieg*, p. 30; Halder, *Halder Diaries*, vol. 6, p. 148; and Chief of Staff, Army Command Norway, Results of the German-Finnish Conference in Helsinki, 3–5 June 1941, 7 June 1941, NARA T-312/994/9187113. A brief summary of this document is in *DGFP*, vol. 12, no. 592, p. 963.

55. *DGFP*, vol. 12, no. 431, p. 685.

56. *DGFP*, vol. 11, no. 532, p. 901.

57. Gosztony, *Hitlers Fremde Heere*, p. 58, IMT, *TTMWC*, Doc. 2353-PS, vol. 30, p. 279; and OKH to Army Group South, Lessons from the Russo-Finnish War, 2 October 1940, NARA T-312/256/000703.

58. *DGFP*, vol. 12, no. 431, p. 685; Halder, *Halder Diaries*, vol. 6, p. 154; and *KTB*/German General at the Headquarters of the Royal Hungarian Armed Forces, 14 June 1941, BA-MA RH 31 V/1.

59. See, for example, 239th Infantry Division, Basic Instructions for German Units in Romania, 3 April 1941, NARA T-315/1713/000835.

60. Commander of the Luftwaffe to Fourth Air Fleet, 18 February 1941, BA-MA RL 2 II/271.

61. DLM, Commitment and Missions of Colonel Bassenge's Liaison Staff to the General Staff of the Royal Romanian Air Force, 15 June 1941, NARA T-405/49/4887905, *DGFP*, vol. 12, no. 644, p. 1049; and J. L. Roba and C. Crăciunoiu, *Seaplanes over the Black Sea: German-Romanian Operations 1941–1944* (Bucharest: Editura Modelism, 1995), p. 7.

62. Halder, *Halder Diaries*, vol. 6, p. 154; and *DGFP*, vol. 12, no. 644, p. 1048.

63. Hixson and Cooling, *Combined Operations in Peace and War*, pp. 206–207; and DiNardo, "Dysfunctional Coalition," p. 715.

64. Schmidt, *Hitler's Interpreter*, p. 205. See also Jürgen Förster, *Stalingrad: Risse im Budnis 1942/43* (Freiburg: Verlag Rombach, 1975), p. 16.

65. *DGFP*, vol. 11, no. 381, p. 662; Joseph C. Drăgan, *Antonescu: Marshal and Ruler of Romania (1940–1944)*, trans. Andrei Bartas (Bucharest: Europa Nova, 1995), p. 220; Schmidt, *Hitler's Interpreter*, p. 205; Richthofen Diary, 6 June 1942, Nachlass Richthofen, BA-MA N 671/9; Kershaw, *Hitler 1936–1945*, p. 383; Hitler, *Hitler's Table Talk*, p. 49; and Förster, *Stalingrad*, p. 16.

66. *KTB*/German General at the Headquarters of the Royal Hungarian Armed Forces, 17 June 1941, BA-MA RH 31 V/1; and Hartmann, *Halder,* p. 266. The duties of military attachés in countries that also hosted a German army-level headquarters is laid out in OKH, Position of German Army Headquarters in Foreign Countries as Opposed to Military Attachés, 23 June 1941, NARA T-77/711/1928122.

67. Warlimont, *Im Hauptquartier der deutschen Wehrmacht,* p. 160; Rintelen, "Operational Command in the German-Italian Coalition," 19 February 1948, Nachlass Rintelen, BA-MA N 433/5; and USAMHI, MSS no. P-108, Part I, p. 11.

68. Warner, *Marshal Mannerheim and the Finns,* p. 179. An outline of Finland's mobilization schedule is in Halder, *Halder Diaries,* vol. 6, p. 148.

69. Chief of the General Staff of Army Command Norway, Results of the German-Finnish Conference in Helsinki, 3–5 June 1941, 7 June 1941, NARA T-312/994/9187113; *DGFP,* vol. 12, nos. 669, 675, pp. 1079, 1083; Halder, *Halder Diaries,* vol. 6, p. 175; Erfurth, *Der Finnische Krieg,* p. 39; and *DGFP,* vol. 13, no. 15, pp. 19–20.

70. Weinberg, *World at Arms,* p. 271; Erfurth, *Der Finnische Krieg,* p. 36; and Vehviläinen, *Finland in the Second World War,* p. 95.

71. Vice Admiral Friedrich Ruge, *The Soviets as Naval Opponents 1941–1945* (Annapolis, Md.: Naval Institute Press, 1979), pp. 22–23.

72. Erfurth had very little to say about this in his book. Erfurth, *Der Finnische Krieg,* p. 43; and Halder, *Halder Diaries,* vol. 6, p. 263.

73. *DGFP,* vol. 13, nos. 262, pp. 417–418; and Gerd Ueberschär, "Kriegführung und Politik in Nordeuropa," in *Das Deutsche Reich und der Zweite Weltkrieg,* vol. 4, p. 852.

74. *DGFP,* vol. 13, nos. 228, 248, pp. 356, 396; and Erfurth to OKW, 27 August 1941, NARA T-312/1010/9205523.

75. *DGFP,* vol. 13, no. 349, p. 550; Keitel to Mannerheim, 22 September 1941, NARA T-77/786/5514544; Erfurth to OKW Staff, National Defense Section, 25 September 1941, NARA T-312/1010/9205513; Mannerheim to Keitel, 1 October 1941, NARA T-77/786/5514539; Halder, *Halder Diaries,* vol. 7, p. 80; Erfurth, *Der Finnische Krieg,* p. 66; and Ueberschär, "Kriegführung und Politik in Nordeuropa," p. 853.

76. Liaison Officer to Finnish III Corps, Report on the Discontinuation of the Attack of the Finnish III Corps in Mid November 1941, 21 November 1941, NARA T-312/1010/9205549.

77. Franz Schreiber, *Kampf unter dem Nordlicht: Deutsch-Finnische Waffenbruderschaft am Polarkreis* (Osnabrück: Munin Verlag, 1969), p. 127; and Ueberschär, "Kriegführung und Politik in Nordeuropa," p. 820.

78. *DGFP,* vol. 13, nos. 493, 507, pp. 814, 855; Warner, *Marshal Mannerheim and the Finns,* p. 187; Vehviläinen, *Finland in the Second World War,* p. 101; and Ueberschär, "Kriegführung und Politik in Nordeuropa," p. 856.

79. USAMHI, MSS, no. P-108, Part II, p. 104; and Corum, "*Luftwaffe* and Its Allied Air Forces in World War II," p. 14.

80. Halder, *Halder Diaries,* vol. 7, p. 92; Erfurth, *Der Finnische Krieg,* pp. 94–95; 169th Infantry Division, Basic Conduct of Forest Combat Against the Red Army, 12 July 1941, NARA T-314/876/000838; Army Group North to OKH, 22 October 1942, NARA T-311/72/7093941; and Army Group North to OKH, 11 December 1942, NARA T-311/72/7093952.

81. *DGFP,* vol. 12, nos. 614, 644, pp. 1004, 1048–1049. Axworthy suggests that Killinger informed Antonescu of the precise date of the attack just prior to the 11 June meeting, but contemporaneous sources dispute this. Axworthy, Scafes, and Craciunoiu, *Third Axis/Fourth Ally,* p. 43; and Halder, *Halder Diaries,* vol. 6, p. 154.

82. *DGFP,* vol. 12, nos. 614, 644, pp. 1005, 1048.

83. Ruge, *Soviets as Naval Opponents,* p. 63; and Axworthy, Scafes, and Craciunoiu, *Third Axis/Fourth Ally,* pp. 327–329.

84. Ruge, *Soviets as Naval Opponents,* pp. 64–65; and Axworthy, Scafes, and Craciunoiu, *Third Axis/Fourth Ally,* p. 331. During the same day the German Navy Mission reported the presence of a Soviet aircraft carrier in the Black Sea, a sighting of which the DLM was rightly skeptical. DLM to Bassenge, 26 June 1941, 1035 Hours, NARA T-405/49/4888373.

85. Colonel Bassenge's Liaison Staff, Organization of Coastal Shipping in the Black Sea, 25 August 1941, NARA T-405/49/4887826; Liaison Staff Bassenge to Fourth Air Fleet, Organization of Black Sea Coastal Shipping, 17 September 1941, NARA T-405/49/4887818; DLM, Proposed Organization for *"Flieger Führer Schwarzes Meer,"* 25 August 1941, NARA T-405/49/4887830; Horst Boog, "Die Operationsführung: Luftwaffe," in *Das Deutsche Reich und der Zweite Weltkrieg,* vol. 4, p. 684; and Joel S. A. Hayward, *Stopped at Stalingrad: The Luftwaffe and Hitler's Defeat in the East 1942–1943* (Lawrence: University Press of Kansas, 1998), pp. 50–51.

86. This organization was discussed almost immediately upon the outbreak of hostilities. See DLM, Employment of Staff of JG 52, 23 June 1941, NARA T-405/49/4888412; and DLM, Changes in Fighter Action, 30 June 1941, NARA T-405/49/4888335. See also Roba and Crăciunoiu, *Seaplanes over the Black Sea,* pp. 6–7.

87. DLM, Report on the Defense of the Romanian Oil Area, 14 December 1941, BA-MA RL 9/62; and Alexander Statiev, "Antonescu's Eagles against Stalin's Falcons: The Romanian Air Force, 1920–1941," *Journal of Military History* 66, no. 4 (October 2002): 1102.

88. Chief of the German Military Mission in Romania to Bassenge, 17 July 1941, NARA T-405/49/48871.

89. *DGFP,* vol. 11, no. 84, p. 145.

90. Statiev, "Antonescu's Eagles against Stalin's Falcons," p. 1093; and DLM, Commitment and Missions of Colonel Bassenge's Liaison Staff to the General Staff of the Royal Romanian Air Force, 15 June 1941, NARA T-405/49/4887905.

91. Statiev, "Antonescu's Eagles against Stalin's Falcons," p. 1094; and German IV Air Corps Situation Reports, 22–23 June 1941, BA-MA RL 8/31.

92. See, for example, IV Air Corps Situation Report, 5 July 1941, BA-MA RL 8/31.

93. Statiev, "Antonescu's Eagles against Stalin's Falcons," pp. 1100–1111.

94. *DGFP,* vol. 11, no. 532, p. 901; and Friedrich Forstmeier, *Odessa 1941: Der Kampf um Stadt und Hafen und die Räumung der Seefestung 15 August bis 16 Oktober 1941* (Freiburg: Verlag Rombach, 1967), p. 18.

95. Axworthy, Scafes, and Craciunoiu, *Third Axis/Fourth Ally,* p. 45.

96. DHM, Build-up and Action of the Romanian Army since the Start of the German Military Mission, 18 January 1942, NARA T-501/269/000069.

97. OKH, Foreign Armies East, Handbook on the Romanian Army, February 1940, NARA T-501/281/000004; and German Liaison Staff with the Romanian I Mountain Corps and Romanian 4th Mountain Brigade to Chief of the General Staff of the DHM, 23 April 1941, NARA T-501/275/000284.

98. Axworthy, Scafes, and Craciunoiu, *Third Axis/Fourth Ally,* p. 45; and DHM, Build-up and Action of the Romanian Army since the Start of the German Army Mission, 18 January 1942, NARA T-501/269/000069.

99. XXX Corps to Eleventh Army, Evening Report, 23 June 1941, NARA T-314/823/000279; and XXX Corps, Corps Order No. 7, 25 June 1941, NARA T-314/823/000282.

100. XXX Corps, Personnel List (Reporting Period 22–30 June 1941), 27 March 1942, NARA T-314/823/000258.

101. XXX Corps, Warning Order for *München,* 25 June 1941, NARA T-314/823/000290; and DHM, Report and Map Annexes of the German Second Liaison Command on the Campaign of the Romanian Fourth Army, 25 October 1941, NARA T-501/275/000605.

102. Seaton, *Russo-German War,* p. 136; *DGFP,* vol. 12, no. 57, p. 66; and DHM, Report and Map Annexes of the German Second Liaison Command on the Campaign of the Romanian Fourth Army, 25 October 1941, NARA T-501/275/000605.

103. Air Force General Officer for Captured Aerial Material, Instructions for the Collection and Handling of Material Captured in Operations, 30 June 1941, NARA T-405/49/4887889. For a good example of an individual service's approach to this, see Air Force General Officer for Captured Aerial Material, Conference with General Ionescu of the Romanian Air Force, Major Bindner Captain Peschken, Commanders of Air Material Staffs 16 and 5, Collection of Material Captured in the Joint Operations of German and Romanian Troops in Bacau on 28 June 1941, 30 June 1941, NARA T-405/49/4887887.

104. General Staff, 1st Border Division, Instructions to the General Order for the Coming Operations in Bessarabia, 3 July 1941, NARA T-501/280/000863. For various views on this question, see German 13th Liaison Command, Final Report of the German 13th Liaison Command, 29 October 1941, NARA T-501/275/000706; and German 15th Liaison Command, Report No. 3 on Romanian 13th Division, 14 July 1941, NARA T-312/359/7932932.

105. DHM, Report and Map Annexes of the German Second Liaison Command on the Campaign of the Romanian Fourth Army, 25 October 1941, NARA T-501/275/000605; German 15th Liaison Command, Status Report No. 3 on Romanian 13th Division, 14 July 1941, NARA T-312/359/7932932; XXX Corps, Order for Preparation for Deployment for *Barbarossa,* 4 June 1941, NARA T-314/823/001300; *DGFP,* vol. 13, no. 135, p. 194; Halder, *Halder Diaries,* vol. 6, p. 214; and German 37th Liaison Command to German 2nd Liaison Command, German Awards for Romanian 1st Border Division, 2 August 1941, NARA T-501/280/000854.

106. Alexander Dallin, *German Rule in Russia 1941–1945: A Study of Occupation Policies,* 2nd ed. (Boulder, Colo.: Westview Press, 1981), p. 90.

107. *DGFP,* vol. 12, no. 614, p. 1004.

108. *DGFP,* vol. 13, no. 57, p. 67; German Eleventh Army, Army Order for the Attack across the Dniestr and the Penetration of the Stalin Line, 13 July 1941, NARA T-312/359/7932955; Major of the General Staff Stephanus, Conversation with Major

General Zaharescu, Chief of the General Staff of the Romanian Third Army, 14 July 1941, NARA T-312/359/7932935; and Ernst Klink, "Die Operationsführung: Heer," in *Das Deutsche Reich und der Zweite Weltkrieg,* vol. 4, p. 477.

6. *Playing* "va banque"

1. *DGFP,* vol. 13, no. 7, p. 9.

2. Hitler, *Hitler's Table Talk,* p. 66.

3. German Eleventh Army to Army Group South, 5 August 1941, NARA T-312/360/7934222, German IV Air Corps, Situation Report 23 July 1941, 24 July 1941, BA-MA RL 8/31; Axworthy, Scafes, and Craciunoiu, *Third Axis/Fourth Ally,* p. 65; and Seaton, *Russo-German War,* p. 140.

4. DHM, Build-up and Action of the Romanian Army since the Start of the German Army Mission, 18 January 1942, NARA T-501/269/000069; German Eleventh Army, Army Order for the Attack across the Dniestr and the Penetration of the Stalin Line, 13 July 1941, NARA T-312/359/7932955; Halder, *Halder Diaries,* vol. 6, p. 251; and Forstmeier, *Odessa 1941,* p. 19.

5. Inspection Report of Major (General Staff) Stephanus of 25 and 26 July 1941 to German XXX and XI Army Corps Romanian Third Army, 26 July 1941, NARA T-312/359/7933496; Romanian Third Army to German Eleventh Army Quartermaster, Memo on Supply of the Romanian Third Army East of the Bug River, 21 August 1941, NARA T-312/354/7927680; and German Seventeenth Army Quartermaster, Incorporation of Captured Material, 11 August 1941, NARA T-312/664/8297707. The issue of German horse-drawn transport in *Barbarossa* is considered in Richard DiNardo, *Mechanized Juggernaut or Military Anachronism? Horses and the German Army of World War II* (Westport, Conn.: Greenwood Press, 1991), pp. 35–54.

6. German XXX Army Corps to German Eleventh Army, Message on Performance of Attached Romanian Troops, 20 August 1941, NARA T-312/360/7934932; German XXX Corps to German Eleventh Army, Combat Value of Romanian Units, 9 October 1941, NARA T-314/824/000989; and Axworthy, Scafes, and Craciunoiu, *Third Axis/Fourth Ally,* pp. 66–67.

7. *DGFP,* vol. 13, nos. 188, 204, pp. 299, 317; Antonescu to Schobert, 17 August 1941, NARA T-312/360/7934779; German Eleventh Army, Chief of Staff's Memorandum, 19 August, 1941, NARA T-312/360/7934773; and Forstmeier, *Odessa 1941,* p. 23.

8. *DGFP,* vol. 13, nos. 200, 216, pp. 313, 342; Forstmeier, *Odessa 1941,* p. 24; Förster, "Die Entscheidungen der 'Dreierpaktstaaten,'" pp. 885–886; and Drăgan, *Antonescu,* p. 311.

9. Forstmeier, *Odessa 1941,* p. 29.

10. German Third Liaison Command to DHM, Situation Report, 15 August 1941, NARA T-312/360/7934911; German Thirteenth Liaison Command, Final Report of the German Thirteenth Liaison Command, 29 October 1941, NARA T-501/275/000069; and Statiev, "Antonescu's Eagles against Stalin's Falcons," p. 1104.

11. Forstmeier, *Odessa 1941,* p. 48; Halder, *Halder Diaries,* vol. 7, p. 54; and Statiev, "Antonescu's Eagles against Stalin's Falcons," p. 1100.

12. Halder, *Halder Diaries,* vol. 8, p. 56.

13. DHM, Build-up and Action of the Romanian Army since the Start of the German Military Mission, 18 January 1942, NARA T-501/269/000069; and Forstmeier, *Odessa 1941,* p. 50.

14. German Thirteenth Liaison Command, Final Report of the German Thirteenth Liaison Command, 29 October 1941, NARA T-501/275/000706; Axworthy, Scafes, and Craciunoiu, *Third Axis/Fourth Ally,* p. 53; and Forstmeier, *Odessa 1941,* p. 55.

15. Halder, *Halder Diaries,* vol. 7, p. 118; and Axworthy, Scafes, and Craciunoiu, *Third Axis/Fourth Ally,* p. 54.

16. Halder, *Halder Diaries,* vol. 7, p. 122; and Hitler to Antonescu, 5 October 1941, NARA T-311/292/000931.

17. Bassenge to Chief of the General Staff of the Romanian Air Force, Establishing Positions Relating to the Support of Attacks on Odessa by the German Luftwaffe, 10 October 1941, NARA T-405/49/4887810.

18. German Thirteenth Liaison Command, Final Report of the German Thirteenth Liaison Command, 29 October 1941, NARA T-501/275/000706; DHM, Build-up and Action of the Romanian Army since the Start of the German Army Mission, 18 January 1942, NARA T-501/269/000069; Dragan, *Antonescu,* p. 314; Forstmeier, *Odessa 1941,* pp. 83–86; and Navy High Command, Overview of the Situation in the Mediterranean, Aegean and Black Seas from 16–31 December 1941, 31 December 1941, BA-MA RM 7/115.

19. See, for example, XI Corps to Romanian First Infantry Division, 5 February 1942, NARA T-314/486/000232; XI Corps to Army Group South, Daily Report, 7 February 1942, NARA T-314/486/000291; and Romanian First Division Report to XI Corps, 23 February 1942, NARA T-314/486/000584.

20. German Second Liaison Command to Subordinate Liaison Commands, 30 July 1941, NARA T-501/280/000971.

21. *DGFP,* vol. 11, no. 532, p. 900; and Förster, "Die Gewinnung von Verbundeten in Südosteuropa," pp. 355–356.

22. *DGFP,* vol. 12, nos. 306, 371, 392, pp. 509, 581–586, 622; *KTB*/German General at the Headquarters of the Royal Hungarian Armed Forces, 22 May 1941, BA-MA RH 31 V/1; and Keitel, *Generalfeldmarschall Keitel,* p. 262.

23. Halder, *Halder Diaries,* vol. 6, pp. 97, 144; *DGFP,* vol. 12, nos. 431, 631, pp. 685, 1030; and *KTB*/German General at the Headquarters of the Royal Hungarian Armed Forces, 27–29 May 1941, BA-MA RH 31 V/1.

24. *KTB*/German General at the Headquarters of the Royal Hungarian Armed Forces, 1–12 June 1941, BA-MA RH 31 V/1; Hartmann, *Halder,* p. 266; and *DGFP,* vol. 12, nos. 631, 661, 667, pp. 1030, 1070–1071, 1077.

25. Admiral Nikolas von Horthy, *Ein Leben für Ungarn* (Bonn: Athenäum Verlag, 1953), p. 234; *KTB*/German General at the Headquarters of the Royal Hungarian Armed Forces, 22 June 1941, BA-MA RH 31 V/1; *DGFP,* vol. 13, no. 10, pp. 13–14; and Förster, "Die Gewinnung von Verbündeten in Südosteuropa," p. 359.

26. *DGFP,* vol. 13, no. 54, p. 64; Mario D. Fenyo, *Hitler, Horthy and Hungary* (New Haven, Conn.: Yale University Press, 1972), p. 25; Horthy, *Ein Leben für Ungarn,* p. 235; Macartney, *History of Hungary,* vol. 2, p. 21; Rich, *Hitler's War Aims,* vol. 2, p. 242; and *KTB*/German General at the Headquarters of the Royal Hungarian Armed Forces, 23 June 1941, BA-MA RH 31 V/1.

27. The story of Kassa as a German provocation is laid out in Horthy, *Ein Leben für Ungarn*, p. 236; Fenyo, *Hitler, Horthy and Hungary*, p. 16; and Förster, "Die Gewinnung von Verbündeten in Südosteuropa," 4, p. 360. Standard German documentary sources are *KTB*/German General at the Headquarters of the Royal Hungarian Armed Forces, 26 June 1941, BA-MA RH 31 V/1; *DGFP*, vol. 13, no. 22, p. 25; and notably for its silence, *KTB/OKW*, 27 June 1941, vol. 1, p. 421. The bombing of Kassa as a Russian mistake is set forth in Macartney, *History of Hungary*, vol. 2, p. 32; and Fenyo, *Hitler, Horthy and Hungary*, pp. 22–23.

28. Macartney, *History of Hungary*, vol. 2, p. 35.

29. Niehorster, *Royal Hungarian Army*, p. 68; and *KTB*/German General at the Headquarters of the Royal Hungarian Armed Forces, 27 June 1941, BA-MA RH 31 V/1.

30. Niehorster, *Royal Hungarian Army*, pp. 69–70; and Gosztony, *Hitlers Fremde Heere*, p. 156.

31. *KTB*/German General at the Headquarters of the Royal Hungarian Armed Forces, 28 June 1941, BA-MA RH 31 V/1; and *DGFP*, vol. 13, no. 58, p. 68; Halder, *Halder Diaries*, vol. 6, p. 260; Charles Messenger, *The Last Prussian: A Biography of Field Marshal Gerd von Rundstedt 1875–1953* (London: Brassey's, 1991), pp. 148–149; and *KTB/OKW*, 4 July 1941, vol. 1, p. 427.

32. Niehorster, *Royal Hungarian Army*, pp. 71–76; Gosztony, *Hitlers Fremde Heere*, p. 157; Miklós Szabó, "The Development of the Hungarian Aircraft Industry, 1938–1944," *Journal of Military History* 65, no. 1 (January 2001): 67; First Panzer Group, Instructions for the Command and Action of Italian and Hungarian Air Units, 19 August 1941, NARA T-313/6/7231639; Fenyo, *Hitler, Horthy and Hungary*, p. 28; and Messenger, *Last Prussian*, p. 149.

33. Niehorster, *Royal Hungarian Army*, p. 196; and *KTB*/German General at the Headquarters of the Royal Hungarian Armed Forces, 4 July 1941, BA-MA RH 31 V/1.

34. *KTB/OKW*, 5–11 July 1941, vol. 1, pp. 427–432; Niehorster, *Royal Hungarian Army*, p. 159; and *KTB*/German General at the Headquarters of the Royal Hungarian Armed Forces, 8 July 1941, BA-MA RH 31 V/1.

35. Dumitrescu to German Eleventh Army, 15 August 1941, NARA T-312/360/7934785.

36. Halder, *Halder Diaries*, vol. 7, p. 87; and Keitel, *Generalfeldmarschall Keitel*, p. 279.

37. *DGFP*, vol. 12, no. 584, pp. 940–951; Cavallero, *Diario*, p. 192; Ciano, *Diary*, pp. 431–432; and Corvaja, *Hitler and Mussolini*, pp. 215–217.

38. Cavallero, *Diario*, pp. 188, 200; Ciano, *Diary*, pp. 436; and *DGFP*, vol. 12, no. 660, p. 1066. Outside of an editor's note in *DGFP*, vol. 12, p. 924, there is no other documentary source establishing that a meeting between Marras and Hitler took place.

39. *DGFP*, vol. 12, no. 660, p. 1068; and Förster, "Die Entscheidungen der 'Dreierpaktstaaten,'" p. 898.

40. *DGFP*, vol. 13, no. 7, p. 9; Ciano, *Diary*, pp. 438, 440; and Dennis Mack Smith, *Mussolini's Roman Empire* (New York: Viking Press, 1976), p. 243. On the subject of Cavallero's influence on Mussolini, see Ceva, *La condotta italiana della guerra*, pp. 36–37.

41. *DGFP,* vol. 13, nos. 50, 62, pp. 58–59, 72.
42. A complete order of battle for the CSIR is in Ceva, *Le forze armate,* pp. 519–525. Cavallero, *Diario,* p. 208; Rintelen, "The Italian Expeditionary Corps in Russia," 1947, Nachlass Rintelen, BA-MA N 433/4; Corvaja, *Hitler and Mussolini,* p. 225; and Knox, *Hitler's Italian Allies,* p. 115.
43. OKW, Commitment of the "Corpo di spedizione italiano in Russia," 4 August 1941, NARA T-312/360/7934173; Halder, *Halder Diaries,* vol. 6, p. 260; First Panzer Group, Instructions for the Command and Action of Italian and Hungarian Air Units, 19 August 1941, NARA T-313/6/7231369; and Förster, "Die Entscheidungen der 'Dreierpaktstaaten,'" p. 899.
44. German Eleventh Army to Army Group South, 6 August 1941, NARA T-312/360/7934169.
45. German Eleventh Army to Army Group South, 6 August 1941, NARA T-312/360/7934169; Messe to Pasubio Division, Employment of the Pasubio Division, 7 August 1941 NARA T-312/360/7935323; German Eleventh Army to Army Group South, 7 August 1941, NARA T-312/360/7934168; and After Action Report of Liaison Officer to the Italian Motorized Division "Pasubio," 15 August 1941, NARA T-312/360/7934956.
46. Giovanni Messe, *La Guerra al Fronte Russo,* 4th ed. (Milan: Rizzoli, 1964), pp. 124–125, 156–161; J. Lee Ready, *The Forgotten Axis* (London: McFarland, 1987), p. 147; and DiNardo, "Dysfunctional Coalition," p. 727.
47. Messe, *La Guerra al Fronte Russo,* p. 140.
48. After Action Report of Liaison Officer to the Italian Motorized Division "Pasubio," 15 August 1941, NARA T-312/360/7934956; and German Liaison to Italian Fifth Air Fleet, Report of Liaison Officer to Italian Fifth Air Fleet in North Africa to Commanding General X Air Corps, 19 May 1941, BA-MA RL 2 II/38.
49. After Action Report of Liaison Officer to the Italian Motorized Division "Pasubio," 15 August 1941, NARA T-312/360/7934956; Ceva, *Le forze armate,* p. 552; and Messe, *La Guerra al Fronte Russo,* p. 150.
50. Corvaja, *Hitler and Mussolini,* p. 227; and Mack Smith, *Mussolini,* p. 269.
51. *DGFP,* vol. 13, no. 156, p. 222; Corvaja, *Hitler and Mussolini,* p. 227; and Knox, "Italian Armed Forces," p. 156. The effect of Bruno's death on Mussolini is described in Mack Smith, *Mussolini,* p. 284. A rather different interpretation of the relationship between Mussolini and Bruno is in Bosworth, *Mussolini,* p. 386.
52. Keitel, *General Feldmarschall Keitel,* p. 282; Corvaja, *Hitler and Mussolini,* pp. 239–241; and Messenger, *Last Prussian,* p. 150.
53. *DGFP,* vol. 13, nos. 156, 242, pp. 222, 387; OKW, Discussion Points between the Chief of OKW and General Cavallero, 29 August 1941, BA-MA RL 2 II/38; and Cavallero, *Diario,* p. 225.
54. Ciano, *Diary,* p. 468–469; and *DGFP,* vol. 13, no. 521, p. 902.
55. IMT, *TTMWC,* Doc. 1456-PS, vol. 27, pp. 220–221; and Dallin, *German Rule in Russia,* p. 307. Dallin's study remains the best work on this topic.
56. Ueberschär, "Kriegführung und Politik in Nordeuropa," p. 851; Leni Yahil, *The Holocaust: The Fate of European Jewry, 1932–1945* (New York: Oxford University Press, 1990), p. 577; Wuorinen, *Finland and World War II,* p. 121; and OKW, Special Instructions for German Units Staying on Finnish Sovereign Territory, 10 June 1941, NARA T-77/488/1652397.

57. *DGFP*, vol. 13, nos. 204, 210, pp. 317, 325; OKW, Transcript of Agreement on the Security, Administration and Economic Exploitation of the Regions between the Dniestr and the Bug (Transnistria) and the Bug and the Dniepr (Bug-Dniepr Region), 30 August 1941, NARA T-77/544/1719430; Army Group South, Special Orders No. 10, 31 August 1941, NARA T-501/55/000571; OKH, Security and Administration of the Area between the Dniestr and the Dniepr, 7 October 1941, NARA T-77/544/1719429; and Dallin, *German Rule in Russia,* p. 90.

58. Dallin, *German Rule in Russia,* p. 90; OKW, Transcript of Agreement on the Security Administration and Economic Exploitation of the Regions between the Dniestr and the Bug (Transnistria) and the Bug and Dniepr (Bug-Dniepr Region), 30 August 1941, NARA T-77/544/1719430; and Rich, *Hitler's War Aims,* vol. 2, p. 252.

59. Dallin, *German Rule in Russia,* p. 379; and IMT, *TTMWC,* Doc. 1017-PS, vol. 26, p. 550.

60. OKW, Transcript of Agreement on the Security Administration and Economic Exploitation of the Regions between the Dniestr and the Bug (Transnistria) and the Bug and the Dniepr (Bug-Dniepr Region), 30 August 1941, NARA T-77/544/1719430.

61. *KTB*/German General at the Headquarters of the Royal Hungarian Armed Forces, 8 July 1941, BA-MA RH 31 V/1; and Commander of Rear Area, Army Group South, Order for the Commitment of the Royal Hungarian Carpathian Group in the Army Group's Rear Area, 13 August 1941, NARA T-501/5/000679.

62. Horthy, *Ein Leben für Ungarn,* p. 117; Yahil, *Holocaust,* p. 184; and DiNardo and Hughes, "Germany and Coalition Warfare in the World Wars," p. 189.

63. Horthy, *Ein Leben für Ungarn,* pp. 140–141; Theo Schulte, *The German Army in Occupied Russia* (Oxford: Berg, 1989), p. 113; and Excerpt from Report of *SS* Officer Attached to the OKW Staff, 18 September 1942, NARA T-175/21/2526491.

64. Yahil, *Holocaust,* p. 345; Rich, *Hitler's War Aims,* vol. 12, p. 256; Antonescu to Schobert, 17 August 1941, NARA T-312/360/7934779; Romanian Propaganda Leaflet, c. August 1941, NARA T-312/360/7934382; Commander of Romanian Third Army, Instructions for the Establishment of a Good Administration and Defense of the Liberated Areas of the Ukraine, August 1941, NARA T-501/278/001114; Representative of the Chief of Security Police and the SD with the Rear Area Commander of Army Group South and Einsatzgruppe D to German Eleventh Army, Report on the Behavior of Romanian Occupation Troops, 2 September 1941, NARA T-501/278/001109; and 553rd Army Rear Area Command to German Eleventh Army, Encroachments of German Police Agents in the Romanian Administrative Area, 5 October 1941, NARA T-501/55/000691.

65. German General at Romanian Headquarters to German Eleventh Army, Report on Observations in Romania, 4 November 1941, NARA T-501/278/001087; and Axworthy, Scafes, and Craciunoiu, *Third Axis/Fourth Ally,* p. 143.

66. *DGFP,* vol. 13, no. 466, p. 773; Axworthy, Scafes, and Craciunoiu, *Third Axis/Fourth Ally,* pp. 142–143; and Yahil, *Holocaust,* pp. 346–348.

67. David M. Glantz, *The Battle for Leningrad 1941–1944* (Lawrence: University Press of Kansas, 2002), p. 46.

68. Förster, *Stalingrad,* p. 16; Goebbels, *Goebbels Diaries,* p. 445; and Rich, *Hitler's War Aims,* vol. 2, p. 252. Romanian behavior in its part of occupied Russia

does call into question the argument of some that Romanian policy as formulated by Antonescu was basically nonideological. For contending sides of these questions, see Haynes, *Romanian Policy towards Germany,* p. 177; Dragan, *Antonescu,* p. 228; and Ioanid, *Sword of the Archangel,* p. 193.

69. See, for example, German Thirteenth Liaison Headquarters, Final Report of the German Thirteenth Liaison Headquarters, 29 October 1941, NARA T-501/275/000706.

70. OKW, Discussion Points between the Chief of OKW and General Cavallero, 29 August 1941, BA-MA RL 2 II/38; and Ceva, *La condotta italiana della guerra,* p. 58.

71. *KTB/OKW,* 20 March 1942, vol. 1, p. 489; DiNardo, *Mechanized Juggernaut or Military Anachronism?* p. 50; and Megargee, *Inside Hitler's High Command,* p. 174.

72. Gosztony, *Hitlers Fremde Heere,* p. 190.

73. Hitler, *Hitler's Table Talk,* p. 66; and DHM, Build-up and Action of the Romanian Army since the Start of the German Army Mission, 18 January 1942, NARA T-501/269/000069.

74. DHM, Build-up and Action of the Romanian Army since the Start of the German Army Mission, 18 January 1942, NARA T-5-1/269/000069.

75. OKW, Air Attaché in Budapest, Report on Losses of Hungarian Armed Forces in Action against Russia, 27 December 1941, NARA T-77/711/1928095; Niehorster, *Royal Hungarian Army,* p. 74; Szabó, "Development of the Hungarian Aircraft Industry," p. 65; IMT, *TTMWC,* vol. 30, Doc. 2353-PS, p. 279; and USAMHI, MSS no. P-108, Part I, p. 84.

7. Disaster at Stalingrad

1. Antonescu to Army Group South, 15 January 1942, NARA T-501/278/000370.

2. Ciano, *Diaries,* p. 526.

3. Hoth to Manstein, 3 January 1943, NARA T-311/270/000020.

4. George E. Blau, *The German Campaign in Russia: Planning and Operations (1940–1942)* (Washington, D.C.: Department of the Army, 1955), p. 88.

5. *KTB/OKW,* 15 February 1942, vol. 2, p. 298; Seaton, *Russo-German War,* p. 240.

6. 10th Panzer Division, Report on Effective Tank Strength, 21 December 1941, NARA T-315/568/001661; Rolf-Dieter Müller, "Das Scheiten der wirtschaftlichen 'Blitzkriegstrategie,'" in *Das Deutsche Reich und der Zweite Weltkrieg,* vol. 4, p. 974; and Reich Economic Ministry, Monthly Industrial Production Report, December 1941, NARA T-71/97/598713.

7. Seaton, *Russo-German War,* p. 258; Weinberg, *World at Arms,* p. 409; Megargee, *Inside Hitler's High Command,* p. 175; and Germany, Auswärtiges Amt, *Akten zur Deutschen Auswärtigen Politik 1918–1945* (Göttingen: Vandenhoeck und Ruprecht, 1969–1979), Series E, vol. 1, Doc. nos. 62, 63, 64, pp. 105, 116, 119 (hereafter cited as *ADAP,* vol. 1, no. 53, p. 94; all references to *ADAP* are from Series E).

8. Warlimont, *Im Hauptquartier der deutschen Wehrmacht,* p. 265.

9. Bernd Wegner, "Die Mobilisierung der Verbündeten," in *Das Deutsche Reich und der Zweite Weltkrieg,* vol. 6, p. 829; Erfurth, *Der Finnische Krieg,* p. 119; *KTB/OKW,* 4 June and 5 June 1942, vol. 2, pp. 402, 404; and Earl F. Ziemke and

Magna E. Bauer, *Moscow to Stalingrad: Decision in the East* (Washington, D.C.: U.S. Government Printing Office, 1987), p. 226.

10. Glantz, *Battle for Leningrad*, pp. 230–231; Ziemke and Bauer, *Moscow to Stalingrad*, p. 232; and *KTB*/Army Command Lapland, 27 March 1942, NARA T-312/1009/9204205.

11. Robert Goralski and Russell W. Freeburg, *Oil and War: How the Deadly Struggle for Fuel in WWII Meant Victory or Defeat* (New York: Morrow, 1987), p. 177; *KTB/OKW*, 13 April 1942, vol. 2, p. 320; Weinberg, *World at Arms*, p. 410; Hartmann, *Halder*, p. 315; and Blau, *German Campaign in Russia*, p. 121.

12. Axworthy, Scafes, and Craciunoiu, *Third Axis/Fourth Ally*, p. 75; Antonescu to Army Group South, 15 January 1942, NARA T-501/278/000370; *ADAP*, vol. 1, no. 244, pp. 444–453; and Keitel, *Generalfeldmarschall Keitel*, p. 280.

13. DiNardo and Hughes, "Germany and Coalition Warfare in the World Wars," p. 174; Förster, *Stalingrad*, p.17; German Military Attaché in Hungary to OKH, Army General Staff Attaché Section, Hungary's Military-Political Situation in the Years 1941/1942, 13 December 1941, NARA T-77/711/1928099; *ADAP*, vol. 1, no. 244, p. 450; and Axworthy, Scafes, and Craciunoiu, *Third Axis/Fourth Ally*, p. 75.

14. *ADAP*, vol. 1, no. 130, pp. 234–238; Fenyo, *Hitler, Horthy and Hungary*, pp. 39–41; Horthy, *Ein Leben für Ungarn*, p. 240; Macartney, *History of Hungary*, vol. 2, p. 68; and Wegner, "Die Mobilisierung der Verbündeten," pp. 824–825.

15. *ADAP*, vol. 1, no. 244, p. 453; *ADAP*, vol. 2, no. 182, p. 308. Oddly, Ciano made no mention of this in his description of the meeting in his diary. Ciano, *Diary*, pp. 514–516; *ADAP*, vol. 3, nos. 8, 12, 47, pp. 14, 18–22, 77; Förster, *Stalingrad*, p. 18.

16. Ciano, *Diary*, pp. 454–455; *DGFP*, vol. 13, no. 424, p. 695; and Mack Smith, *Mussolini*, p. 276.

17. *DGFP*, vol. 13, no. 501, p. 826; Rintelen, "The Italian Expeditionary Corps in Russia," 19 December 1947, Nachlass Rintelen, BA-MA N433/4; *ADAP*, vol. 1, no. 164, p. 293; and Wegner, "Die Mobilisierung der Verbündeten," 818.

18. Ceva, *Le forze armate*, p. 552.

19. USAMHI, MSS no. T-15, General Friedrich Schulz, "Reverses on the Southern Wing," n.d., pp. 291–292; Ciano, *Diary*, p. 526; Knox, *Common Destiny*, p. 163; Messe, *La Guerra al Fronte Russo*, p. 263; and Knox, *Hitler's Italian Allies*, p. 121.

20. Steven J. Zaloga and James Grandsen, *Soviet Tanks and Combat Vehicles of World War Two* (London: Arms and Armor Press, 1984), p. 129. The Germans were also well aware of this. See OKH, Experiences in Combating Tanks and Conclusions for Anti-tank Defense in the Defensive, 15 September 1942, NARA T-315/785/000410.

21. Antonescu to Army Group South, 15 January 1942, NARA T-501/278/000370; OKW/WiRüAmt, Appointment of *Wehrmacht* Representatives Authorized for Oil Questions in Romania, Hungary, and Croatia, 28 January 1942, NARA T-77/544/1719322; DHM, Directive No. 5 for Training Personnel of the DHM, 26 May 1942, NARA T-501/274/000568; and DHM, Handbook for German Trainers in Romania, 23 September 1942, NARA T-501/286/000522.

22. OKW, Exchange and Delivery from German Armed Forces to Italian Units, 30 May 1942, NARA T-77/544/1719120; Horthy, *Ein Leben für Ungarn*, p. 240; and Fenyo, *Hitler, Horthy and Hungary*, p. 101.

23. Walter J. Spielberger, *Panzer IV and Its Variants* (Atglen, Pa.: Schiffer Military/Aviation History, 1993), p. 80; Macartney, *History of Hungary*, vol. 2, p. 98;

DHM, Report on the Condition of the Romanian Units in May 1942, 12 May 1942, NARA T-501/269/000153; DHM, Report on the Condition and War Organization of the Romanian Third Army (2nd Wave), 12 May 1942, NARA T-501/269/000156; Organization of Romanian Infantry Division, 1942, NARA T-501/278/001030; and Wegner, "Die Mobilizierung der Verbündeten," p. 819.

24. DHM, Report on the Condition of the Romanian Units in May 1942, 12 May 1942, NARA T-501/269/000153; German Liaison Staff to Romanian 6th Infantry Division to DHM, 12 May 1942, NARA T-501/269/000168; German Liaison Staff to Romanian 7th Infantry Division to DHM, 12 May 1942, NARA T-501/269/000179; German Liaison Staff to Romanian 2nd Mountain Division to DHM, 12 May 1942, NARA T-501/269/000182; and Manfred Kehrig, *Stalingrad: Analyse und Dokumentation einer Schlacht* (Stuttgart: Deutsche Verlags-Anstalt, 1974), p. 64.

25. OKW, Agreement between the German and Italian Armed Forces on the Action of an Italian Army in the USSR, 16 June 1942, NARA T-312/1614/000319; and OKH, Directive for the Supply of the Royal Italian Eighth Army and Royal Italian Units, 26 June 1942, NARA T-312/1615/000016.

26. The Italian Eighth Army, for example, was supported by a mere fifty aircraft. Knox, *Hitler's Italian Allies,* pp. 83–84. It is very difficult to determine how many aircraft, if any, supported the Hungarian Second Army.

27. Axworthy, Scafes, and Craciunoiu, *Third Axis/Fourth Ally,* p. 291; and DLM, Orientation Booklet on Romania 1942, 19 January 1942, BA-MA RL 9/39. See also Corum, "*Luftwaffe* and Its Allied Air Forces in World War II," p. 12.

28. DLM, War Organization of German Fourth Air Fleet, 11 August 1941, NARA T-405/49/4887856.

29. Richthofen Diary, 12 August 1942, Nachlass Richthofen, BA-MA N 671/9.

30. Axworthy, Scafes, and Craciunoiu, *Third Axis/Fourth Ally,* p. 293; Hayward, *Stopped at Stalingrad,* pp. 208–209; and Richthofen Diary, 9 October 1942, Nachlass Richthofen, BA-MA N 671/9.

31. *KTB*/Navy Group South, 3 January 1942, BA-MA RM 35 III/19; Ruge, *Soviets as Naval Opponents,* p. 79; *KTB*/Navy Group South, 5 January 1942, BA-MA RM 35 III/19; and Navy Group South, Overview of the Transport of S, R and U Boats to the Black Sea, 20 May 1942, BA-MA RM 7/248.

32. *KTB*/Navy Group South, 1 January 1942, BA-MA RM 35 III/19; and Hayward, *Stopped at Stalingrad,* p. 50.

33. *KTB*/Navy Group South, 14 January 1942, BA-MA RM 35 III/19; Navy Group South to Group Commands, 5 February 1942, BA-MA RM 7/248; and Antonescu to Navy Group South, 20 March 1942, BA-MA RM 7/248.

34. Martienssen, *Führer Conferences on Naval Affairs,* p. 262; Naval High Command, Overview of the Situation in the Mediterranean, Aegean and Black Seas from 16–30 April 1942, BA-MA RM 7/115; Naval High Command, Overview of the Situation in the Mediterranean, Aegean and Black Seas from 16–31 May 1942, BA-MA RM 7/115; and Naval High Command, Overview of the Situation in the Mediterranean, Aegean and Black Seas, from 1–13 June 1942, BA-MA RM 7/115.

35. Hayward, *Stopped at Stalingrad,* pp. 41, 53; OKM to Navy Group South, 17 April 1942, BA-MA RM 7/248; and Navy Group South to OKM, Cooperation of German and Italian Naval Forces in the Black Sea, 11 May 1942, BA-MA RM 7/248.

36. Navy Group South to Group Commands, 5 February 1942, BA-MA RM 7/248; Antonescu to Navy Group South, 20 March 1942, BA-MA RM 7/248; and Navy Group South to OKM, Cooperation of German and Italian Naval Forces in the Black Sea, 11 May 1942, BA-MA RM 7/248.

37. Navy High Command, Overview of the Situation in the Mediterranean, Aegean and Black Seas, from 1–15 May 1942, BA-MA RM 7/115; Ruge, *Soviets as Naval Opponents,* p. 78; and Hayward, *Stopped at Stalingrad,* p. 78.

38. Navy High Command, Overview of the Situation in the Mediterranean, Aegean and Black Seas, from 14–30 June 1942, BA-MA RM 7/115; Hayward, *Stopped at Stalingrad,* p. 107; and Ruge, *Soviets as Naval Opponents,* pp. 79–80.

39. Reply to the Proposal of the Commander of German Navy Group South of 28 July 1942, 7 August 1942, BA-MA RM 7/248; and Roba and Crăciunoiu, *Seaplanes over the Black Sea,* pp. 39–40.

40. Navy High Command, Missions of the Nikolaev Shipyards, 8 August 1942, BA-MA RM 7/248; and Ruge, *Soviets as Naval Opponents,* p. 95.

41. Navy High Command to Naval Attaché in Rome, 18 July 1942, BA-MA RM 7/248; Navy High Command to Navy Group South, 1 August 1942, BA-MA RM 7/248; and Martienssen, *Führer Conferences on Naval Affairs,* p. 290.

42. The activity of the Axis and Soviet naval forces on the Black Sea remains one of the least explored aspects of the eastern front.

43. German 107th Liaison Command, Annex 6 to *KTB*/German 107th Liaison Command, Experiences, 17 September 1942, NARA T-501/282/000194; and German 107th Liaison Command, Roster of German 107th Liaison Command, ca. September 1942, NARA T-501/282/000184. For examples of German reports noting the linguistic capabilities of their Romanian counterparts, see DHM, Report on the Condition and War Organization of the Romanian Third Army (2nd Wave), 12 May 1942, NARA T-501/269/000156.

44. Army Group Ruoff to Army Group A, Interpreters, 2 September 1942, NARA T-312/706/8343809; and German Seventeenth Army to OKH, Interpreter Training, 20 October 1942, NARA T-312/706/8343816.

45. Bernd Wegner, "Der Beginn der Sommeroffensive," in *Das Deutsche Reich und der Zweite Weltkrieg,* vol. 6, p. 933; and Ziemke and Bauer, *Moscow to Stalingrad,* p. 358.

46. Förster, *Stalingrad,* p. 24; Drăgan, *Antonescu,* p. 370; Field Marshal Erich von Manstein, *Lost Victories* (1958; repr., Novato, Calif.: Presidio Press, 1982), p. 292; and Hitler, *Hitler's Table Talk,* p. 294.

47. Kehrig, *Stalingrad,* p. 46; Bernd Wegner, "Stalingrad," in *Das Deutsche Reich und der Zweite Weltkrieg,* vol. 6, pp. 980–981; Förster, *Stalingrad,* p. 24; and Axworthy, Scafes, and Craciunoiu, *Third Axis/Fourth Ally,* p. 84.

48. *ADAP,* vol. 3, no. 85, p. 142; and Compilation Presented to the Royal Romanian Supreme Headquarters to the Redress of the Shortage of Supplies in the Third and Fourth Armies, ca. December 1942, NARA T-311/269/00642.

49. OKW, Agreement between the German and Italian Armed Forces on the Action of an Italian Army in the USSR, 16 June 1942, NARA T-312/1614/000319.

50. Knox, *Hitler's Italian Allies,* p. 156. The effects of frostbite are graphically described in Eugenio Corti, *Few Returned: Twenty-eight Days on the Russian Front,*

Winter 1942–1943, trans. Peter Edward Levy (Columbia: University of Missouri Press, 1997), p. 235. For the condition of the Italian Eighth Army in November 1942, see Förster, *Stalingrad,* p. 28; and German General at Italian Eighth Army to Army Group B Quartermaster, Daily Report on Condition of the Italian Eighth Army, 9 November 1942, NARA T-312/1616/000149.

51. Ciano, *Diary,* pp. 484–485; Corti, *Few Returned,* p. 78; and Excerpt from Report of SS Officer Attached to OKW Staff, 18 September 1942 and NARA T-175/21/2526491.

52. *KTB/OKW,* 22 May 1942, vol. 2, p. 376. Atrocities committed by elements of the Hungarian Occupation Group are covered by Truman O. Anderson, "A Hungarian *Vernichtungskrieg?* Hungarian Troops and the Soviet Partisan War in Ukraine, 1942," *Militärgeschichtliche Mitteilungen* 58, no. 2 (1999): 345–366, directly contradicting the assertion in Gosztony, *Hitlers Fremde Heere,* p. 258.

53. Halder, *Halder Diaries,* vol. 7, pp. 369–370; and Niehorster, *Royal Hungarian Army,* p. 82.

54. Király interview, 20 December 1993; DiNardo, "Dysfunctional Coalition," p. 729; and German Military Attaché in Hungary to OKH, Army General Staff Attaché Section, Hungary's Military Political Situation on the Changing Years 1941/1942, 13 December 1941, NARA T-77/711/1928099.

55. German Sixth Army Quartermaster, Estimate of the Supply Situation, 28 July 1942, NARA T-312/1449/000162; German Sixth Army Quartermaster, Report on Supply Situation to Quartermaster of OKH, 21 October 1942, NARA T-312/1450/000435; and DiNardo, *Mechanized Juggernaut or Military Anachronism?* pp. 59–60.

56. DHM to General Steflea, Chief of the Royal Romanian General Staff, Operational Memorandum Nr. 14, 19 October 1942, NARA T-501/286/000369; DHM Mobile Staff to Steflea, Operational Memorandum Nr. 16, 26 October 1942, NARA T/501/286/000318; and German Liaison Staff to the Romanian Third Army, The Battles of the Romanian Third Army on the Don From 19–23 November 1942, 15 December 1942, NARA T-311/269/000661.

57. German Liaison Staff to the Romanian Third Army, The Battles of the Romanian Third Army on the Don From 19–23 November 1942, 15 December 1942, NARA T-311/269/000661; and Axworthy, Scafes, and Craciunoiu, *Third Axis/Fourth Ally,* p. 86.

58. Steflea to Hauffe, 20 October 1942, NARA T-501/286/000341; Antonescu to Hauffe, 22 October 1942, NARA T-501/286/000347; German 110th Liaison Command, Condition of the Romanian 9th Infantry Division, mid-September 1942, NARA T-501/282/000053; and DHM Mobile Staff to Steflea, Operational Memorandum Nr. 16, 26 October 1926, NARA T-501/286/000318.

59. German Liaison Staff to the Romanian Third Army, The Battles of the Romanian Third Army on the Don From 19–23 November 1942, 15 December 1942, NARA T-311/269/000661; Geoffrey Jukes, *Hitler's Stalingrad Decisions* (Berkeley: University of California Press, 1985), p. 110; and Kehrig, *Stalingrad,* p. 66.

60. Rolf Stoves, *Die 22. Panzer-Division, 25. Panzer-Division, 27. Panzer-Division und die 233. Reserve-Panzer-Division: Aufstellung—Gliederung—Einsatz* (Bad Nauheim: Podzun-Pallas-Verlag, 1985), p. 38; DHM to Steflea, 23 June 1942,

NARA T-501/278/000995; *KTB*/XLVIII Panzer Corps, 10 November 1942, NARA
T-314/1160/000012; Axworthy, Scafes, and Craciunoiu, *Third Axis/Fourth Ally,* p.
87; Kehrig, *Stalingrad,* p. 271; and Wegner, "Stalingrad," p. 1005.

61. German Liaison Staff to the Romanian Third Army, The Battles of the Romanian Third Army on the Don from 11–23 November 1942, 15 December 1942,
NARA T-311/269/000661; Axworthy, Scafes, and Craciunoiu, *Third Axis/Fourth
Ally,* p. 89; DHM Mobile Staff to Steflea, Operational Memorandum Nr. 16, 26
October 1942, NARA T-501/286/000318; and XLVIII Panzer Corps to 22nd Panzer
Division, 16 November 1942, NARA T-315/785/000484.

62. Louis Rotundo, ed., *Battle for Stalingrad: The 1943 Soviet General Staff
Study* (New York: Pergamon-Brassey's, 1989), pp. 79–86; David M. Glantz and
Jonathan House, *When Titans Clashed: How the Red Army Stopped Hitler* (Lawrence: University Press of Kansas, 1995), p. 133; Axworthy, Scafes, and Craciunoiu,
Third Axis/Fourth Ally, p. 93; German Liaison Staff to the Romanian Third Army,
The Battles of the Romanian Third Army on the Don from 11–23 November 1942,
15 December 1942, NARA T-311/269/000661; Richthofen Diary, 19 November
1942, Nachlass Richthofen, BA-MA N 671/9; and Weichs to Army Group Don, 21
November 1942, NARA T-501/278/000869.

63. German Liaison Staff to the Romanian Third Army, The Battles of the Romanian Third Army on the Don from 11–23 November 1942, 15 December 1942,
NARA T-311/269/000661; *KTB*/XLVIII Panzer Corps, 20 November 1942, NARA
T-314/1160/000046; *KTB*/XLVIII Panzer Corps, 21 November 1942, NARA T-
314/1160/000052; and DiNardo, "Dysfunctional Coalition," pp. 715–716.

64. The actions of the two divisions are covered in Stoves, *Die 22. Panzer-Division,* pp. 51–72; and Axworthy, Scafes, and Craciunoiu, *Third Axis/Fourth Ally,* pp.
92–101; *KTB*/XLVIII Panzer Corps, 28 November 1942, NARA T-314/1160/000079.
Very critical of Heim's conduct is USAMHI, MSS no. T-15, General Friedrich Schulz,
"Reverses on the Southern Wing," n.d., pp. 27–28.

65. Richthofen Diary, 22 November 1942, Nachlass Richthofen, BA-MA N
671/9; Hayward, *Stopped at Stalingrad,* pp. 230–232; Glantz and House, *When
Titans Clashed,* p. 134.

66. Manstein, *Los.t Victories,* pp. 308–309; Bernd Wegner, in "Die Vernichtung
der 6. Armee," *Das Deutsche Reich und der Zweite Weltkrieg,* vol. 6, p. 1027; and
Hayward, *Stopped at Stalingrad,* pp. 234–235.

67. Kehrig, *Stalingrad,* pp. 354–369; Wegner, "Der Vernichtung der 6. Armee," pp.
1035–1943; Helmut Heiber and David M. Glantz, eds., *Hitler and His Generals: Military Conferences 1942–1945* (New York: Enigma Books, 2003), pp. 22–23; Manstein,
Lost Victories, p. 332; Seaton, *Russo-German War,* pp. 326–328; and Walter Görlitz,
Paulus and Stalingrad (New York: Citadel Press, 1963), pp. 254–255.

68. German 102nd Liaison Command to Army Group Don, via German 2nd Liaison Staff, 4 January 1943, NARA T-501/290/000742; German 103rd Liaison Command to German 2nd Liaison Command, 4 January 1943, NARA T-501/290/000734;
Report of the German 16th Liaison Command with the Romanian VI Corps, 3 January
1943, NARA T-501/290/000751; Chief of Liaison Staff to Romanian Fourth Army
to Army Group Don, 11 January 1943, NARA T-501/290/000727; German 121st
Liaison Command to Army Group Don, 5 January 1943, NARA T-501/290/000730;
Corti, *Few Returned,* pp. 24–25; Italian Eighth Army to Army Group B, 6 January

1943, NARA T-312/1620/000166; German General with Italian Eighth Army, Discussion with General Marras, 5 January 1943, NARA T-312/1620/000195; *ADAP,* vol. 4, no. 303, p. 542; Extract from the After-Action Report of the German General with the Hungarian Second Army, January 1943, NARA T-78/333/6290832; and Extract from After-Action Report of the Commander of the German 618th Artillery Regimental Staff for Special Duty, January 1943, NARA T-78/333/6290829.

69. Ceva, *Le forze armate,* p. 323; German 17th Liaison Command to Army Group Don, 8 January 1943, T-501/290/000746; Commander of Fourth Air Fleet to Army Group Don, Action of Fourth Air Fleet in the Area of Army Group Don on 18 December 1942, 18 December 1942, NARA T-311/269/000521; Commander of Fourth Air Fleet to Army Group Don, Action of Fourth Air Fleet in the Area of Army Group Don on 19 December 1942, the Night of 19–20 December 1942, 20 December 1942 NARA T-311/269/000374; and Hayward, *Stopped at Stalingrad,* p. 272.

70. Ceva, *Le forze armate,* p. 323; Knox, *Hitler's Italian Allies,* p. 84; and Corti, *Few Returned,* p. 227.

71. Axworthy, Scafes, and Craciunoiu, *Third Axis/Fourth Ally,* p. 114; Fenyo, *Hitler, Horthy and Hungary,* p. 108; and Niehorster, *Royal Hungarian Army,* p. 94.

72. Hauffe to OKH, 28 December 1942, NARA T-501/288/000223; *KTB/OKW,* 25 January 1943, vol. 3, p. 70; and DHM to Chief of the Romanian General Staff, General Steflea, 27 January 1943, NARA T-501/288/000290. This proved to be Hauffe's final major duty with the DHM, as he was appointed to the command of a division. His successor was Erich Hansen, commander of the LIV Corps in 1941. Chief of DHM to Romanian General Staff, 18 January 1943, NARA T-501/288/000229.

73. Rintelen, "The Italian Expeditionary Corps in Russia," Neustadt, 19 December 1947, Nachlass Rintelen, BA-MA N 433/4; Knox, *Hitler's Italian Allies,* p. 84; Macartney, *History of Hungary,* vol. 2, p. 139; and Niehorster, *Royal Hungarian Army,* p. 95.

74. German Liaison Staff to Romanian Third Army, Memorandum on Treatment of Romanian Soldiers, 24 November 1942, NARA T-312/1452/000026; and Corti, *Few Returned,* pp. 45–69. Bela Király described all the German liaison officers he dealt with, save one, as "arrogant." The exception was an Austrian who Király described as "very *gemütlich.*" Király interview, 20 December 1993.

75. German General with Italian Eighth Army, Discussion with General Marras, 5 January 1943, NARA T-312/1620/000195; Antonescu to Hauffe, 22 October 1942, NARA T-501/286/000347; Romanian Royal Headquarters to *DHM,* 23 November 1942, NARA T-501/278/000896; Romanian Royal Headquarters Operations Section to DHM, 27 November 1942, NARA T-501/278/000878; Dumitrescu to Army Group B, 26 November 1942, NARA T-501/278/000881; Extract from the After-Action Report of the German General with the Hungarian Second Army, January 1943, NARA T-78/333/6290832; Richthofen Diary, 21 January 1943, Nachlass Richthofen, BA-MA N 671/10; Hoth to Manstein, 3 January 1943, NARA T-311/270/000020; and Förster, *Stalingrad,* p. 146.

76. Erfurth, *Der Finnische Krieg,* pp. 125, 142, 149; *ADAP,* vol. 4, no. 243, p. 432; Warner, *Marshal Mannerheim and the Finns,* p. 192; Bernd Wegner, in "Die historische Ort des zweiten Feldzuges gegen die Sowjetunion," *Das Deutsche Reich und der Zweite Weltkrieg,* vol. 6, p. 1101; and Vehviläinen, *Finland in the Second World War,* p. 120.

77. Steflea to Commanders of the Romanian Third and Fourth Armies, 24 November 1942, NARA T-501/278/000880; *ADAP*, vol. 4, no. 303, p. 542. Oddly enough, Ciano makes no mention of Hitler's comment in his diary. Ciano, *Diary*, p. 572.

78. Förster, *Stalingrad*, p. 49; Romanian Royal Headquarters Operations Section to DHM, 27 November 1942, NARA T-501/278/000878; Dumitrescu to Army Group B, 26 November 1942, NARA T-501/278/000881; and Drăgan, *Antonescu*, pp. 346–355.

79. Manstein to Antonescu, 15 December 1942, NARA T-311/269/000647; and Romanian Royal Headquarters Operations Section, Order of the Day Nr. 33, 27 November 1942, NARA T-501/278/000879. Heim's relief has been a matter of long-standing controversy. Some sources consider it to be unfair. See, for example, Stoves, *Die 22. Panzer-Division*, p. 78. A more critical view is in USAMHI, MSS no. T-15, pp. 27–28. Heim's life was supposedly saved by the intervention of Hitler's adjutant, Rudolf Schmundt. Kershaw, *Hitler 1936–1945*, p. 543. How seriously Hitler wanted to pursue Heim's death sentence seems questionable, however, as Heim was later appointed commandant of Boulogne. Weinberg, *World at Arms*, p. 450; and DiNardo, "Dysfunctional Coalition," p. 723.

80. *ADAP*, vol. 5, no. 136, p. 237; Horthy, *Ein Leben für Ungarn*, p. 254; and Wegner, "Der historische Ort des zweiten Feldzuges gegen die Sowjetunion," p. 1101.

81. DHM, Report on the Condition of the Romanian Units, 12 May 1942, NARA T-501/269/000153; *KTB/OKW*, 27 October 1942, vol. 2, pp. 867–868; and German Liaison Staff to the Romanian Third Army, The Battles of the Romanian Third Army on the Don from 11–23 November 1942, 15 December 1942, NARA T-311/269/000661.

82. *KTB/XLVIII* Panzer Corps, 20 November 1942, NARA T-314/1160/000046.

83. Förster, *Stalingrad*, pp. 131–132.

8. Desert Sands II

1. Ciano, *Diary*, p. 530.

2. Liddell-Hart, *Rommel Papers*, p. 321.

3. *ADAP*, vol. 1, no. 62, p. 110; *KTB/OKW*, 25 January 1942, vol. 2, p. 258; Ciano, *Diary*, p. 489; Liddell-Hart, *Rommel Papers*, p. 183; Panzer Army Africa, Army Order for the Conduct of Further Combat, 14 February 1942, NARA T-314/2/000630; Mellenthin, *Panzer Battles*, pp. 103–106; and Reinhard Stumpf, "Der Beginn der zweiten deutsch-italienischen Offensive in Nordafrika und der Kampf um Malta," in *Das Deutsche Reich und der Zweite Weltkrieg*, vol. 6, pp. 583–585.

4. *KTB/OKW*, 21 April 1942, vol. 2, p. 326; *ADAP*, vol. 2, no. 165, p. 273; and Corvaja, *Hitler and Mussolini*, p. 248.

5. *ADAP*, vol. 2, no. 182, p. 307; and Ciano, *Diary*, p. 515.

6. *ADAP*, vol. 2, no. 183, p. 315; Cavallero, *Diario*, p. 384; Stumpf, "Der Beginn der zweiten deutsch-italiensichen Offensive in Nordafrika und der Kampf um Malta," p. 592; Corvaja, *Hitler and Mussolini*, p. 251; *KTB/OKW*, 20 May 1942, vol. 2, p. 370; and Ciano, *Diary*, p. 515. In his memoirs, Kesselring makes no mention of the meeting. Hitler's lunchtime harangue seems to have exhausted his

thoughts on the war for that day, as he made no mention of the meeting that night over dinner at the *Berghof*. Hitler, *Hitler's Table Talk,* pp. 448–450.

7. Liddell-Hart, *Rommel Papers,* p. 192; *ADAP,* vol. 2, no. 183, p. 315; and Ciano, *Diary,* p. 516. Ceva contends that German strategy in the Mediterranean after the fall of 1941 was essentially defensive. Ceva, *La condotta italiana della Guerra,* p. 41.

8. Rintelen, "German-Italian Military Cooperation in the Second World War," Nachlass Rintelen, BA-MA N 433/6; and Panzer Army Africa, Training Memorandum, 1 February 1942, NARA T-314/2/000620.

9. *KTB/90th Light Division,* 12 May 1942, NARA T-315/1156/000726; and Commander of Panzer Army Africa, Army Order for Salvage of Captured Material, 23 May 1942, NARA T-313/480/000512.

10. Navy High Command, Overview of the Situation in the Mediterranean, Aegean and Black Seas from 1–15 April 1942, BA-MA RM 7/115; Gundelach, *Die Deutsche Luftwaffe im Mittelmeer,* vol. 1, p. 344; and Sadkovich, *Italian Navy in World War II,* p. 223.

11. Winton, *Ultra at Sea,* pp. 178–179; and Sadkovich, *Italian Navy in World War II,* pp. 244–246.

12. Borghese, *Sea Devils,* pp. 164–165; Macintyre, *Battle for the Mediterranean,* pp. 140–141; Naval High Command, Overview of the Situation in the Mediterranean, Aegean and Black Seas from 1–15 April 1942 and 16–30 April 1942, BA-MA RM 7/115; Sadkovich, *Italian Navy in World War II,* p. 229; and Liddell-Hart, *Rommel Papers,* p. 192.

13. Some of the more standard accounts include Barrie Pitt, *The Year of Alamein 1942* (New York: Paragon House, 1990), pp. 28–82; Barnett, *Desert Generals,* pp. 136–171; Mellenthin, *Panzer Battles,* pp. 107–137; Liddell-Hart, *Rommel Papers,* pp. 191–242; and Reinhard Stumpf, "Der Feldzug nach El Alamein (Unternehmen 'Theseus')," in *Das Deutsche Reich und der Zweite Weltkrieg,* Vol. 6, pp. 595–623.

14. Pitt, *Year of Alamein,* p. 55; and Stumpf, "Der Feldzug nach El Alamein (Unternehmen 'Theseus')," p. 609.

15. Liddell-Hart, *Rommel Papers,* pp. 214–216; and Stumpf, "Der Feldzug nach El Alamein (Unternehmen 'Theseus')," p. 621. In his account of the disastrous attack launched by the British on 5–6 June, Barrie Pitt states that the poorly handled attack ran afoul of German antitank gunners. A look at Pitt's own map, however, shows clearly that the Ariete bore the brunt of the attack. Pitt, *Year of Alamein,* pp. 63–64. The Italo-German units holding the covering positions had to make do without air support because Rommel had decided to mass Waldau's aircraft against Bir Hacheim.

16. *KTB/90th Light Division,* 21 June 1942, NARA T-315/1156/000765; Rintelen, "German-Italian Military Cooperation in the Second World War," 1952, Nachlass Rintelen, BA-MA N 433/6; Stumpf, "Der Feldzug nach El Alamein (Unternehmen 'Theseus')," p. 629; Ciano, *Diary,* p. 530; and *KTB/OKW,* 24 June 1942, vol. 2, p. 446.

17. Cavallero, *Diario,* pp. 410–411; Ciano, *Diary,* p. 531; Liddell-Hart, *Rommel Papers,* p. 235; Irving, *Trail of the Fox,* p. 221; and Macksey, *Kesselring,* p. 121. It is worth pointing out that as a field marshal, Rommel had right of direct access to Hitler.

18. Cavallero, *Diario,* pp. 413–416; Rintelen to OKW, 28 June 1942, NARA T-78/451/6427069; *KTB/OKW,* 24 June 1942, vol. 2, p. 446; and Stumpf, "Der Feldzug nach El Alamein (Unternehmen 'Theseus')," p. 634.

19. *KTB/OKW,* 26 June 1942, vol. 2, p. 452.

20. Sadkovich, *Italian Navy in World War II,* p. 242.

21. This issue is closely discussed in Stumpf, "Der Feldzug nach El Alamein (Unternehmen 'Theseus')," pp. 642–647.

22. *KTB/OKW,* 27 June 1942, vol. 2, p. 454; Rintelen to OKW, 28 June 1942, NARA T-78/451/6427069; Ciano, *Diary,* p. 533; and Corvaja, *Hitler and Mussolini,* p. 263.

23. Pitt, *Year of Alamein,* pp. 121–127; Barnett, *Desert Generals,* p. 170; Mellenthin, *Panzer Battles,* pp. 163–164; *KTB/OKW,* 29 June 1942, vol. 2, p. 458; *ADAP,* vol. 3, no. 122, p. 212; Liddell-Hart, *Rommel Papers,* p. 251; and *KTB/OKW,* 21 July 1942, vol. 2, p. 515.

24. 15th Panzer Division, Request for Interpreters, 7 August 1942, NARA T-315/665/000792; and 15th Panzer Division, Activity Report for 16–29 August 1942, 29 August 1942, NARA T-315/665/000798.

25. John Terraine, *The Right of the Line: The Royal Air Force in the European War 1939–1945* (London: Hodder and Stoughton, 1985), pp. 375–377; *KTB/OKW,* 12 July 1942, vol. 2, p. 495; and Navy High Command, Situation Report on the Mediterranean, Aegean and Black Seas from 1–16 July 1942, BA-MA RM 7/115.

26. *ADAP,* vol. 3, no. 153, p. 262; and Williamson Murray, *Luftwaffe* (Baltimore: Nautical and Aviation Co. of America, 1985), p. 124.

27. Navy High Command, Situation Report on the Mediterranean, Aegean and Black Seas From 1–16 July 1942, BA-MA RM 7/115.

28. Ceva makes a particularly compelling argument here. Ceva, *La condotta italiana della Guerra,* pp. 99–106.

29. Liddell-Hart, *Rommel Papers,* p. 233; *KTB/OKW,* 7 July 1942, vol. 2, p. 483; Navy High Command, Situation Report on the Mediterranean, Aegean and Black Seas from 16–31 July 1942, BA-MA RM 7/115; Commander of the German 556th Army Rear Area to Commander of Panzer Army Africa, Advocacy of German Interests and Consequences in the Army Rear Area, 1 October 1942, NARA T-313/480/000590; Panzer Army Africa, German-Italian Protocol on the Port of Tobruk, 2 October 1942, NARA T-313/480/000597; and Reinhard Stumpf, "Seekrieg und Nachschub 1942/43," in *Das Deutsche Reich und der Zweite Weltkrieg,* Vol. 6, p. 754. A contrary view is Sadkovich, *Italian Navy in World War II,* p. 288.

30. Cavallero noted on 27 June 1942 that the Italian navy was beginning to reach its last fuel reserves. Cavallero, *Diario,* p. 418.

31. Ralph Bennett, *Ultra and Mediterranean Strategy* (New York: Morrow, 1989), p. 140; Reinhard Stumpf, "Das Ringen um El Alamein," in *Das Deutsche Reich und der Zweite Weltkrieg,* vol. 6, pp. 672–687; German General at Italian Armed Forces Headquarters, Transport Situation to Africa in August and the Beginning of September 1942, 6 September 1942, BA-MA RM 7/115; OKW Staff, Draft Memorandum on Supply of Panzer Army Africa, 13 September 1942, NARA T-313/476/8774573; *ADAP,* vol. 4, no. 98, p. 165; and Stumpf, "Seekrieg und Nachschub 1942/43," pp. 754–756.

32. For the consequences of the lack of an armored shield on the Italian 47mm antitank gun, see the photo in Knox, *Hitler's Italian Allies,* p. 142; Barnett, *Desert Generals,* p. 274; and Ceva, *Le forze armate,* pp. 348, 552.

33. Rommel to OKW and OKH, 22 September 1942, NARA T-313/476/8774586.

34. Stumpf, "Das Ringen um El Alamein," p. 689.

35. The effectiveness of Montgomery's initial offensive has been the subject of robust debate. See, for example, Pitt, *Year of Alamein,* pp. 297–339; and Barnett, *Desert Generals,* pp. 276–286. For the German view of Italian performance in El Alamein, see *KTB/OKW,* 25 October 1942, vol. 2, p. 862; 15th Panzer Division, Battle Report of the 15th Panzer Division on the Battle in the El Alamein Position and the Retreat to the Mersa El Brega Position, 23 October–25 November 1942, November 1942, NARA T-315/666/000275; Liddell-Hart, *Rommel Papers,* p. 325; and Hans von Luck, *Panzer Commander* (Westport, Conn.: Praeger, 1989), p. 93.

36. Rommel partly blamed Kesselring for sending reports back to Hitler that were unjustifiably optimistic. It is interesting to note that Kesselring glides over that episode in his memoirs. See Liddell-Hart, *The Rommel Papers,* pp. 323–326; and Kesselring, *Memoirs of Field Marshal Kesselring,* pp. 135–136.

37. *ADAP,* vol. 4, no. 146, p. 257. Ciano makes no mention of this in his diary. Ciano, *Diary,* p. 560.

38. *ADAP,* vol. 4, no. 165, p. 282; and Ciano, *Diary,* pp. 561–562.

39. German General at Italian Armed Forces Headquarters, Complete Overview of the Italian Army, 20 November 1942, NARA T-78/343/6300371; and German General at Italian Armed Forces Headquarters, Report on Status of the Italian Army, 20 November 1942, NARA T-78/343/6300382.

40. Rommel thought Kesselring was entirely too optimistic and air-centric in his thinking. Liddell-Hart, *Rommel Papers,* pp. 352, 363; Fraser, *Knight's Cross,* p. 386; Bennett, *Ultra and Mediterranean Strategy,* p. 176; and Reinhard Stumpf, "Der Rückzug der Deutsch-Italiensichen Panzerarmee bis zur tunesischen Grenze (4 November 1942 bis 4 Februar 1943)," in *Das Deutsche Reich und der Zweite Weltkrieg,* vol. 6, p. 730.

41. Liddell-Hart, *Rommel Papers,* p. 365; Heiber and Glantz, *Hitler and His Generals,* pp. 49–50; and Hitler to Mussolini, 28 November 1942, NARA T-313/476/8774590.

42. Heiber and Glantz, *Hitler and His Generals,* p. 11; Cavallero to Kesselring, 28 December 1942, NARA T-313/416/8709223; Richard L. DiNardo, *Germany's Panzer Arm* (Westport, Conn.: Greenwood Press, 1997), p. 107; Weinberg, *World at Arms,* pp. 441–443; Murray, *Luftwaffe,* p. 155; Kesselring, *Memoirs of Field Marshal Kesselring,* p. 147; and Bennett, *Ultra and Mediterranean Strategy,* pp. 194–195.

43. *ADAP,* vol. 4, no. 303, pp. 545–547; Rintelen, Operational Command in the German-Italian Coalition, 19 February 1948, Nachlass Rintelen, BA-MA N 433/5; Ciano, *Diary,* p. 572; and Kershaw, *Hitler 1936–1945,* p. 546.

44. Fraser, *Knight's Cross,* pp. 405–406; Liddell-Hart, *Rommel Papers,* pp. 401–402; *KTB/OKW,* 31 January 1943, vol. 3, p. 87; and Irving, *Trail of the Fox,* p. 329.

45. Commando Supremo, Mission of the Chief of the Italian Liaison Staff with Army Group Africa, 2 March 1943, and Commando Supremo, Instructions for the German Chief of Staff of the First Army, 2 March 1943, BA-MA RH 31 VIII/2; and *KTB/OKW*, 9 April 1943, vol. 3, p. 262. Messe saw the position as an attempt by Cavallero to get rid of him. Ciano, *Diary*, p. 584.

46. Liddell-Hart, *Rommel Papers*, p. 352; Kesselring, *Memoirs of Field Marshal Kesselring*, p. 167; Ciano, *Diary*, p. 586; *ADAP*, vol. 5, no. 84, p. 154; *KTB/OKW*, 2 February 1943, vol. 3, p. 94; and Rintelen, "Operational Command in the German-Italian Coalition," 19 February 1948, Nachlass Rintelen, BA-MA N 433/5.

47. Mack Smith, *Mussolini*, p. 279; Bosworth, *Mussolini*, pp. 395–397; *ADAP*, vol. 5, no. 99, pp. 175–176; and Ciano, *Diary*, p. 587.

48. Liddell-Hart, *Rommel Papers*, p. 419; Irving, *Trail of the Fox*, p. 341; Kesselring, *Memoirs of Field Marshal Kesselring*, p. 167; and Macksey, *Kesselring*, pp. 156–157.

49. *ADAP*, vol. 5, nos. 135, 192, pp. 229, 377; Corvaja, *Hitler and Mussolini*, p. 276; and OKW, Minutes of Conference in Klessheim Castle, 9 April 1943, NARA T-77/780/5506550.

50. Bennett, *Ultra and Mediterranean Strategy*, pp. 216–218; Alan J. Levine, *The War against Rommel's Supply Lines, 1942–1943* (Westport, Conn.: Praeger, 1999), pp. 146–181; Weinberg, *World at Arms*, p. 446; and Mack Smith, *Mussolini*, p. 290.

51. Murray, *Luftwaffe*, p. 155.

52. OKW, Minutes of Conference in Klessheim Castle, 9 April 1943, NARA T-77/780/5506550.

53. Knox, "Italian Armed Forces," p. 150; and DiNardo, "Dysfunctional Coalition," p. 728.

54. See, for example, Kesselring, *Memoirs of Field Marshal Kesselring*, p. 130; and Liddell-Hart, *Rommel Papers*, p. 363.

55. Panzer Army Africa, German-Italian Protocol on the Port of Tobruk, 2 October 1942, NARA T-313/480/000597; Rommel to OKW, OKH, 22 September 1942, NARA T-313/476/8774586; and Rintelen, "German-Italian Military Cooperation in the Second World War," 1952, Nachlass Rintelen, BA-MA, N 433/6.

9. All Fall Down

1. Keitel to OKH, OKM, OKL, and OKW, Cooperation with Japan, 30 July 1943, NARA T-82/90/0246978.

2. Louis P. Lochner, ed. and trans., *The Goebbels Diaries 1942–1943* (New York: Doubleday, 1948), p. 429.

3. Hugh Trevor-Roper, ed., *Final Entries 1945: The Diaries of Joseph Goebbels* (New York: Putnam's, 1978), p. 191.

4. Macartney, *History of Hungary*, vol. 2, p. 139; *KTB/OKW*, 9 April 1943, vol. 3, pp. 258–259; and Förster, *Stalingrad*, p. 46.

5. Förster, *Stalingrad*, p. 49; *ADAP*, vol. 5, no. 174, pp. 337–338; Horthy, *Ein Leben für Ungarn*, p. 257; OKH, Foreign Armies West, Report on the Situation in Italy, 30 June 1943, NARA T-78/451/6426935; Macksey, *Kesselring*, p. 160; Bosworth, *Mussolini*, pp. 398–399; *ADAP*, vol. 4, no. 243, p. 432; and Erfurth, *Der Finnische Krieg*, p. 142.

6. Carlo D'Este, *Bitter Victory: The Battle for Sicily, 1943* (New York: Dutton, 1988), p. 187.

7. German General at Italian Armed Forces Headquarters, Report on Status of Italian Army, 20 November 1942, NATA T-78/343/6300382; and Commander of German Twelfth Army to Italian Liaison Officer, Lessons from the Major Landing Attempt at Dieppe, 1 September 1942, NARA T-312/466/8054726.

8. OKW, Minutes of Conference in Klessheim Castle, 9 April 1943, NARA T-77/780/5506550; and OB Southeast, Transport Situation in the Month of August 1943, 7 September 1943, NARA T-311/173/000203.

9. Macksey, *Kesselring,* pp. 162–163; D'Este, *Bitter Victory,* pp. 196–198; General Fridolin von Senger und Etterlin, *Neither Fear Nor Hope* (New York: Dutton, 1964), p. 126; and German Naval Attaché to OKM, Conversation with Admiral Giartosio, 1 July 1943, NARA T-78/451/6426933.

10. D'Este, *Bitter Victory,* pp. 207–208; and DiNardo, *Germany's Panzer Arm,* p. 46.

11. Rintelen, "German-Italian Military Cooperation in the Second World War," 1952, Nachlass Rintelen, BA-MA N 433/6; Knox, *Hitler's Italian Allies,* p. 43; Ceva, *Le forze armate,* pp. 345–346; and Study Group for the History of Aerial Warfare, "Aircraft Procurement," 1955, p. 435, Karlsruhe Collection, AFHRA; Corum, "*Luftwaffe* and Its Allied Air Forces in World War II," p. 11; and Johannes Steinhoff, *Messerschmitts over Sicily: Diary of a Luftwaffe Fighter Commander* (Mechanicsburg, Pa.: Stackpole Books, 2004), p. 168.

12. Liddell-Hart, *Rommel Papers,* p. 430; D'Este, *Bitter Victory,* p. 454; and Senger und Etterlin, *Neither Fear Nor Hope,* p. 146. D'Este's work is still the most comprehensive study of the campaign.

13. Martienssen, *Führer Conferences on Naval Affairs,* p. 348; and D'Este, *Bitter Victory,* p. 515. Kershaw, following Kesselring's account, gives Kesselring credit for the decision to mount the evacuation. Kesselring, *Memoirs of Field Marshal Kesselring,* p. 165; and Kershaw, *Hitler 1936–1945,* p. 599.

14. Westermann, *Flak,* p. 232; Combined Services Detailed Interrogation Center (CSDIC) (United Kingdom), SRIG Report 355, Interrogation of Italian Rear Admiral Who Was Captured in Sicily on 20 August 1943, 19 November 1943, AFRHA; and D'Este, *Bitter Victory,* pp. 514–515.

15. Ziemke, *Stalingrad to Berlin.* p. 137; Seaton, *Russo-German War,* p. 365; and Heiber and Glantz, *Hitler and His Generals,* p. 166.

16. IMT, *TTMWC,* vol. 31, 2911-PS, 2929-PS, 2954-PS, pp. 274, 309, 392; and *ADAP,* vol. 5, no. 318, p. 648. See also Carl Boyd, *Hitler's Japanese Confidant: General Ōshima Hiroshi and Magic Intelligence, 1941–1945* (Lawrence: University Press of Kansas, 1993), pp. 77–79.

17. German Military Attaché in Japan to OKW, 20 July 1943, NARA T-82/92/0250069; German Military Attaché in Japan to OKW, 25 July 1943, NARA T-82/92/0250073; Memo from Keitel to OKH, OKM, OKL, and OKW, Cooperation with Japan, 30 July 1943, NARA T-82/90/0246978; *ADAP,* vol. 6, no. 364, p. 607; and Meskill, *Hitler and Japan,* p. 180.

18. *ADAP,* vol. 6, no. 159, pp. 264–275. Compare also Kershaw, *Hitler 1936–1945,* p. 593; and Corvaja, *Hitler and Mussolini,* pp. 301–305.

19. *KTB/OKW,* 25 July 1943, vol. 3, p. 830; Bosworth, *Mussolini,* pp. 400–401; and Mack Smith, *Mussolini,* pp. 294–298.

20. Lochner, *Goebbels Diaries,* p. 408. The quotation is from Kershaw, *Hitler 1936–1945,* p. 594. The classic account on the relationship between Hitler and Mussolini during the period 1943–1945 remains F. W. Deakin, *The Brutal Friendship* (New York: Harper and Row, 1962).

21. Lochner, *Goebbels Diaries,* p. 411; Heiber and Glantz, *Hitler and His Generals,* pp. 228–229; and OB Southeast to Subordinate Commands, Command Relationships in Greece, 20 August 1943, NARA T-311/173/000168.

22. OKW, Summary Notes of Conference with the Italians in Tarviso on 6 August 1943, 1500–1730, 6 August 1943, NARA T-77/780/5506479; *ADAP,* vol. 6, no. 217, p. 381; and Heiber and Glantz, *Hitler and His Generals,* p. 252.

23. *ADAP,* vol. 6, no. 291, pp. 501–502; and Bragadin, *Italian Navy in World War II,* pp. 316–318.

24. Kershaw, *Hitler 1936–1945,* pp. 600–601; Kesselring, *Memoirs of Field Marshal Kesselring,* p. 187; Bosworth, *Mussolini,* p. 403; and Mack Smith, *Mussolini,* p. 300.

25. *ADAP,* vol. 6, no. 303, pp. 519–520; *KTB/OKW,* 7 September 1943, vol. 3, p. 1068; and OKW, New Oath for Loyal Italian Soldiers Who Are Posted in the Areas of the German Armed Forces, 7 October 1943, NARA T-77/893/5643944.

26. Gerhard Schreiber, *Die italienischen Militärinternierten im Deutschen Machtbereich 1943–1945* (Munich: R. Oldenbourg, 1990), p. 30; CSDIC (Middle East), Report 779(G), 27 September 1943, AFRHA; OKW Staff, Oil Section, List of Fuel Captured from Italian Stocks from 8 September–31 October 1943, NARA T-77/522/1693015; *KTB/OKW,* 9 September 1943, vol. 3, p. 1085; and German Navy Command Constanza to Navy Group South, Securing of Italian Personnel and Material by the Romanian Navy, 1 December 1943, BA-MA RM 7/248.

27. Bosworth, *Mussolini,* p. 404; and Kesselring to OKW, 6 October 1943, NARA T-77/780/5506485. An example of German treatment of Italy as occupied territory can be found in Gerhard Schreiber, *Deutsche Kriegsverbrechen in Italien: Täter, Opfer Strafverfolgung* (Munich: Verlag C. H. Beck, 1996), pp. 130–132.

28. Compare Lochner, *Goebbels Diaries,* p. 455, with Kesselring to OKW, 6 October 1943, NARA T-77/780/5506485, and Kesselring, *Memoirs of Field Marshal Kesselring,* p. 180. Rintelen had been relieved of his position at the end of August 1943, after an extraordinarily long tour of seven years in that post. Rintelen, "Remarks on the Selection and Training of German Officers for Service as Military Attachés," 1951, Nachlass Rintelen, BA-MA N 433/23; Warlimont, *Im Hauptquartier der deutschen Wehrmacht,* p. 389; Schreiber, *Die italienischen Militärinternierten im Deutschen Machtbereich,* p. 36; and Yahil, *Holocaust,* pp. 421–427.

29. Warlimont, *Im Hauptquartier der deutschen Wehrmacht,* p. 391; OKH, Chief of Army Equipment and Commander of the Replacement Army, Final Assembly of Italian Divisions, 18 January 1944, NARA T-77/893/5643849; USAMHI, MSS no. D-032, Lieutenant General Rudolf von Tschudi, "The Italian Second 'Litorio' Division," November 1943–1945, n.d., pp. 2, 6, 10; and Higher SS Commander and Police Chief in Italy to Fourteenth Army, 8 October 1943, NARA T-175/223/2760992.

30. *ADAP,* vol. 7, no. 168, pp. 329–330; Corvaja, *Hitler and Mussolini,* pp. 347–349; and Mussolini to OKW, Outline of the Situation, June 1944, NARA T-77/893/5643740.

31. Mack Smith, *Mussolini,* pp. 319–320; and Bosworth, *Mussolini,* pp. 411–412.

32. Erfurth, *Der Finnische Krieg,* p. 149; and *ADAP,* vol. 4, no. 243, p. 432; and *ADAP,* vol. 5, no. 80, pp. 149–150.

33. *ADAP,* vol. 6, no. 140, pp. 239–240; Erfurth, *Der Finnische Krieg,* pp. 136–137; and Mannerheim, *Memoirs of Marshal Mannerheim,* p. 466.

34. Vehviläinen, *Finland in the Second World War,* p. 123.

35. Erfurth, *Der Finnische Krieg,* p. 153.

36. Vehviläinen, *Finland in the Second World War,* p. 109; and USAMHI, MSS no. P-108, Part II, p. 131.

37. Vehviläinen, *Finland in the Second World War,* p. 126; and Ziemke, *Stalingrad to Berlin,* p. 270.

38. Glantz and House, *When Titans Clashed,* p. 202; and Weinberg, *World at Arms,* p. 703.

39. Glantz, *Battle for Leningrad,* pp. 429–454.

40. Weinberg, *World at Arms,* p. 703; Ziemke, *Stalingrad to Berlin,* p. 391; and Vehviläinen, *Finland in the Second World War,* p. 148.

41. Warner, *Marshal Mannerheim and the Finns,* p. 204; and OKW, QM2 (North) to Twentieth Mountain Army, OKH, OKL, and OKM, 5 September 1944, NARA T-77/786/5514499.

42. Heiber and Glantz, *Hitler and His Generals,* p. 523; and Schreiber, *Kampf unter dem Nordlicht,* p. 313.

43. *ADAP,* vol. 5, no. 306, pp. 595–596; Kershaw, *Hitler 1936–1945,* p. 582; and Horthy, *Ein Leben für Ungarn,* p. 253.

44. *ADAP,* vol. 5, no. 315, pp. 626–627; Kershaw, *Hitler 1936–1945,* p. 582; Lochner, *Goebbels Diaries,* p. 335; and Horthy, *Ein Leben für Ungarn,* p. 254.

45. DHM to Chief of the Romanian General Staff, General Steflea, 27 January 1943, NARA T-501/288/000290; and Niehorster, *Royal Hungarian Army,* p. 93.

46. Axworthy, Scafes, and Craciunoiu, *Third Axis/Fourth Ally,* p. 144. See also Office of the Reichsführer SS, Pamphlet for SS Officers on SS Volunteers from the German Population in Romania, ca. October 1943, NARA T-175/474/2996144.

47. OKW Foreign Relations Section, Report on Romanian-Hungarian Relations in the Political and Economic Areas, October 1943, NARA T-77/711/1928090; and Report of Howard K. Travers, American Chargé d'Affaires in Hungary and William W. Shott, Second Secretary of the American Legation at Budapest, c. 1944, Box 40B, William J. Donovan Papers, USAMHI.

48. Inspector General of Panzer Troops to Adjutant to Chief of the General Staff, 19 August 1944, NARA T-312/366/6328496.

49. DiNardo, "Dysfunctional Coalition," p. 718; Macartney, *History of Hungary,* vol. 2, pp. 166–167; Study Group for the History of Aerial Warfare, "Aircraft Procurement," p. 437, 1955, Karlsruhe Collection, AFHRA; Szabó, "Development of the Hungarian Aircraft Industry, 1938–1944," pp. 72–74; and Corum, "*Luftwaffe* and Its Allied Air Forces in World War II," p. 16.

50. *ADAP,* vol. 3, no. 312, p. 551.

51. Colonel K. G. Jacob, "The German Passive Air Defense System," Part I, 1957, pp. 127–128, AFHRA; USAMHI, MSS no. P-108, Part II, p. 170; and James Dugan and Carroll Stewart, *Ploesti: The Great Ground-Air Battle of 1 August 1943,* rev. ed. (Dulles, Va.: Brassey's, 2002), p. 28.

52. Westermann, *Flak,* p. 221; Jacob, "The German Passive Air Defense System," Part I, p. 128, AFHRA; and Dugan and Stewart, *Ploesti,* pp. 28, 222.

53. Jacob, "The German Passive Air Defense System," Part I, p. 133, AFHRA; Westermann, *Flak,* p. 225; Report of Commander of German Fighters in Romania, Colonel Neumann, on His Activity in Romania, 1944, BA-MA RL 8/210, USAMHI; WiRüAmt, Oil Situation in Romania and Hungary, 15 May 1944, NARA T-77/489/1653445, MSS no. P-108, Part II, p. 170; and Dugan and Stewart, *Ploesti,* p. 262.

54. Reich Minister of Aviation and Commander of the *Luftwaffe* to German Ambassador, Air Attaché in Romania, Oil Exports from Romania to Sweden, 9 July 1943, NARA T-405/60/4902857; and Air Attaché in Romania to Reich Minister of Aviation and Commander of the *Luftwaffe,* Oil Exports from Romania to Sweden, 27 July 1943, NARA T-405/60/4902856.

55. Romanian Undersecretary of Aviation to Commander of DLM in Romania, 29 July 1943, NARA T-59/4900615; Study Group for the History of Aerial Warfare, "Aircraft Procurement," p. 442a, Karlsruhe Collection, AFHRA; and Corum, "*Luftwaffe* and Its Allied Air Forces in World War II," p. 12.

56. Gosztony, *Hitlers Fremde Heere,* p. 380; Seaton, *Russo-German War,* p. 424; and Alex Buchner, *Ostfront 1944: The German Defensive Battles on the Russian Front 1944* (West Chester, Pa.: Schiffer, 1991), p. 139.

57. Buchner, *Ostfront 1944,* pp. 100–101; Ruge, *Soviets as Naval Opponents,* p. 130; Martienssen, *Führer Conferences on Naval Affairs,* p. 377; Axworthy, Scafes, and Craciunoiu, *Third Axis/Fourth Ally,* p. 132; and Warlimont, *Im Hauptquartier der deutschen Wehrmacht,* p. 427.

58. Seaton, *Russo-German War,* p. 430.

59. Buchner, *Ostfront 1944,* p. 137; and Ruge, *Soviets as Naval Opponents,* p. 132, give much higher numbers for those evacuated. More reliable are Glantz and House, *When Titans Clashed,* p. 191; Axworthy, Scafes, and Craciunoiu, *Third Axis/Fourth Ally,* p. 344; Seaton, *Russo-German War,* p. 431; and Werner Haupt, *Die Schlachten der Heeresgruppe Süd* (Bad Nauheim: Podzun-Pallas-Verlag, 1985), p. 420.

60. At the end of June 1944, Model was replaced by General Josef Harpe, while in late July 1944 Schörner was replaced by General Johannes Friessner. Andris J. Kursietis, *The Wehrmacht at War 1939–1945* (Soesterberg, Netherlands: Aspekt, 1999), p. 21.

61. Inspector General of Panzer Troops to Adjutant to the Chief of the General Staff, 19 August 1944, NARA T-312/366/6328496; Army Group Wöhler, Report of the Trip of the Army Group Commander to the Romanian 1st Armored Division, 13 June 1944, NARA T-312/69/7588409; and Axworthy, Scafes, and Craciunoiu, *Third Axis/Fourth Ally,* p. 163.

62. Army Group Wöhler, Report of the Trip of the Army Group Commander to the Romanian 1st Panzer Division, 13 June 1944, NARA T-312/69/7588409. For comparative purposes, see Commander of Training Staff II of the DHM in Romania, Situation Report, 7 February 1941, NARA T-315/680/000134.

63. Axworthy, Scafes, and Craciunoiu, *Third Axis/Fourth Ally,* p. 157; *KTB/* Army Group Wöhler, 5 June 1944, NARA T-312/69/7588455; and Commanding General of the German Air Force in Romania, Special Order of the Day, 9 July 1944, BA-MA RL 9/81/1.

64. Axworthy, Scafes, and Craciunoiu, *Third Axis/Fourth Ally,* p. 175.

65. Glantz and House, *When Titans Clashed,* pp. 218–219.

66. Guderian described the meeting as civil. Heinz Guderian, *Panzer Leader* (1952; repr., Washington, D.C.: Zenger, 1979), p. 365; Kershaw, *Hitler 1936–1945,* p. 723; and Seaton, *Russo-German War,* p. 473. Romanian-based accounts characterized the meeting as being more rancorous. Axworthy, Scafes, and Crăciunoiu, *Third Axis/Fourth Ally,* pp. 160–161; and Drăgan, *Antonescu,* pp. 396–397.

67. Seaton, *Russo-German War,* p. 477.

68. Extract from the After-Action Report of the German General with the Hungarian Second Army, January 1943, NARA T-78/333/6290832; and Horthy, *Ein Leben für Ungarn,* p. 254.

69. Niehorster, *Royal Hungarian Army,* p. 96; Macartney, *History of Hungary,* vol. 2, p. 165; and Horthy, *Ein Leben für Ungarn,* p. 257.

70. OKH, Organization Section, Arms Stocks for the Hungarian Army, 6 June 1944, NARA T-78/444/6382332; and Niehorster, *Royal Hungarian Army,* pp. 108–109.

71. *ADAP,* vol. 7, no. 275, pp. 517–518; Kershaw, *Hitler 1936–1945,* pp. 627–628; and Horthy, *Ein Leben für Ungarn,* pp. 264–266.

72. Kershaw, *Hitler 1936–1945,* pp. 734–735; Horthy, *Ein Leben für Ungarn,* pp. 284–289; and *ADAP,* vol. 8, no. 274, p. 505. Horthy was imprisoned by the Germans at Schloss Hirschberg in Bavaria. Although his SS guards apparently had standing orders to execute him in case the Americans appeared, they fled at the approach of American troops, who captured Horthy on 1 May 1945. Although interrogated a number of times, he was never tried as a war criminal. In 1948 he was released from custody and moved to Portugal. Horthy, *Ein Leben für Ungarn,* p. 299; and Eby, *Hungary at War,* p. 297.

73. Extract from Report of SS Officer Attached to OKW Staff, 18 September 1942, NARA T-175/21/2526491; Lochner, *Goebbels Diaries,* p. 335; and Horthy, *Ein Leben für Ungarn,* p. 259.

74. OKH, Instructions for Members of the German Armed Forces Who Come into Contact with Hungarian Commanders or with Members of the Hungarian Armed Forces, 17 February 1944, NARA T-77/711/1927887; and Yahil, *Holocaust,* pp. 501–519.

75. OKH, Organization Section, State of the Hungarian Army, 6 June 1944, NARA T-78/414/6382329; OKH, Organization Section, Arms Stocks for the Hungarian Army, NARA T-78/414/6382332; OKW to Chief of Army Equipment and Commander of the Replacement Army, Armaments Production Capacity of Hungary, 8 May 1944, NARA T-78/414/6382333; and OKH to OKW, Demands to Hungary, 1 June 1944, NARA T-78/414/6382339.

76. Army Group South to Commander of Hungarian First Army, 26 October 1944, NARA T-311/159/7209496; Army Group South to Army Group Fretter-Pico, Army Group Wöhler and General of the German Armed Forces in Hungary, 6 November 1944, NARA T-311/159/7209870; and Army Group South to OKH, 10 November 1944, NARA T-311/159/7209926.

77. DiNardo, "Dysfunctional Coalition," p. 718; and Rintelen, "German-Italian Military Cooperation in the Second World War," 1952, Nachlass Rintelen, BA-MA N 433/6.

78. Warlimont, *Im Hauptquartier der deutschen Wehrmacht,* p. 427.

79. *ADAP*, vol. 4, no. 303, pp. 545–547; Ciano, *Diary*, p. 572; Kershaw, *Hitler 1936–1945*, p. 582; and Drăgan, *Antonescu*, p. 340.

10. Germany and Coalition Warfare

1. DHM, Handbook for German Trainers in Romania, 23 September 1942, NARA T-501/286/000522; emphasis in original.

2. Rintelen, "German-Italian Military Cooperation in the Second World War," 1952, Nachlass Rintelen, BA-MA N 433/6.

3. USAMHI, MSS no. P-108, Part I, p. 62; and Jurgen Förster, "The Dynamics of *Volksgemeinschaft*: The Effectiveness of the German Military Establishment in the Second World War," in *Military Effectiveness*, vol. 3, p. 198.

4. German Air Staff, Agreement on the Action of Italian and German Air Forces in the Central and Eastern Mediterranean and Its Surrounding Areas, 31 August 1941, BA-MA RL 2 II/38; Sadkovich, *Italian Navy in World War II*, p. 223; and Corum, "*Luftwaffe* and Its Allied Air Forces in World War II," p. 10.

5. Förster, "Die Entscheidungen der Dreierpaktstaaten," p. 888; Jacob, "The German Passive Air Defense System," Part I, 1957, Karlsruhe Collection, AFHRA; and Westermann, *Flak*, p. 221.

6. Smith, *Into the Assault*, p. 65; Knox, *Hitler's Italian Allies*, p. 65; Study Group for the History of Aerial Warfare, "Aircraft Procurement," 1955, pp. 435–436, AFHRA; German Liaison Officer to the Italian Fifth Air Fleet, Report of the Liaison Officer to the Italian Fifth Air Fleet in North Africa to the Commanding General of the X Air Corps, 19 May 1941, BA-MA RL 2 II/38; and Corum, "*Luftwaffe* and Its Allied Air Forces in World War II," p. 11.

7. *ADAP*, vol. 3, no. 312, p. 551; Report of Commander of German Fighters in Romania, Colonel Neumann, of His Activity in Romania, 1944, BA-MA RL 8/210; and Jacob, "The German Passive Air Defense System," Part I, 1957, Karlsruhe Collection, AFHRA.

8. Kelshall, *U-Boat War in the Caribbean*, p. 175; Naval High Command, Overview of the Situation in the Mediterranean, Aegean and Black Seas from 16–30 November 1941, BA-MA RM 7/115; and Navy High Command to Naval Attaché in Rome, 18 July 1942, BA-MA RM 7/248.

9. DiNardo, "Dysfunctional Coalition," p. 718; and Rintelen, "German-Italian Military Cooperation in the Second World War," 1952, Nachlass Rintelen, BA-MA N 433/6.

10. After-Action Report of the German Liaison Officer to the Italian Motorized Division Pasubio, 15 August 1941, NARA T-312/360/7934956; Compilation Presented to the Royal Romanian Supreme Headquarters to the Redress of the Shortage of Supplies in the Third and Fourth Armies, c. December 1942, NARA T-311/269/000642; German Liaison Staff to Romanian Third Army, Memorandum on Treatment of Romania Soldiers, 24 November 1942, NARA T-312/1452/000026; and Axworthy, Scafes, and Craciunoiu, *Third Axis/Fourth Ally*, p. 163.

11. See chapters 6 and 7.

12. Rintelen, "German-Italian Military Cooperation in the Second World War," 1952, Nachlass Rintelen, BA-MA N 433/6.

13. *ADAP*, vol. 1, no. 244, p. 453; *ADAP*, vol. 2, no. 182, p. 308; *ADAP*, vol. 3, nos. 8, 12, 47, pp. 14, 18–22, 77; Förster, *Stalingrad,* p. 18; and OKW Foreign Relations Section, Report on Romanian-Hungarian Relations in the Political and Economic Areas, October 1943, NARA T-77/711/1928090.

14. Warlimont, *Im Hauptquartier der deutschen Wehrmacht,* p. 160; and Weinberg, *Foreign Policy of Hitler's Germany,* vol. 1, p. 8.

15. See chapters 4 and 8.

16. See chapters 6 and 7.

17. Hitler, *Hitler's Table Talk,* p. 66; and *DHM*, Report on the Condition of the Romanian Units in May 1942, 12 May 1942, NARA T-501/269/000153.

18. Ceva, *La condotta italiana della guerra,* pp. 99–106; and DiNardo and Hughes, "Germany and Coalition Warfare in the World Wars," pp. 176–177.

19. Wedermeyer, *Wedemeyer Reports!* pp. 49–54; Boog, *Die Deutsche Luftwaffenführung,* p. 405; and Corum, *Luftwaffe,* pp. 253–254.

20. Hartmann, *Halder,* pp. 35–36; Keitel, *Generalfeldmarschall Keitel,* pp. 19–21; Gunther Just, *Alfred Jodl: Soldat ohne Furcht und Fadel* (Hannover: National Verlag, 1971), pp. 13–14; and DiNardo and Hughes, "Germany and Coalition Warfare in the World Wars," p. 190.

21. Wilhelm Deist, "The Road to Ideological War," in *Making of Strategy,* pp. 378–379.

BIBLIOGRAPHY

Documentary Sources

AIR FORCE HISTORICAL RESEARCH CENTER, MAXWELL AFB, ALABAMA

Combined Services Detailed Interrogation Center
Karlsruhe Collection

BUNDESARCHIV-MILITÄRARCHIV, FREIBURG-IM-BREISGAU, GERMANY

MSg 1/1914 Karl von Kaganeck Diary
Msg 1/2517/2 Karl von Kaganeck Diary
N 77 Nachlass Ludendorff
N 247 Nachlass Seeckt
N 362 Nachlass Freytag von Loringhoven
N 433 Nachlass Rintelen
N 671 Nachlass Richthofen
PH 5I Army Group von Mackensen
RH German Army
RM German Navy
RL German Air Force

NATIONAL ARCHIVES, COLLEGE PARK, MARYLAND

Microfilm Series
T-77 German Armed Forces High Command
T-78 German Army High Command
T-82 German Institutions with Interests Related to the Far East
T-175 Office of the Reichsführer SS and Chief of German Police
T-311 German Army Groups
T-312 German Field Armies
T-313 German Panzer Groups and Armies
T-314 German Corps
T-315 German Divisions
T-321 German Navy
T-405 German Air Force
T-501 German Rear Area Commands

PERSONAL INTERVIEWS

Bela Kiraly, 20 December 1993

UNPUBLISHED PAPERS

Muller, Richard R. "Germany's Satellite Air Forces: Coalition Air Warfare on the Eastern Front, 1941–1944." Paper presented at Society for Military History Conference, Ontario, Canada, May 1993.
Wedemeyer, Captain Albert C. "German General Staff School." Berlin: U.S. Embassy, 1938.

UNPUBLISHED MANUSCRIPTS AND PAPERS, UNITED STATES MILITARY HISTORY INSTITUTE, CARLISLE, PENNSYLVANIA

Gianni Bai-Maccario Papers
William J. Donovan Papers
MSS No. B-661, General Gunther Blumentritt. "Wartime Alliances." 1947.
MSS No. C-061, Field Marshal Albert Kesselring. "Italy as a Military Ally." July 1948.
MSS No. D-024, Major General Hans Henning von Holtzendorf. "Grunde für Rommels Erfolge in Afrika 1941/1942." 27 March 1947.
MSS No. D-032, Lieutenant General Rudolf von Tschudi. "The Italian Second *Littorio* Division, November 1943–1945." N.d.
MSS No. P-108, Major General Burkhard Müller-Hillebrand. "Germany and Her Allies in World War II." 2 pts. 1953.
MSS No. T-15, General Friedrich Schulz. "Reverses on the Southern Wing." N.d.

Published Collections of Documents

Germany, Auswärtiges Amt. *Akten zur Deutschen Auswärtigen Politik 1918–1945.* Series E. 8 vols. Göttingen: Vandenhoeck und Ruprecht, 1969–1979.
International Military Tribunal. *Trial of the Major War Criminals.* 42 vols. Nuremberg: U.S. Government, 1947–1949.
Schramm, Percy Ernst, ed. *Kriegstagebuch des Oberkommando der Wehrmacht 1940–1945.* 4 vols. Frankfurt am Main: Bernard und Graefe Verlag für Wehrwesen, 1965.
United States State Department. *Documents on German Foreign Policy 1918–1945.* Series D. 13 vols. Washington, D.C.: U.S. Government Printing Office, 1949–1956.

Published Works

Addington, Larry H. "Operation *Sunflower:* Rommel versus the General Staff." *Military Affairs* 31, no. 3 (Fall 1967): 120–130.
Afflerbach, Holger. *Falkenhayn: Politisches Denken und Handeln im Kaiserreich.* Munich: R. Oldenbourg, 1996.
Agnew, Lieutenant Colonel James B. "The Improbable Alliance: The Central Powers and Coalition Warfare, 1914–1918." *Parameters* 1, no. 3 (Winter 1972): 36–49.
Alvarez, David. "Axis Sigint Collaboration: A Limited Partnership." *Intelligence and National Security* 14, no. 1 (Spring 1999): 1–17.

Anderson, Truman O. "A Hungarian *Vernichtungskrieg?* Hungarian Troops and the Soviet Partisan War in Ukraine, 1942." *Militärgeschichtliche Mitteilungen* 58, no. 1 (1999): 345–366.

Andreopoulous, George J., and Harold E. Selesky, eds. *The Aftermath of Defeat: Societies, Armed Forces and the Challenge of Recovery.* New Haven, Conn.: Yale University Press, 1994.

Axworthy, Mark, Cornel Scafes, and Christian Craciunoiu. *Third Axis/Fourth Ally: Romanian Armed Forces in the European War, 1941–1945.* London: Arms and Armor, 1995.

Badoglio, Pietro. *Italy in the Second World War.* 1948. Reprint, Westport, Conn.: Greenwood Press, 1976.

Barnett, Correlli. *The Desert Generals.* New and enlarged edition. Bloomington: Indiana University Press, 1982.

———. ed. *Hitler's Generals.* New York: Grove Weidenfeld, 1989.

Bennett, Ralph. *Ultra and Mediterranean Strategy.* New York: Morrow, 1989.

Bessel, Richard, ed. *Fascist Italy and Nazi Germany: Comparisons and Contrasts.* New York: Cambridge University Press, 1996.

Blau, George E. *The German Campaign in Russia: Planning and Operations (1940–1942).* Washington, D.C.: Department of the Army, 1955.

———. *The German Campaign in the Balkans (Spring 1941).* Washington, D.C.: Department of the Army, 1953.

Bloch, Michael. *Ribbentrop: A Biography.* New York: Crown, 1992.

Bock, Field Marshal Fedor von. *The War Diary 1939–1943.* Ed. Klaus Gerbet. Atglen, Pa.: Schiffer Military History, 1996.

Boog, Horst. *Die Deutsche Luftwaffenführung 1935–1945: Führungsprobleme, Spitzengliederung, Generalstabausbildung.* Stuttgart: Deutsche Verlags Anstalt, 1982.

Borghese, J. Valerio. *Sea Devils.* Chicago: Henry Regnery, 1954.

Borowski, Lieutenant Colonel Harry R., ed. *The Harmon Memorial Lectures in Military History 1959–1982.* Washington, D.C.: Office of Air Force History, 1988.

Bosworth, R.J.B. *Mussolini.* London: Arnold, 2002.

Boyd, Carl. *Hitler's Japanese Confidant: General Ōshima Hiroshi and Magic Intelligence, 1941–1945.* Lawrence: University Press of Kansas, 1993.

Bragadin, Commander Marc Antonio. *The Italian Navy in World War II.* Annapolis, Md.: United States Naval Institute, 1957.

Buchner, Alex. *Ostfront 1944: The German Defensive Battles on the Russian Front 1944.* West Chester, Pa.: Schiffer, 1991.

Bucholz, Arden. *Moltke, Schlieffen, and Prussian War Planning.* Oxford: Berg, 1993.

Bullock, Alan. *Hitler: A Study in Tyranny.* Rev. ed. New York: Harper and Row, 1964.

———. *Hitler and Stalin: Parallel Lives.* New York: Knopf, 1992.

Bullock, Alan, and Brian R. Sullivan. *Il Duce's Other Woman.* New York: Morrow, 1993.

Cannistraro, Philip V., ed. *Historical Dictionary of Fascist Italy.* Westport, Conn.: Greenwood Press, 1982.

Cavallero, Ugo. *Diario 1940–1943.* Ed. Giuseppe Bucciante. Rome: Ciarrapico Editore, 1984.

Cecil, Lamar. *Wilhelm II.* 2 vols. Chapel Hill: University of North Carolina Press, 1989–1996.

Cervi, Mario. *The Hollow Legions: Mussolini's Blunder in Greece, 1940–1941.* Garden City, N.Y.: Doubleday, 1971.

Ceva, Lucio. *La condotta italiana della guerra: Cavallero e il Commando Supremo 1941/1942.* Milan: Feltrinelli Editore, 1975.

———. *Le forze armate.* Torino: UTET, 1981.

Ciano, Count Galeazzo. *Diary 1937–1943.* Eds. Robert L. Miller and Stanislao Pugliese; trans. Robert L. Miller. New York: Enigma Books, 2002.

Clark, Alan. *Barbarossa: The Russian-German Conflict 1941–45.* New York: Morrow, 1965.

Clausewitz, Carl von. *On War.* Ed. and trans. Michael Howard and Peter Paret. Princeton, N.J.: Princeton University Press, 1984.

Cohen, Eliot A., and Gooch, John. *Military Misfortunes: The Anatomy of Failure in War.* New York: Vintage Books, 1990.

Conrad von Hötzendorf, Field Marshal Franz Baron. *Aus Meiner Dienstzeit 1906–1918.* 5 vols. 6th ed. Vienna: Rikola Verlag, 1921–1925.

Corti, Eugenio. *Few Returned: Twenty-eight Days on the Russian Front, Winter 1942–1943.* Trans. Peter Edward Levy. Columbia: University of Missouri Press, 1997.

Corum, James S. *The Luftwaffe: Creating the Operational Air War, 1918–1940.* Lawrence: University Press of Kansas, 1997.

———. "The *Luftwaffe* and Its Allied Air Forces in World War II: Parallel War and the Failure of Strategic and Economic Cooperation." *Air Power History* 51, no. 2 (Summer 2004): 4–19.

———. *The Roots of Blitzkrieg: Hans von Seeckt and German Military Reform.* Lawrence: University Press of Kansas, 1992.

———. "The Spanish Civil War: Lessons Learned and Not Learned by the Great Powers." *Journal of Military History* 62, no. 2 (April 1998): 313–334.

Corvaja, Santi. *Hitler and Mussolini: The Secret Meetings.* New York: Enigma Books, 2001.

Coverdale, John F. *Italian Intervention in the Spanish Civil War.* Princeton, N.J.: Princeton University Press, 1975.

Cramon, August von. *Unser Österreichisch-Ungarischer Bundesgenosse im Weltkrieg. Erinnerungen aus meiner vierjahrigen Tatigkeit als bevollmachtiger deutscher General beim KuK Armeeoberkommando.* Berlin: E. S. Mittler und Sohn, 1922.

Cramon, August von, and Paul Fleck. *Deutschlands Schicksalsbund mit Österreich-Ungarn: Von Conrad von Hötzendorf zu Kaiser Karl.* Berlin: Verlag für Kulturpolitik, 1932.

Crozier, Brian. *Franco.* Boston: Little, Brown, 1967.

Cruikshank, Charles. *Greece 1940–1941.* Newark: University of Delaware Press, 1976.

Dallin, Alexander. *German Rule in Russia 1941–1945: A Study of Occupation Policies.* 2nd ed. Boulder, Colo.: Westview Press, 1981.

Deak, Istvan. *Beyond Nationalism: A Social and Political History of the Habsburg Officer Corps.* New York: Oxford University Press, 1990.

Deakin, F. W. *The Brutal Friendship*. New York: Harper and Row, 1962.

de Gaulle, Charles. *The Enemy's House Divided*. Trans. Robert Eden. Chapel Hill: University of North Carolina Press, 2002.

D'Este, Carlo. *Bitter Victory: The Battle for Sicily 1943*. New York: Dutton, 1988.

DiNardo, Richard L. "The Dysfunctional Coalition: The Axis Powers and the Eastern Front in World War II." *Journal of Military History* 60, no. 4 (October 1996): 711–730.

———. "German Armor Doctrine: Correcting the Myths." *War in History* 3, no. 4 (November 1996): 384–397.

———. *Germany's Panzer Arm*. Westport, Conn.: Greenwood Press, 1997.

———. *Mechanized Juggernaut or Military Anachronism? Horses and the German Army of World War II*. Westport, Conn.: Greenwood Press, 1991.

DiNardo, Richard L., and Daniel J. Hughes. "Germany and Coalition Warfare in the World Wars: A Comparative Study." *War in History* 8, no. 2 (April 2001): 166–190.

Dönitz, Karl. *Memoirs: Ten Years and Twenty Days*. 1958. Reprint, Annapolis, Md.: Naval Institute Press, 1980.

Drăgan, Joseph C. *Antonescu: Marshal and Ruler of Romania (1940–1944)*. Trans. Andrei Bartas. Bucharest: Europa Nova, 1995.

Duffy, Christopher. *The Army of Frederick the Great*. New York: Hippocrene Books, 1974.

———. *The Military Life of Frederick the Great*. New York: Hippocrene Books, 1986.

Dugan, James, and Carroll Stewart. *Ploesti: The Great Ground-Air Battle of 1 August 1943*. Rev. ed. Dulles, Va.: Brassey's, 2002.

Dyakov, Yuri, and Tatyana Bushuyeva, eds. *The Red Army and the Wehrmacht*. Amherst, N.Y.: Prometheus Books, 1995.

Eby, Cecil D. *Hungary at War*. University Park: Pennsylvania State University Press, 1998.

Erfurth, Waldemar. *Der Finnische Krieg, 1941–1945*. Revised and expanded edition. Wiesbaden: Limes Verlag, 1977.

Erickson, Edward J. "Strength against Weakness: Ottoman Military Effectiveness at Gallipoli, 1915." *Journal of Military History* 65, no. 4 (October 2001): 981–1011.

Falkenhayn, General Erich von. *The German General Staff and Its Decisions 1914–1916*. New York: Dodd, Mead, 1922.

Fenyo, Mario D. "The Allied Axis Armies and Stalingrad." *Military Affairs* 29, no. 2 (Summer 1965): 57–72.

———. *Hitler, Horthy and Hungary*. New Haven, Conn.: Yale University Press, 1972.

Fest, Joachim C. *Hitler*. New York: Harcourt, Brace and Jovanovich, 1974.

Field, Geoffrey G. *Evangelist of Race: The Germanic Vision of Houston Stewart Chamberlain*. New York: Columbia University Press, 1981.

Fischer, Fritz. *Germany's War Aims in the First World War*. New York: Norton, 1967.

Foerster, Lieutenant Colonel Wolfgang. "Generalfeldmarschall von Mackensen 90 Jahren alt." *Militärwissenschaftliche Rundschau* 4, nos. 5 and 6 (December 1939): 597–604.

———. *Mackensen: Briefe und Aufzeichnungen des Generalfeldmarschalls aus Krieg und Frieden.* Leipzig: Bibliographisches Institut, 1938.

Förster, Jürgen. *Stalingrad: Risse im Budnis 1942/43.* Freiburg: Verlag Rombach, 1975.

Forstmeier, Friedrich. *Odessa 1941: Der Kampf um Stadt und Hafen und die Räumung der Seefestung 15 August bis 16 Oktober 1941.* Freiburg: Verlag Rombach, 1967.

Fraser, David. *Knight's Cross: A Life of Field Marshal Erwin Rommel.* New York: HarperCollins, 1993.

Emperor Friedrich III. *Das Kriegstagebuch von 1870–1871.* Ed. Heinrich O. Meissner. Berlin: K. S. Kohler, 1926.

Giurescu, Dinu C. *Romania in the Second World War (1939–1945).* Boulder, Colo.: East European Monographs, 2000.

Glantz, David M. *The Battle for Leningrad 1941–1944.* Lawrence: University Press of Kansas, 2002.

Glantz, David M., and Jonathan House. *When Titans Clashed: How the Red Army Stopped Hitler.* Lawrence: University Press of Kansas, 1995.

Goda, Norman J. W. *Tomorrow the World: Hitler, Northwest Africa and the Path toward America.* College Station: Texas A&M University Press, 1998.

Goodspeed, D. J. *Ludendorff: Soldier, Dictator and Revolutionary.* London: Rupert Hart-Davis, 1966.

Goralski, Robert, and Russell W. Freeburg. *Oil and War: How the Deadly Struggle for Fuel in WWII Meant Victory or Defeat.* New York: Morrow, 1987.

Görlitz, Walter. *The History of the German General Staff.* New York: Praeger, 1957.

———. *Paulus and Stalingrad.* New York: Citadel Press, 1963.

Gosztony, Peter. *Hitlers Fremde Heere: Das Schicksal der nichtdeutschen Armeen im Ostfeldzug.* Düsseldorf: Econ Verlag, 1976.

Graham, Dominick, and Shelford Bidwell. *Coalitions, Politicians and Generals: Some Aspects of Command in the Two World Wars.* London: Brassey's, 1993.

Grant, Jonathan. "The Sword of the Sultan: Ottoman Arms Imports, 1854–1914." *Journal of Military History* 66, no. 1 (January 2002): 9–36.

Greene, Jack, and Alessandro Massignani. *The Naval War in the Mediterranean 1940–1943.* London: Chatham, 1998.

———. *Rommel's North African Campaign.* Conshohocken, Pa.: Combined Publishing, 1994.

Guderian, Major General Heinz. *Achtung—Panzer!* Trans. Christopher Duffy. London: Arms and Armor, 1992.

———. *Panzer Leader.* 1952, Reprint, Washington, D.C.: Zenger, 1979.

Gundelach, Karl. *Die Deutsche Luftwaffe im Mittelmeer 1940–1945.* 2 vols. Frankfurt am Main: Peter D. Lang, 1981.

Halder, General Franz. *The Halder Diaries.* 7 vols. Washington, D.C.: Infantry Journal, 1950.

Hartmann, Christian. *Halder: Generalstabschef Hitlers 1938–1942.* Paderborn: Ferdinand Schöningh, 1991.

Hartung, Fritz. "Die geschichtliche Bedeutung des Weltkriegs." *Militärwissenschaftliche Rundschau* 4, no. 4 (November 1939): 443–455.

Haupt, Werner. *Die Schachten der Heeresgruppe Süd*. Bad Nauheim: Podzun-Pallas-Verlag, 1985.

Haynes, Rebecca. *Romanian Policy towards Germany, 1936–1940*. New York: St. Martin's Press, 2000.

Hayward, Joel S. A. *Stopped at Stalingrad: The Luftwaffe and Hitler's Defeat in the East 1942–1943*. Lawrence: University Press of Kansas, 1998.

Heiber, Helmut, and David M. Glantz, eds. *Hitler and His Generals: Military Conferences 1942–1945*. New York: Enigma Books, 2003.

Herring, George C., Jr. *Aid to Russia 1941–1946*. New York: Columbia University Press, 1973.

Herwig, Holger. *The First World War: Germany and Austria-Hungary 1914–1918*. London: Arnold, 1997.

———. "Generals versus Admirals: The War Aims of the Imperial German Navy, 1914–1918." *Central European History* 5, no. 3 (September 1972): 208–233.

Higgins, Trumbull. *Hitler and Russia: The Third Reich in a Two Front War 1937–1943*. New York: Macmillan, 1966.

Hitler, Adolf. *Hitler's Second Book*. Ed. Gerhard L. Weinberg; trans. Krista Smith. New York: Enigma Books, 2003.

———. *Hitler's Table Talk 1941–1944*. Trans. Norman Cameron and R. H. Stevens. 1953. Reprint, New York: Enigma Books, 2000.

———. *Mein Kampf*. Trans. Ralph Manheim. Boston: Houghton Mifflin, 1971.

Hixson, Lieutenant Colonel John, and Benjamin Franklin Cooling. *Combined Operations in Peace and War*. Rev. ed. Carlisle, Pa.: U.S. Army, 1982.

Höbelt, Lothar. "Schlieffen, Beck, Potiorek und das Ende der gemeinsam deutsch-österreichisch-ungarischen Aufmarschpläne im Osten." *Militärgeschichtliche Mitteilungen*, no. 36 (February 1984): 7–30.

Hoffman, Peter. "The Gulf Region in German Strategic Projections, 1940–1942." *Militärgeschichtliche Mitteilungen*, no. 44 (February 1988): 61–73.

Holmes, Terence M. "The Reluctant March on Paris: A Reply to Terence Zuber's 'The Schlieffen Plan Reconsidered.'" *War in History* 8, no. 2 (April 2001): 208–232.

Horthy, Admiral Nikolas von. *Ein Leben für Ungarn*. Bonn: Athenäum-Verlag, 1953.

Hughes, Daniel J., ed. and trans. *Moltke on the Art of War: Selected Writings*. Novato, Calif.: Presidio Press, 1993.

Ioanid, Radu. *The Sword of the Archangel: Fascist Ideology in Romania*. Boulder, Colo.: East European Monographs, 1990.

Irving, David. *The Trail of the Fox*. New York: Avon Books, 1977.

Jacobsen, Hans Adolf, and Jürgen Rohwer, eds. *Decisive Battles of World War II: The German View*. New York: Putnam's, 1965.

Jomini, Antoine Henri Baron. *The Art of War*. Philadelphia: Lippincott, 1862.

Jukes, Geoffrey. *Hitler's Stalingrad Decisions*. Berkeley: University of California Press, 1985.

Just, Gunther. *Alfred Jodl: Soldat ohne Furcht und Fadel*. Hannover: National Verlag, 1971.

Kannengiesser, Hans. *The Campaign in Gallipoli*. London: Hutchinson, 1927.

Kehrig, Manfred. *Stalingrad: Analyse und Dokumentation einer Schlacht*. Stuttgart: Deutsche Verlags-Anstalt, 1974.

Keitel, Wilhelm. *Generalfeldmarschall Keitel: Verbrecher oder Offizier?* Ed. Walter Görlitz. Berlin: Musterschmidt Verlag, 1961.

Kelshall, Gaylord T. M. *The U-Boat War in the Caribbean.* Annapolis, Md.: Naval Institute Press, 1994.

Kershaw, Ian. *Hitler 1889–1936: Hubris.* New York: Norton, 1999.

———. *Hitler 1936–1945: Nemesis.* New York: Norton, 2000.

Kessel, Eberhard. *Moltke.* Stuttgart: K. F. Koehler, 1957.

Kesselring, Field Marshal Albert. *The Memoirs of Field Marshal Kesselring.* 1953. Reprint, London: Greenhill Books, 1977.

Kiesling, Eugenia C. *Arming against Hitler: France and the Limits of Military Planning.* Lawrence: University Press of Kansas, 1996.

Kiszling, Rudolf. "Bündniskrieg und Koalitionskriegführung am Beispiel der Mittelmächte im Ersten Weltkrieg." *Wehrwissenschaftliche Rundschau* 10, no. 12 (1960): 630–640.

Kleinfeld, Gerald R., and Lewis A. Tambs. *Hitler's Spanish Legion: The Blue Division in Russia.* Carbondale: Southern Illinois University Press, 1979.

Knox, MacGregor. *Common Destiny: Dictatorship, Foreign Policy and War in Fascist Italy and Nazi Germany.* Cambridge: Cambridge University Press, 2000.

———. *Hitler's Italian Allies: Royal Armed Forces, Fascist Regime, and the War of 1940–1943.* New York: Cambridge University Press, 2000.

———. *Mussolini Unleashed 1939–1941: Politics and Strategy in Fascist Italy's Last War.* New York: Cambridge University Press, 1982.

Koburger, Charles W., Jr. *Naval Warfare in the Eastern Mediterranean 1940–1945.* Westport, Conn.: Praeger, 1993.

Koschorrek, Günther K. *Blood Red Snow: The Memoirs of a German Soldier on the Eastern Front.* London: Greenhill Books, 2002.

Kriebel, Colonel Rainer. *Inside the Africa Corps: The Crusader Battles, 1941–1942.* Ed. Bruce I. Gudmundsson. London: Greenhill Books, 1999.

Kronenbitter, Gunther. "Die Macht der Illusionen. Julikrise und Kriegsausbruch 1914 aus der Sicht des deutschen Militärattachés in Wien." *Militärgeschichtliche Mitteilungen* 57, no. 2 (1998): 519–550.

Kühn, Volkmar. *Mit Rommel in der Wüste.* Stuttgart: Motorbuch Verlag, 1987.

Kurowski, Franz. *Der Kampf um Kreta.* Herford: Maximilian Verlag, 1965.

Kursietis, Andris J. *The Wehrmacht at War 1939–1945.* Soesterberg, Netherlands: Aspekt, 1999.

Leggiere, Michael V. *Napoleon and Berlin: The Franco-Prussian War in North Germany, 1813.* Norman: University of Oklahoma Press, 2002.

Levine, Alan J. *The War against Rommel's Supply Lines, 1942–1943.* Westport, Conn.: Praeger, 1999.

Liddell-Hart, B. H., ed. *The Rommel Papers.* New York: Harcourt, Brace and Company, 1953.

Liman von Sanders, Otto. *Five Years in Turkey.* Annapolis, Md.: Naval Institute Press, 1927.

Lochner, Louis P., ed. and trans. *The Goebbels Diaries 1942–1943.* New York: Doubleday, 1948.

Luck, Hans von. *Panzer Commander.* Westport, Conn.: Praeger, 1989.

Ludendorff, Erich. *Der totale Krieg.* Munich: Lundendorffs Verlag, 1936.

———. *Meine Kriegserinnerungen 1914–1918*. Berlin: E. S. Mittler und Sohn, 1919.

Lützow, Rear Admiral. "Zur strategisch Lage im Mittelmeer." *Militärwissenschaftliche Rundschau* 6, no. 1 (March 1941): 73–92.

Luvaas, Jay, ed. and trans. *Frederick the Great on the Art of War*. New York: Free Press, 1966.

Macartney, Carlile A. *A History of Hungary 1929–1945*. 2 vols. New York: Praeger, 1956.

Macintyre, Donald. *The Battle for the Mediterranean*. New York: Norton, 1965.

Mack Smith, Denis. *Mussolini: A Biography*. New York: Knopf, 1982.

———. *Mussolini's Roman Empire*. New York: Viking Press, 1976.

Macksey, Kenneth. *Kesselring: German Master Strategist of the Second World War*. London: Greenhill Books, 1996.

Malaparte, Curzio. *Kaput*. Trans. Cesare Foligno. New York: Dutton, 1946.

Mallet, Robert. *The Italian Navy and Fascist Expansionism 1935–1940*. London: Frank Cass, 1998.

Mannerheim, Marshal Carl. *The Memoirs of Marshal Mannerheim*. London: Cassell, 1953.

Manstein, Field Marshal Erich von. *Lost Victories*. 1958. Reprint, Novato, Calif.: Presidio Press, 1982.

Markus, Georg. *Der Fall Redl*. Vienna: Amalthea Verlag, 1984.

Martienssen, Anthony, ed. *Führer Conferences on Naval Affairs 1939–1945*. Annapolis, Md.: Naval Institute Press, 1990.

May, Arthur J. *The Passing of the Habsburg Monarchy 1914–1918*. 2 vols. Philadelphia: University of Pennsylvania Press, 1966.

Megargee, Geoffrey P. *Inside Hitler's High Command*. Lawrence: University Press of Kansas, 2000.

Mellenthin, Major General F. W. von. *Panzer Battles*. 1956. Reprint, New York: Ballantine Books, 1971.

Meskill, Johanna Menzel. *Hitler and Japan: The Hollow Alliance*. New York: Atherton Press, 1966.

Messe, Giovanni. *La Guerra al Fronte Russo*. 4th ed. Milan: Rizzoli, 1964.

Messenger, Charles. *The Last Prussian: A Biography of Field Marshal Gerd von Rundstedt 1875–1953*. London: Brassey's, 1991.

Michalka, Wolfgang, ed. *Der Zweite Weltkrieg*. Munich: Piper, 1989.

Militärgeschichtlichen Forschungsamt. *Das Deutsche Reich und der Zweite Weltkrieg*. 7 vols. Stuttgart: Deutsche Verlags Anstalt, 1974–2002.

Millett, Allan R., and Williamson Murray, eds. *Calculations: Net Assessment and the Coming of World War II*. New York: Free Press, 1992.

———. *Military Effectiveness*. 3 vols. Boston: Allen and Unwin, 1988.

Moltke, Colonel General Helmuth von. *Erinnerungen-Briefe-Dokumente 1877–1916*. Ed. Eliza von Moltke. Stuttgart: Der Kommende Tag A.G. Verlag, 1922.

Moltke, Field Marshal Helmuth Graf von. *Ausgewählte Werke*. 4 vols. Ed. F. von Schmerfeld. Berlin: Reimar Hobbing, 1925.

Mombauer, Annika. *Helmuth von Moltke and the Origins of the First World War*. Cambridge: Cambridge University Press, 2001.

Moorehead, Alan. *Gallipoli*. New York: Harper and Brothers, 1956.

Müller, Rolf-Dieter, and Hans-Erich Volkmann, eds. *Die Wehrmacht: Mythos und Realität.* Munich: R. Oldenbourg, 1999.

Murray, Williamson. *The Change in the European Balance of Power, 1938–1939: The Path to Ruin.* Princeton, N.J.: Princeton University Press, 1984.

———. *Luftwaffe.* Baltimore: Nautical and Aviation Co. of America, 1985.

Murray, Williamson, MacGregor Knox, and Alvin Bernstein, eds. *The Making of Strategy: Rulers, States, and War.* New York: Cambridge University Press, 1994.

Niehorster, Leo W. G. *The Royal Hungarian Army, 1920–1945.* Bayside, N.Y.: Axis Europa Books, 1998.

Overy, R. J. *Göring: The "Iron Man."* London: Routledge and Kegan Paul, 1984.

———. *War and Economy in the Third Reich.* Oxford: Oxford University Press, 1994.

Padfield, Peter. *Dönitz: The Last Führer.* New York: Harper and Row, 1984.

———. *Himmler: Reichsführer-SS.* New York: Holt, 1990.

Paret, Peter, ed. *Makers of Modern Strategy.* Princeton, N.J.: Princeton University Press, 1986.

Pearton, Maurice. *Oil and the Romanian State.* New York: Oxford University Press, 1971.

Perkins, John. "'Coins for Conflict' Nickel and the Axis, 1933–1945." *Historian* 55, no. 1 (Autumn 1992): 98.

Petersen, Jens. "Deutschland und der Zusammenbruch der Faschismus in Italien im Sommer 1943." *Militärgeschichtliche Mitteilungen*, no. 37 (January 1985): 51–69.

Petre, F. Loraine. *Napoleon's Conquest of Prussia—1806.* 1907. Reprint, New York: Hippocrene Books, 1977.

———. *Napoleon's Last Campaign in Germany—1813.* 1912. Reprint, New York: Hippocrene Books, 1974.

Pitt, Barrie. *Western Desert 1941.* London: Jonathan Cape, 1980.

———. *The Year of Alamein 1942.* New York: Paragon House, 1990.

Probst, Just. *Hungarian Armored Forces 1929–1945.* Copenhagen: Privately published, 1976.

Proctor, Raymond L. *Hitler's Luftwaffe in the Spanish Civil War.* Westport, Conn.: Greenwood Press, 1983.

Ready, J. Lee. *The Forgotten Axis.* London: McFarland, 1987.

Rich, Norman. *Hitler's War Aims.* 2 vols. New York: Norton, 1973–1974.

Ritter, Gerhard. *The Schlieffen Plan: Critique of a Myth.* New York: Praeger, 1958.

———. *The Sword and the Scepter: The Problem of Militarism in Germany.* 4 vols. Coral Gables, Fla.: University of Miami Press, 1968–1972.

Roba, J. L., and C. Crăciunoiu. *Seaplanes over the Black Sea: German-Romanian Operations 1941–1944.* Bucharest: Editura Modelism, 1995.

Röhl, John C. G. *The Kaiser and His Court.* Cambridge: Cambridge University Press, 1994.

Rohwer, Jürgen. *Axis Submarine Successes, 1939–1945.* Annapolis, Md.: Naval Institute Press, 1983.

Rothenberg, Gunther E. *The Army of Francis Joseph.* West Lafayette, Ind.: Purdue University Press, 1976.

————. *The Art of Warfare in the Age of Napoleon*. Bloomington: Indiana University Press, 1978.

Rotundo, Louis, ed. *Battle for Stalingrad: The 1943 Soviet General Staff Study*. New York: Pergamon-Brassey's, 1989.

Ruge, Vice Admiral Friedrich. *The Soviets as Naval Opponents 1941–1945*. Annapolis, Md.: Naval Institute Press, 1979.

Sadarananda, Dana V. *Beyond Stalingrad: Manstein and the Operations of Army Group Don*. New York: Praeger, 1990.

Sadkovich, James J. "German Military Incompetence through Italian Eyes." *War in History* 1, no. 1 (March 1994): 39–62.

————. *The Italian Navy in World War II*. Westport, Conn.: Greenwood Press, 1994.

Schafranek, Hans, and Robert Streibel, eds. *22 Juni 1941: Der Überfall auf die Sowjetunion*. Vienna: Picus Verlag, 1991.

Schindler, John R. *Isonzo: The Forgotten Sacrifice of the Great War*. Westport, Conn.: Praeger, 2001.

Schmider, Klaus. "The Mediterranean in 1940–1941: Crossroads of Lost Opportunities?" *War and Society* 15, no. 2 (October 1997): 19–41.

Schmidt, Paul. *Hitler's Interpreter*. New York: Macmillan, 1951.

Schreiber, Franz. *Kampf unter dem Nordlicht: Deutsch-Finnische Waffenbruderschaft am Polarkreis*. Osnabrück: Munin Verlag, 1969.

Schreiber, Gerhard. *Deutsche Kriegsverbrechen in Italien: Täter, Opfer Strafverfolgung*. Munich: C. H. Beck, 1996.

————. *Die italienischen Militärinternierten im Deutschen Machtbereich 1943–1945*. Munich: R. Oldenbourg, 1990.

Schulte, Theo. *The German Army in Occupied Russia*. Oxford: Berg, 1989.

Schwarzmüller, Theo. *Zwischen Kaiser und Führer. Generalfeldmarschall August von Mackensen: Eine Politische Biographie*. Paderborn: Ferdinand Schöningh, 1996.

Seaton, Albert. *The Russo-German War 1941–45*. New York: Praeger, 1970.

Senger und Etterlin, General Fridolin von. *Neither Fear Nor Hope*. New York: Dutton, 1964.

Seyfert, Gerhard. *Die militärischen Beziehungen und Vereinbarungen zwischen dem deutschen und dem österreichischen Generalstab vor und bei Beginn des Weltkrieges*. Leipzig: J. Moltzen, 1934.

Shanafelt, Gary W. *The Secret Enemy: Austria-Hungary and the German Alliance, 1914–1918*. Boulder, Colo.: East European Monographs, 1985.

Showalter, Dennis E. "German Grand Strategy: A Contradiction in Terms?" *Militärgeschichtliche Mitteilungen*, no. 48 (February 1990): 65–102.

————. *Tannenberg: Clash of Empires, 1914*. Dulles, Va.: Brassey's, 2004.

————. *The Wars of Frederick the Great*. New York: Longman's, 1996.

————. *The Wars of German Unification*. London: Arnold, 2004.

Smith, Peter C. *Into the Assault*. Seattle: University of Washington Press, 1985.

————. *The Stuka at War*. New York: Arco, 1971.

Sondhaus, Lawrence. *Franz Conrad von Hötzendorf: Architect of the Apocalypse*. Boston: Humanities Press, 2000.

Spielberger, Walter J. *Panzer III and Its Variants*. Atglen, Pa.: Schiffer Military/ Aviation History, 1993.

————. *Panzer IV and Its Variants.* Atglen, Pa.: Schiffer Military History, 1993.

Statiev, Alexander. "Antonescu's Eagles against Stalin's Falcons: The Romanian Air Force, 1920–1941." *Journal of Military History* 66, no. 4 (October 2002): 1085–1114.

Stein, George H. *The Waffen SS: Hitler's Elite Guard at War.* Ithaca, N.Y.: Cornell University Press, 1966.

Steinhoff, Johannes. *Messerschmitts over Sicily: Diary of a Luftwaffe Fighter Commander.* Mechanicsburg, Pa.: Stackpole Books, 2004.

Stone, Norman. *The Eastern Front 1914–1917.* New York: Scribner's 1975.

Stoves, Rolf. *Die 22. Panzer-Division, 25. Panzer-Division, 27. Panzer-Division und die 233. Reserve-Panzer-Division: Aufstellung—Gliederung—Einsatz.* Bad Nauheim: Podzun-Pallas-Verlag, 1985.

Strachan, Hew. *The First World War.* Vol. 1, *To Arms.* Oxford: Oxford University Press, 2001.

Stürgkh, Count Josef von. *Im deutschen Grossen Hauptquartier.* Leipzig: Paul List Verlag, 1921.

Sugar, Peter F., and Péter Hanák, eds. *A History of Hungary.* Bloomington: Indiana University Press, 1994.

Sullivan, Brian R. "From Little Brother to Senior Partner: Fascist Italian Perceptions of the Nazis and Hitler's Regime, 1930–1938." *Intelligence and National Security* 13, no. 1 (Spring 1998): 85–108.

Szabó, Miklós. "The Development of the Hungarian Aircraft Industry, 1938–1944." *Journal of Military History* 65, no. 1 (January 2001): 67.

Taylor, Fred, ed. and trans. *The Goebbels Diaries 1939–1941.* New York: Putnam's, 1983.

Terraine, John. *The Right of the Line: The Royal Air Force in the European War 1939–1945.* London: Hodder and Stoughton, 1985.

————. *The U-Boat Wars 1916–1945.* New York: Putnam's, 1989.

Trevor-Roper, Hugh, ed. *Final Entries 1945: The Diaries of Joseph Goebbels.* New York: Putnam's, 1978.

Tunstall, Graydon A., Jr. *Planning for War against Russia and Serbia.* Boulder, Colo.: Social Science Monographs, 1993.

Unsigned. "Der Angriff im italienischen Heer." *Militärwissenschaftliche Rundschau* 4, no. 1 (January 1939): 125–137.

Vehviläinen, Olli. *Finland in the Second World War: Between Germany and Russia.* New York: Palgrave, 2002.

Villari, Luigi. *Italian Foreign Policy under Mussolini.* New York: Devin-Adair, 1956.

Wallach, Jehuda L. *Uneasy Coalition: The Entente Experience in World War I.* Westport, Conn.: Greenwood Press, 1993.

Warlimont, Walter. *Im Hauptquartier der deutschen Wehrmacht 1939–1945.* Frankfurt am Main: Bernard und Graefe Verlag für Wehrwesen, 1962.

Warner, Oliver. *Marshal Mannerheim and the Finns.* Helsinki: Otava Publishing Company, 1967.

Wawro, Geoffrey. *The Austro-Prussian War: Austria's War with Prussia and Italy in 1866.* New York: Cambridge University Press, 1996.

Wedemeyer, General Albert C. *Wedermeyer Reports!* New York: Holt, 1958.

Wegner, Bernd, ed. *From Peace to War: Germany, Soviet Russia and the World, 1939–1941.* Oxford: Berghahn Books, 1997.

Weinberg, Gerhard L. *The Foreign Policy of Hitler's Germany.* 2 vols. Chicago: University of Chicago Press, 1970–1980.

———. *Germany and the Soviet Union 1939–1941.* Leiden: Brill, 1954.

———. *A World at Arms.* New York: Cambridge University Press, 1994.

Weitz, John. *Hitler's Diplomat: The Life and Times of Joachim von Ribbentrop.* New York: Ticknor and Fields, 1992.

Westermann, Edward B. *Flak: German Anti-aircraft Defenses, 1941–1945.* Lawrence: University Press of Kansas, 2001.

Wetzell, General Georg. "Der Bündniskrieg." *Militär Wochenblatt* 122, no. 14 (2 October 1937): 833–841.

———. "Der Bündniskrieg." *Militär Wochenblatt* 122, no. 15 (8 October 1937): 897–903.

———. "Der Bündniskrieg." *Militär Wochenblatt* 122, no. 16 (15 October 1937): 961–967.

———. "Der Bündniskrieg." *Militär Wochenblatt* 122, no. 17 (22 October 1937): 1025–1030.

———. "Der Bündniskrieg." *Militär Wochenblatt* 122, no. 18 (29 October 1937): 1089–1094.

———. *Von Falkenhayn zu Hindenburg-Ludendorff: Der Wechsel in der deutschen Obersten Heeresleitung im herbst 1916 und der rümanische Feldzug.* Berlin: E. S. Mittler und Sohn, 1921.

Whealey, Robert. *Hitler and Spain: The Nazi Role in the Spanish Civil War.* Lexington: University Press of Kentucky, 1989.

Willmott, H. P. *Empires in the Balance.* Annapolis, Md.: Naval Institute Press, 1982.

Winton, John. *Ultra at Sea: How Breaking the Nazi Code Affected Allied Naval Strategy during World War II.* New York: Morrow, 1988.

Wood, Derek, and Derek Dempster. *The Narrow Margin: The Battle of Britain and the Rise of Air Power 1930–1940.* New York: McGraw-Hill, 1961.

Wuorinen, John H., ed. *Finland and World War II 1939–1944.* 1948. Reprint, Westport, Conn.: Greenwood Press, 1983.

Yahil, Leni. *The Holocaust: The Fate of European Jewry, 1932–1945.* New York: Oxford University Press, 1990.

Zaloga, Steven J. "Romanian Armor in World War II." *Military Modeling,* November 1987, 800–803.

Zaloga, Steven J., and James Grandsen. *Soviet Tanks and Combat Vehicles of World War Two.* London: Arms and Armor Press, 1984.

Ziemke, Earl F. *Stalingrad to Berlin: The German Defeat in the East.* Washington, D.C.: U.S. Army, 1968.

Ziemke, Earl F., and Magna E. Bauer. *Moscow to Stalingrad: Decision in the East.* Washington, D.C.: U.S. Government Printing Office, 1987.

Zuber, Terence. *Inventing the Schlieffen Plan: German War Planning, 1871–1914.* Oxford: Oxford University Press, 2002.

———. "The Schlieffen Plan Reconsidered." *War in History* 6, no. 3 (July 1999): 262–305.

INDEX

282 *Index*